The Newspapers Handbook

Third edition

Richard Keeble

Routledge
Taylor & Francis Group

LONDON AND NEW YORK

First published 1994 by Routledge
11 New Fetter Lane, London EC4P 4EE

Simultaneously published in the USA and Canada
by Routledge
29 West 35th Street, New York, NY 10001

Reprinted 1995, 1997

Second edition published 1998
Reprint 1999, 2000, 2004

Third edition published 2001

Routledge is an imprint of the Taylor & Francis Group

Typeset in Times and Helvetica
by Florence Production Ltd, Stoodleigh, Devon
Printed and bound in Great Britain
by TJ International Ltd, Padstow, Cornwall

British Library Cataloguing in Publication Data
A catalogue record for this book is available from the British Library.

Library of Congress Cataloging in Publication Data
Richard Keeble, 1948–
   The newspapers handbook / Richard Keeble.—3rd ed.
      p .cm.
   Includes bibliographical references and index.
   1. Newspaper publishing—Handbooks, manuals, etc.
   2. Journalism—Handbooks, manuals, etc.   I. Title.
   PN4783.K44 2001
   070.1'72–dc21   00–067065

ISBN 0–415–24083–2 (pbk)
ISBN 0–415–24082–4 (hbk)

Dedicated to the memories of my
former students Sophie O'Neill, Sirr Anai
Kelueljang, David Irwin, William Nyadru-Mia
and Zodwa Mshibe and to Henry Clother,
caring teacher, committed trade unionist and
charming man who died in December 2000

The struggle to learn, to describe, to understand, to educate is a central and necessary part of our humanity. The struggle is not begun at secondhand after reality has occurred. It is itself a major way in which reality is continually formed and changed.

Raymond Williams, *Communications*

Contents

Notes on contributors   viii
Preface   ix
Acknowledgements   x

1   **Behind the Hollywood myths: the journalist's job**   1

2   **Efficks, ethics or politics?**   21

3   **Sourcing the news**   41

4   **The art of interviewing**   61

5   **Learning the language of news**   81

6   **News reporting: beyond the five Ws**   95

7   **Planning for the unforeseen: covering transport accidents, fires, demonstrations and human interest stories**   113

8   **More news assignments: meetings, press conferences, reports, speeches and eye-witness reporting**   134

9   **Powerful information: reporting national and local government**   147
John Turner

10   **Law and disorders: covering the courts**   173
Henry Clother

11   **Investigative reporting: why and how**   183
David Northmore

12   **Feature writing: thinking visually, painting pictures with words**   194

13   **Some specialist areas: personal columns, reviewing, freelancing**   216

14   **New technology: how journalism can damage your health**   231

15   **On and off the job – or both? Training and careers**   235

Glossary   241
Bibliography   254
Index   261

Notes on contributors

Henry Clother was a lecturer in journalism at City University from 1977 until 1996. His career in journalism included working as news editor on *The Teacher* and as first industrial reporter and then education correspondent at the IPC (pre-Murdoch) *Sun*. From 1970 to 1977 he was head of public relations for the National Union of Teachers.

David Northmore is an award-winning author and investigative journalist who has contributed to the *Guardian, Observer, Independent, Independent on Sunday, Sunday Times* and a range of periodicals. He wrote the *Freedom of Information Handbook* (London: Bloomsbury, 1990) which won the MBC University Press Best General Reference Book 1990 award; *How to Get Publicity for Free* (London: Bloomsbury, 1993); *Lifting the Lid: A Guide to Investigative Research* (London: Cassell, 1996); and *Censored: The News They Don't Want You to Read* (London: Vision Paperbacks, 2000).

John Turner is a Principal Lecturer in the Department of Politics at Oxford Brookes University where he lectures in British politics, media policy and electoral studies. He has been a member of the Midlands Regional Consultative Committee of the Independent Television Commission and is a consultant with ICM Research carrying out opinion surveys and focus groups for the *Guardian* and *Observer*. He has published *The Tories and Europe* (Manchester University Press, 2000), which examines how the issue has split the modern Conservative Party.

Preface

...........:............................

This remains a textbook on newspaper reporting skills with a difference. It has attempted to draw together two traditions so often in conflict. There is a dominant newspaper culture which stresses learning skills 'on the job'. Then there is a tradition, embedded in many journalism and communication courses, which encourages a more reflective, critical approach to the press. As a result of this split, journalists and media theorists speak different languages: they seem to inhabit different worlds. So this book is rooted in the ever-changing, everyday skills of newspaper reporting but at the same time it draws on theoretical writings and new research in examining reporters' routines, news values and myths.

I have completely rewritten it for this third edition, updating all the sections. Virtually all the cuttings are new, my comments on them intended to spark discussions. The selection of journalistic assignments is aimed at helping journalism students, freelances wondering how to break into the somewhat intimidating world of reporting and at the general reader seeking a different perspective on newspapers.

I would particularly like to thank my colleagues in the journalism department at City University for supporting me over a sabbatical year during which I was able to complete the book; Helen Montgomery (*Cambridge Evening News*); Richard Garner (the *Mirror*); Angella Johnson; Dipankar De Sarkar and Alex Whiting (Gemini); Sarah Knight (*Derby Trader*); Phillip Knightley; Claude-Jean Bertrand; Tessa Mayes; Nol van der Loop; Waltraud Boxall; Professor Thom Blair, and Christopher Cudmore (of Routledge). Thanks to David Northmore and John Turner for updating their invaluable chapters (Henry Clother sadly died shortly after submitting his revised text). And special thanks to Maryline Gagnère and Gabi Keeble.

If you have any comments on this book, please send them to me at City University, Department of Journalism, Northampton Square, London EC1V OHB or R.L.Keeble @city.ac.uk

Acknowledgements

The author and publishers gratefully acknowledge permission to reproduce copyright material from the following:

The Guardian News Service Limited for permission to reprint John Vidal, 'City under siege as the world looks on', *The Guardian*, 1 December 1999

The Bury Free Press for permission to reprint Mark Baxter, 'Please end this misery', April 7, 2000, front page

Mirror Syndication International for permission to reprint Jenny Johnston, 'Virginie's secret',

The Mirror, Wednesday Feb 23, 2000, page 3

World Entertainment News Network for permission to reprint the picture of Virginie Ledoyen and Louis used in 'Virginie's secret', by Jenny Johnston, page 3, *The Mirror*, Wednesday Feb 23, 2000

The Voice for permission to reprint Vic Motune, 'Youngsters Flock to Praise Christ',

The Voice, December 20 and 27, 1999

Cambridge Newspapers Ltd for permission to reprint 'Bingo: Eyes down for that elusive jackpot', by Richard Keeble, *Cambridge Evening News*, 15 January 1977

Anne Robinson for permission to reprint 'Anne Robinson' column, *The Times Weekend*, Saturday April 15, 2000

The Morning Star for permission to reprint Mike Parker, 'A few wisps of smoke', *The Morning Star*, May 4, 2000, page 9

Every attempt has been made to obtain permission to reproduce copyright material. If any proper acknowledgement has not been made, we would invite copyright holders to inform us of the oversight.

1 Behind the Hollywood myths

....

The journalist's job

One of the most striking features of the British press is its diversity. There are many 'journalisms'. The poorly paid journalist on a local freesheet is living almost in a different world from a top columnist on a national. The reporter on an ethnic minority weekly, similarly, has little in common with a freelance travel writer. Their salaries, sources and working routines will all be different. So might their ethical values and notions of what they expect to achieve through their jobs.

The London-based national mainstream press comprises 11 Sundays (*Sport First* being launched in 1998) and 12 dailies (*Today* being the most recent casualty, closed by Rupert Murdoch in November 1995). The regional mainstream press incorporates 1,400 titles: dailies, weeklies, Sundays, freesheets (roughly half the total) and paid-fors (Peak and Fisher 1999: 36). By 2000, 85 per cent of regional papers were online.

Behind the diversity: DOMINATION
....

Yet behind the façade of extraordinary diversity lies an industry dominated by monopolies and conformism. There is a lively 'alternative' press including leftist, religious, municipal, trade union and ethnic minority publications. But their circulations are relatively small and their impact on the national debate only marginal. Power, influence and financial resources lie with the mainstream local and national press. Here competition has not promoted variety. By 1974 only London, Edinburgh and Belfast had directly competing local morning or evening papers. Since then, the concentration of media ownership has intensified, reducing many newspapers to tiny outposts of vast, highly profitable multinationals (G. Williams 1994).

Yet even in the face of the internet-inspired technological revolution of the late 1990s, the local press remained the country's second largest advertising medium. As Colin Sparks comments:

> Newspapers in Britain are first and foremost businesses. They do not exist to report the news, to act as watchdogs for the public, to be a check on the doings of government, to defend the ordinary citizen against abuses of power, to unearth scandals or to do any of the other fine and noble things that are sometimes claimed

for the press. They exist to make money just as any other business does. To the extent that they discharge any of their public functions, they do so in order to succeed as businesses.

(Sparks 1999: 46)

Monopolies rule: AT THE LOCAL LEVEL

The mid-1990s witnessed a major shake-up in the ownership structure of the regional press. In November 1995, the Chester-based Trinity International Holdings, which grew out of the *Liverpool Post* group in the 1980s, purchased Thomson Regional Newspapers (for £327.5 million) making it the largest group in the UK with well over 130 titles, while Newsquest bought out Reed Regional Newspapers, the UK's largest free newspaper publisher (for £205 million). Also in this month, Southnews bought Portsmouth and Sunderland Newspapers for £12.95 million. Then in July 1996, Johnston Press paid £211.1 million for Emap Regional Newspapers while in the following month Pearson sold its regional newspaper business, Westminster Press, to Newsquest for £305 million. In all, 77 per cent of the regional press changed ownership between 1996 and 1999. Yet the overall monopoly structure of the regional press remained intact. In June 1998 a survey by the Newspaper Society, representing UK regional and local newspapers, showed that the top 20 publishers accounted for 92 per cent of the total weekly audited circulation.

In the late 1990s the financial successes of the local press began to attract the attention of US companies and in June 1999, the US media giant Gannett (owner of 74 papers including *USA Today* and 22 television stations all with their interlocking websites) purchased Newsquest, UK's largest local group with 63 paid-for titles and 120 frees, for £904 million. The following month Trinity became the UK's largest newspaper group with its £1.5 billion merger with the Mirror Group. The new company, named Trinity-Mirror, included the *Mirror, Sunday Mirror, Sunday People, Sunday Record* and *Sunday Mail* in Scotland along with 155 regional papers. By 2000, just four companies – Northcliffe (part of Associated Newspapers), Trinity-Mirror, Johnston Press and Newsquest – controlled the bulk of the regional newspaper industry.

Monopolies rule: AT THE NATIONAL LEVEL

Monopoly ownership has similarly intensified at the national level. In 1947, the three leading corporations accounted for 62 per cent of the national daily circulation and 60 per cent of national Sunday circulation. By 1988 these figures had increased to 73 and 81 per cent. Kevin Williams (1998: 228) comments: 'In the post-war period the press has become integrated into British finance and industry. So much so that today there is no national newspaper or major regional newspaper group that does not have a tie through cross-ownership to interests outside publishing and the media.' Overall, the trend in ownership of the British press since 1945 has been towards concentration, conglomeration and internationalisation. By 2000, Fleet Street was dominated by just four companies. This trend is best typified in Rupert Murdoch, whose four London-based nationals (*The Times, Sunday Times, Sun* and *News of the World*) constitute a small subsidiary of a vast empire, which includes the following:

- A principal share in British Sky Broadcasting (BSkyB) satellite TV company, which distributes programmes throughout Europe with exclusive screening rights to many top sporting events such as Premiership football, golf's Ryder Cup and the cricket World Cup. The *Guardian* (27 March 2000) described him as having 'an iron grip on sports broadcasting'.
- Newspapers in Australia, Hungary, Fiji, Papua New Guinea and Hong Kong.
- 20th Century Fox Hollywood studios (producers of *Titanic*, *Independence Day* and *Star Wars*) and 33 TV stations. Programmes include *The Simpsons* and the *X-Files*.
- Asia's dominant satellite company, Star TV (by satellite to more than fifty countries); and stakes in television companies in India, Indonesia, Bulgaria and Japan.
- Book publishing houses in the US, UK and Australia.
- A growing interest in internet services in the UK, US and Australasia. In June 1995 Murdoch's company, News Corporation, announced the launch of a joint deal with the *People's Daily*, the powerful newspaper of the Chinese Communist Party, to explore a range of possibilities in the information technology sector including electronic publishing, online information databases, data transmission networks and digital mapping. In 2000 an agreement with Yahoo! (the world's most popular website) looked likely to lead to Sky programming going online.
- In March 1998 Murdoch's Fox Group purchased the LA Dodgers baseball team for $350 million (£212 million). In English football, he has stakes in Sunderland, Chelsea, Leeds United, Manchester City and Manchester United though his plan to take over Manchester United was blocked by the Blair government.

News Corporation's financial report for 1997 indicated that it controlled globally 780 'entities'. Its net assets amounted to A$12.4 billion with a net operating profit of A$41 million. In June 2000, Murdoch planned 'the biggest flotation of a media company' spinning off the satellite television businesses (including BSkyB, Star TV, Stream in Italy, Sky Brazil, Sky Mexico and Sky PerfecTV of Japan) from News Corp. The valuation of Sky Global Networks was expected to rise to $40 billion, placing it on a par with the total worth of News Corp.

Accompanying this monopoly ownership has been a serious decline in sales: since their peak in the mid-1950s nationals' sales have slumped 20 per cent while the paid-for local and regional newspapers have been in even sharper decline. In April 1990, the three Sunday red-top tabloids sold 10.5 million copies every week. Ten years later they were selling just 7.4 million. Figures released in March 2000 showed a 'grim' sales decline in the regional press – apart from weeklies, which managed a rise, but of only 0.1 per cent, on the previous figure.

What it takes

Journalism remains a job carrying enormous personal rewards. It is difficult, challenging (politically, ethically, physically) and fun. It requires a formidable range of knowledge and skills. Reporters must be both literate and numerate. They need to master the law as it affects newspapers and the social skills to develop contacts and interview different kinds of people. Many will want to speak at least one foreign language. All will need to possess computer and internet searching skills. Reporters should be curious, persistent, imaginative and daring. Or in the words of Nicholas Tomalin, the *Sunday Times* foreign correspondent killed on the Golan Heights in 1973, journalists should cultivate 'rat-like cunning, a plausible manner and a little literary ability'. In addition, he said, they should be able to display 'an ability to believe passionately in second-rate projects' and possess 'well-placed relatives' and 'an implacable hatred of spokesmen, administrators and public relations men'. There is a glamorous side to the job which Hollywood has helped to promote. No wonder the queues for entering the industry are so long.

The jobs revolution

Since the arrival of new technology, the job has been through many changes – not all of them positive. Staffing levels have been reduced at both national and local levels. In the regions, newspapers lost hundreds of jobs as owners 'downsized' reducing staffing levels in advance of selling off titles to the emerging conglomerates. At the same time, working hours have been extended, with early Saturday morning 'sunrise' editions adding further demands to provincial journalists.

Local branches (chapels) of the 25,000-strong National Union of Journalists (NUJ) have been left fighting for recognition and personal contracts have been increasingly forced on staffers: the recognition deal signed by the NUJ with T.R. Beckett, part of the Johnston Press, in March 2000, was significantly its first with a regional newspaper group for more than a decade. Accompanying these trends has been growing casualisation. Many staffers have been turned into 'permanent part-timers'. Managements have found it cheaper, while job insecurity always promotes conformism. With the decline in unions' power, opportunities for exploitation by management have increased. Only time would tell if the Employment Rights Act 2000, giving bargaining rights to unions where they had 50 per cent or more of the workforce in membership, would help resurrect the NUJ's fortunes.

Multi-skilling or de-skilling?

One consequence has been 'de-professionalisation', with reporters forced to perform promotional, distribution and other non-professional tasks. 'Multi-skilling' schemes are being introduced on some papers with reporters, photographers and subeditors (those handling text and layout) learning from each other – and sparking fears of further job cuts and a decline in standards. Many local papers are training reporters in subediting skills, not primarily as a way of improving their overall journalistic skills, but so they can fill in during absences. 'Flexibility' is the buzzword.

As newspapers move increasingly into the internet and cable television, the demands on journalists are likely to mount. Anthony Thornton, editor of http://www.nme.com, one of Britain's most popular websites, commented: 'Now the journalist needs to be a writer, sub editor, designer, photographer, camera person, editor, technician and radio presenter to carry out online journalism effectively'. In the United States, reporters are increasingly having to write a story, appear on television, broadcast on radio and then file a quick update for the newspaper's internet site. How long will it be before these multimedia demands are routinely faced by British journalists? Young reporters have had to fund their own training; some work without any contractual protection. Many entrants, desperate to get their foot in the door, are being cynically exploited by managements, having to work long periods on unpaid attachments. 'Commercial features' geared to promoting business and info-tainment specials (reflecting the growing power of market researchers on editorial content) have mushroomed; serious investigative journalism has been marginalised.

The tabloid values of junk journalism (and trash TV) have crept into the serious and regional press. As Harold Evans, the legendary former editor of *The Times* and *Sunday Times*, commented: 'Sexual allegations make the front pages and the decision to do that is defended on the grounds the story is about "character". This is no more than prurience on stilts.' He continued: 'If only one tenth of the energy spent on snooping on private lives can be spent on monitoring real power, on analysis, on improving the writing and the accuracy, we will be a helluva lot better off.'

Many press commentators have argued that, in a period of hyper-competition, profits are the prime concern of managements rather than editorial quality. Roy Greenslade, former editor of the *Mirror* and *Guardian* media analyst, argues: 'The pressure is constantly on managing directors and directors. They must cut costs, they must make savings. This means redundancies and greater productivity from those who stay.' And he adds: 'The most important person on a newspaper is no longer the editor. It is the managing directors. They rule the roost.' Foreign staffs have been cut to the bone, with the overfifties the most likely to be chopped.

Money matters: THE SCANDAL OF LOW PAY

Salaries for many in the newspaper industry remain scandalously low: for trainees they can be appalling. A 1996 survey by the NUJ found that 11.1 per cent in provin-cial newspapers earned less than £10,000 and 22 per cent between £10,000 and £15,000. Across all media sectors one-fifth of the sample earned between £15,000 and £20,000. The survey also identified significant gender differences: whereas 33 per cent of the male members earned £30,000 and above, only 19 per cent of the women did so.

Significantly, in December 1999, the then president of the Society of Editors, Chris Elliott, had the courage to speak out over what he called the 'downright disgraceful' salaries of some regional journalists; a week later he was fired as editor of the *News*, Portsmouth. 'We are now exploiting people and it makes me very uncomfortable,' he said. He gave the example of a journalist in his twenties on just £12,500. At the same time top executives and columnists on national newspapers can earn £100,000 plus. On 28 January 2000, for instance, *The Times* reported that Paul Dacre, editor-in-chief of Associated Newspapers, earned £637,000 including a £100,000 bonus. Suzanne Moore was said to be earning £140,000 a year for one column a week for the *Mail on Sunday*. In contrast, for many freelances salaries have either stood still over recent years or dropped, while payments to them can take up to a year (Beck 1999).

The news machine

Reporters work in close liaison with their news desk. The number of titled executives on the desk will differ according to the size of the operation. A weekly free-sheet may have just one news editor doubling up as deputy editor and feature writer.

An evening paper may have a city desk headed by a news editor alongside a district desk organising (through computer link-up) the operations of the district offices. In contrast a national may have as many as five journalists assigned to the home news desk. They will be drawing up the diary and news lists, liaising by phone with reporters out on stories and feeding in follow-up ideas into the operation. In addition, they will be monitoring the news agency wires, the other media and the flow of copy from staff reporters, attending news conferences to review past issues and plan future ones.

The amount of initiative allowed to individual reporters differs from paper to paper. General reporters on local weeklies and dailies will be 'fed' a considerable number of their stories by their news editor. They will arrive in the office at 7.30 a.m., say, often with no idea of what they are to cover until they are briefed by the news editor. Specialists, who are generally more experienced reporters, will tend to originate far more of their own material. An evening might have them assigned to crime, education, industrial, local government, farming (where relevant) and environment beats. A national broadsheet's specialisms, on the other hand, might include education, the environment, crime, arts, the media, consumer affairs, the countryside, defence, Westminster, health, religion, politics, transport, the law, Ireland, social services, technology (but significantly neither peace nor race relations).

At the core: the conference

At the centre of the news operations of all but small weeklies will be the conference. A national broadsheet may have as many as six in one day; a regional evening two or three; a weekly just one at the start of an operation. Attendance differs from paper to paper. At a small newspaper all the staff will attend. At a national, one meeting may be open to all staffers while at other times only heads of departments such as features, sports, finance, news, foreign and arts together with top executives (often called the backbench team) will be present. Discussions tend to focus around the news list extracted from the diary with reporters and where relevant photographers, graphic artists and cartoonists being assigned tasks.

In and out of the office?

One of the consequences of new technology and the staffing cuts has been the increased amount of newsroom-based work by reporters. Many local reporters say that as much as 90 per cent of their work is done by phone; national reporters can spend 70 per cent of their time and more in the office. Reporting is an increasingly desk-bound job. As investigative reporter Nick Davies says of working journalists: 'They spend such a lot of time trapped in newsrooms where they are not allowed to be real reporters. They simply process PA copy and PR quotes and have no time or encouragement to go and dig-up old-fashioned stories.'

The role of the subs

Once the story has passed the news editor, it will go through the computer system to a copy taster (often in a group of copy tasters), the much-analysed media content 'gatekeepers' of sociological theory. They will check for accuracy, see, for instance, if someone or some group criticised has had the opportunity to answer any allegations, establish whether the intro is the strongest one and decide, finally, whether the story is worth using. The story at this stage may be sent back to the reporter for revision. If the story is not rejected ('killed' or 'spiked' in the jargon) by the taster, it then moves on to the subeditors, who work entirely at the screen manipulating text and images with their mouse.

The subeditors will further check for accuracy, with the reporter contacted if there are queries, and for legal problems such as libel and contempt. (In addition, nationals have teams of lawyers to offer advice.) They may re-jig the story if a clearer structure is required or reduce its length if necessary. They will ensure style is followed throughout and compose any accompanying headlines, captions, standfirsts and panels. They design the pages normally using the QuarkXpress desktop publishing program and PhotoShop for image manipulation – increasingly directly on the screen without drawing out a sketch of the layout in pencil beforehand. This basic structure has many variants. For instance, in some newspapers the news editor and deputy operate as 'tasters'. At the *Western Morning News* reporters type their stories straight into the page and add the headlines, with the subs checking for errors on a full-size tabloid page proof. Other former subs spend their time developing content.

The amount of subbing of copy differs from paper to paper and from section to section. But all reporters have to accept that their copy may be hacked about. News copy on a national tabloid might be almost entirely rewritten to fit the small space available though features on the same paper may be only slightly touched by the subs. National broadsheets are 'reporters' papers' and their copy is generally only lightly subbed. Given the number of words, there is not the time to do regular re-jigs. Journalists new to local papers will tend to have their copy subbed a lot as they get used to house style. Once settled, their copy will tend to be heavily subbed only rarely. Indeed, reporters come to sub their own copy (checking style, clarity, conciseness, flow, punctuation, spelling and factual accuracy) before passing it on.

Writing with a visual sense

Designers and art editors are responsible, particularly in large publications, for the overall appearance of the newspaper: its use of pictures, fonts, column widths, even the use of white space in the layout, together with features such as graphs, maps and sophisticated computer-generated artwork. Their work is becoming increasingly important as newspapers reduce the text and extend their picture/graphic elements. Accordingly reporters are having to consider the representation of their stories on the page more and more as they write. A reporter composing a long feature, for instance, will often accompany it with a smaller one. This will help add tonal variety to the text on the page and also provide the sub with the material for an interesting layout. Or a reporter will help research details for a complex graphic. At the *Eastern Daily Press* (*EDP*), reporters and photographers are encouraged to think together about the best ways of displaying their stories. As Pete Waters, *EDP* special projects editor and author of *The Guide to the Tabloid: Best Practices for a Better EDP*, commented: 'If the best form [of presenting a story] is a graphic and the reporter is asked to research details rather than write a story, then that is what we must do.'

To illustrate the day-to-day practicalities of the job, five journalists from differing sectors talk about the challenges, routines, stresses, necessary skills and rewards of working in the media. A local evening, a local free weekly, a national tabloid and broadsheet and an 'alternative' news agency are represented.

More routine: BUT MORE SATISFACTION

Profile | Helen Montgomery, news editor
Cambridge Evening News

Helen Montgomery grew up in a family where all the national newspapers were present every day. Her father had been an eminent Fleet Street sports reporter and so it is perhaps not surprising that she followed in his journalistic footsteps. But she is quick to stress:

> I don't think you are a born journalist. Newspapers have always been a big part of my life. I've seen that being called up all the time is not particularly glamorous but I've also seen how exciting it can be, the buzzes it gives. The crucial skills are being able to talk and get on with people – and these are skills you have to learn.

Montgomery, 28, trained on the Westminster Press scheme in Hastings in 1995 and worked on the *St Albans Herald* and *Welwyn and Hatfield Times* before moving to the *Cambridge Evening News* (*CEN*) in December 1996 as a senior reporter. After becoming assistant news editor, she was promoted to news editor in November 1998.

> I'm a pretty calm person and don't get flapped at deadlines. But my new job is more stressful mainly because I have more responsibilities. I'm caught in the middle – with pressures from above and below – and the phone is always ringing. At the same time I get more out of the job and as part of middle management I have some considerable influence on the direction of the paper.

Her work routine has also changed dramatically. As a reporter each day was different. She could be out and about interviewing sources, attending council meetings, covering fires and accidents, following up press releases and national stories with local angles. As news editor she tends to follow a set pattern each day, organising the copy flow from twenty reporters, attending editorial conferences, planning future editions. making sure all the deadlines are met. 'The flip side to having more influence on the paper is that there is more routine. But I don't mind that. And I don't miss news writing as much as I thought.'

Under the editorship of Colin Grant since November 1998, the *CEN* has made a number of changes to make itself more accessible to its readers. Montgomery stresses:

> In the past I think we were perhaps too 'authority led', covering councils, committees and health bodies, say, rather than the actual people affected by their decisions. Stories would sometimes go over readers' heads. We are now trying to 'humanise' our reporting.

As part of these moves, the newspaper has decided to replace its specialist reporters (in the areas of education, health, science and crime) by spreading coverage among all the reporters. Montgomery says:

> With a relatively small staff it didn't make sense to have a specialist in say the health area. If they were off ill for two weeks it would be difficult to arrange coverage. Now the reporters like the new system because it gives them a variety of stories to cover. Someone may concentrate on covering schools but education won't be all they will cover. It means we are building up a team of really good all-rounders.

Part of the Yattendon group, the *CEN* has district offices in Haverhill, Saffron Walden, Royston, St Ives, Newmarket and Ely. The paper went full colour in April 1992 and moved to full page design (using QuarkXpress) the following year. Currently it has twenty subeditors and three graphic designers; of the twenty reporters (with seven based in the district offices) fourteen are women and seven trainees. With a circulation of around 42,000 on weekdays and 35,000 on Saturdays, it has six local editions Mondays to Fridays and one on Saturday. In addition, since September 2000 it has published a lifestyle magazine on Saturdays and its lively website (http://www.cambridge-news.co.uk), launched in May 1996, has thousands of hits every day. 'If a major news story, such as a serious crash on the A14, broke after the last edition had gone we would have no hesitation in putting it on the website,' says Montgomery.

Campaigns form an important ingredient of the newspaper's activities. For instance, a petition linked to its campaign to improve road safety on the notorious A14 drew 10,000 signatures and *CEN* won praise from Prime Minister Tony Blair for supporting a government study of the road by distributing a questionnaire. A 'human interest' campaign focused on the plight of a local 6-year-old boy suffering from meningitis who had lost his leg but was denied benefits after he was considered to be 'coping well with his life'. Supported by local firms and Eurostar, the boy (with a *CEN* reporter and photographer in tow) travelled to Paris to see England footballers play in Euro2000 and meet the team. The campaign ended on a high note when the boy won most of his benefits back. Another campaign has backed Cambridge United's moves to build a 10,000 all-seater football stadium in the face of opposition from local allotment holders.

A DAY IN THE LIFE OF HELEN MONTGOMERY

7 a.m.: arrives at *CEN* offices (away from the historic centre of Cambridge in the outlying village of Milton). She then has just 15 minutes to finish copy-tasting any breaking overnight stories for the first three news pages. A conference the previous day has decided on the page leads but overnight stories may spark a rethink.

7.15 to 8 a.m.: attends conference with editor, deputy editor, chief sub, sports editor and picture editor where the decisions on the first three pages are 'firmed up'. In addition, the Press Association (PA) sends three pages of national news 'ready' for publication. PA's choice of stories is discussed and sometimes changes are needed. Copy for the six local editions is also discussed.

8.50 a.m.: first edition copy deadline: all news has to be with the chief sub-editor except front page copy, which has a 9.05 a.m. deadline.

Throughout the day: reads post, faxes, emails, press releases; constantly answers phone; makes sure there is copy for the fourteen overnight pages (the prime responsibility of her deputy); develops story ideas; prepares the diary for the days ahead; liaises with the picture desk. Copy prepared for the six local editions (Cambridge and towns in the south of the region; St Neots; Saffron Walden/St Ives/Peterborough; Huntingdon; Ely; Newmarket) printing starting at 10.15 a.m. and continuing at hourly intervals.

12.15 to 12.45 p.m.: conference to discuss final Cambridge city edition. Then some kind of lunch break.

3 p.m.: conference to discuss next day's editions. Every Thursday afternoon there is a meeting to discuss the week ahead. Overnight copy prepared.

4.30 p.m.: usually finishes but can work on to 7 p.m. and even later if a major news story breaks.

Resigned: AND HEADING OFF TO PR

Profile Sarah Knight, features editor
Derby Trader

It is Tuesday and Sarah Knight, 34, is on the point of quitting her job as features editor of the four *Trader* titles after ten years' service. But she expects no special event in her honour to be provided by the company. 'We may just go for a drink at the pub,' she says, somewhat resigned.

Public relations is to be her new challenge. She has formed her own company, Messenger Press and PR, and with just three commercial clients already snapped up they are likely to earn her £12,000 in the year ahead – equivalent to her current salary. 'The move was really forced on me with having three young children but I'm looking forward to it,' she says.

During the 1990s she has witnessed ownership of her papers shift a number of times – from the original Trader Group, through Thomson to Midland Independent Newspapers. But there have been few changes to her day-to-day routines. In 1996 she was news editor with a single reporter, but more recently she has been features editor alongside two reporters and an editor – so work has been much less stressful. Some 90 per cent of her time is spent on the telephone. 'It's easier and I just don't have the time to go out and interview sources.' She has also often found writing property features 'extremely boring'. 'But I didn't think about it. I just bashed them out.' One of her more interesting assignments has been organising the annual Miss Derby beauty pageant.

She accesses internet sources routinely in researching features, using slack periods in the office to surf the internet, and receives many press releases over email. But one site she and her colleagues never visit is that of their main competitor, the *Derby Evening Telegraph*. 'We don't rely on it at all. We get our own information from our own sources.' She also never uses email for interviewing. 'I prefer contacting people by phone or interviewing them face to face, using faxes for getting information confirmed.'

Sarah had always wanted to be a journalist but worked from 1984 to 1990 first for an airline company and then a travel agency. 'The Gulf war finished us off.' This spurred her to write to local and national papers asking for jobs. Robert Maxwell's *The European* took her on and from June to December 1990 she helped to research news and features. Then after three months at Stradbroke journalism training centre, she began as a trainee reporter in the Heanor office of the Thomson weekly, known then as the *Derby Herald and Post*, moving to become news editor in September 1996.

On the necessary characteristics of a reporter, she points to perseverance and tenacity.

A lot of people just won't talk to you. They assume that whatever they say will be twisted. You get that an awful lot. You have to have enthusiasm for the subjects you tackle. If you are interviewing someone and you're not interested it will show. And you have to write succinctly in a simple way. It's not something that comes naturally. You have to learn it.

A WEEK IN THE LIFE OF SARAH KNIGHT

Monday: each day she works from 9 a.m. to 3 p.m., only occasionally with lunch breaks. Today spent working on property features for the *Burton Trader*.

Tuesday: the most stressful day with numerous deadlines. Completing some features for the Burton paper and working on property features for the *Long Eaton Trader*. Also spends time preparing articles for the *Long Eaton Advertiser* and commercial features for *Nu News*, based in Melbourne, Derbyshire.

Wednesday: works on features for the *Derby Trader* and property features for the *Ilkeston and Ripley Trader*. Sarah also has to fit in composing features for the special A4 glossy magazines produced regularly by her company. Little free time until she leaves.

Thursday: a relatively quiet day spent catching up on administration, letters and surfing the web. 'It's a day for a lot of paperwork.'

Friday: spent planning next week's features.

From Fleet Street to South African flesh spots: THEN BACK TO BRITAIN

Profile | Angella Johnson
Johannesburg Weekly Mail and Guardian

'I don't feel fear easily. In any case, I was too excited to be frightened,' says Angella Johnson, reflecting on her extraordinary three years reporting in South Africa. Formerly a journalist on the *Guardian*, Angella left in April 1996 for the Johannesburg *Weekly Mail and Guardian* and ended up covering brutal murders, rapes, prostitution, high politics and swinging sex in the suburbs – where fearlessness was constantly required.

> Crime is a burgeoning industry today in South Africa, growing faster even than the birth rate. And rape is a sort of national pastime for men. But I didn't do stupid things such as driving in the wrong area at the wrong time of night. I got to know the people in my neighbourhood. But after three years I felt my luck could be running out. Statistically it was all there ready to happen to me. So I thought: 'Time to go home.' And I felt I'd achieved everything I wanted journalistically.

On arrival in Johannesburg, Johnson had been thrown immediately into the crime beat covering drugs, taxi crime, car hijacking, child prostitution and 'terribly depressing murders'.

> When horrific crimes happen almost hourly you become immured – from the regularity and viciousness. People weren't even bothering to report them. But for me they were terrible and I wrote them up in a 'terrible, shock' sort of way. After a while other newspapers, television and radio even suggested that I had brought a new dimension to crime reporting. Nothing was acceptable: a child abduction was not acceptable; a black child found with his genitals cut off was unacceptable.

After a year she was made principal profiler and managed to ruffle a lot of prominent feathers in the process. Unlike many mainstream journalists still syco-phantic towards the newly elevated African National Congress (ANC) leaders, Johnson was not afraid to criticise. So she was called 'that Bolshie woman from Britain', a 'foreigner'. 'I was accused of being vicious and did get carried away at times.' Winnie Mandela took her aside and berated her at a cocktail party. Even President Nelson Mandela, whom she followed on a state visit, attacked her for asking an 'unpatriotic' question over Libya at a press conference in Scotland. 'But I said: "What's patriotism got to do with it? I'm a journalist".'

Her final post, as columnist, was probably her most rewarding and enjoyable. She surprised some of her friends by accepting the logo 'View From A Broad' to accompany her pieces. 'But I wasn't offended. It's a pun; it's funny. "Broad" suggests to me a woman who is sassy and confident. A friend could call me "nigger" and there would be no problem. But coming from someone I didn't know: that would be different.' Generally fearless Johnson, however, does admit to one fear: that of the gaping hole in the paper she had to fill every week with her 1,500-word column. But her efforts, in the end, brought her national celebrity status. 'I'd go into a restaurant and the head waiter would immediately clear a table for me because he was a fan. I enjoyed that.' One assignment had her standing in a 'short little number' alongside prostitutes in Oxford Street, downtown Johannesburg. 'I acted all innocent like a virgin on her first date. Men (99 per cent of them white) would drive up in their BMWs and ask me to do such and such. And I'd say: "No, not tonight".' On another occasion she went undercover with a friend to a sex club.

> There were private rooms and three rooms for communal sex where you could watch or take part. My friend was sweating and shaking like a leaf. But what I'd do to get a story! I needed proof that I'd spoken to someone so I let a German put his business card on my breast. After that my friend dragged me out.

Johnson has had a colourful career since studying English and History at Leicester University. She took the newspaper training course at City University, London, and then reported on a six-month programme funded by the European Commission in Brussels. After freelancing for Thames News and the BBC World Service and eighteen months on the *Slough Observer*, she did short spells on *The Times* and Robert Maxwell's ill-fated *London Daily News* before ending up on the *Guardian* in 1987. Current, hush-hush plans to ghost write an autobiography of a 'well-known person' appear to have come unstuck. Fleet Street beckons.

A WEEK IN THE LIFE OF ANGELLA JOHNSON

Friday: her newspaper has learned about a doctor, Michael Swango, who is alleged to have killed a number of patients at a rural hospital in Zimbabwe and fled to the US. Johnson is assigned to follow up the story. Spends day phoning Bulawayo hotel, sorting out car hire and booking coach. Main contact is the daughter of a former prime minister. Official response from the government is 'not helpful'.

Sunday morning: start of eleven-hour coach drive. Once in Bulawayo establishes name of Swango's solicitor.

Monday: goes to local paper and secures name of the hospital. Drives from noon to 3 p.m. and then 'hangs about' at the hospital (funded by the Swedish government) talking and drinking tea with the nurses. One tells off-the-record how she had suspected Swango and at the last minute had stopped him injecting poison into a pregnant woman. Also reveals that a man who had his leg amputated by Swango was living in a distant rural village. Spends night in guest house.

Tuesday: spends day trying to locate the man with the amputated leg, aided by a young woman trader in cloth. Eventually finds him living with his wife in a mud hut. After a short interview and taking a picture of him leaning on his crutch by his mud hut, heads back 'like a bat out of hell' to Bulawayo. There she interviews Swango's one-time landlady and lawyer. Night spent at Bulawayo hotel.

Wednesday: the bus lands her right outside the *Weekly Mail and Guardian*'s offices and she briefs editor Phillip Van Nekierk. Starts writing up the story and takes laptop home to continue.

Thursday: writes through the night. In the morning hands over the 2,000-word story which makes the front page splash. Mission accomplished.

Why reporting for the *Mirror* is simply not cricket

Profile   **Profile of Richard Garner, education correspondent** *Mirror*

Richard Garner, education correspondent on the *Mirror* since 1990, found one Sunday that it was just not cricket to be rung up by a colleague.

> I was watching a very exciting match between Middlesex and Durham at Southgate when my mobile went off with a call from our lobby correspondent wanting to discuss the government's comprehensive spending review due in a few days. In the end the stand turned totally against me and ejected me for ruining their cricket-watching. I had to walk out of the stand and continue my conversation there.

The mobile phone, along with its bleeper, has become an indispensable feature of Garner's working life. Although it means he is on call to his newspaper anywhere – and at any time – he doesn't object. Chatting in the canteen on the twenty-first floor of the snazzy Canary Wharf complex (with a perfect view of the Millennium dome below), 50-year-old Garner stresses that after a period of management upheaval, the *Mirror* has settled into a period of welcome stability.

> We've gone back to the coverage of more serious news. Piers Morgan, the longest serving editor since I joined, is a man you can approach and discuss things with while most of his working day is spent on the editorial floor. And now there are more mechanisms for feeding ideas into the operation of the newspaper.

Investigative reporter Paul Foot is one of the journalists he most admires. 'He nagged away at his campaigns – over the Bridgewater and Hanratty cases for instance – and never let them drop. Yet at the same time he writes fluently and amusingly.' Since the 1997 general election, the *Mirror*'s campaign style has changed significantly.

When the Tories were in power we could highlight stories of classes with 70 students; for instance. It was all good, knock-about stuff. Now our stance is that of a 'critical friend' of Labour. We are responding more positively to government initiatives and understanding their problems back at base while at the same time we are not slow to criticise when necessary and say 'Hang on a minute, minister'. We are still there to prick their conscience.

Garner, one of the longest serving education correspondents on Fleet Street, is particularly proud of the way his paper has covered race issues. He cites the coverage of a primary school in King's Cross, London, where twenty-seven first languages are spoken. It had won praise from inspectors and gained impressive results in national curriculum tests.

We gave it a double page spread, with a big picture showing the children from all the different cultures. And we pointed out the huge advantages of having so many cultures in spreading understanding of the wider world. We did exactly the same thing in our coverage of White Hart Lane secondary school in Tottenham. There, fifty first languages are spoken with a quarter of the 1,500 pupils asylum seekers. We quoted the head on how she coped with the influx of refugees and on the advantages for teaching in a multi-cultural environment.

The Press Complaints Commission (PCC) code of practice is also taken very seriously at the *Mirror*, he stresses. In 1996 when teachers were taking action against unruly pupils, names of 'thug like' 13 year olds would be printed. Today the 'more responsible' *Mirror* will not 'name and shame'. Despite his many years as an education specialist, Garner admits that one of the most difficult aspects of his £57,600 job is interviewing children. 'In fact, partly because I don't have children of my own, I feel more nervous talking to them than I do to the head teachers. I tend to "dumb down" my questions to them unnecessarily and am not quite as natural with them.'

In recent years, Garner has become a regular radio pundit on educational issues. Intriguingly, one of his first jobs after school in 1967 was as a disc jockey at a discothéque, even being auditioned for Radio 1. 'They thought I might have a good voice for late night listening on Radio 2. I thought about it for a while but in the end realised as a career move it was the kiss of death.' Eventually he took the plunge, taking the journalism training course at Harlow and joining the *North London Press*, Islington, in 1970. It was his news editor on a later job at the *Camden Journal* who was to have a great impact on his journalistic thinking. 'He taught me that reporting was not simply about listening but campaigning on issues.'

His path toward becoming *Mirror* education correspondent began in earnest in 1974 when he was appointed local government correspondent on the *Kent Evening Post*, Chatham while four years later he became education specialist on the *Birmingham Evening Mail*. 'It was a right-wing tabloid with a definite slant on its political stories. They were obsessed with supposed Marxist infiltration of the local trade council. They were always going on about how teachers didn't work hard.' He was left devising various ingenious ways of subverting that bias. In 1980 he moved to the paper's London office as a general reporter and then to Rupert Murdoch's *Times Educational Supplement* where the following year he rose to become news editor. In 1990, to the amazement of many of his colleagues, he left to join the *Mirror*.

He uses shorthand all the time and only rarely a tape recorder. The BBC's online news service, with three dedicated education specialists, he finds particularly useful (though he has yet to use email for an interview) while the *Mirror*'s electronic database of cuttings from 1992 is one of his most valuable resources.

A WEEK IN THE LIFE OF RICHARD GARNER

Thursday: back after a two-week break. His normal train from Hertford is held up half an hour so he arrives at the specialist desk (grouping him with the crime, royal, medical, consumer, and business and labour correspondents) in the enormous open-plan office at 10.30 a.m.

> Luckily within five minutes of arriving I had a call from a freelance journalist, Francis Beckett, who was working for the Campaign Against Selective Education. He told me the last group – in Trafford – wanting to get a ballot to end selective education in their education authority had finally decided to withdraw because they could not get enough signatures. It was a sad story from the *Mirror*'s perspective because it meant that despite legislation giving parents power to campaign for an end to selective education all 164 grammar schools in the country were safe because no group had managed to get a ballot. Cynics believe the legislation was framed specifically to help the government avoid getting into a battle over the future of grammar schools. I tend to think they are right.

Spends most of the rest of the day following up the story on the telephone. Over a year, he calculates that half his time is spent outside the office – 'far more than many other education correspondents'. He completes twenty pars (400 words) but only eight make the paper. 'It's still difficult seeing stories cut and it hurts when they spike my copy. But I could see why it happened because it was a very heavy news day.' That day the paper had covered the government's own 'glossy mag' performance update. Piers Morgan comes up to the specialist desk and asks each to compose their own 300-word report on the government's performance. 'He wanted it to be more objective and in no way sycophantic.' Later appears in his regular Thursday slot on LBC radio's *Julia Somerville Show* giving his views for ten minutes on government moves to force parents to attend lessons in parenthood if their children are found playing truant. Finishes at 6.30 p.m.

Friday: 10.30 a.m. and off to the High Court where the National Union of Teachers' (NUT) case against performance related pay proposals is being heard.

> I must confess I didn't realise the serious repercussions that granting the injunction could have so as I was going there in the morning I wasn't sure if I was on to a good story or not. So it is one of those occasions when you are sitting through the judge's ruling and it suddenly dawns on you that you

have a big story with the government facing its biggest legal shambles since the election.

When the judgment – for the NUT – finishes at 12.30 p.m. he is on the mobile immediately to the news desk trying to explain the implications. He writes 700 words (of which 500 make the paper) and it forms the page two lead story ('the best you can do on a Saturday').

Begins to prepare story for the coverage of the major public spending review announcement due the following week but all his contacts are more keen to talk on the pay ruling. On the way home, he is paged to appear on the BBC's *The World Tonight*. The radio car appears at 10 p.m. in his road and he is interviewed live by a journalist in the studio.

Sunday: often has to work on the 'day of rest', following up newspaper and television coverage. Working with his exclusive, off-the-record sources he predicts the spending review will apportion £10 billion to education (in the end it is £12 billion). The copy-taker tells him their screen has gone down so has to ring back – just as a long-lost friend arrives at his home. 'So I had to say: "Hi Alan, nice to see you" and then keep him waiting for ten minutes.' Then off to the cricket match.

Monday: off to Church House, Westminster for a Church of England press conference about an amendment to a bill on stressing the importance of marriage in the school curriculum.

> Ultimately it wasn't very interesting because it was a bland statement. The government accepted it anyway, so there was no element of conflict. But then Conservative Baroness Young proposed that the curriculum should stress marriage is the best way to bring up a child. And both the Church of England and the government opposed this since they felt it could stigmatise children who came from a non-marriage background.

Back to the office to write up story.

Picked up the government's emergency statement on performance related pay and gathers reactions by phoning contacts. Next interviews by phone four students who have attended summer schools in a scheme launched by millionaire philanthropist Peter Lampl aimed at increasing recruitment to Oxford, Cambridge, Bristol and Nottingham universities from inner city schools and backed by the *Mirror*. 'I have to reassure them they don't need to worry since if the results on 17 August show they are not successful I wouldn't then carry their profiles.'

Tuesday: it is the day of the public spending review announcement. Works on features for university supplement due after A level results are announced, and composes 900-word 'end of term' report on the government's education record for *Education* magazine. At 3.30 p.m. watches the statement by the Education Secretary David Blunkett on television. Immediately afterwards, the Department for Education and Employment's press office rings giving 10 minutes of background information. Telephones contacts for follow-ups. 'Now the teachers' unions are incredibly well organised and will fax me within minutes of any major announcement.' Completes 700-word story by 7.15 p.m., just before his 7.30 p.m. deadline.

Tiny outfit with a massive ambition

Profile   Gemini News Service

From its cramped offices in north London, Gemini News Service is a tiny operation with a massive ambition – to challenge the anti-Third World bias of the media. In some respects it has succeeded. Though largely unknown in Britain, in many Third World countries Gemini is more famous than such giants as Reuters and Agence France Presse.

The agency was founded on 1 January 1967 by Derek Ingram, formerly of the *Daily Mail*, and Oliver Carruthers, a British journalist who had been based in Zambia. A Sri Lankan, Gamini Seneviratne, was the first staff reporter. Ingram, who remained editor until 1993, commented:

> I was particularly concerned to promote reporting about Commonwealth countries from a London base. During the late 1960s, with the end of decolonisation, I saw newspapers in the Third World swamped with material written by British journalists. I wanted to see work about India, say, by Indians, about Zambia by Zambians. Gemini aimed to promote just that.

During the 1970s, the United Nations Educational, Scientific and Cultural Organisation (Unesco) became embroiled in controversies over development journalism, the New World Information and Communication Order (NWICO) and challenges to the international news system dominated by five leading agencies: the United Press International, Associated Press, Reuters, Agence France Presse and Tass. As Ingram commented: 'We were at the nub of the NWICO debate – but before Unesco had even thought of it.'

Since the heady days of the 1970s, Gemini's ownership, staffing numbers and news service have, not surprisingly, gone through many changes. Part of the Guardian Group during the 1970s, it became wholly independent in 1982. Later it was owned by a foundation (chaired by newscaster Trevor McDonald) whose deeds entrenched its editorial independence while in April 1999 it was taken over by Panos, an international information and communications nongovernmental organisation that works closely with journalists.

Dipankar De Sarkar, editor-in-chief, has twenty-one years' experience as a journalist – with the United News of India, India Abroad News Service, *India Express*, *India Today* magazine and New Delhi TV. In 1996, he became InterPress Service (IPS) London correspondent and Panos editor of features before moving over to Gemini at the takeover. He is convinced that, despite the increasing focus globally on business news and the monopoly trends in newspapers, there is 'still room for southern perspectives in the mainstream media in any country'. But he acknowledges that there are probably more opportunities in the developing world than in First World countries. Currently the service's 150 stringers around the world supply 1,000-word features to 50 subscribers in 27 countries – in the Middle East, Asia, Africa, North America and Europe. Newspapers include the *New Straits Times*, the *Kenyan Standard*, the *Deccan Herald* of Bangalore, the *Sowetan*, the *Daily Despatch* of Johannesburg, *Ottawa Citizen* and *Montreal Gazette*. In addition, 25 individuals receive the service by post.

A recent batch of Gemini features (plus graphics) highlights a range of important issues marginalised in the mainstream press: one examined the trial of the perpetrators of the Cambodian genocide; another profiled the Organisation of American States after novelist Mario Vargas Llosa condemned it as a 'decrepit institution'; a third focused on the Malaysian government's decision to back fixed monthly wages for plantation workers. But De Sarkar is keen to extend Gemini's remit to promote otherwise marginalised perspectives on European stories. For instance, after 58 Chinese immigrants were found suffocated to death at the back of a lorry in Dover in June 2000, Gemini carried a story from the Chinese city of Fujian. 'It defied western media stereotypes that portrayed the people of Fujian as living in poverty, reporting instead that here migration was the outcome of riches.'

In recent years most subscribers have shifted to receiving the service online: much less hassle, obviously, for Gemini than the old, laborious method of posting them off. With reduced resources, the service is down from offering twelve features a week to seven – but a relaunch is planned for the autumn offering ten features a week in two packages. The service's website (http://www.oneworld.net/gemini), being revamped by project manager and editorial assistant Alex Whiting, will provide subscribers access to Panos Pictures, a unique resource containing a quarter of a million images on southern issues and relevant artwork in both black and white and colour. A special search engine will help guide users through issues and countries, graphics and texts. In addition Gemini continues its scheme allowing a senior journalist and a Canadian graduate student to spend a few months at the London office before heading off to a Third World country on a reporting assignment for the rest of the year.

A WEEK IN THE LIFE OF GEMINI

Monday: Whiting (her background in television documentaries and magazine production) arrives at 9 a.m. and checks the emails for copy ideas. At an editorial meeting with De Sarkar, last week's features are assessed; future ones (not just for the current week) are planned. Panos's in-house database on upcoming events is invaluable. For instance, the Sydney Olympics were due to begin in September so the commissioning of stories on that event begins. Whiting handles queries from subscribers, makes sure none of the emails with copy have bounced back and works on changes to the website logo, along with the Panos press office. Ends around 6 p.m.

Tuesday: De Sankar discusses story selection with the two subeditors. Out of around twenty stories considered at the beginning of the week, five are killed, five are 'put on hold' while eleven are worked on. From these most of the eventual seven will come. The subs work on two stories each, emailing the writer any queries. 'Often our queries are seen as providing a form of training to the reporters,' says Whiting. A balance is sought between local and British styles of writing. The other authors are told their stories are being considered and to expect emailed queries the next day.

Wednesday: at the second editorial meeting of the week, the freelance graphic artist is given a run-down on the stories and graphics are discussed. The artist works closely with the subs who help find the facts and figures for the graphics. One of the two interns may be present to work on the stories or research their own. Work finishes at 7 p.m.

Thursday: editor and subeditors continue work on the chosen stories with the close involvement of the graphics artist: 8 p.m. finish.

Friday: 'Often there's a desperate hunt for the last two stories,' says De Sarkar. Slots are kept open for news-pegged features that may turn up at the last minute. Very often, a feature is pulled out at the last moment – and features based on breaking news are updated. The final seven stories are checked by the subs, editor and Whiting. The text format is arranged by a Panos information management specialist before distribution. A summary of the week's package is prepared for regular correspondents. Finish at 9 p.m.

2 Efficks, ethics or politics?

Mainstream journalists are often sceptical about the value of ethical debate. As media specialist Raymond Snoddy (1993) commented: 'It certainly sets the British press apart from newspapers in the US where on the whole the word "ethics" can be uttered without hoots of derision.' One journalism lecturer tells of when he invited a prominent Fleet Street editor to talk to his students about ethics. 'Efficks, What's that?' the editor asked, bemused and proceeded to tell a string of stories about his life and times in the industry.

There are a number of reasons for this scepticism. Many journalists are profoundly idealistic, concerned about ethical issues and determined to improve standards. Yet the dominant attitude in the mainstream press prioritises 'getting the story' and the demands of the deadline above all else. Ethical and political concerns are secondary, if they are ever considered at all. Linked to this attitude is the belief that the best way to learn reporting is 'on the job'. Practical-based training is tolerated but theoretical studies are generally thought a waste of time.

More importantly, many journalists (in particular young ones) are deeply sceptical about the power they have as individuals to improve media standards. Newspapers seem too committed to entrenched routines and mythologies, too prone to stereotyping and crude sensationalising, too closely tied to the political establishment and to the rigours of surviving in a market-led economy. Most newspaper operations are hierarchically organised with power to those (usually white men) at the top. Many lower down the pecking order often see themselves as impotent (and largely dispensable) cogs in a much larger machine. There is much talk of press freedom but little of the journalists' freedom to influence the organisation for which they work.

Adding to this ethical malaise are the theatrical, unreal elements at the heart of the current debate. A major controversy developed during the 1990s over the use of telephoto lenses and bugging devices by journalists following various controversies involving royals and other celebrities. Yet these issues confront only a tiny minority of journalists for a small part of their time. Far more significant political issues, such as the impact of advertisers or the role of the vast military/industrial complex on the coverage of wars, are marginalised.

The ethical tensions in the industry

Mainstream journalists' scepticism over standards is, in part, a consequence of the ethical contradictions within the newspaper industry. Its central position as a largely monopolistic industry in a profit-oriented economic system means business and entertainment priorities dominate. News becomes, above all, a commodity to be sold. Yet journalists' rhetoric promotes notions of the public interest, the right to know and the free press which are often in conflict with the priorities of the marketplace. Moreover, while journalists stress the importance of 'objectivity' and 'truth' (news being a mirror of reality), these notions conflict with the actual production of bias, myth and state propaganda by the press.

The ethics of everyday journalism

Journalists' widespread scepticism about ethics is strange given the importance of the job's moral and political dimensions. All journalists talk of news 'values'. Moreover, representations of good and bad, the just and the unjust/criminal predominate in the media (Cohen 1980). Read any red-top tabloid and you will see stories about 'evil' rapists, 'monsters' who attack old ladies, 'evil' mums who lead their children into prostitution, 'Nazi' Serbs who butcher innocent Bosnians. The 1991 Gulf conflict carried this reporting genre to its extreme with representations of President George Bush as 'good, pacific and heroic' engaged in a personal battle with President Saddam Hussein of Iraq, the 'evil, bully, Butcher, new Hitler of Baghdad'. During the Nato attacks on Serbia in 1999, President Slobodan Milosevic was also demonised as 'evil' and a 'new Hitler'. Jostein Gripsrud (1992) relates this moralising dimension of newspapers to the emotional excesses of the nineteenth-century morality play. Today it is the press (and mass media in general) which provide moral tales, stories that give lessons in and define what is good and bad, normal and abnormal.

The notion of standards is also central to any concept of professionalism. This concept emerged in the latter half of the nineteenth century as the radical, dissident, partisan working class-based newspapers collapsed following the ending of the Stamp Tax in 1855 and mainstream newspapers became integrated into the market-led economy (Curran and Seaton 1994: 11–48). Linked to this process of professionalisation came the stress on concepts such as objectivity, neutrality, fairness, accuracy and the separation of fact from opinion. The concern of unions and management since the Second World War to promote journalism training has been closely tied to notions of standards and professionalism.

The politics of everyday journalism

Many journalists challenge such notions as professionalism, objectivity and the free press and stress the mainstream media's function as one of social reproduction in the interests of dominant groups and classes. As Brian McNair (1996: 33) comments: 'News is never a mere recording or reporting of the world "out there" but a synthetic, value-laden account which carries within it dominant assumptions and ideas of the society within which it is produced.' Journalists committed to such principles often opt, for political and ethical reasons, either to work critically within mainstream media or for an 'alternative' outlet such as a leftist or gay newspaper, trade union or environmental campaigning publication. Other journalists are inspired by religious or humanistic convictions to work critically within mainstream media or for 'alternative' publications.

Some everyday ethical dilemmas

Beyond these general observations let us identify some everyday ethical issues that can confront journalists:

- Should journalists ever lie or use deceit in the pursuit of a story?
- Should they ever edit a direct quote?
- Is it legitimate to tape a conversation and not inform the interviewee of this?
- Should journalists accept freebies? Should they do so only on certain conditions? Are there any significantly different ethical issues in being offered a book for review, a free ticket to review a play and a free trip to the Seychelles for a travel feature?
- Which special considerations should journalists have when interviewing children?
- Is chequebook journalism (paying sources) justified. (Phil Hall, the editor of *News of the World*, in November 1996 said that in almost 10 per cent of stories subjects were paid.)
- Is it legitimate to invade someone's privacy for a story? Do different standards apply to public figures and members of the general public?
- Is it legitimate ever to break an embargo?
- To what extent does newspaper language reinforce militarist and ageist stereotypes and how can journalists confront these issues?
- What ethical issues are raised by business sponsorship of newspaper editions?

To relate this ethical discussion to the practicalities of the job, you might talk to journalists from Britain and abroad about these issues. What do they consider to be the most important ethical issues facing them in their jobs?

A brief history of moves to improve press standards

Since the Second World War, press standards have attracted constant concern from governments, politicians and the general public. Royal Commissions have reported, surveys into press content have been conducted, committees have pondered such issues as bias, sensationalism, trivialisation, invasions of privacy, proprietorial intervention. The impact on the industry is uncertain. Many of the calls for reform have been simply ignored by the industry.

The first Royal Commission in 1947 arose out of concerns over growing monopolies, with Lord Rothermere, owner of the *Daily Mail*, Lord Beaverbrook, of the *Daily Express*, and Lord Kemsley, of the *Daily Sketch*, *Daily Graphic* and *Sunday Times*, coming under particular scrutiny. Beaverbrook was frank before the commission, saying he ran his paper 'purely for the purpose of making propaganda and with no other motive'. Yet the commission failed to conclude that the industry was endangered by increasingly powerful monopolies. Nor did it discover any concerted efforts by advertisers to influence newspapers. But the commission did express concerns over political bias, inaccuracies and trivialisation. It rejected measures to limit newspaper circulations or profits as well as legislation to halt intrusions into privacy.

Most significantly, the commission recommended a General Council of the Press be set up to safeguard press freedoms and encourage the development of a sense of public responsibility among journalists. It was four years before the council first met on 21 July 1953. Its first ruling was that a *Daily Mirror* poll on whether Princess Margaret should marry Group Captain Pater Townsend was 'contrary to the best traditions of British journalism' (how royal reporting has changed!). A second Royal Commission, set up in 1961, also followed mounting concern over monopolies. Chaired by Lord Shawcross, a former Labour Attorney-General, it criticised the industry over its poor response to the 1949 commission's recommendations and stressed the importance of including a lay element on the General Council. Thus, the Press Council came into being in July 1963 – with twenty industry representatives and five lay members.

The first commission had predicted no significant trends towards further concentration of ownership. Events had proved it wrong. By 1962 the top three proprietors' slice of the national daily press had risen to 89 per cent, major monopolies were growing in the periodical press and only in local weeklies was concentration 'negligible'. To contain this trend it proposed a Press Amalgamations Court. Legislation in 1965 incorporated some elements of this idea with major takeovers having to be approved by the Secretary of State. Yet virtually all the acquisitions of newspaper companies by major press groups during the period 1965–99 were allowed.

The Younger Committee on Privacy was established in 1970 after a Private Member's bill seeking to introduce a general right of privacy was rejected by the Labour government. It considered a wide range of issues: for instance, how the right to know could conflict with the right to be protected from intrusive reporters; how reporting could cause personal suffering which might outweigh any claims of public interest. In the end it decided against the introduction of a right to privacy law. A third Royal Commission (1974–7) reported with concern that three owners dominated the national daily and Sunday markets, while in the regions morning, evening and weekly papers were being owned by the same group. The commission was also critical of the performance of the Press Council, making twelve recommendations to transform its operating procedures. However, these were largely rejected and the council remained a weak body, lacking the confidence of both the managers and the NUJ (Robertson 1983).

Calcutt report into privacy and related matters

In 1989, following a spate of controversies over press intrusions into private grief, Margaret Thatcher's government authorised a committee to investigate the possible introduction of a privacy law. Chaired by David Calcutt, master of Magdalene College, Cambridge, the committee heard evidence from a wide range of people. For instance, the father of an *EastEnders* actor who had committed suicide complained of press harassment. In the end, the committee came out against a privacy law but recommended making physical intrusion an offence. The industry, however, reacted quickly to the call to set up a self-regulatory Press Complaints Commission in place of the Press Council and so attempt to ward off legislation. The first of many versions of a Code of Practice was introduced and most of the national newspapers also appointed ombudsmen to consider readers' complaints. They were to prove to have only very limited influence.

Second Calcutt report on privacy and the press

In January 1993, Calcutt (by then Sir David) presented a second report focusing on press and privacy issues. The PCC was accused of being ineffective and too dominated by the industry. Calcutt singled out its handling of revelations contained in Andrew Morton's (1992) biography of Diana, Princess of Wales, various sex scandals (involving such prominent figures as Paddy Ashdown, leader of the Liberal Democrats, and David Mellor, National Heritage Minister and Chelsea supporter) and the *People*'s contemptuous treatment of the commission after it printed pictures of an infant royal running naked.

In response Calcutt proposed new offences carrying maximum fines of £5,000 for invasions of privacy and the use of surveillance and bugging devices in certain cases. In defence, journalists could claim the material was obtained for preventing, detecting or exposing crime or antisocial behaviour, or to prevent people being misled by some statement or action of the individual concerned. John Major's government responded positively and later in the year proposed the introduction of a privacy law. Yet it was determined not to apply the restrictions to the security services. As the *UK Press Gazette* of 6 September 1993 commented:

> The greatest invasion of privacy is carried out every day by the security services, with no control, no democratic authorisation and the most horrifying consequences for people's employment and lives. By comparison with them the press is a poodle.

The PCC responded to all this controversy by introducing new clauses to the code on bugging and the use of telephoto lenses and a lay majority (though only of the great and the good) was created among its members. In addition it appointed Professor Robert Pinker, of the London School of Economics, as its special privacy commissioner.

How the privacy debate hit fever pitch

In November 1993, 'peeping Tom' photographs taken secretly of a reclining Princess Diana working out at a gym and published in the *Sunday Mirror* and *Mirror* refuelled the privacy debate – though it continued to be focused narrowly on the problems faced by Britain's aristocracy and political elite. As John Tulloch (1998: 80) comments: 'The impression remains that the PCC, constructed out of a pact between the great and the good and the newspaper establishment, is most concerned to look after its own.'

A *Sunday Times* sting operation in July 1994 against two Conservative Members of Parliament (MPs) which revealed them accepting £1,000 from a journalist to ask questions in Parliament, provoked more controversy. The newspaper was originally backed by the PCC but predictably condemned in April 1995 by the Commons Privileges Committee (with its built-in Conservative majority) for 'falling substantially below the standards to be expected of legitimate journalism'. Then surprisingly, in March 1996, the PCC reversed its decision, ruling that the newspaper did not first gather enough information since an issue of serious public interest was at stake.

In October 1994, the *Guardian* began its own long campaign to expose sleaze among Conservative MPs taking cash handouts in return for asking parliamentary questions. *Guardian* editor Peter Preston admitted that his reporters sent a 'cod fax' to the Ritz Hotel in Paris in the hunt for financial information about Cabinet minister (former journalist and great-nephew of *Daily Express* owner Lord Beaverbrook) Jonathan Aitken, using a mock-up of the House of Commons notepaper to protect the source. The privacy debate duly reached fever pitch (Leigh and Vulliamy 1997).

Preston was summoned to explain his use of the fax to Parliament's Sergeant-at-Arms and resigned from the PCC. Soon afterwards, Premier John Major set up a committee, chaired by Lord Nolan, which eventually drew up guidelines for the ethical behaviour of politicans and lobbyists. After being discovered lying over the payment of a bill at the Paris Ritz during a libel case against the *Guardian*, Aitken was duly jailed for 18 months in July 1999 (though in the end he served only 30 weeks) and the newspaper went on to win award after award for its fearless investigation.

The newly appointed PCC chairman, the Tory grandee Lord Wakeham, in early 1995 gave a strong warning to editors not to abuse the public interest defence when facing complaints over invasions of privacy. Soon afterwards the PCC criticised the *News of the World* for publishing pictures, gained through the use of a long-lens camera, of yet another aristocrat, a frail-looking Countess Spencer, sister-in-law of the Princess of Wales, in the garden of a private health clinic. After her husband, Earl Spencer, complained, Professor Pinker contacted Rupert Murdoch, owner of the *News of the World*, who publicly reprimanded its editor, Piers Morgan. Murdoch described Morgan as 'a young man' who 'went over the top' in his coverage. The editor duly apologised – and went on to even greater fame as editor of the *Mirror* (Browne 1996). Then in July 1995, the government's long-awaited White Paper appeared – but it retreated from imposing any privacy legislation (Department of National Heritage 1995). Instead, it called for

- the PCC to pay compensation from an industry fund to victims of privacy intrusion
- a 'hotline' between the chairman and editors to head off breaches of the code
- non-industry members to sit on the PCC's code committee
- the code to be tightened up to include a clearer definition of privacy.

Tory backbenchers greeted the announcement with jeers; the Labour Party expressed disappointment. Yet the privacy issue hit a new peak of intensity after the death of Princess Diana in Paris in a car crash on Sunday 31 August 1997 (Hanstock 1999). Blame initially fell on the paparazzi following the royal Mercedes and on the press which had so mercilessly pursued the Princess (though it was generally acknowledged that she had exploited the press when it suited her). New guidelines on the use of paparazzi photographs were introduced; in revising the code, Lord Wakeham redefined 'a private place' as covering the interior of a church, a restaurant and other places 'where individuals might rightly be free from media attention'.

Money matters: CHECKING OUT CHEQUEBOOK
JOURNALISM

The Major government did threaten to intervene in the controversial area of 'cheque-book journalism'. Following payments by newspapers to nineteen witnesses in the Rosemary West multiple murders trial, the Lord Chancellor, Lord Mackay of Clashfern, in October 1996, proposed bringing in a criminal law to ban such payments. The PCC responded predictably by lauding the benefits of self-regulation and revising its code again to highlight the importance of full disclosure. The issue was even taken up by the Labour government in February 2000 when the Lord Chancellor, Lord Irvine, announced that the government was to review payments by the press to witnesses in criminal trials. Guy Black, PCC director, immediately responded by claiming that the issue had arisen only five times in the past fifty years so such legislation was unnecessary.

Earlier, a series of newspaper payments to criminals drew some intriguing rulings from the PCC. After two nurses, jailed in Saudi Arabia for murder, were released early, in May 1998, newspapers raced to dangle chequebooks in front of them. Deborah Parry was 'bought' by the *Express* and Lucille McLaughlan by the *Mirror*. Soon afterwards the PCC ruled that their stories were in the public interest. Payment controversies also erupted after *The Times* serialised Gitta Sereny's (1998) biography of child murderer Mary Bell and after the *Daily Mail* paid £40,000 to the parents of au-pair Louise Woodward, convicted of the manslaughter of baby Matthew Eapen in Boston: again the PCC ruled that there were clear public interest defences. But the *Daily Telegraph* was censured by the PCC in July 1999 for paying Victoria Aitken about £1,000 for writing about her jailed father's plight since it could not be defended in the public interest. The code's guidelines on payments to criminals also meant that the commission investigated the £65,000 paid by the *Sunday Times* to serialise Aitken's memoirs, though it was done only on the condition that the money went straight to the creditors of the former cabinet minister.

The politics of sleaze reporting

An unprecedented number of political resignations occurred in the three years after John Major's election victory of 1992 and his launch of a 'Back to Basics' moral crusade, many of them following 'scandalous' revelations in the press. Such scandals were not confined to Britain. Hardly a country was unaffected as ruling elites bickered among themselves following the ending of the Cold War and the demise of the old Soviet enemy. In all, there were fourteen resignations on the grounds of scandal in Britain over the three years: about half the cases involved sexual activities and about half financial irregularities. All were men.

The *Independent on Sunday* (23 July 1995) claimed that a five-year period (1990–5) saw thirty-four Conservatives, one Liberal Democrat and four Labour scandals; of these, at least a quarter involved sex. Furthermore, a study of parliamentary reporting in the nationals between 1990 and 1995 found that 'scandal and personal misconduct' was the third most frequently reported topic, way ahead of major issues such as health (eighth), education (tenth), social services (thirty-fifth) and race (thirty-eight) (Franklin 1997: 32). Sleaze also dogged the Labour government. The breakdown of the marriage of Robin Cook, Foreign Secretary, and the failure of Peter lson, Minister without Portfolio, to declare how a gift from Geoffrey Robinson, a Cabinet minister, had helped him purchase a London house (leading to the resignations of both Mandelson and Robinson) were among the most celebrated scandals to hit the headlines (Baston 2000: 192–209).

Underlying newspapers' coverage of sleaze lies the operation of consensual news values. As Hogan (1998) comments: 'The problem with the coverage of sleaze was how scandal of a predominantly sexual nature spread from Sunday tabloids to Sunday evening BBC and ITN news. By Monday the broadsheet press were covering the scandals.' Behind the formation of such a consensus, the political factors remain the most interesting and significant (Keeble 1998). Now little distinguishes the three major parties in Britain. Tony Blair, the Labour leader, proclaimed himself a follower of Margaret Thatcher, mouthed Thatcherite rhetoric with consummate ease and dutifully followed Thatcherite politicies (Hay 1999). The emergence of New Toryism as New Labour represents, in one respect, the death of (classical) politics. Peter Mair (2000) talks of the 'assault on partisan politics' and the 'depoliticised democracy'. In its place has emerged the politics of personality, of sexual scandal and sleaze. The Bill Clinton/Monica Lewinsky scandal represents the ultimate manifestation of this process in the United States. Newspapers no longer draw their central inspiration from politics but from the worlds of Hollywood, entertainment generally, television and sport.

Privacy legislation: BY THE BACK DOOR?

While in opposition, the Labour Party had appeared largely sympathetic to calls for privacy legislation as a way of curbing press excesses. When in office, its tune changed. Soon after its May 1997 landslide victory, New Labour made it clear it was not planning to introduce privacy laws unless newspapers behaved in an 'intolerable fashion'. Journalists disguising themselves as doctors was given as an example of such behaviour.

Fears grew among prominent journalists that the European Convention on Human Rights, which the government was due to incorporate into British law, could introduce privacy legislation 'by the back door'. But on 11 February 1998, Tony Blair pledged in the Commons that the government had no such intention. Article 8 of the convention, incorporated into British law in October 1999, states: 'Everybody has the right to respect for his private and family life, his home and his correspondence.' But balancing this, Article 10 guarantees freedom of expression. Significantly, on 16 January 1998, the European Commission of Human Rights had ruled that Earl Spencer and his former wife had insufficient grounds for starting a case in court under the European Convention of Human Rights over the government's failure to protect them against press intrusions.

Then in April 2000, the PCC condemned the *News of the World* in what Roy Greenslade, media commentator of the *Guardian*, described as a 'landmark' judgment on privacy. A typical kiss 'n' tell story by the former fiancé of *Coronation Street* actress, Jacqueline Pirie, was said to have breached clause 3 of the code: 'Everyone is entitled to his or her private and family life, home, health and correspondence'. As Greenslade (2000) concluded: 'In other words, the one-sided account by Pirie's ex-fiancé, even though its truth has not been disputed, was considered to have invaded her privacy.'

To relate this coverage to the practicalities of the job why not ask some journalists their views on the introduction of a privacy law. Some prominent journalists, such as Alan Rusbridger, editor of the *Guardian*, and Selina Scott (victim of a 1995 *News of the World* contrived sexposé) have come out in favour of a privacy law. Do your local journalists (on mainstream and non-mainstream media) agree? Have they ever used a bugging device in pursuit of a story? Or do they find ethical controversies largely irrelevant? Do newspapers in your area offer readers a right of reply?

Sex matters: COMBATING SEXISM

There are no easy answers to the many ethical dilemmas in journalism. Even when people agree on the importance of certain principles (such as anti-sexism, anti-racism, anti-militarism) differences may emerge over strategies for implementing them. While certain attitudes and routines predominate throughout the mainstream media, each newspaper still has its unique culture. What is possible at one will be impossible at another. Thus in tackling sexism within the industry there are many strategies available. For instance, once you have secured your first job, you may choose to lie low on ethical issues and wait until you have established your credibility before speaking out.

You may work on ethical or political issues through the National Union of Journalists. Your newspaper may routinely carry page three-type images of women and glorify macho images of men. In this context, you may choose to work discreetly, raising issues in discussions with colleagues, using any freedom you have in choosing features and sources to tackle sexist assumptions. Some journalists even opt out of mainstream media for ethical reasons. For them, working in the mainstream involves too many ethical compromises. They may see racist, sexist and class biases too firmly entrenched. Constant confrontations over these issues can prove both exhausting and counter-productive. In contrast, they may find a culture away from the mainstream press more open to progressive ideas. Wherever you choose to work, a sense of humour and a willingness to subject your own views to searching criticism will always prove invaluable.

The questioning approach

Since ethical debate remains remote from the dominant journalists' culture, simply raising pertinent questions can become an important first step. Many ethical questions stem from the unjust distribution of power in society; they are, at root, political issues. The focus tends to fall on the 'oppressed' – women, children, elderly people, disabled people and ethnic minority groups. The dominant questions focus around how discrimination and stereotyping can be reduced. But is there not a danger here of focusing on these groups as victims (of oppression and consequent stereotyping) while the problem groups are really the oppressors – men, adults, the able-bodied, the dominant ethnic groups?

The question of sexism

The 1990s witnessed a few advances for women in the mainstream press. In May 1991, Eve Pollard became the first woman editor of the *Sunday Express* while, in

April 1998, Rosie Boycott became the first woman editor of a broadsheet (the strug-gling *Independent on Sunday*) before moving on first to the editorship of the *Independent* and then – in April 1998 – of the *Express*. At the *Sunday Mirror*, editorial control in November 1996 was in the hands of three women: managing director Bridget Rowe, deputy managing director Pat Moore and acting editor Amanda Platell. This was the first time in Fleet Street history that an all-female executive triumvir-ate had held power on a national newspaper. In May 2000, Rebekah Wade, at 31, became editor of the *News of the World*, the world's biggest-selling English-language newspaper, and in the same month Rebecca Hardy, at 34, became the first woman editor of the *Scotsman*. At the local level, the *Diss Express* was staffed entirely by women. On 8 March 2000, to mark International Women's Day the *Western Mail* changed its name to the *Western Femail* and was edited by Pat English with Michelle Bower as head of content. As Norren Taylor (2000) comments, male newspaper owners had 'realised that winning women readers and attracting female-targeted advertising is best achieved by promoting women'.

Yet all the same, research by Women in Journalism (WiJ) pressure group published in 1996 revealed a 'pervasive and flexible strand of stereotyping through coverage of women in the news'. Newsrooms tended to be male-dominated and traditional sexist attitudes survived unscathed. WiJ concluded: 'It seems clear that sometimes news desks go on autopilot, trotting out clichés and stereotypes when, in fact, the woman in the story before them is unique.' A later report from WiJ, *Real Women: The Hidden Sex*, in November 1999 highlighted the sexist use of images of women to 'lift' pages.

Most political editors and lobby correspondents remain male. 'So,' according to Harriet Harman (2000), 'political news is reported in a way that appeals to and inter-ests men. Issues of particular concern to women are inevitably lower on the agenda. This reinforces the sense among women that politics is a male activity of no relev-ance to them.' Research has also shown the general bias in news reporting towards male sources (Allan 1999: 141). Margareta Melin-Higgins (1997) found that most of the female journalists she interviewed were concerned that the recruitment system was disadvantageous to women in an industry where an 'old-boys network loomed large'. Significantly, *Mirror* editor Piers Morgan in October 1998 said his newspaper employed just 62 women to 204 men – but female staff had quadrupled since 1983. In July 2000, only seven local newspapers were edited by women.

Women journalists too often face ridicule from their male colleagues. Ginny Dougary (author of *Executive Tarts and Other Myths*) was criticised for being an 'ambitious girl reporter' (she was 38) after her revealing profile of Chancellor Norman Lamont was published in *The Times* magazine in September 1994. As Amanda Platell comments on the institutionalised sexism in the press,

> it's about pigeonholing women journalists, denying equality of pay and conditions and opportunities, demeaning them and making assumptions about them. It's about a widespread and inherent belief by some men that women can't cut it, that news-papers are a man's world, that women are only good for one thing – 'features' – and that ritual humiliation is a way of keeping girls in their place.
>
> (Platell 1999: 144)

All reporters should be aware of the major feminist and post-feminist texts (e.g. Spender 1983; Paglia 1995) and try to combat the routine marginalisation of women's voices in the media. Reports and features, where possible, should reflect the gender (as well as the race, age and class) diversity of the society. Editors need to be convinced that women's issues should not be confined to special pages and soft features. Just as newspapers have defence and environment specialists, should they not have specialists producing news with a women's focus?

Men and sexism

All these issues 'problematise' women. Instead, let us focus on men. To what extent are male roles stereotyped in the press with images glorifying macho firmness, violence, power, militarism, heroism and success? Do not reviewers have a responsibility to challenge such representations in films, plays and books? To what extent does the press encourage men to question their emotional unease, their career obsessions or their traditional roles away from the home and child-rearing? To what extent are men challenged over their responses to sexual violence towards women or to the sexual harassment of women in the workplace?

To add a further complexity to the debate, it can be argued that sexism sometimes works in favour of women. Women foreign correspondents often say the 'invisibility' of women in some cultures helps give them access to places where men would be banned or harassed (see Leslie 1999). Editors are sometimes said to favour women as profile writers since men are considered more likely to open up to a female interviewer. Even the new head of the Equal Opportunities Commission (EOC), Julie Mellor, said that men were the new victims: 'Men look at what women have achieved and they would like the same thing – more part-time work, more flexible hours. But the long hours culture prevents them thinking about it.'

Man-made language

The marginalisation of women in the press and the glorification of macho or laddish values do not usually come from any deliberate policy. They emerge within a political culture where certain attitudes are routinely adopted and certain questions are routinely eliminated. One area where sexism is most evident is in language. Very often the male bias of language can render women invisible (Spender 1980; Mills 1991). Or it can infantilise them. For instance, when the Labour victory of 1997 was accompanied by a large new influx of women MPs they were immediately dubbed (in sexist terms) 'Blair's babes'.

Challenging this bias is no easy task. Some newspaper-style books avoid all mention of sexist language issues except in relation to the use of 'Ms', 'Miss' and 'Mrs'. Most newspapers now accept the use of 'Ms' where appropriate and avoid using 'he' when 'he or she' or 'they' (as a singular bisexual pronoun) is more accurate. Phrases such as 'the common man' and the 'man in the street' are also widely avoided. Discussions over style book changes, then, provide opportunities to raise language issues. But style book revisions are often monopolised by an editorial elite. In certain situations it might be appropriate to work with your colleagues in the NUJ to confront sexist stereotyping in language. To assist such campaigns, the union has drawn up an *Equality Style Guide* suggesting words to be avoided and alternatives. Here are some examples:

businessman	business manager, executive, boss, business chief, head of firm
cameraman	photographer, camera operator
dustman	refuse collector
fireman/men	firefighter, fire services staff, fire crews
foreman	supervisor
gentleman's agreement	verbal agreement
ice cream man	ice cream seller
mankind	humanity, people
newsman	journalist, reporter
nightwatchman	caretaker, security guard
policeman/men	police officer, police
salesman/girl	assistant, shop worker, shop staff, representative, sales staff
spaceman	astronaut
stewardess/air hostess	airline staff, flight attendant, cabin crew
workmen	workers, workforce

Even where style books fail to acknowledge these issues, there is often a certain degree of stylistic freedom available to the reporter to use such language.

Race and anti-racism: NOT JUST A BLACK AND WHITE ISSUE

It could be argued that the British press is at its worse when engaging in racist, overtly xenophobic rhetoric. Attacks on 'Arab rats', 'funny Frogs', 'boring Belgians' or 'lazy Irish' are commonplace in the patriotic pops (Searle 1989; Gordon and Rosenberg 1989). In March 2000, for instance, the *Sun* directed its venom at East European 'beggars' and 'Gypsy scroungers' yet failed to turn its attention to proprietor Rupert Murdoch, 'who has managed to avoid paying corporation tax in this country for years' (Wheen 2000). The PCC received hundreds of complaints from readers following crudely racist, anti-German coverage in the tabloids during the Euro96 football tournament.

But since racist oppression is historically rooted in Britain's imperial past, is it not inevitable that the press, so much a part of the dominant economic system and its consensual news values, should reflect this? As Max Hastings, editor of the London *Evening Standard*, commented: 'We're hideously racist in our approach to news. Because people in Bosnia look like us and speak quite good English we're more interested in what happens to them and we sympathise with them more than we do with the Sudanese.' Along with institutional racism goes the overt racism of some journalists. For instance, the *Sun*'s acting editor was recorded as saying: 'I'm not having pictures of darkies on the front page' (Hollingsworth 1990: 132).

A major report by Anthony Delano and John Henningham (1995) of the London College of Printing concluded that less than 2 per cent of British press, radio and television journalists were black or ethnic while out of around four thousands national newspaper journalists only two or three dozen are black. Moves to increase the number of black journalists through special training grants and other means need to be supported. Too often newspaper coverage of ethnic minority groups and asylum seekers focuses on 'problems' such as 'riots', violence, crime, 'welfare scrounging' and drug abuse. Alongside this representation go media images of Muslim fanatics as mad and threatening global stability. The sensational coverage given to race issues feeds on people's fears and reinforces them.

Tackling racism

There are no easy answers. As Allan (1999: 182) comments: 'The ways in which racist presuppositions are implicated in the routinized practices of news production, from the news values in operation to "gut instincts" about source credibility, are often difficult to identify let alone reverse.' But there are some useful strategies. Language used uncritically can play a crucial role in perpetuating racism (van Dijk 1991). Thus be wary of using 'black' in a negative context. Should alternatives be found for blackspot (accident site) and blackleg (strike-breaker)? The NUJ has drawn up guidelines for race reporting and for covering racist organisations which are worth consulting.

Mainstream journalists also need to extend their range of contacts to incorporate ethnic minority groups. The *Washington Post*, for instance, has a diversity committee which reviews ethnic and racial composition of staff, a correspondent dedicated to race relations issues, and a series of informal lunches where staff and the ombudsman meet to discuss the way the paper reports race issues. In London, scholarships are reserved for minority journalists at City University but all newspapers should develop strategies for recruiting, retaining and promoting ethnic staff and consider the appointment of race relations specialists. Similarly, journalists need to be far more aware of the major religions of the world.

The *Leicester Mercury* has half a dozen correspondents from the city's Asian communities who file news and pictures regularly. The Nottingham *Evening Post* has launched an ethnic awareness programme for all its editorial staff. Bradford *Telegraph and Argus* has had an Asian columnist, Anila Baig, tackling such subjects as trips back to Pakistan and the cultural difficulties that young Asians can encounter (A. Moore 1999). Journalists need to be made aware of alternative and ethnic media, (such as *Muslim News*, *Q News*, *Eastern Eye*, *Asian Times*, *Voice*, *New Nation*, *Jewish Chronicle* and *Race and Class*) their different ethical standpoints and their opportunities for offering alternative careers away from mainstream stereotyping – and the anti-racist campaigns of journals such as *Socialist Worker*, *Searchlight* and *New Left Review*.

Handling disability: PEOPLE FIRST?

Government research suggests that there are 8.6 million adults with disabilities in Britain (including 23,000 deaf people and people with impaired hearing) yet they are marginalised, rendered invisible or stereotyped in the press and throughout the media ('Disabled Lives', *New Internationalist*; Oxford; July 1992). Scope, the organisation for people with cerebral palsy, in a survey of press coverage of disabled people, concluded: 'There remains an imbalance between the reality of people's lives, hopes and aspirations and the way they are written about. Too often stereotypes are used and false assumptions indulged.'

Covering people with disabilities poses a number of ethical issues for journalists which have been highlighted in a campaign 'People First' by the NUJ and the Campaign for Press and Broadcasting Freedom (with leaflets available for partially sighted people, in braille and on tape). The campaign suggests that, as a reporter, you should never assume that your audience is able-bodied. When advertising events (in listings, entertainment reviews, travel and eating out features), newspapers have a responsibility to identify the provision for access by disabled people. Similarly, traditional news values which marginalise the concerns of people with disabilities and confine them to specialist columns and publications need to be challenged.

The campaign also raises some other pertinent questions: how often are the voices of disabled people represented in the press by 'able-bodied' experts? How much is coverage of disabled people over-sentimentalised? Too often, stereotypes of disability promote the idea that charity can solve their 'problems' while marginalising the view that political and economic changes are needed to end the discrimination they confront. Similarly, disabled people are often associated with being courageous, tragic victims, eternally cheerful, grateful, pathetic and asexual. How often is it recognised they may be black, or lesbian or gay?

Language

As a number of style books point out, it is better to refer to 'disabled people' rather than 'the disabled', which depersonalises them and focuses entirely on their disability. Words such as 'cripple', 'deaf and dumb' and 'abnormal' should be avoided. Negative words and phrases should not be linked with disabilities as in 'lame duck', 'blind stupidity' and 'deaf to reason'. 'Physically challenged' is not generally accepted as a substitute for 'disabled'. Use 'wheelchair user' but not 'wheelchair bound'.

Avoiding the victim syndrome:

HANDLING AIDS STORIES

Journalists face special ethical issues when compiling AIDS-related stories. Reporting of AIDS-related diseases in the early 1980s was minimal because those affected – gays, drug users and Africans – were already marginalised by the press. Since then coverage of AIDS-related stories has too often been either sensationalised, with the creation of 'moral panics' exploiting and perpetuating fears of the fatal condition, and of sexuality in general, or more recently marginalised. Some style books have identified areas where special care is needed. For instance, on reporting claims for an AIDS cure, the Reuters style book commented:

> If a story making dramatic claims for a cure for AIDS or cancer does not come from a reputable named source it must be checked with recognised medical experts before being issued (or spiked). If such a story is issued it should include whatever balancing or interpretative material is available from such authorities.

A leaflet produced by the NUJ and the Health Education Authority, *HIV and AIDS: A Guide for Journalists*, suggests that stories should not perpetuate myths that AIDS can be spread through casual contact such as kissing. It can be spread only through intimate sexual contact, by the sharing of needles by drug addicts, by blood transfusion or from mother to infant in pregnancy. Some reports about children with HIV, it says, have provoked anxieties among pupils and parents. Confidentiality about infection by either a child or adult should always be respected. No pressure should be put on people to reveal their identities. Even when names and addresses have been supplied by the police, these should be revealed only with the consent of those concerned.

The NUJ has also drawn up a useful guide for covering AIDS (acquired immune deficiency syndrome) stories. Instead of 'carrying AIDS' or 'AIDS carrier' or 'AIDS positive' (which confuses the two phases of being infected with HIV and having AIDS) it suggests 'people with HIV'. 'AIDS test' is to be avoided since the most commonly used test detects antibodies to HIV (human immunodeficiency virus). Someone who proves positive, and thus infected with HIV, does not necessarily go on to develop AIDS. A better phrase is 'HIV antibody test'. When the distinction is made clearly between HIV and AIDS, there is no need to use the term 'full-blown AIDS'. Nor is it possible to 'catch AIDS' like colds or flu. Better to say 'contract HIV'. People do not 'die of AIDS' but of cancers or pneumonia that develop because of a weakened immune system.

Many people with HIV express concern over the way the press has represented them as helpless victims. Reports should avoid phrases such as 'AIDS sufferer' or 'AIDS victim' since someone with AIDS can continue working for some time after diagnosis. Better to say 'person with AIDS'. Also avoid 'innocent victim' since this suggests that others are guilty. The style guide suggests avoiding using the term 'high risk groups' since there is risk behaviour rather than risk groups. In addition, the NUJ has drawn up a model, nine-point house agreement promoting employment protection for those infected with HIV or who have AIDS.

Censorship and self-censorship

It might seem strange to journalists on a small weekly to raise the issue of censorship. The problem at their newspaper might not be censorship but the opposite: finding enough material to fill the next edition. Proprietorial interference may be non-existent. As for the advertisers, they might take up more space than is ideal but that is reality in a market-driven economy, isn't it? Yet, for all journalists, censorship issues are relevant. At the most basic level, the dominant news values prioritise certain sources and perspectives and marginalise or eliminate others. In a way, isn't that a form of censorship?

The impact of advertisers

The impact of advertisers on the press is enormous. Occasionally they will put pressure on editors to highlight favourable stories and downgrade or remove others. Freesheets, entirely dependent on advertisers, are particularly vulnerable to this. As Donald Trelford (2000), former editor of the *Observer*, comments: 'There are certainly some parts of newspapers, usually in consumer areas such as travel, motoring and property where the choice of subject and the editorial treatment dance to a tune set by the advertisement department'. But in general, the pressure is far more subtle.

Within the general economic environment, advertisers promote the values of materialism and consumerism as well as a conservative respect for the status quo.

Curran and Seaton (1994: 32–48) argue that the emergence of an advertisement-based newspaper industry in the late nineteenth century helped stifle the development of a radical press. Even as late as 1964, the Labour-backing *Daily Herald* closed with a readership far larger than that of *The Times* and *Financial Times* combined. It had crucially failed to win the support of the advertisers.

The impact of proprietorial intervention:

THE MAXWELL FACTOR ET AL.

The film *Citizen Kane* captured all the mystique and romance that surround the media mogul in the cultural history of the West. Men like the American media tycoon William Randolph Hearst, on whom Kane was based, and Northcliffe, Beaverbrook, Rothermere, Rowland, Murdoch and Maxwell have cultivated images which have made them seem almost larger-than-life: eccentric, egocentric, super-powerful, super-rich. There are many accounts of these proprietors interfering in the day-to-day operations of their newspapers. Editorials have been written or rewritten, layouts have been altered. Partisan politics (largely right-wing and belligerent during crises and wars) have been promoted. Favoured journalists have risen through the ranks; others have been sacked or pressurised into leaving. Newspapers end up being, not public watchdogs, but press lords' poodles (Bower 1988; Leapman 1983; Shawcross 1992). Fleet Street's history is often portrayed as a fascinating saga revolving around these figures (Wintour 1990).

Most serious has been the cumulative impact of these devout defenders of the free press on narrowing the consensus in British newspapers. Given the links between the major media throughout the UK that censorship has seriously distorted news values, even in the provinces. Most national newspapers have plumped predictably, and often ferociously, for the Conservative Party, or more recently the newly respectable, right-wing Labour Party.

In particular, the integration of the media barons' empires into the world of international finance and industry has given rise to a host of potential no-go areas for newspapers. Understandably, newspaper proprietors are reluctant to have reporters probing into their more murky activities. Robert Maxwell managed to keep the scandal of his pension fund rip-off secret during his lifetime through a mixture of intimidation, a merciless use of the courts and libel laws and through exploiting journalists' desire for the quiet life (Greenslade 1992). As even the investigative reporter Paul Foot commented: 'When Maxwell was at the *Mirror* I used to have a list on the wall of his friends – and they covered a wide section of British industry. Immediately a story came in about one of those people, I had to be completely on my guard.'

Moreover, media moguls have inevitably promoted their own financial interests through their newspapers. Tiny Rowland's *Observer* campaigned against the Al Fayed family following their purchase of Harrods. Maxwell constantly publicised himself and his many 'charitable' and political activities. Murdoch has promoted his television, publishing and internet interests through his many outlets and opposed the BBC at every opportunity. All the same, there is a danger of exaggerating the power of the proprietors. All have been or are colourful personalities. But virtually every industry today is led at local, national and international levels by a small group of companies. Media moguls are merely the newspaper manifestations of this trend: typical monopoly holders within advanced capitalism. Stressing their power serves to boost their egos while exonerating journalists from some of their worst excesses.

Big Brother?

Censorship by the state has served to create a climate of intimidation and 'emergency' at critical moments. But overt interventions by the state into the operations of newspapers have been the exceptions to the rule. Various other factors, such as the impact of advertisers, the role of the dominant news value system, proprietorial pressure, journalists' self-censorship and the growing number of repressive laws are more important in maintaining conformity and the mainstream press's propaganda role (Hillyard and Percy-Smith 1988).

The state has, in any case, interfered more with broadcasting than the press, perhaps because the fervently right-wing owners of newspapers have been less independent of the government than the broadcasting companies. One of the most notorious cases of the Conservative government slipping on a censorship banana skin followed its long-drawn-out, farcical and ultimately futile attempts to prevent publication of *Spycatcher* by a retired MI5 officer, Peter Wright (1987). In June 1986, the *Observer* and the *Guardian*, which had published some of Wright's allegations of sedition by the secret service in advance of publication, were served with injunctions. Then the short-lived *News on Sunday*, the *Sunday Times* and the *Independent* were each fined £50,000 for having intended to prejudice legal proceedings in the original case through publishing information from the book (in fact, so boring nobody would have bothered to read it had not the government tried to ban it). Eventually these fines were set aside on appeal. Similarly injunctions against the *Observer* and *Guardian* were set aside and the Law Lords ruled that, in view of the world-wide publication, national security could in no way be damaged by publication in the UK.

More recently the Labour government proved itself equally heavy-handed and authoritarian in its response to various revelations by a disgruntled MI5 officer, David Shayler, in the *Mail on Sunday* in August 1997. Among his allegations, Shayler claimed that the security services had files on various members of the Labour government. Injunctions were served on the British news media from airing any more of his allegations and again in August 1998 after Shayler threatened to disclose details of a 1996 plot by MI6 to assassinate President Muammar Gadafi of Libya. But the *Guardian* cleverly got round this injunction by reproducing a *New York Times* report on the Gadafi plot. Shayler was jailed in Paris pending extradition to Britain to face charges under the Official Secrets Act. Then in November 1998, he was surprisingly released from jail – after the French judge argued that extradition could not go ahead since his revelations had been political – and began his life on the run (Hollingsworth and Fielding 1999).

When in February 2000, Shayler and the *Mail on Sunday* were sued by the government for breaches of confidence and of contract and he sent the media names of two intelligence officers involved in the Gadafi plot, newspapers obeyed instructions not to publish. Yet still the government continued its harassment of the media and went to the High Court demanding that the *Guardian* and *Observer* hand over material sent them by Shayler. The judge's final rejection of the police's demands in July 2000 was hailed as a 'ringing endorsement of freedom of expression'. Then in October 2000, concerns of freedom of information campaigners mounted again after a High

Court judge found *Punch* magazine guilty of contempt for publishing an article by Shayler on the IRA's bombing campaign – even though he found no evidence it had damaged national security.

The wrong arm of the law

David Northmore (1990) has calculated there are well over a hundred laws prohibiting disclosure of information. He concludes, along with many other commentators, that Britain is the most secretive state in the so-called developed world (see also Ponting 1990). In 1994, the Guild of Editors listed forty-six laws restricting disclosure of information of particular relevance to journalists, including the Trade Union Reform and Employment Rights Act 1993 and Young Persons Act 1993. Moreover, the Criminal Procedures and Investigations Act 1996 gave the courts even more powers to impose reporting restrictions. Privatised utilities (such as gas, water and electricity) once accountable to Parliament, have been criticised even by the Confederation of British Industry for their lack of accountability and openness in decision-making. There are an estimated 6,424 quasi-autonomous non-governmental organisations (quangos) in Britain responsible for £63 billion of taxpayers' money, yet there is no legal obligation on them to disclose information. Employee contracts often contain restrictive 'gagging' clauses (Johnson 1996).

In 1989, the secret state was further strengthened with a new Official Secrets Act (OSA). The 1911 OSA had proved notorious, particularly after civil servant Sarah Tisdall was jailed in 1983 for leaking to the *Guardian* government plans for the timing of the arrival of cruise missiles in England. National security seemed hardly threatened by the disclosure. Then came the acquittal of top civil servant Clive Ponting, charged under Section 2(1) of the Act after he leaked information showing the government had misled the House of Commons on the sinking of the Argentine ship, the *General Belgrano*, during the Falklands conflict.

The 1911 legislation was proving an embarrassment to the government and the 1989 Act was introduced to sort out the mess. In an Orwellian piece of doublethink, the Home Secretary, Douglas Hurd, claimed the Act represented 'a substantial, unprecedented thrust in the direction of greater openness'. The opposite is nearer the truth. The Act covers five main areas: law enforcement, information supplied in confidence by foreign governments, international relations, defence, and security and intelligence. The publishing of leaks on any of these is banned. Journalists are denied a public interest defence; nor can they claim in defence that no harm had resulted to national security through their disclosures. After a disgruntled former officer, Richard Tomlinson, sent a synopsis of a book about his four years in MI6 to a publisher in Australia, he was jailed for six months in December 1997. He became the first MI6 officer to be prosecuted for secrets offences since George Blake, thirty-six years earlier.

As the secret state's powers steadily mounted, in 1993 the Intelligence Service Act allowed MI6, with the permission of the Foreign Secretary, to commit acts abroad which, if carried out in Britain, would be illegal. It also created the Intelligence and Security Committee which meets in secret to overview the security services' activities. Apart from France, virtually every other western country has independent oversight of intelligence agencies. In 1996 the Security Service Act extended MI5's functions to 'act in support of the prevention and detection of crime' while the Labour government continued its moves to extend the secret state, allowing intelligence services and other government agencies to conduct covert surveillance including bugging phones and property. The government proceeded, somewhat reluctantly, to introduce a Freedom of Information (FoI) Bill, but its critics claimed that it would be more protective of law enforcers than the law in any other country with a FoI Act.

Good news appeared to come with a landmark decision on 20 December 1996 by the High Court, which ruled that a blanket ban by the government a year earlier on journalists interviewing prison inmates was illegal and an unjustified restriction of freedom of speech. The ruling came after freelance journalist Bob Woffinden and BBC Wales reporter Karen Voisey refused to sign undertakings not to publish material obtained during visits to two prisoners whose life sentences for murder they were investigating as possible cases of miscarriages of justice. The appeal court renewed the ban. But this decision was finally overruled by the Law Lords on 8 July 1999.

As another exercise, ask journalists to what extent the 'culture of secrecy' impedes them in their work. How many say they enjoy freedom to write whatever they want? Given that the links between the security services and mainstream media have always been close, how many of them have been invited by MI5 or MI6 to work for them as paid agents?

See *Statewatch* magazine, PO Box 1516, London N16 0EW; tel: 020-8802 1882; fax: 020-8880 1727; email: office@statewatch.org; website: http://www.statewatch. org[.] See also literature produced by the anti-censorship body Article 19, 33 Islington High Street, London N1 9HL; tel: 020-7278 9292; fax: 020-7713 1356; email: info@article19.org; website: http://www.gn.apc.org/article19[.] For a global view see *Index on Censorship*, 33 Islington High Street, London N1 9LH; tel: 020-7278 2313; fax: 020-7278 1878; email: contact@indexoncensorship.org; website: http://www. indexoncensorship.org[.] Amnesty has a special network campaigning for imprisoned journalists. Contact Nora Cranston 0207-7417 6370; email: nora.cranston@amnesty. org.uk; website: http://www. amnesty.org.uk/journos

Principled or pointless: CODES OF CONDUCT

Journalists work under many constraints, from proprietors, advertisers, laws and so on. One way in which journalists have regulated their own activities, with the aim of improving ethical standards, is through codes of conduct.

Starting the ball rolling: the NUJ

One of the most enduring is the National Union of Journalists' code drawn up in the late 1930s (accessible at http://www.nuj.org). In February 1998, the NUJ agreed to an amendment to the code to outlaw misrepresenting news through digital manipulation of photographs. The new clause prohibits use of manipulated photographs unless they are labelled with an internationally recognised symbol within the image area. The thirteen-clause code relies on generalised statements of high principle. On the one hand this has clear benefits. As Nigel Harris (1992: 67) argues, detailed sets of regulations foster a 'loophole-seeking attitude of mind'.

On the other hand, the code incorporates principles broken every day all over the country by NUJ members. What is the point of having them if they are not backed up by any penalties? As Bill Norris (2000: 325) argues: 'Every story is different and every reporter is driven by the compulsion to get the story and get it first. To imagine that he or she is going to consult the union's code of ethics while struggling to meet a deadline is to live in cloud-cuckoo land.' Attempts to impose the code through a disciplinary procedure and since 1986, an NUJ ethics council, have proved difficult.

The Press Complaints Commission's Code of Practice

Following stern warnings from the first Calcutt committee that the press should clean up its act or face statutory regulation, the PCC drew up a detailed Code of Practice (accessible at http://www.pcc.org.uk). Since then it has been amended many times. A new controversy blows up and so new changes are made to the code. For instance, after statutory threats emerged over bugging and the use of telephoto lenses, the code was amended appropriately.

The move to greater detail in the code marks a shift towards the American tradition where codes of conduct can cover a wide range of categories such as conflicts of interests, special privileges enjoyed by journalists (such as freebies), plagiarism and the use of shocking pictures (Goodwin 1994). Many mainstream journalists argue that the PCC's Code has had a positive impact on standards, particularly since the death of Princess Diana. But critics have accused the PCC of being a toothless watchdog, a cosy gathering of 'the great and the good' too concerned to preserve the interests of the elite. As Mike Jempson, of PressWise Trust, which backs those with complaints and aims to raise standards in journalism, argues: 'All the signs are that the PCC has created a sort of cordon sanitaire around the press and woe betide anybody who tries to upset the applecart.'

As an exercise you might interview (or simply talk to) journalists about their views on codes of conduct. Are they aware of their existence? What impact do they have on their work? Do a survey of newspapers in your region and see how many incorporate the PCC Code into their style books.

3 Sourcing the news

At the heart of journalism lies the source. Becoming a journalist to a great extent means developing sources. As a journalist you need to know a lot, where to go for information, whom to ask. For career development, contacts are crucial.

The contacts book

One of the most treasured possessions of any journalist is their contacts book in which sources' phone numbers, addresses, fax and pager numbers, email and website details are listed. To be safe, journalists should keep a duplicate in a secure place since the loss or theft of a sole contacts book can be disastrous. Many journalists have contacts on a computer file as a further back-up or use personal digital assistants which, at best, can combine the functions of contacts book, notepad and word processor. Reporters investigating sensitive issues (national security, spying, the arms or drugs trade, share dealings) tend to keep details of important, exclusive sources in their heads. Police have been known to raid the homes and computers of journalists involved in sensitive areas and thus every step should be taken to preserve the anonymity of such contacts.

The importance of the phone to the journalist means that one of the most vital sources is the telephone directory (online or offline). You are researching a story on Islam. Just go to the directory and see which local and national organisations are listed (and try Muslim at the same time). Telephone directories are also a source for feature ideas. Diamond cutters, chimney sweeps, feminist car repairs, fallout shelters or robots may be listed and worth a follow-up.

Sourcing: GENERAL COMMENTS

Immediacy and newsiness

Sourcing conventions help provide the news dimension of many stories. An issue may be long-running but new information or opinion from a source will bring it into the news. The state of the national economy is an issue of constant concern. The

Chancellor of the Exchequer warning of further 'inevitable' bankruptcies over the next year becomes news, just as the release of a report by a group of Cambridge University economists highlighting the plight of small businesses is newsworthy.

Elitism and hierarchy

Media research suggests journalists use a remarkably limited range of sources (McQuail 1992: 112–59). The components of the hierarchy will differ from newspaper to newspaper. Television soap stars and showbiz celebrities feature far more in the national tabloids than in the broadsheets, for instance, yet there exists a remarkable consensus over news values and sourcing routines throughout the mainstream press. Some sources will be prominent, others marginalised or generally covered in a negative way. Elitism is particularly evident in foreign reporting. Moreover, this consensus over news sourcing is reinforced by the growing centralisation and secrecy of government and the ever-narrowing consensus between the three major political parties.

Primary and secondary sources

Many journalists divide their sources into two major categories: primary and secondary (Aitchison 1988). At the local level, councils, Members of Parliament and of the European Parliament, courts, police, fire brigade, ambulance service, hospitals, local industries and their representative bodies, trade unions and trades council and the local football and cricket clubs are defined as primary sources. Schools and colleges, churches, local clubs and societies, army, naval and air force bases, local branches of national pressure groups and charities are secondary sources. Other contacts in this category in rural areas may include village postal workers, publicans and hotel keepers, agricultural merchants, livestock auctioneers, countryside rangers or wardens. In coastal areas they include coastguards, harbour officials and lifeboat station personnel.

The stress on primary and secondary sources reflects the hierarchical assumptions underpinning conventional news values. Significantly, the definition eliminates a wide range of sources loosely termed 'alternative'. These might include representatives of religions other than Christian, ethnic minority groups, members and representatives of political parties other than the dominant three; feminist, lesbian and gay groups; pacifist, environmental and animal rights campaigning groups.

Journalists' sourcing routines tend to reflect the distribution of power in society, representatives of leading institutions and public services dominate having easier access to the press. Representatives of 'alternative' bodies are either marginalised or eliminated from the local and national press which reinforces their relative powerlessness in society. Women and ethnic minorities are marginalised by the political system just as they are marginalised in the press (Allan 1999: 141).

Professional routines: on- and off-diary sources

Sources are often defined according to their relation to journalistic routines of news gathering. Thus, on-diary routine sources will include on a national newspaper the government, parliament and select committees, the major political parties, the Confederation of British Industry (CBI), Church of England Synod meetings, prominent court cases, press conferences arranged by prominent bodies such as campaigning groups (Amnesty International), companies, the police, trade unions and charities. At the same time a system of 'calls' institutionalises this sourcing routine. The news editor, news desk member or specialist correspondent will contact by phone at regular intervals (as often as every hour) such bodies as the police, ambulance service or fire brigade to check on any breaking news. Such bodies are increasingly providing taped news updates so local reporters will often 'call in' for chats to help personalise the contacts.

Similarly a local reporter will meet at regular intervals locally important people (such as vicars, business leaders, prominent campaigners and trade unionists) for informal chats from which news angles may or may not emerge. Bob Franklin and David Murphy (1991), in a study of 865 stories in the local press, found local and regional government, voluntary organisations, the courts, police and business accounted for 66.7 per cent of the total. Such groups and individuals are described as on-diary sources since details of their activities are listed in diaries traditionally in book form supplemented by dated files but increasingly now on screens.

Representation

Linked to journalists' sourcing routines are certain notions about representation. A source, other than a celebrity in their own right, tends to assume a significance for a journalist when they can be shown representing not just their personal views but those of a larger group or institution. Thus, usually accompanying the name of a source is their title or other description. Ms X may have believed Tony Blair ought to have resigned from the premiership over the bombing of Serbia in 1999. But her views will mostly be of interest to a journalist if they can be shown to represent a larger group such as the local Labour Party, of which she is the treasurer.

Journalists are sometimes tempted, because of sourcing conventions, to invent a title when none exists. During the early 1980s when the Greenham Common women were protesting outside the US airbase near Newbury, journalists often represented the relatively few people they quoted as 'spokeswomen' for the camp. In fact, the women sought to challenge traditional hierarchical notions of representation. Each woman spoke for herself. The group did not have representatives as such. By describing them as 'spokeswomen' journalists were failing to understand or respect an important political dimension of their struggle.

Credibility and authority

Accompanying journalists' sourcing routines and linked closely to views about representation are notions relating to credibility and authority. The views of party politicians tend to be prominent in the national and local press because they are seen as having been democratically elected to represent certain widely held views. Along with that representative element goes authority and credibility. Ms A may have very strong views about abortion. But on what authority does she speak and how credible are those views? Those short titles or descriptive phrases accompanying the name of the person quoted answer that kind of question. Ms B might be described as having 'launched a campaign against abortion at her parish church'. This immediately identifies her commitment to the cause and her authority as a source. Similarly when someone is described as 'an eye-witness to a road accident', their authority is established (though they may be mistaken and must not be seen to allocate blame). Inclusion of such details immediately 'hardens' the story. In the same way, the presence of 'ordinary people' (without any title or representative function) 'softens' the story.

Bias and neutrality

Reporters use sources to distance themselves from the issues explored. Rather than express their views on a subject, reporters use sources to present a range of views over which they can appear to remain objective and neutral. The title or descriptive phrase accompanying the quoted person clarifies the bias. But this is the bias of the source, not the reporter. Sourcing routines also reinforce notions of balance. A campaigning group accuses a local authority of inadequate provision. It is the responsibility of the reporter to contact the authority to balance the report with their response to the allegations. But such a process eliminates a range of other views. Indeed, many media theorists question journalists' notion of balance and the existence of an objective reality. Considering the highly selective process of news gathering, the financial, political and legal pressures on newspapers and the absence of any neutral language, they argue that objectivity is unattainable and a myth.

Experts

Experts are often sought by journalists as sources. They play a crucial role since authority and independence are associated with their views. Journalists often use experts such as academics, think-tank members and pressure group campaigners (sometimes even fellow reporters) to provide background information, which is not necessarily used in copy, and ideas for future, more newsy contacts. But they can also use them more subtly to add extra weight to a view they (or their proprietors) wish to promote. The *Sun,* for instance, often quotes psychiatric 'experts' on the alleged insanity or otherwise of people in the news (such as 'madman' Saddam Hussein and Tony Benn of the 'loony left'). But experts can be wrong.

Professional status

Journalists enjoying close contact with people at the top of the sourcing hierarchy tend to have a high professional status. On a national broadsheet, the parliamentary correspondent enjoys high status just as the posting as a foreign correspondent (with all the contacts with presidents and other VIPs this will involve) ranks as a journalistic top job. At the local level, the journalist whose everyday contacts are councillors enjoys high status; the journalist dealing with the Women's Institute reports or the children's page is usually low on the professional ladder. As Bob Franklin (1994: 19–20) comments: 'Journalists are conscious of being sited in a finely graduated hierarchy which influences their access to politicians . . . Acknowledging and exploiting to the full the advantages which their position in the hierarchy bestows is a precondition for journalistic advancement.'

Journalists' reputations can be built on the ability to extract good quotes from sources. 'Did you get any good quotes?' is often asked by colleagues when they return from an assignment.

Professionalism as a construct generally implies a certain objectivity and neutrality towards sources. In reality this is difficult to maintain. Many argue that journalists often get too close to their sources. Journalists' regular contact with elite sources means they are often accused of disseminating a range of conflicting elite perspectives. Journalists tend to be part of the same social milieu as the political elite, they speak the same language and often come from similar social and educational backgrounds.

Press poachers: THE MEDIA AS A SOURCE

All journalists spend some considerable time each day going through the media. They have to know what is going on, what is being covered and more particularly what is not being covered. They become 'media junkies'. Whatever your feelings about the heavies or popular press, it is important to read as many papers as possible. You may despise the red-tops for their blatant racism and sexism but they are increasingly setting the national news agenda and need to be watched. Similarly, you may find the heavies tedious and long-winded but (while their omissions are often more significant than their contents) they carry masses of important national and international news which might even spark ideas for follow-ups. Most newspaper offices stock all nationals and leading locals. Freelances will often buy their two favourite papers and a different third paper each day to help build up their cuttings files.

Don't concentrate all the time on the nationals and your mainstream locals. They are just one (though the most powerful) ingredient of a diverse range of journals available. Look at the lively ethnic press (*New Nation, Voice, Caribbean Times, Asian Times, Eastern Eye*), the religious press (*Q News, Jewish Chronicle, Methodist Recorder, Catholic Herald, Church Times*), the left press (*Tribune, Socialist Worker, Morning Star, News Line, Lobster, Peace News*) or the gay press (*Gay Times*, the *Pink Paper*). For contact details see the invaluable *Media Guide* series, which is updated every year, edited by Steve Peak and Paul Fisher (London: Fourth Estate). It is worth looking at these publications for a number of reasons:

- They often carry articles by specialists raising issues and perpectives marginalised in the mainstream press and which can be followed up.
- The listings of meetings, conferences, demonstrations, vigils and visits to the UK by potentially newsworthy figures can be followed up.
- Journalists on them are useful contacts and their journals could provide outlets for freelance work (if your contract permits).
- They can prove rewarding places for student work attachments.

Newspapers published outside England, such as the *Scotsman, Glasgow Herald* and *Irish Independent*, should not be ignored. The *International Herald Tribune*, carrying a compilation of reports from the *New York Times* and *Washington Post*, is essential reading for anyone wanting an insight into elite opinion in the United States. See *Mother Jones* or *Covert Action Quarterly* for more dissident perspectives. Most journalists will either speak or want to speak a second language and follow the press in that country. Comparisons with foreign newspapers on elements such as content, use of pictures, design and questions of taste can all throw up interesting insights into the UK press.

It is impossible to buy even a small sample of these publications on a regular basis. You would end up bankrupt. The internet provides easy access to most newspapers while public and university libraries stock a wide range of newspapers and magazines. Most journalists settle for buying on a regular basis a few that they consider vital for their specialist areas. The journalist's own newspaper often provides a source for news. Letters to the editor can provide the basis for a follow-up (but should not be converted into interviews) while an advert asking for sources on a particular topic can often produce good results. Similarly newsworthy letters in other newspapers or magazines can be followed up. National and local newspapers sponsor charity or sporting events or run campaigns which can also provide colourful, exclusive coverage.

Cuttings

Most newspapers have their own cuttings library (often online now) which is a crucial resource. Journalists also create their own filing system. For a freelance without regular access to a cuttings library, it is an essential. The Press Association's cuttings library can also be accessed, but at a cost of £35 an hour. Most journalists, especially freelances, develop specialist areas and tidy filing of cuttings, magazines, photocopies, notes from books and internet sources and jottings of feature ideas can prove enormously useful and time-saving during research. But reporters can get details and quotes wrong. Unless cuttings are treated critically, there are dangers of reporters repeating each other's errors. In its March 1992 report, the PCC even criticised journalists' over-reliance on cuttings: 'Cuttings are an essential part of newspaper research but too many journalists now seem to act in the belief that to copy from 10 old stories is better than to write a new one with confirmation by proper fresh enquiry.'

Follow-ups

The follow-up of an item in the news is a constant feature of newspaper coverage. As controversy emerges in the national press, a local paper will 'do a follow-up' carrying the views of relevant local people and providing local information on the issue. Similarly, a report in a local paper, say about an educational controversy considered sufficiently sensational, unusual or with wider implications, will be followed up by a national with new sources and new information.

Newspapers routinely tape selected radio and television news programmes, build up stories from interviews on these media and perhaps do follow-ups on others. A great deal of the coverage in the Sunday heavies comprises follow-ups on the main stories of the previous week. On Mondays (following the relatively dead news days of Sunday) nationals are in the habit of carrying reports on interviews given by prominent politicians on weekend television and radio programmes (McNair 2000: 100–2). Investigations by Sunday newspapers can be followed up by the national press. Sometimes a reporter will 'lift' a story from another newspaper, rewording it slightly, perhaps adding only a few original pars.

Columnists on both national and local newspapers often base some comment on an event or opinion highlighted in a national. Journalists will also habitually use other reporters as sources. Sometimes a specialist in the field will be contacted by other reporters new to the area for contacts and ideas. It is a matter for the individual journalist how much they co-operate with such requests. The issue is complicated when the questions come from a friend or colleague on a competing paper. Some journalists say no to all such requests. Others supply basic information and contacts and keep to themselves special sources gained only after considerable effort. Journalists are often used as 'hard sources' for media-related sources. Often in foreign stories, the views of local journalists are considered informed and authoritative.

Reinforcing the consensus

As competition intensifies between newspapers, pressures to conform to the dominant news agenda grow. Rather than feeling confident and pursuing their own news values, newspapers constantly look over their shoulders to see what their competitors are up to. Consequently, the range of views and experience expressed narrows and newspapers become increasingly predictable (Chomsky and Herman 1994). The media's over-reliance on the media also promotes a passive form of journalism. Investigative reporter Tom Bower (1992) has spoken of the 'culture of inactivity' Reporting becomes a reactive activity, requiring little imagination and courage. Office-based, it becomes a glorified form of clerking.

Disinformation dangers

Histories of the secret services show the extent to which newspapers are used for misinformation, disinformation and propaganda purposes (Pilger 1998: 492–9; Bloch and Fitzgerald 1983: 134–41). As Roy Greenslade, former editor of the *Mirror*, commented: 'Most tabloid newspapers – or even newspapers in general – are playthings of MI5. You are the recipient of the sting' (quotes in Milne 1995: 262). For instance, a contrived story alleging various atrocities by a certain anti-US movement might be planted in a foreign newspaper, perhaps financially backed by the secret service. It might then be picked up by the major international news agencies. That first report provides the authenticity and credibility for the ensuing coverage.

Media used to combat censorship

Sometimes journalists send copy unsuitable for their own newspaper to another outlet (say *Private Eye*). Media in one country can be used to break through censorship regulations in another. In 1986 the Israeli anti-nuclear campaigner Mordechai Vanunu used the *Sunday Times* to reveal details of the secret Israeli nuclear programme which lay hidden behind a rigid censorship regime. (He was later captured by Mossad, the Israeli secret service, and sentenced to eighteen years in jail.) During the lead up to the Gulf conflict of 1991, after details of the 'allied' stategy were stolen from a Defence Ministry official's car, a D-Notice banning newspapers from reporting the event was issued by a special government committee. News of it leaked to an Irish paper. Thus it became public knowledge and London-based papers went ahead and carried their own reports. National security did not appear to be seriously damaged.

On and off the record

On the record

The basis for any good contact between a journalist and source is trust. When that trust is broken, the source is lost. Most news is given on the record. A press release is issued; someone talks to you on the telephone or face to face or over the email; you report a conference. All this information and opinion you gain on the record.

Off the record

An off-the-record briefing is completely different. Information is given but because of its sensitive nature should not be reported. If the off-the-record undertaking is broken, trust is lost. At the same time, such an undertaking leaves the journalist free to try to acquire the same information from another source who might be prepared to go on the record. Public meetings are on the record. If someone says during one, 'Oh, incidentally, that comment was off the record', you have no obligation to treat it as such. Similarly, private conversations are on the record unless otherwise established. Though it is tempting for students to submit copy to their lecturers drawn from off-the-record interviews (with the interviewee presuming no publication is intended) they will be indulging in an unreal form of journalism – which should be avoided.

Unattributable or background comments

Halfway between off-the-record and on-the-record comments lie unattributed or 'for background only' comments. Reports can carry these quotes but attribution is deliberately vague to conceal identities. In Britain, phrases such as 'sources close to the Prime Minister', 'diplomatic sources', 'sources close to the Conservative leadership' are constantly appearing in the national press. During the 1992 saga of the Prince Charles–Princess Diana split such phrases as 'sources close to Buckingham Palace' or 'sources close to the Princess' were prominent. Off-the-record unattributed briefings hold benefits for both the source and journalist. The reporter can be informed on complicated details of which they may have no specialist knowledge and will learn of the source's bias. Sources often speak more openly at these meetings. And for the source, the briefing provides an opportunity to impress their perspectives on the journalist. As Rodney Tiffen comments:

> covert manoeuvres are commonly deployed to shape interpretations of public events, of success and failure, of intentions and portents. In complex or technical developments, briefings can highlight the 'essential meaning' of the details, to provide what journalists will welcome as a short-cut through the maze, but by doing so affording the briefer convenient scope for convenient selectivity. The meaning of opinion polls and some election results, of economic reports and indicators, of international agreements often pass into the news after the filters of briefings.
>
> (Tiffen 1989: 112)

Dominant groups, individuals and institutions have the power and access to the press to organise such briefings and the chance to attempt to influence the news agenda.

Weaker groups and individuals have much-reduced opportunities for such man-oeuvring. Campaigning journalist John Pilger (1996) offers this advice: 'Beware all background briefings, especially from politicians. Indeed, try to avoid, where possible, all contact with politicians. That way you find out more about them.'

Fact, fiction or faction?

Unattributed and anonymous comments can also blur the distinction between fact and fiction. For instance, the *Sunday Express* ran an exclusive in 2000 headlined 'Isabella: the blonde tipped to be Prince William's wife'. It was pure fantasy. It started with a jokey story in the December 1999 *Tatler* about Isabella Anstruther-Gough-Calthorpe 'tipped to be a fairytale princess'. *GQ* and the Edinburgh University student paper followed up the prediction. By the time the *Sunday Express* carried it, a jokey 'tip' had become a 'fact' supported by anonymous sources: 'Royal insiders say the 19-year-old blonde has formed a close bond' with the Prince, it reported. In fact, Isabella and the Prince had never met.

Keeping it confidential

There are other occasions when journalists will legitimately want to protect the iden-tify of a source. For instance:

- Given the high unemployment figures, people are reluctant to criticise their employers for fear of the consequences. Nurses may not dare to speak out on the impact of the financial cutbacks on the health service – some who have spoken to the press have been intimidated. Teachers may be reluctant to put their names to protests over the radical education changes of recent years. Journalists should respect this reserve and not try to tease out names, simply to harden up their story.

- Interviews with people who talk about intimate aspects of their lives such as sexual problems, illnesses and domestic violence are often carried with fictitious names. Relevant places, ages and descriptions are either changed or omitted. The news-paper ought to indicate this style at the start of the article. If it is left until the end the reader may feel cheated. Thus, the *East Anglian Daily Times* (7 April 2000) began a story about child sexual abuse: 'Rebecca (not her real name) and her sister Lizzie . . .'

- When an investigative journalist has acquired information without disclosing their professional identity, the newspaper does not then normally carry the sources' names. For instance, Esther Oxford (1992) explored the world of rent-a-male agencies which provide women with escort and sexual services. She contacted the agencies and described her experiences. Clearly, she could not take her note-book. All quotes and place descriptions had to be written from memory. But the paper left until the end the short disclaimer: 'The names of the men have been changed.'

Leaking in the public interest

According to Rodney Tiffen a leak can be broadly defined as the unauthorised release of confidential information:

However, this umbrella covers many variations – that release may come from a dissident but also from someone in authority seeking political advantage, that confidentiality ranges from the very sensitive to the innocuous, from what was intended to be forever secret to the about-to-be announced.

(Tiffen 1989: 96–7)

Leaks and the use of anonymous quotations by compliant journalists can be manipulated to launch 'trial balloons' or 'fly a kite'. Government officials may release proposals anonymously through leaks to test responses. If an outcry emerges, the government can denounce the plans they drew up, though only reporters pledged to confidentiality will know this. Leaking can lead to institutionalised lying. Leaks by brave whistleblowers can be used to expose corruption – as Paul Van Buitenen found at the European Commission. They can also be used to discredit opponents. Histories of the Harold Wilson administration (Leigh 1989; Dorril and Ramsay 1991) show the extent to which secret service leaks to sympathetic journalists in national newspapers were used systematically to smear the Prime Minister and some of his close associates before his unexpected resignation in 1976.

Because of the aura and glamour surrounding secrecy, information drawn from such sources can be overvalued with an accompanying devaluation of information drawn from other sources. The desire to gain exclusives through privileged access to secret sources can lead to a critical dependency between source and journalist. The lure of the 'exposé' can also make a reporter more reluctant to explore alternative perspectives.

Editors' guidelines

In the United States, attribution rules tend to be tighter than in Britain. Guidelines provided by the editor of the *Cincinnati Enquirer* (Greenslade 1995) to his staff included:

- The identities of all sources must be verified and confidentially disclosed to the editor.
- Misleading information about the true identity of a source may not be used in a story, even to 'throw off' suspicion.
- Information supplied by an unnamed source should be verified independently or confirmed by at least one other source. An exception may be made for individuals who are sole possessors of the information or whose integrity is unassailable.
- The motive of an anonymous source should be fully examined to prevent [journalists] being used unwittingly to grind someone's axe.
- Information attributed to an anonymous source must be factual and important to the story. Peripheral information or a 'good quote' aren't good enough reasons for anonymity.

Hoaxes

Journalists' over-reliance on unattributed sources can make them vulnerable to hoaxes. Some hoaxers, such as Rocky Ryan and Joe Flynn, make a profession of fooling the press. On 17 May 1992, the *Independent on Sunday* revealed that 'one of Fleet Street's most prolific sources of information', particularly about the aviation business, was a conman. He claimed to be a highly placed source within British Airways. He was nothing of the sort. One of the most famous hoaxes of all was when the *Sunday Times* printed what it believed to be the diaries of Adolf Hitler. This was only after they were sold to *Stern* magazine by three German businessmen for £2.5 million and Sir Hugh Trevor-Roper, author of *The Last Days of Hitler*, said that he believed they were genuine. Then in November 1996, Stuart Higgins, editor of the *Sun*, fell victim to an elaborate hoax involving a video that supposedly showed Princess Diana cavorting with a lover. Local papers are by no means no-go areas for hoaxes. New sources, particularly in controversial areas, should be routinely checked and their views and information corroborated by a another reliable source. Journalists should be particularly wary of hoaxes just before 1 April and in letters, emails and on the internet.

Don't Spread The Hoax (http://www.nonprofit.net/hoax/hoax.htm) is a site dedicated to stamping out hoax emails.

Lobby changes: A SIGNIFICANT SHIFT IN THE SECRET STATE?

One of the most famous institutional manifestations of the briefings session is the parliamentary lobby. Every day on which the House sits, Downing Street gives two briefings to accredited lobby correspondents, of which there are around 210 men and 30 women (out of 312 correspondents based at Westminster). The first meeting is at Downing Street at 11 a.m.; the second in the House of Commons at 4 p.m. In addition there are Friday briefings for Sunday journalists, a briefing on Thursdays by the Leader of the House on the following week's business and a weekly Opposition briefing. There are also briefings by ministers or their mouthpieces to groups and individual lobby journalists.

The lobby was launched in 1884 – just five years before the first Official Secrets Act became law. All lobby members were pledged to secrecy, never attaching a name to any information. Instead, phrases such as 'sources close to Downing Street' or 'government sources' or 'members close to the Labour leadership' were used. As Michael Cockerell, Peter Hennessy and David Walker say in their study of the lobby:

> The paradox was that as Britain was moving towards a democracy by extending the vote to men of all classes (women still had 40 years to wait) mechanisms were being created to frustrate popular participation in government and to control, channel and even manufacture the political news.
>
> (Cockerell *et al.* 1984: 34)

Over the years, the lobby has raised enormous passions, pro and anti. For a number of years while Bernard Ingham was Margaret Thatcher's press secretary until October 1991, three high-minded newspapers – the newly launched *Independent*, the *Guardian* and the *Scotsman* together with *The Economist* – withdrew from the system. Ingham used the lobby for blatant disinformation campaigns on political issues and against individuals both inside and outside the cabinet (R. Harris 1990). His immediate successors did not adopt similar tactics and the decision by Christopher Meyer in 1995 to allow off-the-record briefings to be attributed to Downing Street marked the beginnings of changes which were to transform the operations of the lobby. Finally Alastair Campbell, Tony Blair's press secretary (or spin doctor in the jargon), on 13 March 2000, ruled that he could be named as the source of his briefings (rather than the 'Prime Minister's official spokesman'). During the previous month, the twice daily briefings for journalists were put on the Downing Street website, so allowing anyone to gain access to the discussions just hours after they had finished.

What are we to make of these seemingly radical changes? Was a new spirit of openness racing through the corridors of Westminster? Or was it more an attempt by the government to bypass media 'spin' and communicate directly with the electorate via the internet? Soon after Campbell's announcement, Fleet Street heavies printed verbatim versions of a lobby briefing and Fleet Street began mourning the death of the lobby. 'If local reporters in Darlington can access the Downing Street line, what's so special about being in the lobby,' said one lobby correspondent (McCann 2000). Perhaps the UK was heading towards adopting the American system in which televised press conference and a detailed Freedom of Information Act existed alongside the most secret of government machines. Hellinger and Judd (1991: 190–1) speak of the 'covert presidency': 'There now exists a recognizable [sic] pattern of hidden powers, a covert presidency, that rests on centralising presidential direction of personnel, budgets and information, on the manipulation of the media and on the expanding use of "national security" to control the political agenda.'

Controversies over confidentiality

Non-attributable briefings are vital to the journalist on many occasions and the Code of Conduct (clause 7) of the NUJ calls for journalists to preserve the confidentiality of sources. Yet the journalists' right to this confidentiality is not enshrined in law (as it is in most other European countries and the USA) and under Section 10 of the Contempt of Court Act 1981 courts have the right to demand that journalists reveal sources if 'disclosure is necessary in the interests of justice or national security or for the prevention of disorder or crime'.

In 1984 the *Guardian*, under pressure from the courts, handed over material that helped reveal that civil servant Sarah Tisdall had leaked information about the delivery of cruise missiles to Greenham Common. Tisdall was jailed. Then Jeremy Warner, of the *Independent*, was ordered in 1988 to disclose the source of a story on insider dealings and shady takeover bids in the City. He refused and was ordered to pay a £20,000 fine and £100,000 costs in the High Court. His paper paid up for him and received good publicity in the process. He later commented: 'I quite enjoyed it, to tell you the truth. It's a great thing for a young journalist to become a *cause célèbre*' (Lashmar 2000).

In 1990, William Goodwin, a trainee reporter on a weekly trade magazine, the *Engineer*, was fined £5,000 for contempt after refusing to hand over notes of a phone call which revealed confidential information about a computer company's financial affairs. He thus escaped becoming the fourth journalist in the twentieth century in Britain to be jailed for contempt. In 1963, Brendon Mulholland, a *Daily Mail* reporter, and Reginald Foster, of the *Daily Sketch*, were sentenced to six months and three months respectively in Brixton jail for refusing to disclose sources in the Vassall spy tribunal presided over by Viscount Radcliffe. In 1971, Bernard Falk refused to tell the court whether one of two Provisional IRA men he interviewed for the BBC was a man subsequently charged with membership and went to prison for his pains.

However, pressure on the government to enshrine in law a journalist's right to protect the identity of sources intensified after Goodwin took his case to the European Commission of Human Rights. In September 1993, the commission ruled that Goodwin's case was admissible and called on the government to negotiate a 'friendly settlement'. Three years later, the European Court of Human Rights ruled that Goodwin had been right to protect his sources. But still the Lord Chancellor refused to change the Contempt of Court Act. Earlier, Dani Garavelli, then chief reporter for the *Journal*, Newcastle, was threatened under the contempt law for refusing to name a source after being subpoenaed to give evidence to a police disciplinary hearing. Her twenty-month battle ended in 1996 when a High Court ruled against the attempt by two chief constables to jail her. A judge's decision to throw out a Norfolk Police application for the *Eastern Daily Press* and reporter Adrian Galvin, who was backed by the NUJ, to name a source was lauded as a 'landmark judgment' by editor Peter Franzen. Judge Michael Hyman ruled: 'There is undoubtedly a very formidable interest in a journalist being able to protect his sources.'

In September 1999, Ed Moloney, northern editor of the Dublin-based *Sunday Tribune*, faced imprisonment for refusing to hand over notes (dating back ten years) of interviews with a loyalist accused of murdering a Catholic solicitor. Moloney's ordeal ended the following month when Belfast High Court overturned an order by Antrim Crown Court that he should hand over the notes. Then in April 2000, the *Express* overturned a High Court ruling that it had to reveal the source from which financial reporter Rachel Baird obtained confidential documents about a High Court action involving Sir Elton John.

The Prevention of Terrorism Act has also been used by the state in an attempt to intimidate journalists into revealing confidential sources. Thus, in 1988 the BBC was forced to hand over footage of the mobbing of two soldiers who ran into a funeral procession in Belfast. Following a *Dispatches* programme, *The Committee*, by the independent company, Box Productions, in 1991, alleging collusion between loyalist death squads and members of the security forces in Northern Ireland, Channel 4 was committed for contempt for refusing to reveal its source and fined £75,000. Subsequently a researcher on the programme, Ben Hamilton, was charged with perjury by the Royal Ulster Constabulary. Though the charge was suddenly dropped in November 1992, the police retained all items seized from Hamilton. They included his personal computer, all disks, newspaper cuttings and notes of telephone calls and meetings with other journalists interested in the programme. Another journalist involved in the programme received death threats and was forced to leave his home and live incognito at a secret address.

Government plans in 2000 for new terrorism legislation also provoked serious concerns among civil rights campaigners and journalists. The bill, introduced into the Commons on 2 December 1999, radically extended the definition of terrorism to mean: 'The use of serious violence against persons or property or the threat to use such violence, to intimidate or coerce a government, the public or any section of the public for political, religious of ideological ends'. Journalists covering direct action could be caught by clause 18, carrying a five-year sentence for failure to report information received professionally which could lead to a terrorist act (Zobel 2000).

Extra threats

In recent years a number of new threats have emerged to undermine journalists' attempts to keep sources confidential. According to the Police and Criminal Evidence Act (PACE) 1984 a police officer investigating a 'serious offence' can obtain an order requiring the journalist to hand over evidence deemed useful to the court. This can include unpublished notes and photographs. The first major controversy emerged just eight months after PACE passed into law. The *Bristol Evening News* was ordered to hand over film following a drug bust: it refused, lost the case and had the police take away 264 pictures and negatives. Following violent demonstrations outside the premises of Rupert Murdoch's News International in Wapping, east London, in early 1987, the *Independent, Mail on Sunday* and *Observer,* two television companies and four freelance photographers appealed against an order requiring them to hand over pictures.

On 23 May 1988, Mr Justice Alliot ruled that the pictures should be surrendered on the ground that this would not undermine the freedom and independence of the press. All complied except the four freelance photographers who had earlier taken the unprecedented step of sending their materials, via the NUJ, to the International Federation of Journalists in Brussels. In October 1988, the contempt charges against the freelances were thrown out because they were considered no longer to be owners of the material or to possess it. Following the poll tax riots of 31 March 1990 the police applied under PACE for access to 'all transmitted, published and/or unpublished cine film, video tape, still photographs and negatives of the demonstration and subsequent disturbances which was obtained with a view to being of a newsworthy interest'. Some national newspapers complied. Again, the NUJ moved quickly, sending prints and negatives out of the UK. An attempt by the police to force the media to hand over photographs and journalists' notes taken during the riots in the City of London in June 1999 was thrown out by a judge on 2 July 1999.

Managing the new information monster:

THE INTERNET

Over recent years the internet has become a vast, almost unmanageable source of information for journalists. Conceived in the US in the late 1980s, the web was being accessed by millions worldwide by 2000. Globally there were more than 100 million domain names (the vast majority worthless to journalists). In Britain, by March 2000 6.5 million homes (25 per cent) had access, double the figure of the previous year. The *Daily Telegraph* (http://www.telegraph.co.uk) was the first Fleet Street paper to go online – on 15 November 1994 when the word 'internet' was not even included in the *Shorter Oxford English Dictionary*. By 2000, the vast majority of newspapers in Britain had gone online (some of them also providing audio and video); the *Guardian*'s sites, for instance (http://www.guardianunlimited.co.uk) contained an archive of stories going back to 1 September 1998 and were recording 12 million hits a month. Freelances were routinely submitting copy via email while journalists on the smallest of weeklies were surfing the web for sources, using it for interviews and downloading information from databases. Participation in newsgroups was providing access to expert and committed voices around the world. Many reporters were adding their email addresses at the end of their stories encouraging reader feedback. Online supplements and features mushroomed. Dot.com start-ups were providing thousands of new jobs for journalists brave enough to quit the traditional media.

According to internet specialist Milverton Wallace (1996), 24-hour online publishing is revolutionising journalistic practices.

> Most print journalists would recoil in horror at the notion of the death of the deadline. But that is what an online medium does: it eliminates the fixed news deadline. Stories are updated as and when required. This means that the shelf life of the news content is greatly extended, allowing journalists to offer more in-depth information, to craft stories more carefully, to tease out relevant links and provide supporting data.

But as Wayne Ellwood (1996) argued: 'Computerisation is at the core of the slimmed-down, re-engineered workplace that free-market boasters claim is necessary to survive the lean-and-mean global competition of the 1990s. Even factory jobs that have been relocated to the Third World are being automated quickly.' John Naughton, internet specialist on the *Observer* and author of the seminal *A Brief History of the Future: The Origins of the Internet*, reminded his readers (4 July 1999):

> IT is a relatively 'clean' industry – but it also produces serious environmental pollution and needs unconscionable amounts of water. It enables us to do wonderful things but also polarises society into those who are wired and those who are not. It creates 'virtual communities' while wiping out industries which once supported real ones. And the gadgets it sells are often not assembled by hi-tech robots but by sweated labour.

The web (though notoriously vulnerable to virus attacks) has simply revolutionised publishing. Since anyone with a web browser can access almost any site, even the smallest of publishers can register their sites with search engines and directories and achieve instantly a worldwide audience. That is the theory at least. In practice, the web has come to be dominated by big, US-based multinationals. Some 85 per cent of the revenue from internet businesses goes to American firms, which hold 95 per cent of the stock market value of internet properties. US sites are increasingly globalising their activities: Yahoo! for instance, has operations in twenty countries including Brazil, China, Denmark, Japan, Korea, Mexico, Norway, Singapore and Taiwan. As investigative reporter John Pilger (1996) argues: 'Beware celebrating technology until you find out who controls it. The internet is brilliant, but its most fervid bedfellows are the American government and a cluster of multinational companies whose message posting is outstripping all others.' Universities are now largely wired up to the web providing student journalists all the opportunities to surf the information superhighway – for free. Courses on using the internet as a source and electronic publishing (such as the MA at City University, London) are spreading. Yet, as Theodore Roszak (1996) argues: 'If computer literacy does not include material on what computers can't do and shouldn't do, it is advertising, not education.'

Some useful sites for harassed hacks

Most journalists will bookmark their favourite sites for easy access. Here are a few which you should find useful:

- http://www.altpress.org Alternative Press Center
- http://www.paris2.fr/ifp/deontologie Claude-Jean Bertrand's journalism ethics site provides links to a wide range of useful sites
- http://www.bigfoot.com offers a useful list of email addresses
- http://opac97.bl.uk British Library catalogue online
- http://www.bsc.org.uk Broadcasting Standards Commission
- http://www.bt.com/phonenetuk/ BT's PhoneNetUK provides phone books online
- http://www.teldir.com world's phone books
- http://www.biography.com a useful biographical site
- http://www.cpj.org US-based Committee to Protect Journalists campaigning on behalf of harassed/killed journalists worldwide
- http://www.onelook.com OneLook Dictionary searches dozens of online dictionaries when you enter a word
- http://www.disinfo.com disinformation is a US-based site providing stories on government surveillance, counterculture and links to alternative news sources
- http://www.drudgereport.com the alternative gossip site that broke the Clinton–Lewinsky scandal
- http://www.handbag.com describes itself as 'the ultimate destination for women of all ages who want to be informed, empowered and entertained'
- http://www.globalreview.btinternet.co.uk Jim Brennan's look at journalism around the world
- http://www.holdthefrontpage.com provides links to many local newspapers and a useful section on training
- http://crl.com/~jshenry/rig.html Internet Guidebook for Journalists
- http://www.poptel.org.uk/nuj/mike/lecture.htm Mike Holderness's site (with lots of sound advice for journalists on using the internet as a source)
- http://www.NewsDesk-UK.com a massive resource for journalists set up by Vincent Kelly and Alan Bott
- http://ojr.usc.edu *Online Journalism Review*
- http://www.ananova.com PA News Centre (UK)
- http://www.poynter.org site at Poynter Institute, US, has useful focus on journalism and ethics
- http://www.pressgazette.co.uk the trade magazine's important news and comment site
- http://www.quoteland.com a quotation search engine
- http://facsnet.org/ogi-bin/new/facs/18 Randy Reddick's site provides advice to journalists

- http://thesource.dwpub.com has been set up specifically for UK journalists providing access to information from more than 3,000 organisations
- http://www.uta.fi/ethicnet University of Tampere site carries comprehensive list of European journalists' codes of ethics
- http://www.gilest.org Giles Turnbull's site
- http:///www.thesaurus.com *Roget's Thesaurus*
- http://uk.multimap.com a street guide to Britain
- http://www.ukstate.com official information on national and local government, useful for contacting councillors, schools and MPs
- http://upmystreet.com provides local house price figures, crime statistics, school performance data, council and other data
- http://www.mediainfo.co.uk/willings/pressguide.htm Willings Press Guide carrying contact details of all print media in the UK

Taking the slog out of searching

Without search engines, journalists would find tracking down information nearly impossible. They do all the hard work, trawling through web information, indexing it and providing access to sites through keyword searches (Milner 2000). Most of the early search engines, such as AltaVista, Metacrawler and Webcrawler were US-based. But in recent years a large number of UK-specific portals have emerged, building big businesses on the advertising revenue (see www.searchengines galore.com). They include Yahoo! (http://uk.yahoo.com), Lycos (http://www.lycos. co.uk), Excite (http://www.excite.co.uk), Ask Jeeves (http://www.askjeeves.co.uk), Infoseek (http://www.go.com) and MSN Search (http://search.msn.co.uk). Hotbot (http://hotbot.lycos.com) is a US-based engine providing advanced searching facilities. There are countless specialist sites worth checking out (see http://www.search enginewatch.com). For instance, www.switchboard.com provides access to 90 million individual and 10 million business telephone numbers while www.bigfoot.com offers email addresses.

The joy (and pain) of email

With more than thirty years of development, email is one of the most sophisticated tools for reporters. Journalists are increasingly using it to file copy, engage in discussions with readers, receive press releases, search information and interview sources. According to Bill Thompson of the *Guardian*, it is easy to get people to reply to email:

> The medium is fresh enough for most people and many of the barriers we have put up to block unwanted contact have not yet been developed for email. It may be impossible to reach the chief executive by phone but an email may well get a response; a researcher may be travelling but will probably checking email daily.

But Thompson also stresses the limitations of email. 'An email "conversation" is more like an epistolary novel than a live interview and while it does allow some space for reflection, the outcome cannot be compared to a real interview.' Jane Dorner (2000: 32) comments: 'Using email to interview forces you to be more prepared by formulating questions in advance. It's less intrusive, allowing you to ask your questions at any hour of the day without bothering anyone. It's also cheaper than picking up the phone every time you need to check a point.' 'Real-time chat' via email allows immediate follow-up questions and answers and approaches the informality of traditional interviews (Metzler 1997: 137).

There are specific skills in email interviewing. For instance, do not bombard your source initially with a long list of questions. State your background, intentions and target publication and ask for permission first. Then ask a few questions perhaps following up with a few more. But there are serious downsides to the email explosion. They constitute yet another form of communication for the journalist to cope with, thus adding to the demands and stresses of the job. Viruses that can wreak havoc on computer systems often arrive via email. Always remember it is relatively easy to snoop on emails, as secret services and certain managements are only too well aware. Even deleted files can be retrieved.

Chatting on the web: EMAIL DISCUSSION LISTS

Randy Reddick argues that reading or participating in a discussion list can be extremely useful to the journalist. 'It puts reporters in contact with people who generally know a lot about a specific topic. The reporter can then follow up with those people, ask where more information can be found or ask who would be a good source to interview.' The principle of the discussion list is simple: an individual sends a message to a specific address for a particular discussion list and that message is automatically distributed to all subscribers. The address of the list distribution software is known as a Listserv. Indiana University has produced a database of thousands of discussion lists as http://listuniverse.com; Paul Gilster's book *Finding it on the Internet: The Internet Navigator's Guide to Search Tools and Techniques* offers an excellent guide to other email search tools while a visit to Yahoo! or AltaVista can often reveal information about a relevant mailing list. Regular newsletters are also sent through email. Particularly useful for journalists is Free Pint (http://freepint.co.uk) which is sent to subscribers every two weeks and provides tips and tricks on finding useful information on the internet.

Some ethical issues

Since internet technology has developed at such a rapid pace over recent years it is not surprising that journalists have found it difficult to establish the precise implications for their working routines and ethics. No clear rules have emerged. Issues relating to copyrights on internet material, for instance, remain unresolved. Journalist Andrew Bibby advises web users to include a copyright notice on every item. His reads:

> Copyright held by Andrew Bibby. Use for commercial purposes prohibited without prior written permission from the copyright holder. This text has been placed here

as a facility for internet users and downloading is permitted for purposes of private, non-commercial research. The text must not be modified nor this copyright notice removed.

Certainly the temptations towards plagiarism are growing with the internet explosion. Ian Mayes (2000), readers' editor at the *Guardian*, comments: 'Over-reliance on cuttings and now, even more to the point, the ease of electronically cutting and pasting from the internet, may be not simply attractive options, but the only options open to hard-pressed journalists in certain circumstances.' Other issues surround journalists' involvement in discussion groups. When investigating sensitive and dangerous issues, journalists may be justified in seeking anonymity of gathering background information. But Randy Reddick and Elliot King argue:

> Journalists should always identify themselves as such if they plan to use information from discussion lists. In most cases, journalists have the ethical obligation to allow people to choose to go on-the-record or not. To lurk in a discussion list, then quote people who did not know that what they wrote would be used in a different context is as deceptive as posing or going undercover to report a story.
> (Reddick and King 1997: 219)

Though the Americans have developed the concept of 'precision journalism' in relation to the web, journalists have still to be specially careful in assessing the value of material drawn from the internet. Robert Kiley (1999) advises internet users to check always that the information is current: 'A well organised web page will state when it was first written and last updated.' See if there is a named author. If so, then search an appropriate database for their previous publications. 'If there is no identifed author the information should be treated with caution.' Who is funding the site? The owner should be clearly displayed along with details of any sponsorship or advertising. Researchers at the Poynter Institute, in St Petersburg, USA, have also published guidelines for determining the reliability of online content (http://www.poynter.org).

The legal position on internet content remains confused. In theory, online media discussion groups could face problems if they carried material considered defamatory, grossly indecent or offensive, with the website providers subject to a civil action for defamation or charged under the Telecommunications Act 1984. In November 1999, the Lord Chancellor's department had a website closed down because material posted on it criticised five judges. Then in March 2000, Demon Internet paid Lawrence Godfrey, a university lecturer and physicist, £15,000 plus legal fees of around £250,000 in an out-of-court settlement after he was the subject of an allegedly libellous bulletin board posting. Soon afterwards British internet service providers (ISPs) closed two websites – a gay one called Outcast and another devoted (fittingly) to opposing censorship.

Fears that the libertarian view of the internet as a medium immune to censorship is merely a myth seemed justified after Giles Wilson, a BBC journalist, compiled a spoof web page ridiculing a colleague and found most ISPs would pull it in the face of any complaint. As John Naughton commented in the *Observer*: 'ISPs are run by businesses whose main interest is making money, not defending free speech.' To confuse the issue further, in May, a US Supreme Court ruling gave ISPs full protection against libellous or obscene messages sent out over the web, putting them on the same legal footing as telephone companies. Journalists' investigative work and promises of confidentiality appeared also threatened by the Regulation of Investigatory Powers Act 2000. As a result, the contents and details of emails and telephone calls would have become accessible to a wide range of government agencies, police officers and even low-grade council officials.

4 The art of interviewing

The dynamics of every interview are different. They may be short or long, in a pub, airport lounge or sauna. Rex Reed once interviewed singer Bette Midler while she was sitting on a toilet in a gay bathhouse (Silvester 1994: 30). They may be friendly or (occasionally) confrontational. They may be about someone's sex life or high matters of state. Many interviews are unpredictable. Sometimes an interview can change your life. This happened to Fenner Brockway, the late Labour peer, peace activist and journalist, who was 'converted' to socialism following his interview with Keir Hardie. How then to write about such imponderables? One of the most eminent Fleet Street interviewers, Lynn Barber, of the *Observer* and formerly of *Penthouse*, the *Independent on Sunday* and *Sunday Times*, admitted: 'I've made various attempts at instituting a system for organising interviews but have come to the conclusion that, in journalism, panic is the system.'

Here then are a few tips to help you traverse the fascinating territory of the interview. The best way to learn is to go out and do it. But always go about your journalism with a critical hat on. Watch colleagues, see interviewers on television, listen to them on the radio. Notice how they can differ in their techniques. Seek all the time to improve what you are doing.

Why interview?

An interview is intentional conversation. But, as a journalistic convention, it has to be seen in its historical context. It is easy to imagine the interview as a 'natural', unproblematic activity. Christopher Silvester (1994: 4–48) shows, however, in his seminal history that the interview, as a journalistic technique, had to be invented. In fact, the interview between Horace Greeley, editor of the *New York Tribune*, and Brigham Young, the leader of the Mormon Church in 1859, lays claim to being 'the first full-fledged interview with a celebrity, much of it in the question and answer format familiar to modern readers', as Silvester (1994: 4) comments. According to Jean K. Chalaby (1998: 127), the practice of interviewing spread to England in the 1880s, largely pioneered by W.T. Stead, the editor of the *Pall Mall Gazette*.

Journalists should always be aware of the interview's specific purposes: they may be seeking exclusive, new information or confirming established facts; they may be providing opinion or evidence of someone's state of mind. They may be investigating a subject and seeking to expose a lie or a wrong-doing. Observing closely the work or home environment in which the interview takes place can help provide extra details to the picture of the subject being drawn by the journalist. For the source, the interview has a purpose too: they are seeking to convey an opinion or information, hide a secret, or merely articulate their mood. But beware:

• The source may be confused, yet afraid to admit this.
• They may be afraid to speak their true opinion; they could lose their job or face social or professional isolation.
• The source may be lying, conveying misinformation, propaganda or seeking revenge. According to investigative reporter Paul Foot: 'You just have to get into the habit of asking questions and not believing the reply.' Or as Nick Davies comments: 'Almost anyone with a story worth telling has a reason to withhold it.'
• They may be intimidated by the presence of a reporter and so not express their true feelings.
• The source may be flattered by the interest of the journalist and be more extrovert and 'colourful' than they normally are.
• They may forget or hide important details.
• They may be speaking in a foreign language and so unable to express what they mean.
• They may be making fun of the whole process of interviewing.
• The reporter's personality and bias, even their body language, are likely to affect the relationship with the source and the kinds of responses solicited. A reporter may be afraid of their source (for instance, if he is a Balkan warlord) or defer to someone they consider famous or powerful. A different reporter might draw different answers. Someone may respond more openly to a woman reporter, another may feel more relaxed with an older man. Research has shown that interviews by black and white people draw different kinds of responses.

The quickie or grabbed interview

Many interviews are short. You may be covering a parliamentary select committee and want to follow up something said. You have time to ask just a few questions. You have a clear idea of your angle and need extra information and/or quotes to support it. You go to the MP, pen and notebook in hand (tape recorders are not permitted). There are just a few minutes before the MP is off on other business.

Vox pop

This is not about interviewing Madonna or Robbie Williams. It is the jargon term for the short interviews that journalists have with people on a given subject (vox pop derived from the Latin for 'voice of the people'). Do you think a law should be introduced to restrain the press from invading people's privacy? That sort of thing. Newspapers often build up a story around a series of short quotes drawn from street interviews (a photographer accompanying the reporter to provide mug shots for the story) or ring-arounds. A subject is identified and there follows a list of people with direct quotes attached to them. Or a vox pop can constitute part of a feature. The main story can dwell on the news, background and important details. A series of quotes highlights a range of views in an easy-to-read format.

Doorstepping and ambush interviews

Occasionally journalists wait outside people's homes in the hope of gaining an interview. This 'doorstepping' technique is used particularly to gain access to celebrities. It can be abused with the journalistic 'rat-pack' intimidating sources with their constant presence. Similarly a journalist might suddenly swoop down on a source to ask them questions. The 'ambush' technique should be used only when all other means of gaining access have been exhausted and when the issues are serious enough to warrant such treatment. It is most commonly used by television investigative reporters, the ambush itself providing dramatic footage.

Phones and phoney journalism

Phoney journalism is on the increase. Speed is the essence of journalism and the phone provides one of the easiest and quickest ways of contacting a source. It helps in the pursuit of a reluctant source. Journalists have to develop their own 'phone personality'; special 'phone relationships' emerge between reporters and their sources. But the phone has come to dominate the journalist's life far too much. As Christopher Browne (1996) comments:

> The speed and frequency of deadlines means that instead of meeting their sources face to face an increasing number of today's reporters and correspondents rely on mobile and standard telephones, faxes, pagers, teleprinters and computers to get their stories. This creates an artificial barrier between the newsmen [sic] and the news leading to errors, misunderstandings and reports that lack the inimitable freshness of human contact.

As email comes to be routinely used by journalists this distancing between source and reporter will be increased. The advice is clear: whenever you have an opportunity to see a source face to face, take it. If you are to develop that source you will need to meet them.

Phone interviews tend to be shorter than face-to-face contacts. Reporters have to be clear about the questions they are to put and the information they need. There is little time for waffle. Profiles are rarely conducted by phone: the contact between reporter and source is too superficial and impersonal. At the same time, reporters conducting phone interviews have to be extra sensitive to the nuances of speech: a hesitancy, an abruptness, a quivering in the voice all carry meanings which the reporter should be quick to note or respond to.

A reporter should also try to confront the impersonality of the phone and respond emotionally to the conversation. Facial and arm gestures can all help; if you are stressing a point move your hands about; if jokes are made, laugh. Standing up can help provide extra confidence when making a particularly difficult call. Some journalists lodge a phone on their shoulder and type up the conversation at the same time.

Not only can this practice lead to repetitive strain injury (RSI), but also it can be intimidating to the source and the reporter may have to return to note-taking with a pen if no other solution is possible.

Interview phobia

It is common for people new to journalism to find first contact with sources difficult. It is a challenge to ask a stranger questions (maybe in a foreign language) and maintain a coherent conversation while taking a note. Some find the 'distance' provided by the phone reassuring; others find face-to-face interviewing less intimidating. If you are not at ease on the phone you are not alone. According to Dr Guy Fielding, a communications specialist, 2.5 million people in Britain suffer telephone phobia (Rowlands 1993).

In your first few months of reporting it is a good idea to join up with a colleague during assignments. While journalism is an individualistic job, it can succeed only through people working in a team. Joint reporting in no way conflicts with journalistic norms. One of the most famous scoops, the exposé of the Watergate break-in, was the result of a joint effort by Carl Bernstein and Bob Woodward of the *Washington Post*. Investigative reporters often work in pairs or threesomes. It is safer and while one asks the questions the other/s can observe reactions and the environment closely (K. Williams 1998; Spark 1999; de Burgh 2000).

If you are alone on an assignment in those early months, or at any other time, it is fine to ask someone to slow down in their talking. Don't hesitate to ask the interviewee to spell out a difficult word, to repeat a strong quote or important information. Figures, names and titles are worth particular attention. Don't hesitate to ring back to check or extract new information. That merely reflects painstaking efficiency rather than incompetence.

Phone tip-offs

Sometimes journalists are rung at their homes or offices with some news. The journalist has no time to prepare questions. They have to think quickly. Information drawn from an unknown source in this way has to be checked and the source's contact details sought so they can be rung back if necessary.

The role of PROs

If you are contacting pressure groups, political parties or professional bodies you are likely to come into contact with their press relations officer (PRO). It is important to establish good relations with this person. They can be a vital source for background information and sometimes good for a quote. They can provide contact numbers for other sources and help in setting up meetings and interpreters if deaf people or foreign language speakers are being interviewed. But PROs expect a certain amount of background knowledge from reporters. A local government PRO would not expect to have to explain the intricacies of the community tax to an enquiring reporter. Official spokespersons are generally not referred to by name. They are described as 'a spokeswoman for such-and-such body'. They might also refer you to someone else in the organisation with specialist knowledge and responsibility in the area you are investigating.

In case of intimidation

Some people may feel intimidated by a phone call from a journalist. It might be their first contact with this awesome and seemingly powerful institution, the press, so capable of destroying reputations. You may decide to give them time to think about their responses. You could give them a few basic questions which they can respond to when you ring back in say twenty minutes. You have established some trust and they may be more inclined to respond to other questions. If the source is a racist attacking Pakistani or gypsy homes in your area you will adopt a different approach. As so often in reporting, political and ethical issues merge.

Arranging a face to face

Be polite, stay relaxed and sound efficient. It is important straight away to establish the likely length of the interview. The source is likely to have their own diary of engagements to complete. PROs often organise the meetings for celebrities and minor skirmishes are likely over arranging the time and place of the interview.

Negotiating the time-length is important since it provides a shorthand indication of the probable depth of the questioning. Most interviews aiming to extract specific information can last for around half an hour; for a profile of any depth at least three-quarters of an hour is required though they can last up to three hours (with a follow-up phone conversation, as well). Lynn Barber (1999: 198) says that she refuses to do any profile interview for less than an hour. Ginny Dougary, of *The Times*, says she spent two hours with Michael Portillo for her award-winning intereview in which he revealed his gay past – and followed it up with a telephone conversation.

Give a brief indication of the purpose of the interview (whether for a profile, as part of a feature or an investigation) and, in general terms, the kind of questions to be put. Identify clearly the newspaper you are working for and, if you are a free-lance, the target publication you are aiming at. In some cases a subject will be inter-viewed by a group of reporters. In that case, it is a good idea to spell out briefly how your approach is intended to be different. Indicate if you are to be accompanied by a photographer or (where relevant) an interpreter.

Fixing time and place

There are several potential locations:

- *Your territory* (newspaper office if you are a staff writer; your home/office if you are a freelance; college if you are a student). This is rarely adopted by reporters; offices lack the privacy and relative calm needed for interviews and can appear intimidating to members of the public.
- *Their territory* (home, particularly likely if the person is unemployed, office or shop floor). Journalists often visit the source's home when writing a profile. People

tend to feel relaxed there and talk most freely. The home is an expression of their personality: the source might wish to display it. The reporter can certainly use their observations of it and the source's behaviour within it to provide colour in their copy. The reporter might also visit the home when the source considers it too sensitive to hold the interview at their workplace. Visiting homes is not without its problems. The source is extending their hand to the reporter, inviting them into their private territory. The reporter can find it more difficult criticising the source after developing this kind of contact. Investigative reporter Nick Davies advises reporters not to park outside their source's home. 'If they are prompted to look out of the window they will make decisions about you before you introduce yourself.' The source's office is a common site for an interview (factory shopfloor workers are rarely profiled given current news values). The environment can be made relatively free from distractions and relevant information and documents will be at hand.

- *Neutral territory* (a pub or restaurant): useful sites when you are building up contacts. Their informality promotes fruitful contact. The source is being 'entertained' and that helps the conversation flow. The journalist will always go with a specific intention but the informality allows time for digressions, small talk, gossip and jokes. All this helps in the development of the relationship. The journalist can express their own knowledge of and views about the subjects discussed and that, to, helps trust develop.

Reassuring the source

Sometimes a source will need reassuring that they are not opening themselves to attack by agreeing to be interviewed. Members of progressive groups such as peace activists, feminists, trade unionists, gays, lesbians and anti-capitalists have been pilloried in the media and their fears are understandable. Even in today's supposedly democratic Britain, a large number of people are afraid or unwilling to express their views to the media. In these situations it is important to explain whom you are writing for, what you hope to extract from the interview. Never speak to someone on the basis you are writing for one media outlet which they are happy with and then send the copy elsewhere without consulting them. Student journalists might win a difficult interview on the understanding it is not for publication. This makes for unreal journalism (since it is only credible in the context of a target publication) and so should generally be avoided. Certainly the student should resist the temptation to betray the trust and send the copy off to a newspaper.

Submitting questions in advance

Someone might speak to you only on the condition they see a list of questions beforehand. Many politicians and showbiz celebrities are now adopting this line. It is a practice which, in general, should be challenged. Journalists can end up clerical poodles pandering to the whims of the famous. But it is wrong to call for a blanket ban on this request for questions. A journalist might be aware of the interviewee's views; they are more important as a source of information. Since speed is the essence in journalism, the source might plead ignorance and essential information may go missing. They might need to do some research, consult colleagues before answering.

At least the sending of questions gives them time. They cannot plead ignorance during the face-to-face interview.

It might be legitimate when a crucial source is sought and no other way appears possible to agree to send a list of questions. You may even suggest it. At least some response is gained and there is the possibility the source will be impressed by your questions and invite you in for a face to face. An interviewee might first promise half an hour of their time but then running through the previously submitted and impressive questions might easily last for an hour and a half. At the opposite end of the scale from the media-shy person is the self-publicist. Every newspaper office will be harassed by someone desperate for coverage. Reporters need to be on their guard against this kind of person.

Preparing for an in-depth interview

Preparation is essential (Coleman 1993). If you are well informed, you are more likely to extract new and interesting information and be sensitive to the source's bias. Read the cuttings, do the research, talk to friends and colleagues about the subjects likely to be raised. An uninformed reporter becomes the pawn in the hand of the source; they can lie, they can hide crucial information, they can misinform; they can steer the conversation away from tricky subjects. Celebrity interviewer Ginny Dougary says that she prepares for an interview 'like a military campaign'. To help prepare asking difficult questions she psyches herself up with deep breathing, wears smart clothes and makes absolutely sure her tapes are working.

Most professions have their own stock of jargon and a bewildering array of acronyms with which the reporter should have some familiarity. But sources used to handling the press have different expectations of journalists. The specialist is assumed to have more knowledge than the generalist and cub reporter. Never be afraid to express ignorance. Better to clarify a point than flounder or carry mistakes in your copy.

The question of questions

Journalists differ on the extent to which they prepare specific questions. To avoid 'drying up', some argue it is best to write down most of the crucial questions in a logical order and tick them off as the interview proceeds. Many find this can impede free-flowing conversation. Talk moves too fast usually to allow this 'ticking off'. If the detailed list of questions is used it should be on a separate sheet of paper and not buried in a notebook. In any case, interviews can often move in unpredictable directions making it absurd to stick to any pre-planned outline. Another approach is to think through the interview beforehand listing detailed questions in order. The act of writing helps the memory. For the interview, three or four vital headings are listed and around this skeleton the flesh of the interview can be spread.

Dress sense

A journalist should be conscious of the messages put out by their dress. Informal dress will be appropriate on some occasions such as when interviewing members of progressive campaigning groups or think-tanks, formal dress when meeting white-collar professionals or politicians. A journalist will always have at the back of their mind: 'If I dressed differently would the source be more open to me and trusting?'

Preliminary courtesies

First contact is crucial. The reporter should be calm and relaxed, polite but assertive. The greeting should be pleasant with a firm handshake and some eye-to-eye contact. The reporter might need to make clear again the purpose of the interview (though during some investigations the real purpose might be hidden).

If the interview is for some reason off-the-record or unattributable this needs to be established. Politicians and most PROs will be aware of the attribution conventions of newspapers. Many people are not. They may begin to answer questions and then try to designate them as off the record. A journalist should not be willing to permit that kind of arrangement automatically. A source may say something on the record which, in print, could damage them or someone else unnecessarily. In this case the journalist will operate self-censorship. If you are planning to use a tape recorder, make sure this is fine with the source, who might choose to set up their own taping device, after all. You might not wish to bring out your notebook until you have relaxed into the conversation and passed the preliminary courtesies. The notebook should never be over-prominent.

The actual interview: GENERAL POINTS

Note-taking

In your first weeks as a reporter you might find it difficult keeping a conversation going while making notes at the same time. Don't feel self-conscious about that. You may even say: 'That's an important point. Would you mind repeating that?' Selecting the useful information and quotes becomes an art. Sometimes all the notes will be used, usually just a part of them. The writer, confident in their powers of memory, might add more details or comments they remember but did not take down. This has to be handled carefully, particularly if the views are contentious and potentially libellous. Without any notes or tape recording, the journalist has little defence in court.

Presenting your personality

Dennis Barker (1998), former media correspondent and columnist on the *Guardian*, argues that journalists should ask 'questions which the Man on the Clapham Omnibus would ask if he were there' and should not follow their own agenda. But it is impossible to deny your personality in the meeting. The selection and bias of your questions, your manner and your dress will carry the stamp of your personality. The extent to which your personality more overtly intrudes on the interview will differ according to the circumstances.

In most interviews where the focus is on extracting views and information, the reporter's intervention is likely to be limited. An exchange of views and a joke or two are useful for varying the mood and helping conversation flow. In profile interviews your own personality can come more and more to the fore. Someone confronted with a reporter who is nothing more than a blank sheet of a personality merely uttering concise questions can hardly convey their own. But you should never come to dominate a meeting. Your views and experiences are of secondary importance and should be revealed only to entice more out of your subject. Displaying some of your knowledge on the subject can also impress the interviewee and help build up trust. Never show off. And don't be too familiar: it is rarely appropriate to address your source by their first name.

Pacing the interview

Most journalistic training manuals advise reporters to begin always with the non-threatening questions establishing basic information and views. This helps to create trust after which more sensitive questions can be raised. In practice, reporters respond in many different ways to the shifting dynamics of the interview. Some suggest it is best to throw in a difficult question near the start. As Lynn Barber (1991) comments: 'The subject's relief at having survived it so quickly and painlessly may pay dividends for the rest of the interview.' Yet there is always the danger that the interviewee may call a stop to the conversation early on if this strategy fails.

Barber says that at the start of interviews she makes the point of stressing the interviewee's right to refuse: 'Please don't be offended by my questions. If you don't want to answer them, just shake your head and I won't even put no comment.' Questions should be concise. But the interview is not likely to be all questions. It may be fruitful to exchange ideas. Formulate a mix of open-ended questions and specific questions avoiding those which give a yes/no answer.

Active listening

Most interviewers stress that active listening is one of the most crucial skills. Journalists can often be surprised at how open and talkative people are when profiled. Their vanity may be flattered. Here is someone taking an interest in them; however fleeting, a little fame is assured by the coverage. In some respects the press (and the media in general) has taken over the role of the Church as being the site of the confessional, where personal secrets are revealed. Every day the press carries the revelation of some secret: the secret of so-and-so's sex life; the leak of secret divisions in the Cabinet; a secret arms sale. Paradoxically, this is happening in a society where government and industry are becoming increasingly secretive and remote from democratic accountability. Given the willingness to talk, the journalist's role is to listen intelligently and help the conversation along with concise, clearly focused questions.

The flexible approach

Reporters should be relaxed and flexible, ready to abandon their list of questions and follow up more interesting ideas as they emerge. They should always be clear about what they want from an interview. It is dangerous to go into an interview with a vague brief hoping that something will come out of it. It rarely does; the reporter will end up with a lot of waffle. In contrast, continual evasive responses to key questions suggest to the reporter they are on to something important. There is a place for unstructured chat, say over a meal, between journalist and source. Contacts are being maintained and maybe something of interest will emerge. But chat is very different from an interview.

Power games people play

The distribution of power in many communication processes is complex and fluctuating. A source may seek to exploit the reporter to transmit their views, their misinformation or their propaganda. The reporter exploits the source as a 'quote giver' or 'information giver'. In this light, interviews can be seen as a contest. The journalist must be aware as far as possible of the dynamics of the interview and try to be in control, determining the flow. The interviewee should never take over. If they do, by rambling on some irrelevant point, for instance, the journalist should reassert their authority with a pointed question.

Body talk

Eye contact is important but continuous contact is likely to appear intimidating. During profile interviews, other aspects of body language and non-verbal communication, such as sighs, shrugs, silences, coughs or shrugging of shoulders, will be closely observed by the reporter. Interviewing children poses special problems for the journalist. For instance, getting eye contact with them often involves crouching down (Hughes and McCrum 1998). Also be aware of your own body language: is it helping to put the subject at ease?

Dealing with the difficult ones

The hostile interviewee

An interviewee may be hostile for a number of reasons. They may have a poor opinion of the press in general or have been criticised in the past. They may feel threatened or insulted by a particular line of questioning. They may simply dislike the sound of your voice or the colour of your jacket. As a result, you may have to reassure them about the standards you and your newspaper follow, and that understand their sensitivity about a particular issue.

Whatever happens, keep cool. Never argue with an interviewee. Try to steer the conversation towards calmer waters. If the source is particularly important and reacts nervously to your questions, you may agree to show them the copy before publication. Lynn Barber (1999: 197) says 'the best interview ever' was Lillian Ross's profile of Hemingway. Ross sent him the article before publication: he asked for one deletion, which she made. Sometimes the source might walk out on you. That is their privilege.

The over-hasty interviewee

This is the person who says: 'I don't have time to talk to you.' A good response is to say something like: 'I won't take up much of your time but this is an important matter and I want to get it right.' Be sympathetic and straight to the point. They should thaw.

The silent interviewee

You don't seem to be going anywhere. They answer in dull, monosyllabic tones. Give them time to warm up, open-ended questions and lots of encouraging head-nods. If all else fails, fall silent and see what happens.

The 'no comment'

As veteran investigative journalist Phillip Knightley (1998) advises, never take 'no' for an answer. If the source is particularly important, be persistent but don't harass them. If they continue to say 'no comment', you could tell them this looks bad in print. Stress you don't want to write a one-sided story and need their comments, perhaps to correct inaccuracies. Ask why they cannot comment. Someone may try to delay you until the following day. Suggest the story is going to print and will be unbalanced without their quotes.

The dodger

They may claim ignorance of some major detail but be simply trying to avoid controversy. You need to be well briefed to cope. They claim to have been absent at a crucial meeting. 'Ah, but I have looked in the minutes of the meeting and noticed you were present.' That sort of comment should jog their memory.

The waffler

They may habitually be a raconteur and stray away from the main conversational issues. Or they may be trying to evade a delicate issue. Don't let them take command of the conversation. Keep it focused.

Ending the interview

- Sometimes it is worth asking: 'Is there anything else you wish to mention?'
- Appropriate courtesies should be made: thanks for time and so on.
- Arrangements for checking and future contact (perhaps also by a photographer) can be made. If you have interviewed them at their office, it might be useful to have their home number and email details.
- An interviewee might ask to see copy before it is published. You will then have to deal with that issue.

After the interview

This is another crucial period. You might need to ring or email back to clarify some points. They might well contact you again. Often after profile interviews, it is courteous to write back thanking them for their time. Also try to transcribe the tape and compile your article as soon as possible after the event. If you wait you are more likely to forget details, distort others and find your notes incomprehensible.

When the interview is part of a feature investigation, it should similarly be written up as soon as possible and ideas for new interviews and issue to examine should be noted.

Direct quotes

These are best reserved for expressions of opinion. For instance: "She said: 'Tony Blair has already proved himself to be the greatest Prime Minister of the century.'" Direct quotes add newsy elements to stories and provide colour, immediacy, authenticity and the crucial human dimension to copy, hence their prominence. They can add humour. Quotes also help personalise the news. It is always better to have an individual express a view than an impersonal institutional voice. Instead of 'the National Union of Teachers claimed', say 'a spokeswoman for the NUT claimed'. When using a press release, a phone call may be necessary to add this detail.

Lengths of direct quotes will vary. But take any book of quotations and see how short the majority are. Some of the most famous are a matter of a few words. Just as the heavies use longer sentences than the pops, so their quotes tend to be longer. But do people speak in shorter sentences to tabloid journalists?

It is a vexed question among journalists as to how much freedom they have to edit a direct quote. Most will agree that such phrases as 'you know', 'like I said' and 'er, er' slipped into conversation can easily be cut. Beyond that, some argue that a direct quote should never be changed. However, there is a case for editing when someone speaks ungrammatically. Nothing is served by leaving it in other than showing that the source is stupid. Thus, particular care should be given when quoting people for whom English is not their first language. Nonsense is worth quoting when the subject of the piece requires it. For instance, newspapers have focused on the ungrammatical language used by a series of prominent US politicians (Reaganspeak, Haigspeak, Bushspeak), often in off-the-cuff remarks to journalists. Peculiar speech mannerisms and dialect can be quoted to convey the source's typical speech patterns. This has to be done sensitively, mostly in features.

Particular kinds of cliché, jargon and rhetoric do not make good quotes. Thus "The President said: 'This historic meeting of the world's leading industrial states has achieved a lot and we have reason to be proud of what we have done this weekend'." "She was 'very pleased' with the takings from the raffle for handicapped children." These are examples of clichés and rhetoric which can be easily cut.

Reported speech

The conventions of reported speech are simple. Following verbs such as 'said', 'informed', 'claimed', 'warned', 'demanded', 'alleged', 'hinted', 'added' the tense of the verb in reported speech takes one step into the past.

Direct speech	Reported speech
am/are/is	was/were
shall	should
will	would

may	might
was/were	had been
have been	had been
must	had to
could	could have

"Aneurin Bevan said: 'I read the newspaper avidly. It is my one form of continuous fiction'" is using the direct quote. In reported speech it becomes: "Aneurin Bevan said he read the newspaper avidly. It was his one form of continuous fiction." It is wrong to say: "Aneurin Bevan said he reads the newspaper avidly. It is his one form of continuous fiction."

Thus: "He said: 'The trade union movement has been crippled by the Tories' punitive legislation and has little support from the Blair government'" becomes: "He said the trade union movement had been crippled by the Tories' punitive legislation and had little support from the Blair government."

Pronouns are affected by reported speech conventions. "She said: 'We may decide to emigrate to Iceland' becomes: "She said they might decide to emigrate to Iceland."

"She told the council 'Your attempts at promoting equal opportunities in this county are pathetic'" becomes: "She told the council its attempts at promoting equal opportunities in the county were pathetic."

Adverbs are also affected: Thus "He said: 'We shall all meet here soon to plan next week's agenda.'" becomes: "He said they should all meet there soon to plan the following week's agenda." For a longer exposition of reported speech rules see Aitchison (1988) and Hicks (1998: 53–4).

Note the use of reported speech in this article by James Meikie in the *Guardian* of 25 March 2000. Reporting on moves to halt the reprocessing of spent fuel at the Sellafield nuclear plant in Cumbria his story ran:

The state-owned company said there was "no question" of abandoning their work – but in a further demonstration of political support ebbing, the Department of Trade and Industry said the future of reprocessing, and whether there was a market for it, was "a commercial issue for the company".

The latest threat follows the suspension of shipments of spent fuel by Switzerland, Germany and Sweden, a furious row with Japan and warnings about US contracts. The industry inspectorate warned it had powers to close the Thorp reprocessing plant, the newer of two at Sellafield, if safety measures were not implemented.

And he continued:

The Department of Environment said it was developing a national strategy for radioactive discharges over the next 20 years.

- In the first par., following the verb 'said' – reported speech 'was', 'was' and 'was'.

- In the second par., after verb 'warned' – reported speech 'had' 'were not implemented'.

- In the final par., after the verb 'said' – reported speech 'was developing'.

Beware of making reported speech, say in a press release, into direct speech. A release that says: "Former President Nelson Mandela accused the South African government of continuing to suppress black rights" cannot be changed into: "Nelson Mandela said: 'The South African government is continuing to suppress black rights'." There is no proof he said those words. The indirect speech might have been the paraphrase of a longer sentence or a combination of sentences.

Reported speech within a direct quote cannot be converted into direct speech. Thus: "He said he would ask his wife if he should resign tomorrow" cannot become: "He asked his wife: 'Should I resign tomorrow?'"

Most reports of speeches will combine direct and indirect speech. A report concentrating too heavily on indirect speech will lack immediacy and colour; a report almost exclusively in direct quotation conveys the impression the journalist has surrendered their role of selection and interpretation to the source.

Partial quotes

These are used to highlight particular words in sentences. Thus, the Nottingham *Evening Post* reported (25 February 2000):

> Defence Secretary Geoff Hoon today denied British troops were using "lousy equipment" after it emerged that all the Army's standard rifles may have to be recalled because of jamming in extreme temperatures.

Journalists use partial quotes sparingly. They are most commonly used in intros but become confusing if used throughout a story.

Quotation dangers

Two or more people rarely speak in unison. When reporting a public meeting it is strange to have two people identified with the same direct quote. Thus: '"The BBC should be privatised immediately,' two Conservative councillors urged yesterday" is wrong. People can agree on an issue and be linked to a direct quote without any problem. Thus it is perfectly feasible to say: "The BBC should be privatised immediately, two Conservative councillors urged yesterday."

Be careful not to distort reports by over-selective quoting. Someone may devote part of a speech to conveying the pros of an issue, the other part to the cons. One side of the argument may be highlighted; it is irresponsible to eliminate all reference to the other side.

Journalists can let their imagination take over when quoting. The Press Complaints Commission has gone so far as to censure journalists for too frequently resorting to invention in the use of quotes. One of the most famous instances was the *Sun*'s invented interview with the wife of a Falklands war 'hero' killed in battle. (The woman journalist involved went on to edit a national newspaper.)

A variation on the invention theme is the 'words in the mouth' technique. When an interviewee remains unresponsive, the journalist is tempted to feed them quotes. They may ask the interviewee: 'Do you think this scheme for Blackpool transport is outrageous and should never have been backed?' When the hesitant interviewee replies: 'Er, yes', the journalist is able to report: 'She said she thought the transport scheme for Blackpool was outrageous and should never have been backed.' Such a technique should be used sparingly. But former *Sunday Mirror* reporter Wendsley Clarkson (1990) tells of when he met ex-Beatle Paul McCartney in his car with his wife alongside him as he drove out of his country estate. Merely on the basis of a few grunts of the 'Yep, sure do' variety, Clarkson invented an 'exclusive'.

Along with invention can go exaggeration and sensationalism. Two residents are quoted as being opposed to plans for a shopping complex on a school sports site. The story reads: 'Residents are protesting etc.' The report gives a false picture of the strength of opposition for the sake of journalistic hyperbole. If one of the residents was a spokesperson for the residents, then you could intro: 'Residents are protesting etc.' When opposing views are expressed 'rows' have not necessarily broken out, nor have 'wars' nor is one side necessarily 'up in arms'. Disputes at churches need not always be dubbed 'unholy rows'.

There is a danger of placing direct quote marks around a phrase and not making clear the source. Such 'hanging' quotes confuse. Always make the attribution of any quote clear. And be careful not to run two sections of a direct quote together when they were separated by sentences. End the first sentence with double inverted commas. Begin the next sentences with, say: "She added: 'Etc. . . .'"

Quotes punctuation

Most newspapers adopt the following style. They will say:

> She added: "I intend to vote for the Raving Loony Party."

Notice the colon followed by a space, then double inverted commas and a capital letter. At the end of the sentence the full stop is followed by the inverted commas. Variations on that model are considered wrong. Avoid:

> She said, "I intend to vote for the Raving Loony Party".

and

> She said that "I intend to vote for the Raving Loony Party."

When a partial quote is used the punctuation should fall outside the quote marks. Thus:

> He described the US-led attacks on Belgrade as "illegal and barbaric".

> The rail strike is "outrageous", according to Prime Minister Tony Blair.

Normally double quotes are used, with single quotes within quotes. Thus:

> He said: "The Nato attacks on Belgrade are best seen as a 'barbaric slaughter' of innocent Serbian civilians."

First words in partial quotes are not capitalised. Thus: Barbara Tuchman said war was the "Unfolding of miscalculations" is wrong. It should read:

Barbara Tuchman said war was the "unfolding of miscalculations".

Square brackets are used in direct quotations around words inserted by the journalist to make the meaning clear. Thus:

"He [President Clinton] quite obviously backed the bombing of Iraq to deflect attention away from the controversy surrounding his affair with Monica Lewinsky."

Interestingly, American newspapers place square brackets around copy from agencies (such as Reuters or Agence France Presse) which is inserted into stories by staff reporters.

Put an ellipsis (. . .) in a direct quote to indicate irrelevant words are missing. Used more than once it looks as if the reporter is struggling with a poor note or indulging in over-zealous editing. Simpler to change the quote into indirect speech and remove the offending dots.

Attribution verbs

'Said' is most commonly used to convey attribution. It is short, neutral and for these reasons is rapidly read over. To use 'said' on every occasion would be dull and words such as 'replied', 'commented', 'pointed out', 'protested', 'warned', 'indicated', 'explained', 'added', 'hinted', 'revealed', 'claimed' and 'alleged', which have specific meanings, are used, always carefully. They are most often placed in intros where they convey extra emphasis and drama. They should never be used simply to provide colour in news stories though more flexibility is possible in features.

'Claimed' should be used only for controversial statements of alleged fact when there is some reasonable doubt over them. When evidence is undisputed the use of 'claim' throws up unnecessary doubts. When a newspaper reports: 'In its report which follows a detailed review of the operation of the 1976 Race Relations Act, the commission claims ethnic minorities continue to suffer high levels of discrimination and disadvantage,' it is using 'claim' in a subtly racist way to dispute the fact of widespread discrimination.

'Admitted' should be used only when a source is confessing to an error, a failing a limitation, charge or crime. Thus the Nottingham *Evening Post* (of 24 February 2000), on a motorcyclist caught speeding at more than 96 m.p.h. reported:

Learoyd, of Northumberland Avenue, Market Bosworth, admitted speeding when he appeared before Nottingham Magistrates' Court yesterday.

'Added' should be used only after a source has already been quoted. It is wrong to introduce a new source with the words: "She added: 'Etc. . . .'"

'Revealed' should be used only when significant new information is being relayed. 'Stated' is archaic and generally avoided. 'Quipped', 'joked' and 'chuckled' are clichés and best avoided or confined to light features and diary pieces.

An effective way of conveying attribution is to use the phrase 'according to . . .' It is most commonly used in intros as here from the London *Evening Standard* (23 February 2000):

> The world is warming much faster than anyone thought and the process is still accelerating, according to the US National Climate Data Centre.

Getting the quotes down: RECORDING TECHNIQUES

Shorthand

One of the essential skills of the journalist is recording notes effectively. The National Council for the Training of Journalists requires 100 words per minute (wpm) from successful candidates. Many training courses devote considerable time to shorthand and most provincial newspapers will require good shorthand from applicants. The two most popular systems with journalists are Pitmans and Teeline, the latter invented primarily with trainee journalists in mind.

During the nineteenth century the emergence of shorthand as a special journalistic technique (with novelist Charles Dickens demonstrating particular skills) helped in the development of the notion of 'professionalism'. As Anthony Smith (1978) argues: 'It meant that a man could specialise in observing or hearing and recording with precision . . . it gave the reporter an aura of neutrality as he stood between event and reader.'

Today there is a paradox that the higher up the greasy pole of journalistic success you go, the less likely you are to find shorthand competence. Not all Fleet Street writers possess it. Very few other journalistic cultures give shorthand the kind of importance that British provincial newspapers attach to it. Yet it is important for all aspiring journalists to do shorthand to at least 100 words a minute. Nobody regrets the effort put into the learning. For certain jobs, such as covering Parliament, select committees, courts and coroners' courts where tapes are banned, and council meetings, good shorthand is essential. If reporters had better recording techniques, fewer errors would crop up and the habit of inventing quotes and facts would diminish.

Personal shorthands

The most commonly used abbreviation system is Astbury's and you may want to develop your own based on the idea of cutting out vowels. 'Between' becomes 'btwn', 'against' 'agst' and so on. A new shorthand system, AgiliWriting, has been invented by Anne Gresham, which she describes as 'ezy t rd, ezy t wrt and ezy t lrn'. The outstanding feature is that it is accompanied by a computer program allowing the writer to type in shorthand copy and transfer it into longhand. (For more information: 39 Totteridge Lane, London N20 OHD; tel: 020-8446 0086.) Thus, it is possible that in the near future journalists will attend press conferences with their laptop computers, type notes in shorthand form, then send them via a modem to the office for conversion into longhand.

Selective note-taking

Acquiring the skills of selective note-taking is crucial. It is not essential to record everything said. Over-detailed note-taking prevents profitable contact in interviews. The best shorthand writers are not necessarily the best writers. The good journalist knows when something of interest is being said. Their ears prick up and all attention is paid to getting down those facts, those views, that feeling. If you are not certain you have the quote correct, either double check or paraphrase the general meaning (if you are clear about that) and put it in reported speech. David Spark (1999: 47) offers this additional advice: 'If you are in the habit of adorning your notes with comments about the people you are speaking to give up the habit. In court, a rude comment can be construed as showing your evidence-gathering was malicious, not even-handed. In a libel case, malice invalidates a defence of fair comment or a claim to privilege.'

Memory

In some cases, journalists don't take down notes at all. During a risky investigation a journalist may keep their identity hidden. At a particularly sensitive interview a journalist may consider the presence of a notebook impedes conversation and over-formalises the meeting. A source may be prepared to talk but find the notebook intimidating. On these occasions the reporter has to rely on memory. Only those with a good memory should adopt this approach.

Tidiness

Reporters usually use easy-to-handle notebooks that slip easily into pockets and whose pages flip over quickly. Notes should never be made on odd sheets of paper. These can be easily mislaid. A tidy system of keeping used notebooks is essential since back-referencing is sometimes needed. When complaints are made to newspapers over coverage, easy access to the relevant note is essential. The Press Complaints Commission has warned newspapers over their increasing habit of losing important notes. When complaints were made, newspapers had little ground on which to base a defence.

Note-taking from written sources

- For developing background knowledge of people, events and issues, written sources are vital.

- For research in libraries (with CD-ROM, cuttings, the internet and other written sources) you may work with a quiet laptop or more usually with pen and paper. Always make clear the title of the book or article, full name of author, publisher, place and year of publication. These details are usually in small type on the imprint page, before the contents list. It is also advisable to identify the page number as you note the document. This can be important if you go on to write a project or book on the subject. Many journalists work on books in their spare time or on sabbaticals. So it is a useful habit to develop.

- Make clear the distinction between a direct quote from a work and a paraphrase. To lift someone's words directly and not attribute them can lead to allegations of plagiarism.

- Learn to use books, reports, articles and website features selectively. You will rarely read from beginning to end. There is not the time. Sometimes you will rapid-read a work and take detailed notes of the conclusions or recommendations. There may be a vital book or article which is worth reading three times to digest. Use book indexes to go straight to the material you need. Look at the bibliographies for other useful sources.

Tapes: pros and cons

Many journalists are relying increasingly on tape recorders. Their prices range from around £30 up to £200 and beyond. They are small and unobtrusive and few people are intimidated by their presence. If a source challenges a reporter over a quote, nothing is better at ending the controversy than a tape providing the evidence. But courts are aware that tapes can be tampered with. Alastair Brett, a lawyer at Times Newspapers, advises: 'Tape everything you can, every word you utter or is uttered to you.' After a solicitor complained that a *Sunday Times* reporter had 'grossly misled' him, the newspaper had the whole conversation taped and was able to prove otherwise (Spark 1999: 45).

You should inform your source that you are using a tape. Some newspapers have phones set aside for taping while a few journalists have devices on their phones at home. Taping always requires careful handling. Never rely entirely on a tape. You may lose it or may have forgotten to press the vital 'on' switch. The battery may run low; the microphone may pick up unwanted noises. If you put it on the centre of a table during a panel discussion it might not register the voices at the end of the table. Always take a back-up note. The dangers of having a tape erased were highlighted in the case of Jason Connery vs the *Sun* in 1992 when the newspaper's defence failed after a tape that promised to provide crucial evidence was 'lost'. The only record remaining was a transcript of the conversation which the judge said had been 'embellished, added to and altered' (Leyland 1998).

For copy needed quickly, tape recorders can be a positive nuisance. There is not time to wade through the tape to find the relevant quotes and information. Tapes are best used for features and profiles when you have time to note and digest their contents. It is very rare that journalists transcribe all the tape. Take down the most important sections as soon as possible after the interview, then return to it for a more thorough run-through when writing up your story.

Bugging

Bugging devices are available at relatively cheap prices: a study in 2000 by the campaigning body Privacy International found that 200,000 bugs are sold quite legally in Britain every year. Managements use them to snoop on staff – and a few journalists use them during investigations. Investigative reporter Gerry Brown (1995a) highlights the fact that bugging is illegal under the Interception of Communications Act 1985. But recording your own end of a two-way telephone conversation is legal (see also Brown 1995b). He says:

> Quite simply, newspaper reporters who tap people's phones are already breaking the law. I've been doing sneaky investigations for the tabloids for 20-odd years and I've never tapped a phone or been asked by a newspaper to tap a phone. What I do is monitor and record phone calls. The difference is simple. When you hook up to a phone line and listen in to two people without either of them being aware you're eavesdropping, then that's tapping and you're breaking the law. But if you or your contacts are simply recording your own end of a two-way conversation, that's monitoring.
>
> [He continues:] Hide a radio microphone in a room and crouch behind the bushes in the garden to snoop on what's being said, and that's bugging, an offence

under Section 1, the Wireless Telegraphy Act 1949. But if you are in the room yourself with the microphone running to a micro-tape recorder stuffed down your underpants, again, perfectly legal.

The PCC Code of Practice advises against bugging bar exceptional cases. However, the use of bugging by the state and its secret services and by industrial spies is far more widespread (Wingfield 1984; Campbell and Connor 1986).

The law is currently confused on scanners. Possession is not illegal: they can be bought for around £300 in the high street. People use them for listening to citizens' band radio and the weather report from ship to shore. There is even a UK scanning directory listing such sensitive frequencies as airport security, US Air Force bomb disposal units and defence tactical communications. But it is illegal to listen in to official or private conversations and mobile phones are particularly vulnerable to scanning.

5 Learning the language of news

T he language of news today is the product of centuries of linguistic evolution. It is not a 'natural' form of writing. It is a particular discourse with its own rhythms, tones, words and phrases (van Dijk 1988; Fowler 1991). It has to be learnt.

Kiss and tell

Many young reporters from academic backgrounds where writing essays 2,000 words long may be the norm find writing news difficult. Compose a story of 300 words and every one has to count. The sense of news values has to be sharp and that only comes with practice. 'Kiss (*keep it short and simple*) and tell' could be the journalist's motto. Complex sentences overloaded with long subordinate clauses should be avoided. Short, precise sentences are best. As the left-wing novelist and journalist George Orwell advised:

> A scrupulous writer, in every sense he writes, will ask himself at least four questions, thus: 'What am I trying to say: What words will express it? What image or idiom will make it clearer? Is this image fresh enough to have an effect?' And he will probably ask himself two more: 'Could I put it more simply? Have I said anything avoidably ugly?
>
> (Orwell 1984 [1957]: 151–2)

You don't need to count words all the time. But think in terms of a maximum of around 32–5 for a news sentence. The tabloids and many local papers have around 16–20 maximum limit. Take these three examples:

This Norwich *Evening News* (http://www.norfolk-now.co.uk) report (8 December 1999) has 15, 16 and 13 words in its opening pars.

> Police were today hopeful of finding a missing 12-year-old Norwich boy after several reported sightings.
>
> Michael Self was last seen near his home in the West Earlham area at 5.30pm yesterday.
>
> Police combed the area throughout the night and the search was extended today.

These pars from the *Mirror* of 14 September 2000 have 14, 16 and 11:

> Food rationing returned to Britain yesterday as the fuel crisis hit the high street.
>
> Some supermarkets acted to stop panic-buying by shoppers worried that stocks would disappear from the shelves.
>
> And home deliveries were cancelled at other shops to save fuel.

These from the *News Line* (of the Workers' Revolutionary Party) of 13 December 1999 have 20, 19 and 10 words:

> The Russian army suspended its bombing of the Chechen capital, Grozny, on Saturday to allow civilians to flee the city.
>
> Military sources confirmed that air and artillery attacks which have targeted Grozny for weeks stopped early in the day.
>
> Officials said the suspension would last until midnight last night.

Economic base of economical writing

Many factors lie behind the creation of this concise news language. The arrival of the telegraph and telegram during the nineteenth century put a clear cost on elaborate language. With the competition today between advertisers and editorial for space in newspapers, every reported word involves a cost. Economic language helps provide economies in production. Speed is the essence of newspapers. Sentence structure and page design are influenced by the need to help readers move through the newspaper quickly. As the speed of everyday life increases, the average concentration span narrows. Sentences become shorter; headlines end up just a few 'punchy' words. Acronyms proliferate. Words made from acronyms become standards ('yuppie', 'yummie', 'AIDS'). Phrases that compress complex meaning into a few words are everywhere ('the silent majority', the 'new world order'). Newspaper design also influences language and sentence lengths. As Fred Fedler comments:

> Newspapers are printed in small type, with narrow columns, on cheap paper. Long paragraphs – large, gray blocks of type – discourage readers. So reporters divide stories into bite-size chunks that are easy to read. Also, the white space left at the ends of paragraphs helps brighten each page.
>
> (Fedler 1989: 28)

Boil it down

Never use two or three words when one will do. Words and phrase such as 'in order to' (use simply 'to'), 'at the present time' ('now'), 'in the region of' ('about'), 'despite the fact that' ('even though'), 'in view of the fact that' ('because'), 'on the subject of training' ('on training') and 'strike action' ('strike') are all cuttable. Prefer short to long words: 'about' rather than 'approximately', 'show' rather than 'demonstrate', 'after' rather than 'following'. Avoid the over-wordiness of adjectives and adverbs: 'totally destroyed', 'root cause', 'important essential', 'past history', 'invited guest', 'best ever', 'broad daylight', 'close proximity', 'considerable difficulty', 'initial beginning', 'final outcome'. 'Very', 'quite' and 'rather' are meaningless modifiers, eminently cuttable. Beware unnecessary prepositions as in 'divided up', 'circled around', 'fell down'. Try not to repeat a word in the same sentence or any striking words close together unless a specific effect is intended.

The word 'that' can often be cut, as in: 'He admitted that he was guilty of stealing a pen from the office.' Also be careful when using the small word 'of'. Usually you can make a phrase more precise. 'In the northern part of Iraq' is better written 'in northern Iraq'. Use language precisely. Don't confuse decimate/destroy, less/fewer, luxurious/luxuriant, affect/effect, it is/its. Ian Mayes, the *Guardian*'s readers' editor, is constantly having to highlight errors over 'homophones': words pronounced in the same way but differing in meaning or spelling or both – as in bear and bare, sort/sought, diffusing/defusing, censor/censure, rites/rights, yoke/yolk, draws/drawers. Generally try to avoid using 'thing'. It is vague and ugly. (For useful sections on wasteful and commonly misused words and redundancies see Bagnall 1993: 4–11.)

Be active

Rather than: 'A meeting will be held by TUC leaders next week to discuss the government's new privatisation strategy' it is better to say 'TUC leaders will meet next week to discuss the government's new privatisation strategy'.

Fun with puns

Puns are extremely important in newspapers. They play with language and its many-faceted meanings. Some can be forced. But their contrivance is part of their appeal. A certain wit is needed to construct them just as they can convey a certain humour (Fiske 1989). Puns feature particularly in the pops. Their humour contributes to their overall hedonistic appeal. For instance, the *News of the World* (*NoW*) (5 March 2000) carried this (highly contrived) intro section:

Cats the way to give Liam some grrrrrrrrief!

It was a case of (What's The Story?) Morning Roary as Robbie Williams turned into a tiger to taunt his Oasis rival following his double Brit triumph the night before.

In a picture caption, the *NoW* reported:

Rod Stewart has finally found a girl he can look up to . . . and he would if he wasn't below his peak. The 55-year-old 5ft 10in pop star pulled his hat over his eyes as he strolled with Penny Lancaster in the Beverly Hills sun, clearly hoping to disguise his shortcomings. Penny, from Chigwell, Essex, is 6ft even without heels.

The heavies are more likely to reserve puns for soft news stories and headlines. But many of the parliamentary sketch writers, such as Matthew Parris of *The Times*, often build their copy on a simple pun idea.

Clichés: AVOID THEM LIKE THE PLAGUE

Clichés for Fleet Street columnist Keith Waterhouse (1991) count as his no. 1 sin among his 'seven deadly sins' of writing. There are thousands of clichés and they come in many guises. For instance, there are alliterative phrases such as 'safe and sound', 'slow but sure', 'chop and change', 'share and share alike', 'petticoat protest', 'followed in the footsteps', 'few and far between'. They appear as meaningless, over-dramatic adjectives such as in 'driving rain', 'miraculous escape', 'tragic accident', 'brutal murder', 'coveted title', 'sudden death', 'horrific injuries', 'seeping reforms', 'heated argument', 'proud parents', 'bare minimum', 'shock/major/hard-hitting report', 'mercy mission'. There are metaphors gone stale with overuse: 'blanket of snow', 'pillar of strength', 'tower of strength', 'tip of the iceberg', 'sweep under the rug', 'local boy made good'. Some single words such as 'fairytale', 'viable', 'ongoing', 'crisis', 'situation', 'scandal', 'tragedy', 'disaster', 'fury', 'fuming', 'angry', 'shock', 'outrage' amount to clichés.

One of journalism's biggest clichés is 'exclusive', which is constantly devalued through overuse. The *News of the World* of 21 November 1999 had twenty-six 'exclusives' including two 'world exclusives'. On 5 March, the same newspaper had sixteen news 'exclusives', one picture 'exclusive' and in the sports section, five 'exclusives' and four 'world exclusives'. Investigative reporter Phillip Knightley (1998: 44) argues that newspapers, in any case, give 'exclusives' the importance they don't deserve. 'Scoops are a journalist's way of assessing his or her colleagues and of interest only to journalists.'

Newspapers clearly live on clichés. For instance, every day the popular press, in these post-heroic times (when machines and technology have taken the place of humans in so many fields – scientific exploration and warfare to name but two), recreate clichéd images of heroism. During the Gulf conflict of 1991 the press was full of images of 'Top Gun heroes'; the British hostages (sudden 'victims' caught up in the drama of history) were all transformed into 'heroes'. In the *Sun* of 13 November 1999, a child suffering from leukaemia was described as a 'brave angel'. The Bradford *Telegraph and Argus*, won a Newspaper Society award in 2000 for its campaign to honour local 'heroes'.

One of the most prominent clichés revolves around metaphors of violence and warfare. 'Hit out at', '(bitter) battle', 'under siege', 'fight', 'massacre', 'blast', 'axe', 'mount a defence' are everywhere. There are many factors behind this militarisation of language. It reflects the militarisation of culture with the enormous expenditure on the weapons of war and the industrial importance of the arms trade. In addition, there is a high social status enjoyed by the military, the ever-presence of war toys, violent computer games and the media's glorification of violence and macho 'firm-ness'. Just as the culture is brutalised, so is the language of news.

Many stories are built around the drama of conflict and warfare is an obvious metaphor for this. Moreover, as the media are driven to extremes to capture attention, constantly 'bombarding' readers with sensationalised trivia, so the language of violence is used to carry out this 'bombardment'. Politics and sport are the two areas most afflicted by this form of cliché. Thus the *Guardian* of 15 November 1999 reported: 'Tony Blair is to make a full-frontal attack on Ken Livingstone after Labour's selection panel meets tomorrow to decide its shortlist for the party's candidate for election as London's mayor.' On 8 November 1999, the *Mirror* reported: 'Experts are predicting a price war in the health and beauty sector as supermarkets grab a bigger share of the market.' 'Beef war', 'trade war', 'banana war', 'Spice wars', 'tabloid wars' are all common clichés. 'Church wages hi-tech war on thieves', the *Sunday Express* reported on 14 November 1999. The Birmingham-based *Sunday Mercury* of 23 April 2000 reported on a 'dotcom war'.

To simplify the historical record and highlight its confrontational dimension, the press often resorts to categorising. Doves and hawks, hardliners, loony/soft/cuddly/hard left, unilateralists and multilateralists, militants, realists, pragmatists and reformers are constantly 'doing battle' in the press.

Euphemisms: HOW JOB CUTS BECOME RATIONALISATION

Journalists stress their commitment to writing plain English and so it is not surprising that euphemisms (bland expressions) are considered out. Thus never write so-and-so 'passed away' or 'slipped away calmly' – they died. Philip Howard (1984) describes euphemism as the 'British linguistic vice': they are part of the air we breathe. It is impossible for journalists to avoid them. Thus, instead of the emotive sounding 'slump' we have the euphemistic, abstract Latinism of 'recession'. In business, 'rationalisation' and 'restructuring' mean job cuts. Hospitals often describe people seriously hurt as 'comfortable'. The 'spikes' for the tramps of Orwell's day are now the (equally appalling) 'rehabilitation centres' for down-and-outs.

'Wars' today are no longer declared. Bombings of cities are described as 'humanitarian'. People are no longer killed in them (except 'by mistake'). 'Targets' are hit by 'precise', 'clean', 'surgical' missiles. A whole lexicon of euphemistic nukespeak, such as 'independent nuclear deterrent', 'flexible response', 'collateral damage' (for civilian deaths) and 'strategic sufficiency', has emerged to acclimatise our minds to the unspeakable horror of the nuclear holocaust (Aubrey 1982; Chilton 1985).

Jargon: GETTING RID OF GOBBLEDEGOOK

One of the biggest challenges that young journalists face is to cast aside the academic trappings of their backgrounds and the jargon that accompanies it. Each social grouping (local authorities, education, the military, law, computers, librarians, Trotskyists, Conservatives) has its own in-language/jargon and acronymns as a communication aid and 'shorthand'. Academics are in no way peculiar. For instance, General Norman Schwarzkopf contributed this piece of military nonsense during the 1991 Gulf conflict: 'It's not yet possible to get clear BDA in this area of KTO. The continued presence of Triple A means a constant risk of allied personnel becoming KIA or WIA.' With jargon such as this, language becomes a kind of fetish not serving as a communication tool but reinforcing the group's special identity – and excluding uninitiated outsiders.

The reporter's task, often, is to learn rapidly the jargon of a group and translate it into terms comprehensible to a mass readership. It's not easy, particularly when spoken at speed. Journalism has its own jargon (see Glossary). Many of the clichés of journalism (journalese), such as 'probe', 'axe', 'boost', 'jibe', 'shock' and 'blast' all have a currency which bears no relation to their use in conversation.

Times: THEY ARE A-CHANGING

One way to examine the newspaper language of today is to see how *The Times*'s style has changed over the years, just as it will, no doubt, change in the future.

Jan 1

ON THIS DAY

1855

Joseph Sturge (1793–1859) played an important part in the fight to abolish slavery. He was also a member of a deputation from the Society of Friends which went to Russia in 1854 to carry their protest against the Crimean War to the Tsar.

The 'Friends' on the War

THREE NOTABLE members of the Peace Society, and of the Society of Friends, spoke at a Christmas meeting of workmen in Gloucester, on Thursday night, on the subject of the war. Mr. Joseph Sturge, one of the deputation from the Society of Friends to the Czar, Mr. S. Bowly, the peace and temperance advocate, and Mr. T. M. Sturge, of Gloucester.

Mr. Joseph Sturge, after alluding to his mission to St. Petersburg, with the view of bringing about a termination of hostilities, expressed his firm belief, notwithstanding all that had been said against the Emperor of Russia, or whatever might be the evils existing in his Government, that there was no man in Europe who more earnestly desired a return of peace than that monarch, provided it could be done consistently with what he regarded as the honour of his country.

He also alluded to certain accusations which had been made against him in a letter that had been published, he having been accused of a desire to promote the war because it kept up the price of grain, and, in another part of the same letter, he said he was charged with wishing to put an end to the war, simply because it interfered with his trade.

Providence had, however, placed him in such a position that personally he should not feel the effect of the war further than now being unable to obtain grain from where he could formerly procure it; but he was unable now to give employment to as many men as formerly, and he feared matters in this respect would grow worse.

At the present time wheat was, in England, worth about 10s a bushel, whereas in Russia it could be bought for 2s; and thus, as a pecuniary question, it was desirable that the war should be terminated, apart from higher ground of the Christian duty of putting an end to such fearful scenes of bloodshed as were now taking place in the Crimea. He did not wish to say on whom the blame of the war rested, but he was desirous that each of his friends would use his influence to promote peace, should an opportunity of so doing present itself.

Mr. Thomas Sturge recalled to mind the horrors of the wars of the French empire during which period it was computed by the most credible historians that 5,000,000 human beings were slaughtered. During the seven years of the Wellington campaigns 70,000 British lives were destroyed; and at the battle of Waterloo, where there were under 40,000 British engaged, no less than between 800 and 900 officers, and upwards of 10,000 soldiers, were destroyed. And he was of the opinion that if the war in the Crimea continued there would be an equal loss of life.

© Times Newspapers Ltd, 1 January 1992
orig. 1 January 1885

Notice how the language is influenced by the news sense applied. 'Spoke . . . on the subject of war' is too generalised and carries no dramatic weight according to today's news values. The second sentence fails to carry a verb, merely listing the 'three notable members' of the first sentence. Current newspaper style would be stricter on the coverage of the names. Mr Joseph Sturge carries the necessary first name while Bowly and the other Sturge are given only their initials. Today this would be considered an unfortunate disturbance of style. The repetition of Society of Friends is unnecessary.

The second par. is a monster by modern standards – 80 words with five subordinate clauses. There is an over-expansive, literary feel to the par. 'Alluding to', 'with the view of bringing about a termination' and 'notwithstanding' today have an archaic air.

The third par. is also long – 67 words with repetitions of 'war', 'letter' and the awkward 'accusations/accused'. As well as being cluttered with subordinate phrases, it has such unnecessary embellishing words as 'certain' and 'simply' and phrases such as 'a letter that had been published' (better to say 'published letter') and 'to put an end to the war' (better to say 'to end the war'). The letter is contradictory so hardly worth reporting.

The fourth par. has 59 words – still long by today's standards. The next sentence has 63 words. The following two are short in comparison: 38 and 32. The final two are 41 and 21. Notice how the explicit words 'slaughtered' and 'destroyed' are used to describe deaths in battle: there's none of the euphemistic 'collateral damage' jargon of today that aims to hide the horror of warfare. It is also interesting to see that though the report covers a speech, there are no direct quotes.

Converted into the news language of today, the report would read something like:

The Russian Emperor urgently desires peace in the Crimea, Joseph Sturge, who has just returned from a meeting with the Tsar, said on Thursday.

But any peace for the Tsar had to preserve the honour of Russia, he told a meeting of workers in Gloucester.

Mr Sturge, who met the Tsar in St Petersburg on a peace mission for the Society of Friends, said the war had interfered with his buying of grain and he had been forced to lay off some workers.

In England, wheat cost 10s a bushel against 2s in Russia. So it was not only his Christian duty to seek an end to the bloodshed but such a move was needed for financial reasons.

No side could be blamed for the war, and he urged everyone to do their best to promote peace.

Thomas Sturge, also of the Peace Society, said 5m people had been slaughtered during the wars of the French empire. Some 70,000 Britons had died during the seven years of the Wellington campaigns while at the battle of Waterloo between 800 and 900 British officers and 10,000 soldiers had been killed.

He feared there would be an equal loss of life if the Crimean War continued.

This *Times* report (18 January 1940) shows how language and sentence structure were becoming shorter though the copy still lacked the directness of journalism today.

January 18   # ON THIS DAY   1940

FINLAND was invaded by Russia in November 1939, and in spite of heroic resistance was compelled to surrender in March 1940.

FINNS' NEW SUCCESS
UNEQUAL STRUGGLE IN THE AIR

From Our Special Correspondent

Helsinki, Jan. 17

ALTHOUGH THE weather is the coldest for 35 years, the Finnish ski patrols are still active and are distinguishing themselves in the Salla area, where the Russians have been driven back some 12 miles, and are still retreating, pressed by Finnish troops. Today's communiqué states that there was patrol activity north-east of Lake Ladoga between forces of similar strength, in which the Finnish troops routed an enemy company, which lost 70 killed, two tanks, and about 100 rifles.

While the strictly military results of the Russian air raids have been comparatively small, even when attacks were made with 400 machines, the sufferings of the civilian population have been great. Although most of the houses in the provincial towns are still standing, bomb explosions have smashed thousands of windows over wide areas, so that each day more and more houses become uninhabitable in this Arctic winter with temperatures which are exceptional even for Finland.

In the village of Ryttyla, where there are no military objectives, Soviet airmen machine-gunned a funeral procession.

The size of Finland is such that it is impossible to keep the whole of it, or even the most densely populated southern and central districts, adequately supplied with anti-aircraft guns and bomb-proof cellars; but considering that even now Finnish airmen, with rather slow machines, have been able to bring down a good number of enemy aircraft is evidence that a sufficient force of quick, modern fighters is the best means of checking and ending the attacks on civilians. The need for aircraft from abroad is at present the most urgent and decisive issue, the Finns declare.

One example will show the spirit in which the nation is meeting the horrors of air warfare. In a large industrial centre, where there have been frequent air raids, the management of a certain factory asked the employees whether they would be willing to continue to work during air-raid alarms to save time and increase the output of this important factory. The men were offered an extension of their summer holidays in exchange. They answered that they agreed to work during the raids, but would not accept the reward offered them. "We are doing this," they said, "because the Russians must be defeated."

© Times Newspapers Ltd 1940

Of the first five sentences, four begin with subordinate clauses. Newspapers now adopt the opposite style, starting with the main clause except occasionally for variety. Sentence lengths are still long: the first six have 43, 37, 31, 44, 17, 79 words.

The first par. opens without any impact on a subordinate clause about the weather. If the Russians have been driven back, the phrases 'are still active' and 'are distinguishing themselves' are redundant. The second sentence focuses on the communiqué 'stating' rather than on the more dramatic 'routing' of the enemy. The next par. also reflects the passive, low-key coverage. Rather than the active '400 planes attack' it says 'attacks were made with 400 machines'. Similarly, instead of 'civilians have suffered greatly' it says more passively 'the sufferings of the civilian population have been great'. The next sentence repeats the point about the winter coldness made at the start.

Note the bias of the coverage. The Finns, fighting the Nazis, are represented as heroic and the sufferings of innocent civilians are highlighted. In contrast, the enemy Soviets are portrayed as ruthless warriors, even machine-gunning a funeral procession. Coverage of the Soviets was to change dramatically once they changed sides following the Nazi invasion of their country.

At the end of the century, Britain was again at war, backing the US-led Nato attacks on Yugoslavia. Notice how the language and sentence structure have changed.

Hawk Blair stiffens US resolve

From Ben Macintyre in Washington

TONY BLAIR took a message of hawkish resolve on Kosovo to the White House, Congress and the American heartland yesterday as 19 heads of Nato countries converged on Washington for a summit to mark the organisation's 50th anniversary.

The Prime Minister told an audience in Chicago that America must not slip back into isolationism and stand by as Kosovo burns.

Britain and France are urging the US to consider sending ground troops to Kosovo without a peace agreement and the Nato Secretary-General, Javier Solana has agreed that plans for their possible use may be reassessed, but there is no consensus among the allies on deployment against the Serbs in Kosovo.

There is, however, continued support for the campaign of airstrikes which on Wednesday involved bombing President Milosevic's private home in Belgrade.

Nato officials denied that three laser-guided bombs that hit Mr Milosevic's villa were an assassination attempt, which would be illegal under American law. One missile landed in the master bedroom, but the Serb President is believed to sleep in a bunker and was not at home.

"We are targeting the military infrastructure that supports the instruments of oppression in Kosovo . . . we are not targeting President Milosevic or the Serb people," a Pentagon spokesman said. The bombed building was described by US military officials as a "presidential command post".

At the same time, Mr Blair was emphasising Britain's determination that Mr Milosevic should be forced to back down in talks with Senate leaders and in Chicago. The Los Angeles Times noted: "Britain's Prime Minister is emerging as the alliance's most outspoken hawk."

> Mr Blair earlier held intense discussions with President Clinton over the use of ground forces, while Robin Cook discussed the same issue with his American counterpart, Madeleine Albright.
>
> The Foreign Secretary then told reporters that "at some point ground troops will be required to guarantee security and ceasefire". There was no intention to use Nato's soldiers to "fight their way into Kosovo in a ground force invasion", but he said that they could be deployed even if Belgrade had not signed a formal treaty, reinforcing the possibilities that Nato will move when Serb forces are deemed to be sufficiently weakened.
>
> "We have our plans for getting ground troops in the right numbers into Kosovo in permissive circumstances. We cannot tolerate the return of the doctrine of ethnic superiority in Europe," Mr Cook said, comparing the Serb campaign to Nazi atrocities. Ms Albright said that the decision to update military assessments on the use of ground troops was "prudent".

Focusing on the first pars of this front page lead story (the splash) of 23 April 1999, notice how much shorter, in general, the sentences are than in the previous examples: 38, 22, 50, 21, 23, 23, 29, 14, 27.

Precise language and structure

Most sentences begin with the main clause, the language precise and dramatic. The opening par. sets the main news theme (Tony Blair's 'hawkish' talk 'yesterday') with the second par. expanding on this point and reporting where the speech took place. Adjectives and adverbs are used only sparingly in broadsheet hard news; different criteria apply in the tabloids. Here only 'hawkish' stands out. And what a crucial adjective it is. Given the media's liking for 'macho' firmness by 'our leaders', particularly in times of crisis, and Fleet Street's consensus during the Kosovo war in favour of a ground assault on Serbia, 'hawkish' here has a distinctly positive resonance.

Language and the impact of dominant sources

The language of the news is profoundly influenced by the language, biases, jargon, tones and rhythms of the sources quoted. Here the opening pars reflect the bias of traditional elite sources: the British Prime Minister, Nato's Secretary-General, Nato officials, Pentagon spokesman, the British Foreign Secretary. A mainstream US newspaper is used to reinforce the focus on 'hawkish' Blair. No attempt is made to 'balance' the copy with quotes from Serbian sources.

Language tone and contrasts in human interest bias

The tone is dramatic rather than emotional and sensational. The focus is on the leading UK and US spokespeople and their comments. The 'enemy' leader is reported only as the victim of a bomb attack. Nato's denial of any assassination attempt is prioritised. No outrage over the attack is expressed. Significantly during the Gulf war of 1991 and the Kosovo war of 1999 outrage was expressed in the press only once: over the BBC's coverage of the US attack on the al Ameriyya shelter in Baghdad, which killed hundreds of women and children. But consider the outrage that would be expressed if a Serbian missile was fired at Tony Blair's home.

Absence of overt comment and the propaganda function

No overt comment is inserted into the article by the reporter. There is no relaxed, subjective, conversational element to the article. As van Dijk (1988) argues, the language of hard news is impersonal because, though it may be bylined, it is essentially an institutional, bureaucratic voice. At the same time, it becomes clear that a specific propaganda bias affects the selection and arrangement of sources and facts. Nato leaders throughout the Kosovo war constantly referred in their propaganda to the President of Serbia, Slobodan Milosevic, as Hitler and to the Serbs as Nazis. Such references demonise the 'enemy' and legitimise any military action taken against them. Here, Robin Cook is heard yet again making the 'Nazi' references – which are dutifully reported by the press. *The Times* has, in effect, unproblematically adopted the language of the military and government elite.

Language and the simplification process

The language of news also seeks to simplify events, to make the complex dynamics of history intelligible. The personalisation of news is part of this process. Here, the focus on Cook's comparison of Serbian atrocities with those of the Nazi era reproduces the dominant propaganda line which placed all blame for the conflict on the shoulders of 'Milosevic'. At the same time, the roles of US/UK imperialism and militarism, of the International Monetary Fund (IMF) and World Bank strategies to destabilise the Balkans, of Croatian and German nationalism in provoking the conflict are marginalised (Chomsky 1999; Chossudovsky 1998; Keeble 1999).

News language is concrete and non-abstract

On a more fundamental level there is simply not the space to explore the complexities and abstractions of historical factors. News language, as here, is concrete and only rarely abstract.

Word play

One of the most fascinating features of journalism is the way it records society's complex language shifts and at the same time creates new words (neologisms) and new meanings. Many hundreds of new words are recorded and invented every year in newspapers and magazines. For instance, the close political links between President Bill Clinton and his wife, Hillary, gave birth to the word 'Billary'. 'Lunch box' came to describe male genitals.

Many new words emerge from play with well-known prefixes or suffixes. Thus the 'Euro' prefix may provoke 'Eur-wimp' or 'Euro-chic'. The suffix 'mania' has given birth to 'Gorbymania' and 'Spicemania'. The suffix 'ite' has provoked 'Trotsky-ite', 'Thatcherite' and 'Blairite' (but 'Hague-ite' for a follower of the Conservative leader is distinctly absent from the dictionary). Following Watergate, there has been a flood of 'gates': 'Mirrorgate', 'bananagate', 'Zippergate', 'Shaylergate' and so on.

Just as George Orwell coined the words 'doublespeak' and 'newspeak', so they have spawned endless variations: 'nukespeak', 'massacrespeak', 'quangospeak',

'Reaganspeak'. The 1990s saw a new breed of neologism emerge alongside the internet explosion. Virtually any noun could be preceded by an 'e', 'dotcom' or 'cyber': so, for instance, 'email', 'e-commerce', 'e-university', 'e-tailers', 'dotcom economy', 'dotcom advertising', 'cyber-players', 'cyber-verse'. A special e-commerce jargon emerged including 'buzzword compliant' (meaning literate in the latest internetspeak), 'incubators' (companies hatching dotcom start-ups) and 'bizzdev' (business development stage of an internet start-up).

Trade names

There is a long list of registered trade names which journalists can easily mistake for generic terms. For instance, it is tempting to think that Hoover is a general and accepted word for vacuum cleaner, but whenever it is used, the first letter must be capped. Other such trade names include: Aspirin, Aspro, Autocue, Band-Aid, Biro, Burberry, Calor, Catseye (road studs), Dettol, Dictaphone, Duffel, Dunlopillo, Fibreglas (note one 's'), Gillette, Horlicks, Jacuzzi, Jiffy, Kleenex, Lego, Marmite, Martini, Meccano, Plasticine, Polaroid, Portakabin, Scotchtape, Sellotape, Tampax tampons (the two words should always be used together and with a lower case 't' for tampons), Tannoy, Thermos, Vaseline, Yellow Pages.

Doing it in style?

All newspapers have a view about good house style. This is outlined in a document called the style book (occasionally editorial handbook or sheet) though it is increasingly carried on screen. It will tend to focus on such elements as spellings (Peking or Beijing?), punctuation, abbreviations, the use of capitals, titles, Americanisms to avoid, the handling of quotations. Ethical issues, such as the handling of anonymous quotes or AIDS, can also be covered. That is the theory. The reality is very different. As Keith Waterhouse notes, style books are unfortunately 'often peppered with the random idiosyncrasies of editors and proprietors past and present'. Moreover, there is an enormous variation in approaches to house style throughout the industry. Some newspapers, such as the *Mirror*, even manage to survive without a formalised style book. Yet Richard Garner, education correspondent, argues that with more trainees being taken on by the newspaper, the case for introducing a style book is becoming stronger.

The *Guardian*, in contrast, has made its style book, following debates with readers, available on its website. On 'Direct speech' it comments: 'People we write about are allowed to speak in their own, not necessarily the *Guardian*'s style, but be sensitive: do not, for example, expose someone to ridicule for dialect or grammatical errors.' Under a section on 'Disability' it suggests that 'wheelchair-bound' and 'in a wheelchair' should be avoided: better 'wheelchair user'. Rather than 'backward', 'retarded' or 'slow', say 'person with a learning disability'. Under 'Gender issues' it says: 'Phrases such as career girl or career woman are outdated (more women have careers than men) and patronising (there is no male equivalent).' It also recommends special care in handling mental health issues. Terms to avoid because they stereotype and stigmatise include 'victim of', 'suffering from' just as 'a person with' is preferable to 'a person suffering from'. Under 'Clichés to avoid', it includes 'boost (massive or otherwise)', 'dropdead gorgeous', 'luvvies' and 'politically correct'. Other news-papers, such as *The Times* and the *Independent*, have published their style books while Keith Waterhouse's *The Mirror's Way with Words* (1981) is a lively critique of the tabloid's style.

While the subeditors are usually regarded as the ultimate 'guardians' of style, staff reporters, freelances and student journalists should always be aware of the importance of following style and the journalistic disciplines involved. If there is no house style covering an issue, then make one yourself. Thus, if in copy you use 'jail' on first mention it should be similarly spelled throughout. If you spell the President of Libya 'Col. Gadafi' at first mention it should not later change to 'Col. Khadafi' or 'Col. Qaddafi'. And so on.

Presentation of copy

It is vital that all copy, whether for your college, newspaper or freelance outlet, is immaculately tidy and follows basic rules. Untidy copy is simply spiked (thrown away). Freelances should particularly bear this in mind. Copy layout rules differ slightly from paper to paper but the essential principles remain the same throughout the industry. Copy is usually written on screen, transferred to subeditors working on screen and appears in 'hard' form only when printed out in the newspaper. When 'hard' copy is presented (say by freelances, accompanying a computer disk or email attachment), it is always typed in a standard font such as Times New Roman on one side of a white A4 sheet. Hand-written copy is never accepted unless from a big Fleet Street 'name' who can get away with such archaic eccentricity.

All freelances should work on Macs or PCs where possible. Their facilities for providing corrections and clean copy are invaluable, as are their easy filing systems. Always give stories file names which immediately identify them. Don't call them Document 1, Document 2 and so on. Searching through such files can be extremely time-consuming.

Byline

Use the 'header' facility on your Word program to put on the top, left-hand side of the first page your name. Unless otherwise stated, this will be the name on any byline accompanying the story. Then comes an oblique stroke followed by the name of the publication.

Dateline

In the centre goes the date of publication, not the date of writing. This is particu-larly important for weeklies or monthlies. When using words such as 'yesterday' or 'tomorrow' it is advisable to put the day in parentheses afterwards to avoid confusion.

Catchline

At the top right-hand corner goes the catchline. This will usually be one word that clearly identifies the story. Page one of a story about David Shayler will be catchlined

'Shayler 1', page two automatically 'Shayler 2' and so on. Avoid using such words as 'kill', 'dead', 'report', 'story', 'must', 'spike', 'flush', 'splash', 'header' or 'leader' which have specific meanings in newspaper jargon (see Glossary for other words to avoid). When covering a crash, council meeting or fire, don't use the obvious catchlines such as 'crash', 'council' or 'fire'. Similar events may be covered by other journalists and to avoid duplication, words identifying the story's uniqueness should be used.

Copy

Your copy will begin some way down the first folio (page). This leaves space above the start for any subeditorial marks. Copy typed on newspaper computers will be formatted appropriately but freelances should normally present their copy with double-spaced lines. Leave wide margins on both sides of the copy and clear spaces at the top and bottom of the page. Never hyphenate words between lines. Never let a sentence run from one folio to another.

At the foot of each folio except the last (in the 'footer' facility) should be 'more' or 'mf' (short for 'more follows'), usually centred. The story finishes with 'end' centred (you may have to write this in). Bylines, publication, date of publication and catchline will be produced at the top of each folio. Normally no large space is needed between the headers and copy on the second and any subsequent pages.

Copy should always be carefully checked before submission. Never delete the file of your story on disk. Copy can be lost or mislaid. Sometimes you might need to refer back to a previous story. If you send a disk through the post, always make a copy. Whenever there is an unusual spelling, such as 'Smythe' instead of 'Smith' or a name with possible variations such as 'Dennis' or 'Denis', 'Maryline' or 'Marilyn' put 'correct' in square brackets afterwards. The sub should then delete it. Convoluted foreign names should be treated similarly to make clear to the sub that you are aware of the spelling issue and confirming its correctness. The sub should double check anyway.

If submitting copy as a freelance, it is usually advisable to attach a covering letter, reminding the editor of any necessary background to the commission, the payment agreed and add daytime details, address and phone number along with home details. In some cases, a brief outline of your special credentials for writing the story might be appropriate. A word count is also invaluable to editors. If you are including photographs, remind the editor of payment agreed for these – and any expenses, too.

6 News reporting

Beyond the five Ws

For the purpose of simplicity, let us say that hard news is the reporting of issues or events in the past or about to happen. It is largely based on selected details and quotations in direct or indirect speech. Hard news begins with the most striking details and thereafter information progressively declines in importance. Some background details may be needed to make the news intelligible but description, analysis, comment and the subjective 'I' of the reporter are either excluded or included only briefly. Hard news has the highest status in newspapers and tends to fill front pages. But Anne Sebba (Allan 1999: 130) is critical of the emphasis on hard news. 'Writing about numbers of planes shot down and military hardware is the "soft" option male journalists often go for because it is easier and less taxing to one's emotional being.' Hard news differs from a range of newspaper genres which include the following:

* *Soft news*: the news element is still strong and prominent at or near the opening but is treated in a lighter way. Largely based on factual detail and quotations, the writing is more flexible and there is likely to be more description and comment. The tone, established in the intro section, might be witty or ironic. The separation of hard and soft news emerged in the second half of the nineteenth century: the first, linked to notions of accuracy, objectivity, neutrality, was for conveying information; the second was more an entertainment genre.

* *News feature*: usually longer than a straight news story. The news angle is prominent though not necessarily in the opening par./s and quotations are again important. It can contain description, comment, analysis, background historical detail, eye-witness reporting and wider or deeper coverage of the issues and range of sources.

* *Timeless feature*: no specific news angle, the special interest is provided by the subject or sources. For example, a feature could explore youths' experiences of coming out gay (as in Marie Lunn's feature in the *Mirror*'s mag *M* 11 April 2000).

* *Backgrounder/preview/curtain-raiser news story or feature*: emphasis is not so much on the news but on explaining the news or setting the scene for an event about to happen. It might focus on historical background and/or seek to explain

a range of issues and personalities involved. A *retrospective* is a similar feature looking back at an event.

- *Colour feature*: an article of feature length concentrating on description, eye-witness reporting, quotations and the build-up of factual details. It can also contain historical background material, and need not have a strong news angle.
- *Eye-witness news feature*: based on reporter's observations of newsy event, it can incorporate descriptions, conversations, interviews, analysis, comment, jokes. The 'I' of the reporter might also be present.
- *Sketch*: opinionated, colourful, light piece usually associated with Parliament, for example Michael White in the *Guardian*, Matthew Parris in *The Times*, Quentin Letts, formerly of the *Daily Telegraph*, in the *Daily Mail*.
- *Opinion piece/personal/think piece*: emphasis on the journalist conveying their views and experiences (as Mary Killen wrote on the hazards of being a modern mum in the *Daily Telegraph* on 12 April 2000) usually in an idiosyncratic, colourful, controversial fashion. Journalists with regular slots are known as columnists.
- *Diary items*: short, light-hearted, opinionated, gossipy news items are generally grouped together under a single byline.
- *Profile* (sometimes labelled *interview*): description of people usually based on interviews with them and sometimes their friends/critics/relations/work colleagues. A news dimension is often prominent. Jet planes, hotels, shops, Father Christmas and not just celebrities can be profiled. *Obituaries* are profiles appearing after the death of the subject, though often prepared beforehand.
- *Vox pop*: collection of quotes on topical issues, usually accompanied by mug shots of sources (and it is important to be race/gender/age-sensitive over the selection).
- *Reviews*: descriptions and assessments of works of art, television programmes, exhibitions, books, theatre shows, CDs, rock gigs and so on.
- *Lifestyle features*: including advice columns (such as on health or education matters, slimming, gardening, do-it-yourself, computer problems), shopping features, fashion, travel.
- *Editorials*: commentary reflecting the institutional voice of the newspaper. Usually carried in a larger font than that of the basic body text and without a byline. They can be written by the editor but most newspapers have editorial writing specialists.

Going straight to the point

The intro

The intro (known in the US as the lead or nose and in France as the attaque) is the most important par. since it has to draw the reader into the story by creating a sense of urgency and exciting their interest. It should highlight the main theme or angle of the story and set the tone. When a reader surveys a newspaper page, there are a few major foci for attention: pictures, headlines, intros and picture captions. Their grammatical style and content set the tone and character of the whole paper. Choosing the best angle (or news peg in the US) is one of the biggest challenges for a journalist. Reporters often find that once the opening angle has been 'bashed out', the rest 'writes itself'. A good intro also helps the subeditor to think of a suitable headline quickly.

The famous five Ws

'Who', 'what', 'where', 'when' and 'why' are the famous five intro Ws. In addition, some stories have a 'how' element. But the intro should not seek to answer all of those questions, it would be overloaded with words. Usually the intro defines the news angle by selecting two or three of these questions. The rest of the story may go on to answer some of the others.

Journalists tend to feel most at home with the 'who', 'what', 'where', 'when' and 'how' of events coverage. The 'why' factors (the causal linkages) are often complex – and can be missed out, handled superficially or stereotypically. Liz Curtis, in studying the coverage of Ireland, comments:

> The British media's emphasis on 'factual' reporting of incidents, concentrating on 'who what where and when' and leaving out background and significance, appears to be objective and straightforward but is, in fact, very misleading. This type of reporting provides the audience with details of age, sex, type of incident, injuries, location and time of day. But such information says nothing about the causes of the incident making violence appear as random as a natural disaster or accident.
>
> (Curtis 1984: 107)

Take this story from the *Financial Times* (9 November 1999):

> Greek left-wing groups yesterday launched a series of anti-American demonstrations with a mock trial of Nato leaders ahead of an official visit by President Bill Clinton.

Who and where: Greek left-wing groups

What: launched a series of anti-American demonstrations

How: with a mock trial of Nato leaders

When: yesterday, ahead of an official visit by President Bill Clinton.

Here is an intro from the *Saffron Walden Reporter* (6 January 2000):

> A huge operation was launched yesterday to clean-up the devastated field near Great Hallingbury where a Korean Air jumbo jet exploded.

Who: A huge operation

What: was launched

When: yesterday

Why: to clean up the devastated field

Where: near Great Hallingbury where a Korean Air jumbo jet exploded.

Here is an intro from *Eastern Eye* (17 December 1999):

> Visiting Pakistani military leader General Pervez Musharraf met Iran's President Mohammad Khatami last week for talks on relations soured over rivalries in neighbouring Afghanistan.

> *Who*: Visiting Pakistani military leader General Pervez Musharraf
>
> *What*: met Iran's President Mohammad Khatami
>
> *When*: last week
>
> *Why*: for talks on relations soured over rivalries in neighbouring Afghanistan.

Main clause

Most news begins with the main clause as in these three examples. This is because the 'who' and the 'what' tend to be the most important. Readers don't want to wade through dull details, background or comment before arriving at the main point. Thus the *Planet on Sunday* (19 December 1999) did not write:

> The Roman Catholic Church is increasingly concerned over the rising prison population and its broader implications for the country's penal system. Yesterday a Roman Catholic bishop went so far as to call, controversially, for an amnesty for all non-violent prisoners as a gesture to mark the new millennium.

Such an intro delays the impact of the news, opening with an unfocused, scene-setting sentence. In fact, the newspaper went straight and concisely to the news:

> A Roman Catholic bishop has called for an amnesty for all non-violent prisoners to coincide with the new millennium.

People

News often tends to focus on the human angle. Thus, if you were a news agency reporter covering the IRA attack on the Conservative Party conference in 1984 it would have been poor to write:

> The Grand Hotel, Brighton, was rocked today by a Provisional IRA bomb attack during the Conservative Party conference but Mrs Thatcher escaped unhurt.

The focus needed to be on the fate of the Prime Minister. The angle could not wait until the end of the first sentence:

> Premier Mrs Thatcher narrowly escaped an assassination attempt today after the Provisional IRA bombed the Grand Hotel, Brighton, where she was staying for the annual Conservative Party conference.

Given the choice between the structural damage to a hotel and the fate of the Prime Minister, the second provides the better angle.

Descriptions and titles

People in the news are always accompanied by a title or description. The reader needs to know on what authority or on what basis they are speaking: thus *Tribune* (of 24 March 2000) reported on 'Andrew Dogshon, a spokesman for the Transport and General Workers' Union' and 'Martin Barnes, Director of the Child Poverty Action Group'.

People with long titles provide problems for intros. They can clutter them up with words. For instance, 'Mr Doug McAvoy, general secretary of the National Union of Teachers, yesterday claimed'. One way round this problem is to use a phrase such as: 'The leader of a teachers' union yesterday claimed'. Then in the next par. or sentence you might give the name or title. The description of the person in the news does not have to be a formal title such as secretary, MP, councillor or director. It can be looser, for instance, 'of the Green Party' or 'who witnessed the rail crash'. Here the *Sunday Express* (14 November 1999) intros on a descriptive phrase, delaying the name until par. 2.

> A bomber pilot who flew hazardous missions against heavily defended Nazi battle-cruisers has regained his wings with a solo flight at the age of 81.
>
> Former Squadron leader Edward Raw gave up flying after the Second World War but more than 50 years later he has taken to the air in a glider.

Timing

News is rooted in time, the more up-to-date the better. Thus the 'when' element ('yesterday', 'last night', 'earlier today', 'next week') is crucial in many hard news intros. This emphasis on newsiness is commercially driven. The hotter the news, the more sellable it is. But intros hardly ever begin with the basic 'when' words such as 'last night'. Occasionally, when the timing is significant it should be highlighted, as here from the *Guardian* of 20 December 1999:

> Five years after he was diagnosed with Alzheimer's disease, the former US president, Ronald Reagan, is no longer capable of having a conversation that makes sense, his wife, Nancy, has revealed.

Usually is it not necessary to be precise over the 'when' in the intro. Do not say: 'Mrs Gandhi, the Indian Prime Minister, was assassinated by Sikh bodyguards at 2.59 am today.' Sufficient to report 'earlier today'. The precise detail can be added later.

Another popular way of conveying news urgency is used here in Norwich *Evening News* (8 December 1999):

> Researchers at the University of East Anglia have forecast that we are approaching the end of the warmest year if December continues the trend set in the previous 11 months.

and in the *Highbury and Islington Gazette* (24 March 2000):

> An inquiry has been ordered into allegations that unused parking spaces in council estates are being sold to commuters and Town Hall staff in contravention of Islington's anti-car policies.

This eliminates the specific 'when' element from the first sentence. It can be carried later in the story. But weeklies often eliminate specific 'when' references since phrases such as 'last Wednesday' and 'early last week' reduce the news impact.

Where

Local papers will often include the 'where' element prominently in the intro since it stresses the local angle. Thus the Liverpool *Daily Post* (24 November 1999) had this among numerous examples:

> Warships may be built on the Mersey again after it was revealed that Cammell Laird is one of two shipyards short-listed to build two new aircraft carriers for the Royal Navy.

National papers may sometimes delay mention of the 'where' to add an element of vagueness and encourage everyone from all over the country to read on, as here in the *Daily Star* (11 January 2000):

> Three frog garden ornaments were branded neighbours from hell in a courtroom yesterday. They were fitted with sensors to detect movement and croaked non-stop day and night, it was claimed.
>
> Eventually neighbour Catherine Ward got madder than the TV ad chameleons who have to put up with Budweiser frogs – and threw two of the green nuisances on a tip.
>
> But they later reappeared in their original spot . . . and were joined by a third, Glasgow District Court heard.

Most foreign stories carry the 'where' prominently, as here in the *Morning Star* (4 May 2000);

> A Brazilian landless peasant who was wounded on Tuesday during street clashes with police in the southern state of Parana died in hospital yesterday.

Brevity

As the chapter on language identified, intros should be written as concisely as possible. The maximum number of words you should be thinking about for the first sentence is 30, though intros in broadsheets will tend to be longer than in the populars and local papers. The average wordage in the seven stories on the broadsheet *Guardian*'s first two news pages was 30; in the red-top tabloid *Daily Star*, the average in the eight stories on the first two pages was 20 and in the local weekly *Haverhill Echo*, its eight stories averaged 22, while the figure for the black weekly the *Voice*'s seven stories was 25. Here is the *Express* intro (29 February 2000) with just 10 words:

> Austria's controversial Freedom Party leader Joerg Haider resigned last night.

In comparison, the *Guardian* intro for the same story was somewhat overloaded with 41 words:

> Jörg Haider, the controversial far right leader of the Freedom party, whose rise to power has put Austria in turmoil over the last five months, announced his resignation last night in a move that stunned Europe and his own party members.

Brightness

While always remaining true to the style of your publication, be as bright as possible. Try to use active verbs and strong nouns. Take this intro from the *Nottingham and Long Eaton Topper* (22 December 1999): 'Revellers', 'splash out', 'big way', 'snub' and 'celebrations' all carry impact.

> Revellers across Nottingham are all set to splash out on Christmas in a big way – and snub turn of the century celebrations.

Popular tabloids tend to heighten the sensational, emotional content by adding adjectives and adverbs. Take this par. from the *Mirror* (23 February 2000):

> Globetrotting Peter Mandelson notched up an amazing 13 freebie trips in just nine months last year.

'Globetrotting', 'amazing' and 'just' are adjectives aiming to add impact to the intro. Similarly, in this intro from the *News of the World* (9 January 2000):

> Wrinkly romeo Mike Baldwin proudly shows off his bride-to-be blissfully unaware that his busty sex bomb bedded his son on New Year's Eve.

'Wrinkly romeo', 'proudly', 'blissfully unaware' and 'busty sex bomb' are all clichés aiming to heighten interest. But broadsheets also use adjectives and adverbs to dramatise copy. Here is how the *Independent* (4 April 2000) began its story:

> Nato troops mounted a dramatic early-morning raid yesterday to snatch the highest ranking genocide suspect to date, upping the pressure on fugitives accused of war crimes in Bosnia.

'Dramatic', 'mounted raid', 'snatch' and 'highest ranking' all add to the impact.

Quotations

Lively and controversial comments provide material for many intros. But hard news hardly ever begins with direct quotes. There is a 'softness' about a direct quote which is felt more appropriate to 'soft' news, news features or profiles. Such a convention is not universal. In France, hard news stories commonly begin with direct quotes, as here in *Libération* (31 December 1999):

> *"Ce ne sera pas la fin du monde"* a assuré mercredi, à Washington, Bruce McConnell, directeur du Centre international de coopération contre le Y2K (alias "bug de l'an 2000").

Notice, too, how French newspapers often highlight direct quotations by using the italic, sloping typeface. There is no such convention in Britain or the US. Now look at this intro from the *Newmarket Journal* (6 January 2000):

> Leading Newmarket-based vet Tim Greet has described a new report which claims that racehorses in training are suffering from widespread stomach ulcers and bleeding as "sensationalist".

The reporter did not write: "Sensationalist". That's how leading Newmarket-based vet Tim Greet described a new report which claims that racehorses in training are suffering from widespread stomach ulcers and bleeding.' Such copy separating the quote from its source would be too disjointed.

Direct quotes are often reserved for a second or third par. which makes a strong back-up to the intro, expanding on the opening theme. But quotation marks are inserted around words and phrases to highlight them and indicate attribution as here from the Peterborough *Evening Telegraph* (28 January 2000):

> Secretary of State Peter Mandelson has appealed for "cool heads" and patience as the crisis in the Northern Ireland peace process deepened.

Sometimes individual words or short phrases have inverted commas around them without being attributed. This happens usually when colourful/significant words or phrases conveying opinion which the inverted commas imply will be later attributed. Inclusion of the attribution in the intro would overload it. Take this intro from the same edition of the Peterborough *Evening Telegraph*:

> Peterborough has said a final farewell to one of its most "outstanding, upright and loyal" citizens.

That quote is later seen to come from former council leader Charles Swift, whose tribute to Councillor Peter Clarke is reported at some length.

Attribution

Opinion is nearly always attributed clearly in the intro par. Thus, the *Guardian* (27 March 2000) reported:

> Prescription drugs that make the skin more sensitive to sunlight could be linked to a rise in skin cancer, an authority on photosensitivity has warned.

Concise attribution (such as 'it emerged today') can also give a newsy angle to a report of an event in the past, as in this London *Evening Standard* intro (23 February 2000):

> Two black undercover police officers lived as a man and wife on a south-east London estate in an unsuccessful operation to trap racists, it emerged today.

Clear attribution is particularly important when covering allegations and counter-allegations in court cases. Thus the *Express* (29 February 2000) reported:

> Claims that TV footage of the horrors in a Bosnian prison camp was distorted and sensationalised was "wholly false", the High Court heard yesterday.

Tenses

> The lives of elite army cadets are being put at risk by dangerous training, a doctor said yesterday.

The *Mirror* report (11 February 2000) begins with the present tense 'are being put at risk'. Normally with such words as 'warned', 'said', 'declared' or 'criticised', the accompanying clauses follow the rules of reported speech and move back one tense into the past. An intro is one place where these rules are often ignored. This gives an extra sense of urgency to the report. Similarly headlines and picture captions are usually in the present tense though they report on past events. The future tense can also be used, as here in the *Daily Telegraph* (21 November 1999):

> Four out of 10 councils in England are failing to inspect old people's homes in their area regularly, the Government will disclose this week.

Some errors to avoid

Questions

Hard news intros do not normally start with questions, just as question marks do not normally occur in news headlines. Intros are for informing readers, not interrogating them. Occasionally questions can open features and 'soft' news stories.

The 'There is' cliché

Avoid beginning stories 'There was' or 'There is' or 'There will be'. This is dead copy delaying the appearance of the real news. So don't report 'There was a riot in Bow, East London, last night in which four policemen and two youths were injured.' Better to say: 'Two youths and four policemen were injured in riots in Bow, East London, last night.'

Label intros

Label intros are drab sentences showing no news sense. A good intro will do more than say 'a meeting was held', 'a speech was given'. 'Vladimir Putin, President of Russia, gave a long speech at the United Nations in New York yesterday covering issues as diverse as the threat to the rain forests and nuclear disarmament.' A better angle would be more specific: 'President Putin of Russia yesterday called on the world community to introduce a 50 per cent arms trade tax to fight poverty in the Third World. In a wide-ranging, 50-minute speech to the United Nations in New York, he said'.

Present participles

Intro sentences starting with the present participle are to be avoided: 'Referring to humanitarian crisis in Kurdistan, Noam Chomsky' or 'Criticising the government for "monumental ineptitude", William Hague'. Better to say: 'A humanitarian crisis is engulfing Kurdistan, Noam Chomsky warned' and 'The government was accused of "monumental ineptitude" by William Hague'.

Unidentified pronouns

Opening with a subordinate clause is particularly poor when there is an unidentified pronoun, as in 'With what his colleagues described as a clarion call to the party, Al Gore'.

Negatives

There is always a way to avoid using negatives. For instance, instead of 'The Foreign Office would today neither confirm nor deny that two British pilots had been released by Saddam Hussein', say: 'The Iraqis are reported to have freed two British pilots but the Foreign Office was non-committal.'

Numerals

Sentences never begin with numerals. Don't say: '11 people were injured after a bus collided with two stray pigs in Bognor Regis last night.' Instead: 'Eleven people were. . . .'

Varieties of hard news intros

Some of the 68 – and more – varieties of intro include the following.

Clothesline intro

So-called because everything hangs on it. For instance: 'Lady Godiva rode naked through the streets of Coventry today in an attempt to cut taxes.' This contains the six basic ingredients: 'who', 'what', 'where', 'when', 'why' and 'how'.

Immediate identification intro

Used where the person concerned is so important or newsworthy that their presence is a main part of the story. For instance: 'Mr Blair made a sponsored jump from a plane at RAF Brize Norton today and wrecked a three-ton truck after his parachute failed to open.' It would be wrong to say 'A three-ton truck was wrecked after a parachute failed to open after a daring, sponsored jump from a plane at RAF Brize Norton today.'

Delayed identification intro

Used where the person involved is not inherently newsworthy but has become so because of what he or she has done or said. Thus the *Express* reported (14 November 1999):

> The sister of a headteacher jailed in Abu Dhabi on drugs charges yesterday appealed to Prince Charles to make a mercy plea on her behalf.
>   Ann Copsey, whose sister Lynn Majakas, has spent 12 months of a four-and-half year sentence in prison, has written to the Prince, who is due to visit the United Arab Emirates this week, asking him to intervene to help free her before Christmas.

Summary intro

This is used when the reporter, faced with a number of competing angles, none of which stands out, settles for a generalised intro. Thus:

> Prime Minister Tony Blair presented a revolutionary package of disarmament proposals to a historic session of the United Nations General Assembly yesterday.

Single element intro

This contrasts with the summary intro and is used when one angle is particularly strong and needs highlighting. Thus:

> President Chirac of France called the arms race "a crime against humanity which must be halted" at a meeting of the United Nations General Assembly yesterday.

Bullet or staccato intro

This is used where the main point can be covered very briefly. For instance, the front page splash in the Nottingham *Evening Post* (25 February 2000) carried these intro pars alongside a large picture of the baby:

> This is Callum – a living miracle
>   Mum Louise Farmer was just 23 weeks pregnant when he was born at Queen's Medical Centre.
>   Doctors gave him a ten per cent chance of survival and he was baptised immediately.

Personalised intro

Generally news excludes the 'I' of the journalist. It suggests too much subjectivity. The personalised intro subverts that convention and places the 'I' at the centre of the action. The journalist witnessing the event carries its own newsworthiness. Thus, Andrew Meldrum, in the *Observer* (2 April 2000) reported:

> It was a march for peace. But yesterday I watched as President Robert Mugabe's thugs brought it to a violent climax, singling out whites, beating one man unconscious and badly injuring at least a dozen others. As blood streamed down my face, I asked myself: what has become of Zimbabwe?

Comment intro

News often has the appearance of objectivity when, in fact, it is the journalist commenting. For instance, the *Guardian* of 15 November 1999 reported:

> Tony Blair sent a powerful signal yesterday that Labour is moving into election mode when he unveiled a populist proposal to deprive young offenders of their welfare benefits if they fail to obey court orders.

Here 'powerful signal' and 'populist proposal' are opinionated, reflecting a positive attitude to the Prime Minister.

On 13 April 2000, Betty Liu in the *Financial Times* opened with this commenty par.:

> Perhaps it was the pouring rain, but the demonstrators outside the house of Elian Gonzalez yesterday morning were far fewer than in the past few days, seeming to indicate that the fight to keep the Cuban boy in the US is drawing to a close.

Punning intro

This is found particularly in the red tops and some local newspapers (see also Chapter 5). It provides brightness and humour to the copy. Thus the *Star* (16 November 1999) reported:

> Motorist Martin Steele has rustled up a recipe to beat rising petrol prices – he runs his car on cooking oil.

The *Sunday Mirror* of 13 February 2000 ran this intro:

> Fergie will sweep Prince Andrew off his feet for his 40th birthday on Saturday ... with a trip on the London Eye.

The plug intro

Newspapers often like to publicise their own investigations in intros; as the Birmingham-based *Sunday Mercury* did (23 April 2000):

> A self-styled guru is leading a cult which practises exorcisms and ritual slaughter, the *Sunday Mercury* can reveal.

Soft news: INTROS

Soft news stories have the news element at or near the opening. But the news is treated more colourfully and some of the 'rules' of hard news reporting outlined above are broken to provide a 'softer' feel to the copy.

Direct quotation

Starting with a direct quote softens the story, as here from the *Socialist Worker* (31 October 1998):

"When I asked a 30-strong union meeting at my school if they would take industrial action over pay, everyone said yes."

That is how Paul Vernell, secretary of the NUT South Gloucestershire division, describes the bitterness against the government's attempts to effectively freeze teachers' pay with threats to introduce performance related pay.

Questions

Beginning with a question softens the story, as here in the *Independent* (10 March 2000)

What is classical music? The question is being asked not as an academic proposition but as part of a dispute which is about to involve key figures in the music industry.

Naxos, the biggest selling classical music label in the UK, is incensed that its recording of Elgar's Third Symphony has been kept off the top of the classical music charts by William Orbit.

Delayed drop intro

Delaying the main angle is difficult to achieve and needs to be handled with caution. It works by arousing the reader's sense of curiosity and will fail if the reader is not curious to know how it all ends. It is best used when something unusual or eccentric is being reported and the reader is kept in suspense before being let into the secret. Here, from the *Guardian* (15 November 1999), a colourful human interest section precedes the news which comes in par. 3.

He wore sandals without socks which was a daring thing to do in Wigan at the time.

He also sported a cape, goatee beard and long hair, and he painted hundreds of canvases (including a portrait of Mary Whitehouse with five breasts) in an eccentric artistic life dominated by twin passions: alcohol and his mother.

Almost 300 of the paintings of James Lawrence Isherwood, some wild and brilliant, others dark and sombre, went on sale at the weekend in the function suite at Wigan town hall, with prices ranging from £75 to £1,200.

Offbeat intro

A variant of the delayed drop intro, it creates interest and surprise by highlighting an unexpected, obscure aspect of an event or person. Here, the *Independent* (4 April 2000) focused on the seventieth birthday celebrations of former Chancellor Kohl:

> At the inn where Margaret Thatcher had her first encounter with stuffed pig's stomach, a few regulars came together last night to toast their illustrious absent friend.
>
> Helmut Kohl had been due to celebrate his 70th birthday at the Deidersheimer Hof, but the home town feast was cancelled at short notice. Early in the morning Mr and Mrs Kohl were driven away in a black Mercedes, destination unknown.

Eye-witness human interest

Here is an example from *The Times* (8 November 1999):

> Dancing girls, bands and a crowd of several thousand surrounded the Accra airport's tarmac as the Queen, beginning a 48-hour state visit to Ghana, stepped into the cool evening air last night and one of the warmest and noisiest welcomes she has received on a foreign tour for some time.
>
> She even took a brief, unscripted walk along the front of the crowd, safely corralled behind a stout barrier, to acknowledge the cheers and flag waving.

Keep it flowing, keep it clear:
STRUCTURING THE NEWS STORY

News stories, whether of five or thirty-five pars, are formed through the linking of thematic sections. The reader progresses through them in order of importance, except on those few occasions when the punch line is delayed for dramatic reasons. The journalist's news sense comes into operation not only for the intro but throughout the story. Who is the most important person to quote? Who is the next most important person? What details should be highlighted and which left to the end or eliminated? How much background information is required and where is it best included? All these questions are answered according to a set of news values held by the reporter.

Structure

Speed is the essence of news reading just as it is of news gathering. Information should flow logically and easily through copy, the structure being so refined it is invisible to the reader. Only when a story is badly organised with confusing chronology, say, or jumbled up quotes, does the reader become aware of any structure.

Opening section

Intro pars tend to highlight the news angle. Second and third pars can expand on intro angles giving extra information. There is an urgency about hard copy which should be maintained throughout the story but particularly in the opening pars. Unnecessary background information, comment and description should not be allowed to delay the dramatic flow of the copy. Take these pars from the *Highbury and Islington Express* (24 March 2000):

> Labour MP Chris Smith is backing a campaign to save a residential home for the elderly from closure.
>
> The member for Islington South and Finsbury has urged councillors to think again about their plans to close Preedy House, in Muriel Street, Barnsbury.
>
> They were expected to agree to the closure at last night's social services committee even though the decision would leave around 30 elderly people suffering from senile dementia without a permanent home. A final decision is expected to be made in June and the home could close within the next 18 months.
>
> "I've visited the home many times over the years and I have never failed to be impressed by the dedication of the staff and the way in which the residents are looked after," said Mr Smith.

The intro summarises the main angle. The next par. follows up concisely giving extra details about the MP and the residential home. The third par. maintains the dramatic flow by providing a strong news angle ('last night') and more specific details about the home and the plans to close it. The final par. carries a striking quote supporting the main theme from the main source.

Later sections: the inverted pyramids concept

Traditional analysis of news stories stresses the notion of the inverted pyramid with the most important elements at the top and the least important (often defined as background) briefly at the bottom. This notion is useful for stories based in the main on one source. For the vast majority it oversimplifies the writing process. News values operate throughout the individual sections while background can occur anywhere in a news story. Sometimes when a story is unintelligible without background information, it will occur high up.

News stories are never neutral or objective. An overall 'frame of understanding' influences the choice of content, sources, language and quotes used. Within this context, they are usually made up from a mix of quotes (in direct and indirect speech), factual details, background information and occasionally brief analysis. Each of these elements usually comprises a separate thematic section. News values are applied to each section: the most important comes first, the least important last. Thus, instead of a single inverted pyramid it is more useful to think of a series of inverted pyramids within an overall inverted pyramid (see Figure 6.1).

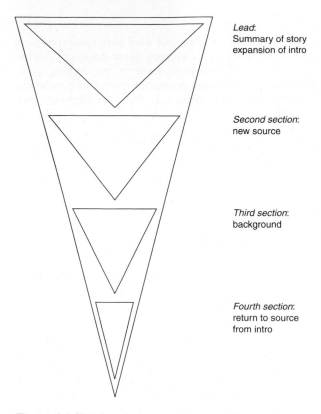

Lead:
Summary of story
expansion of intro

Second section:
new source

Third section:
background

Fourth section:
return to source
from intro

Figure 6.1 The inverted pyramids concept

Thematic structure

Each section will tend to begin with its main subject and most newsy elements associated with it. This could be the most important quote (in direct or indirect speech) or detail. Take this report from the Liverpool *Daily Post* (24 November 1999)

> **D**ISGRACED TORY PEER Lord Archer last night faced the humiliation of his local party chairman calling on him to quit the Conservatives to save their embarrassment.
>
> John Reynolds, who heads the South Cambridgeshire Conservative Association, said: "I actually hope that Lord Archer may consider very carefully over the next few days his position and it may make it easier for the Conservative Party,
>
> both nationally and locally, actually to resign."
>
> "I think that would be in the best long-term interests of the party." The move came as the man who brought him down, Ted Francis, told yesterday of the fateful meal when Lord Archer asked him: "Will you do me a favour?"
>
> Mr Francis said he assumed he was being required to protect Lord Archer from a possible divorce when the peer asked him to lie and say he had been having

dinner together on a night in September 1986.

Mr Francis, whose revelations of the plot to lie in the run-up to the Monica Coghlan 1987 libel case against the *Daily Star* forced Lord Archer to quit the race for Mayor of London, said: "I arrived at the restaurant and we were sitting down with small talk. He (Lord Archer) said: 'What were you doing on September 9 last year?' "

"'I want you to do me a favour and say we were having dinner with somebody else on that night because it would embarrass me with Mary' (Lady Archer)."

Scotland Yard confirmed that the detective who helped jail Jonathan Aitken for perjury has been called in to investigate Lord Archer.

Let's look at the thematic structure:

* *Section 1: par. 1*: first the general details of local Tory Party chairman calling for resignation.

* *Section 2: pars 2–3a*: next comes the name of the chairman together with strong direct quote to support intro angle. Ideally the quote 'I think that would be in the best long-term interests of the party' should have been linked to the previous par., thus making the thematic structure clearer.

* *Section 3: pars 3b–6*: the focus then falls on whistleblower Ted Francis and his account of how he was asked a 'favour' by Lord Archer. The phrase 'The move came as the man' is a typical transitional device helping the copy flow from one section to the next. The 'yesterday' reference maintains the news urgency while the section in par. 5 about the libel trial provides concise but necessary background detail. Notice the use of parentheses in pars 5 and 6. Parentheses are rarely used in hard news stories – except sometimes to clarify details in direct quotes, as here.

* *Section 4: final par.*: Scotland Yard investigation. The reference to Jonathan Aitken cleverly hints at the possible outcome of the investigation.

Take this example from *Eastern Eye* (17 December 1999):

INDIA SAID on Thursday October's military coup in Pakistan had not resulted in a softening of Islamabad's aggressive stance and hostility towards its neighbour.

"The military coup in Pakistan has not altered Pakistan's aggressive approach, hostile policies and propaganda towards India," Foreign Minister Jaswant Singh said in a written response to a question in parliament.

"Pakistan's sponsorship of cross-border terrorism in the state of Jammu and Kashmir and elsewhere in India has continued unabated."

Singh's comments come two days after Pakistan's leader General Pervez Musharraf, who overthrew prime minister Nawaz Sharish, said India had spurned peace overtures.

Musharraf said there would be no peace in South Asia until the two nuclear rivals solved the Kashmir dispute over which they have fought two of their three wars since independence from Britain in 1947.

Singh said Pakistani forces had continued firing across the Line of Control and the international border, which divide the two countries in Kashmir.

India controls around 45 per cent of Kashmir, Pakistan controls just over one-third and China holds the remainder.

"Pakistan has made no moves to withdraw troops from the Line of Control where they had been inducted in large numbers during its armed intrusion and aggression in the Kargil sector," Singh said.

India and Pakistan stood on the brink of a fourth war earlier this year when Indian forces launched a massive offensive to oust hundreds of heavily armed intruders from the strategic Kargil heights near a cease-fire line with Pakistan in Kashmir.

New Delhi has frequently accused Pakistan of sponsoring the decade-old separatist insurgency in Jammu and Kashmir state, but Islamabad says it provides only moral and diplomatic support to the Kashmiri people in their struggle for self determination.

- *Section 1: pars 1–3*
  - *Par. 1*: India's allegation against Pakistan 'on Thursday'
  - *Par. 2*: direct quote supporting main angle; source named
  - *Par. 3*: direct quote continues with focus on Jammu and Kashmir.
- *Section 2: pars 4–5*
  - *Par. 4*: counter allegation by Pakistan's leader. Link phrase 'Singh's comments come two days after'
  - *Par. 5*: Musharraf quoted in indirect speech. Background detail on three wars inserted by journalist (not in indirect speech).
- *Section 3: pars 6–8*
  - *Par. 6*: return to Singh's allegations (somewhat a repetition of par. 3)
  - *Par. 7*: background detail on control of Kashmir provided by reporter
  - *Par. 8*: Singh's allegations continue with reference to Kargil.
- *Section 4: 9–10*
  - *Par. 9*: background on hostilities earlier in the year focused on Kargil: this flows on logically from previous par.'s reference to Kargil.
  - *Par. 10*: more background information based on allegation and counter allegation by India and Pakistan, referred to by their capitals 'New Delhi' and 'Islamabad' – a common device in copy and headlines to avoid repetition.

7 Planning for the unforeseen

Covering transport accidents, fires, demonstrations and human interest stories

Reports of transport accidents and fires feature regularly in local papers. A survey by Durrants press cuttings agency found that during 1997 accidents and disasters secured more newspaper coverage than any other subject. They beat sport into second place with the economy and crime in third position. Indeed, while journalists stress the 'newness' of the news, sociologists often highlight its 'endless repetitiveness' (Rock 1988).

The more serious the consequences, the more prominent will be the coverage. Nationals are likely to cover accidents and fires only if they involve a serious loss of life (and thus amount to disasters) or if some celebrity is involved. Journalists will only rarely witness an accident. News come through tip-offs from the public or more usually from routine calls by reporters to police, hospitals and fire services. In contrast, a major fire might be witnessed by reporters.

Readers relate ambivalently to the coverage. They are drawn in, somewhat voyeuristically, to the tragedy, the human suffering, the drama of any rescue attempt. They are relieved they are not involved. At the same time they are repelled by the event's awfulness, the terrible unpredictability of 'fate' that strikes down one person and leaves another (the reader, for instance) unscathed.

Coverage of transport accidents and fires (as well as natural disasters) falls within a dominant genre which presents news as a series of disconnected 'bad' events and individuals as victims of forces beyond their control. Ideological, economic, cultural and religious factors are more difficult to identify and report, though their historical impact is considerable. An accident, in contrast, can be reported as an isolated event with a beginning and an end. Coverage can slot easily within the dominant routines of journalistic research. The accumulation of details is always important in accident reports. Yet research suggests readers remember little of it. Instead, the coverage contributes to the representation of a powerful, ever-present symbolic world of tragedy, suffering and potential heroism (Bird and Dardenne 1988).

Details to stress

The human interest angle

The most important focus for any report will tend to be on the consequences to human life. The impact on property or means of transport is secondary to this. Thus it is wrong to intro: 'An engineering factory was gutted by a fire in Birmingham yesterday (Monday) in which four employees were seriously injured and two died.' Better to say: 'Two engineering workers died and four were seriously injured in a fire which gutted a Birmingham factory yesterday (Monday).' Similarly, in an accident coverage it would be poor to intro: 'A Rolls-Royce driven by a Cardiff man was seriously damaged in an accident with an Austin Maestro in Doncaster yesterday (Thursday).' In reporting the huge earthquake in Turkey, the *Guardian* (13 November 1999) significantly introed:

> At least 34 people died in a powerful earthquake that rocked Turkey's north-western province of Bolu yesterday, according to the local news channel NTV.

A report of a train crash at Waterloo station, London, in the *Guardian* (11 March 2000) began:

> A passenger was seriously injured and 29 others were hurt when their train hit empty carriages waiting at a platform.

Be specific

Hospitals are usually well prepared to deal with media inquiries following fires and accidents. Spokespersons are available (either in face-to-face or phone interviews) to provide regular bulletins on the conditions of any casualties. Go for specific details. Thus rather than 'Many people were injured after a fire swept through a night club in Bognor Regis last night (Friday)' it is better to report: 'Twelve people were admitted to hospital with serious burns after fire swept through a Bognor Regis night club last night (Friday).'

In fast-breaking fire and accident stories, hospital and ambulance authorities are often unclear about the exact number of casualties. A fire breaks out in a hotel: twelve people are pronounced dead at the scene or in hospital and three others are unaccounted for. In this case it is possible to say: 'At least 15 people were feared dead after fire swept through a hotel overlooking Margate promenade yesterday (Monday).'

Controversial guidelines issued by the Association of Chief Police Officers (ACPO) in May 1999 indicated that, following the Data Protection Act, names of victims and witnesses of road crashes or other accidents were entitled not to have personal details released without their permission. An ACPO survey in June 2000 revealed that thirty-one forces (70.5 per cent) were implementing the guidelines or had similar policies. But journalists throughout the UK challenged them. Sometimes details of work status are provided or can be gathered from friends or relatives. In accident reports it is important in local papers to identify where the accident happened and at what time. The number and types of vehicles need to be identified. The ages of accident victims are usually carried prominently.

Use the past tense

In covering fires and disasters, there is a temptation to use the present tense to convey the drama. For instance: 'Seven people are feared to have died in a fire which gutted a factory in Huddersfield earlier today (Friday). Ten fire appliances are at the scene trying to bring the flames under control.' But by the time the paper appears (and almost certainly by the time the reader sees the copy) the situation is likely to have changed. The fire may well have been contained. All details have to go in to the past tense. 'Seven people were feared dead after a fire gutted a factory in Huddersfield today (Friday).' Take this report from the *East Anglian Daily Times* (10 November 1999).

Hero catches fire victim in dramatic fall

by **RICHARD CORNWELL**

A **TERRIFIED** woman escaped from her burning home by climbing out of a bedroom window and jumping into the arms of a neighbour.

Jan Ryder was recovering from shock and the effects of smoke inhalation yesterday after the fire at her house in Trimley St Mary.

Neighbours raced to her rescue after hearing screams and finding Ms Ryder dangling from a first-floor window, clinging on by her fingertips.

Paul Stansby, 17, and his wife Donna, 22, who live opposite Ms Ryder in St Mary's Close were first on the scene.

"I heard these two screams and turned down the TV, but it was so dark outside you couldn't see at first what was happening," said Mrs Stansby. Then I could see Jan hanging out of the window and trying to keep herself from falling."

SAVED THE DAY:Paul Stansby

Mr Stansby rushed across the road and arrived just at the moment Ms Ryder could hold on no longer and fell from the window ledge.

"I managed to catch her as she fell and fortunately she twisted on to her side as she came down, which made it easier," he said.

"I was so worried she would come down head first and would have been seriously injured or even killed.

"I laid her on the grass and then sat her up as she was coughing so much. She was able to tell us there was no-one else in the house.

"We got her cat out and I went in quickly and checked all the rooms, but I didn't try to tackle the fire. The smoke was so thick – it was just horrible in there."

Three fire crews – two from Felixstowe and one from Ipswich headquarters – attended the Monday night blaze Police and an ambulance also attended.

Ms Ryder, who has two grown up sons, received treatment from paramedics at the scene for smoke inhalation but did not go to hospital. She was not at home yesterday. A Suffolk Fire Service spokeswoman said fire crews were called out to tackle a small blaze in the bedroom that took 20 minutes to control, but caused severe smoke damage to the house.

Drama

The report focuses conventionally and concisely on the drama of the 'heroic' rescue. 'Terrified' in the intro adds to the impact. The chronology of the drama (neighbours race to blaze, see woman dangling from ledge, woman falls into arms of brave neighbour) is clear throughout.

Highlight any uniqueness

Reports of fires and accidents should aim to highlight any uniqueness. The intro of the *East Anglian Daily Times* highlights well the unusual feature of the woman jumping into the arms of her neighbour. The *Haverhill Echo* (11 November 1999) highlighted not only a tragedy but also the unusual feature of an amazing escape.

> Two next door neighbours from Haverhill died in a car crash last week and but for a broken finger a third resident of Fritton Court would have been in the car too.

The causes

In the *East Anglian Daily Times* story no cause of the fire is identified. Ms Ryder was 'not at home yesterday' and consequently the story is missing quotes from her which may have clarified this point. Normally after a tragedy like a fire, one of the first questions to be asked is why did it happen. Thus the 'why' element will often be prominent in fire stories and sourced to an appropriate authority. For instance, a report in the *Guardian* (27 March 2000) introed:

> A spring weather sleep-out in a garden shed ended in tragedy yesterday for three families whose sons died when a candle set fire to bedding and carpets in a cramped shed.

Even if the authorities have no explanation at the time of going to press this is still worth carrying: 'Police were unable to determine the cause of the blaze.' Be careful if the police refuse to confirm or deny rumours that arson took place. They may say: 'We have heard rumours that the fire was started deliberately. At the moment we have no evidence to support that theory. At the same time we are not ruling out the possibility.' You may afterwards look at your note and see 'We have no evidence to support the arson theory'. But the police spokesperson went on to qualify that statement. It would be possible to intro strongly on 'Two elderly women died in a fire in Burnley yesterday (Monday). Afterwards police refused to rule out the possibility of arson.'

Similarly, in transport accidents, one of the major issues to be addressed high up in the story is why it happened. Theories over the immediate causes of the tragedy can be explored (failure of warning lights at the crossing, for instance) but no individuals should be identifiable in the criticisms. Newspapers tend to marginalise the deeper social and economic factors behind many accidents. As Wendy Moore (1999) stresses, accidents are the biggest killers of children today. Government figures indicate that around 500 youngsters die in accidents (mainly as pedestrians, in fires and at the home) every year, but children of poorer families are eight times more likely to be killed by a car and fifteen times more like to die in a fire, than children from better-off families. 'The reason for such inequality is a lethal combination of more dangerous living conditions and fewer safeguards.'

Be careful not to over-hype any information for dramatic effect. The *Guardian*, for instance, described the Ladbroke Grove (near Paddington) crash of 1999 in which thirty-one people died as 'the worst rail disaster in 50 years'. It wasn't: a crash at Harrow and Wealdstone in 1952 claimed 112 lives. And be extra sensitive about the language you use. Following the Ladbroke Grove crash, in which many died from burns, the *Guardian* said the disaster would 'rightly ignite the smouldering debate [about safety]'. Some readers found that 'crass'.

The leading sources

Police
The police examine the causes of the blaze, time of outbreak and how it was discovered; they often provide details of casualties. The police can issue appeal for witnesses (providing contact name and telephone number). After accidents, the police are often able to describe the accident, perhaps on the evidence provided by street surveillance videos (though journalists should be aware of the implications for civil rights posed by those videos). Be careful here not to impute blame to a particular driver. Better to say: 'The cars were in a collision' than 'Car A collided with car B' or even worse 'Car A hit car B'. Under provisions of new Youth Justice and Criminal Evidence legislation, the media are unable to print the names of young persons alleged to be involved in offences, such as under-aged driving, before court proceedings. Some newspapers have opposed these plans, with *The News*, Portsmouth, going so far as to publish the names and photographs of three schoolboys involved in a motorway death crash.

Ambulance services
Ambulance services provide details of number of ambulances (sometimes helicopter ambulances) and paramedics sent to the scene, number of people taken to hospital or treated at scene and sent home.

Hospitals
Hospitals give casualty details, conditions of those in hospitals, kinds of injuries suffered; numbers of those in intensive care; numbers pronounced dead. It is important to avoid such clichés as 'fighting for her life'. Better to say 'in a critical condition'. Remember injuries are not 'received' but 'suffered' or 'sustained'. 'Lacerations' and 'contusions' are medical jargon words to avoid. Instead, use 'cuts' and 'bruises' respectively. Skulls can be 'fractured' but bones are 'broken'.

Relations and friends
Relatives of victims can provide details of funerals. After disasters they often lead campaigns and petitions for changes in safety provisions and the law. For instance, after the October 1999 Ladbroke Grove rail crash, relatives of the victims featured prominently at a *Mirror*-backed demonstration in London calling for the installation of a new train safety system. Depending on the time available before your deadline, you may be able to follow up friends and relatives of anyone killed in an accident for their tributes. Particular sensitivity will be required for these assignments, known

as 'death knocks'. Journalists have sometimes refused to conduct such interviews – and been sacked as a result. Others have simply lied or found an excuse not to do the news desk's wishes.

Fire service

Firefighters can supply details of number of appliances at scene and give accounts of any rescue operation and specific difficulties (practical and psychological) encountered. They might also conduct their own investigations into causes, provide warnings and advice to avoid repeat of tragedy. Avoid using 'firemen' (they may be women). Many style books suggest 'fire service spokesman' or 'spokeswoman'. Because of firefighters' crucial roles in saving lives, plans to close stations can provide a focus for local newspaper campaigns – such as that conducted by *East Anglian Daily Times* in 1999: 'Hands off Sudbury Fire Station' ran the slogan, supported by news stories and editorials.

Survivors, eyewitnesses and neighbours

Members of the public often provide dramatic accounts of how people reacted and, in cases of fires, how buildings and contents were affected. Be wary of using any quotes which blame the fire or accident on any person. Formal inquiries are held to determine that. Eye-witnesses can be mistaken. You may visit the scene of the fire or accident, perhaps accompanied by a photographer or video journalist, which may prove harrowing. Be sensitive to the feelings of anyone involved in the tragedy and any eye-witnesses. They may not be prepared to talk. Photographing them may be unnecessarily intruding on their private grief. However, some might want to talk since it could help to release their anxiety.

Owners of property

Following fires, owners are sometimes able to provide an estimated cost of the damage and details of whether the property was insured. There can often be special 'human interest' dimensions to the tragedy worth highlighting. For instance, the *East Anglian Daily Times* (7 April 2000) carried this quote after a fire: 'One of my hobbies has been collecting cricket memorabilia, which includes more than 500 club ties, and if I had lost them I would have been very upset.'

Motoring organisations and rail companies

The Automobile Association (AA): provides details about the impact of accidents on traffic flows. Rail companies provide information about the impact of accidents on train timetables. The Health and Safety Executive provides reports on transport safety and rail users' consultative committees are on hand to comment about punctuality and general efficiency.

Meteorological Office

This is usually carried as the Met Office: many serious accidents happen in poor weather. The Met Office provides necessary background and can forecast warnings.

Follow-ups

Follow-ups are often possible. In the week following the Ladbroke Grove rail disaster on 5 October 1999, the *Guardian* carried 40,000 words explaining what happened, looking at the apparent causes, trying to provide a political context and exploring some of the ethical issues raised by the media's coverage (Mayes 1999). Casualty lists may change over time and need updating. Emergency services may be criticised for their alleged inefficiency or praised for the speed of their reaction. Coroners' inquiries and sometimes public or local authority inquiries are held to determine the truth. In cases of suspected arson police investigations will need to be followed closely. Calls may come for safety improvements at junctions, at notorious accident spots or to planes. Political parties (often keen to stress the impact of underfunding of public services) and campaigning groups are good sources here.

The emotional trauma of accident and fire victims and of those who witness them generally goes unrecognised, not only by the media but also by health professionals and their families and friends. A feature could highlight their plight and the ways they are overcoming it. For example, Headway, the National Head Injuries Association, of 4 King Edward Court, King Edward Street, Nottingham NG1 1EW (0115-924 0800) has 112 branches and groups around Britain helping accident victims.

Dealing with demos: COVERING MARCHES

Press and political strategies increasingly overlap. Though demonstrations were held long before our mass media age, their media dimension is now crucial. People carry banners with simple slogans, they wear eccentric costumes, they chant, they play music, they choose routes often heavy with symbolism, they distribute leaflets and they attract prominent speakers. They do all this for political reasons. But they also do it hoping to attract media attention. A demonstration serves many purposes. For the participants and organisers, it represents a public statement of solidarity for a cause. When people are angry or concerned they may demonstrate. It is as if the more traditional avenues for debate and political action – the smoke-filled committee room, media, Parliament, the protest meeting – are incapable of containing the feelings involved. They then break out on to the streets.

Demonstrations and vigils are regular occurrences in London and, not surprisingly, the vast majority are ignored by Fleet Street. Even well-attended ones (with numbers in the thousands) often suffer the same fate or are marginalised in various ways. Coverage of a political march may be confined to an aesthetically pleasing picture or over-personalised with stress on the presence or speech of a 'celebrity'. The tone and prominence of coverage is often influenced by the attitude of the newspaper to the event. The massive Campaign for Nuclear Disarmament (CND) demos during the early 1980s received largely negative coverage because of the papers' almost universal opposition to unilateral nuclear disarmament. In contrast, the London march in support of the miners following the Conservative government's sudden announcement of pit closures in 1992 was given generally positive, front-page coverage.

A demo on which violence breaks out is almost always given negative coverage, even though the violence may involve only a tiny fraction of the participants and last for a matter of minutes and may even have been started by the police (Halloran *et al.*, 1970). Sometimes newspapers (bizarrely) intro on the absence of violence: 'The CND demo in London passed off peacefully yesterday with the only problems coming to police in the form of massive traffic jams.' When violence breaks out the blame is often explicitly or implicitly put on the demonstrators. Criticisms of police over-reactions (such as during the 1 May 2000 anti-capitalist demo in London) tend to be marginalised. Sometimes a demonstration can be covered neutrally in the news columns but is attacked or supported in features and/or editorial comments. For local papers a demonstration (even the peaceful variety) can usually provide good copy. Advances are often compiled outlining the plans of the organisers and police.

Guidelines for demo reporting

It is important to report the numbers of people involved. There can often be significant differences between figures given by the organisers and by the police. Figures should always be attributed. Sources might also have views about the numbers attending. They may be delighted at the turn-out or disappointed and blame the weather. Do not take the word of an organiser that the demo is, say, the biggest ever in the town. Claims like that need to be carefully checked. If a demo includes a march indicate its route. Observe the responses of passers-by.

Police in Britain, as in France, Luxembourg and the Netherlands, have introduced voluntary identity card schemes for journalists and possession can sometimes help when covering dramatic events such as riots, disaster and demos (Frost 2000: 49). It is always worth joining the march. Chants and slogans can often provide useful 'eye-witness' colour. In his report on the 1 May 2000 anti-capitalist demo in London, the *Guardian*'s John Vidal carried this exchange:

> "What is happening?" asked a Japanese mother, feeding grain to the pigeons. "Don't worry ma'am." said one man. "We're just overthrowing the state." "I see," replied the woman.

In some cases it is not advisable to identify yourself as a journalist. Some reporters and photographers have been attacked by demonstrators suspicious of the bias of most newspapers. The compliance of some editors with police demands for incriminating photographs following demo violence has not helped protect journalists on such assignments.

Participants can be drawn from a variety of groups, local and national. These are worth identifying. Prominent participants, not necessarily speakers, can also be identified. Demos usually end with rallies at which speeches are given. Coverage will depend on space available. Local papers, operating as 'journals of record' will often cover as many speeches as possible in order of news value. Responses of audience to speeches (applause, jeers, heckling, for example) are worth carrying to convey eye-witness colour.

Background details are often essential. For instance, when the demo is part of a nationwide or European-wide series of protests, that needs to be mentioned to place the local action within its proper context. If violence breaks out or if arrests are made be careful not to sensationalise these elements. Try to convey any conflicting views on causes of violence from police, organisers, participants and eye-witnesses. Police are increasingly detaining and even attacking journalists covering demonstrations. As Andrew Wasley (2000) writes:

SINCE ENVIRONMENTAL activists first resorted to direct action at the Twyford Down anti-bypass siege in 1992–93 protests have attracted media attention like never before. With this, however, there has been an alarming increase in the number of journalists reportedly assaulted, harried and even arrested by the police at such events.

Those covering road protests, hunt sabotage and action against genetically modified crops claim to have been targeted most frequently. Some say they have been arrested as many as seven times, others that they have been beaten by the police, their houses raided and equipment seized. All say their press card credentials have been systematically ignored, in spite of a police-operated PIN number identification scheme.

Some journalists argue that it represents a deliberate and organised attempt on the part of the police to intimidate campaign-sympathetic reporters and to 'manage' the news. The situation is further complicated by reports that private detectives pose as freelance reporters and photographers at demos to gather information.

The importance of risk-assessment

At the same time, demonstrators are becoming increasingly hostile to journalists. Journalists, for instance, came under attack during the 1 May 2000 anti-capitalist demo in London. You should always assess the risks involved before covering any story – but in particular potentially dangerous investigative assignments and demos. Newspapers and training courses in general have been slow to acknowledge the importance of such training. But in 2000, moves were underway to improve matters, with the Rory Peck Trust along with CNN, BBC News, ITN, the *Guardian* and the *Financial Times* launching an initiative to provide safety training to freelances working in hostile environments. The organisation Reporters Sans Frontières (5 rue Geoffroy-Marie, 75009 Paris) has also produced a useful *Survival Manual for Journalists* on dangerous assignments.

It might be more appropriate to cover a demo from a vantage point, high above the demonstrators; if you decide to walk with the protesters, it might be sensible to be accompanied by a colleague and with a mobile phone to keep in regular contact with your news desk. Always be aware of 'get-out' routes in case violence breaks out and protesters are pinned into a confined space by the police. As the safety manual *Danger: Journalists at Work* (International Federation of Journalists, Boulevard Charlemagne, 1 Bte 5, 1041 Brussels, Belgium) stresses: 'No story is worth your life. You are more important than the story. If you are threatened, get out fast.'

All journalists covering dangerous assignments, in particular freelances, should either be aware of or organise their insurance cover. After particularly harassing assignments journalists may suffer Post Traumatic Stress Syndrome. Chris Cramer (2000), a BBC journalist who was caught up in the London Iranian Embassy siege of 1980, commented: 'I was back at work the day after the siege ended. With hindsight, I should have accepted the offers for psychiatric help, as many of my fellow hostages did, and maybe saved myself years of stress and anxiety.'

Reporters covering demonstrations should be aware of the 24 January 1997 High Court judgment. This ruled that, under the offence of trespassory assembly aimed at curbing road protests, police can ban groups of twenty or more meeting in a particular area if they fear 'serious disruption to the life of the community', even if the meeting is non-obstructive and non-violent. The ruling related to the cases of two people who were the first to be convicted of trespassory assembly under the controversial Criminal Justice Act 1994 after taking part in a peaceful demonstration at Stonehenge in 1995.

Journalists covering marches should also be aware of the provisions of the Public Order Act 1986. This gave the police unprecedented new powers. Organisers must give police seven days' notice unless it is not reasonably practical to do so. Police can impose conditions on a march or ban it. Moreover it becomes an offence if the date, time and route differ from that notified to police. Road blocks are now routinely used by the police to stop people from attending major demonstrations. More than 300,000 were estimated to have been stopped by police road blocks during the coal dispute of 1984–5. Peace campaigners and travellers aiming to hold their traditional midsummer festival at Stonehenge have also faced road blocks (Hillyard and Percy-Smith 1988).

Analysis of 'City under siege as world looks on':

Guardian (1 December 1999) John Vidal

Seven in the morning. Dark, wet, cold. 1,500 people have gathered at Victor Steinbrueck park. It is innocent enough. "Down with the WTO", "End Capitalism Now", "Free Tibet", "Fair Trade Not Free" read the banners.

We set off, led by steelworkers and loggers, shouting and singing and drumming. Anita Roddick is there. So, too, the Zapatistas, Tibetan monks, environmentalists, a few British veterans of the anti-GM and Newbury protest and a rainbow collection of young America. A six-man Trojan cow. "Hey ho, hey ho, out with the WTO," shout the protesters.

Across Fifth Street is a line of 30 riot police, and behind them two more lines, horses, armoured cars and dogs. The protesters and police size each other up. The police look like something from Star Wars. Heavy black visors, black handguns, black machine guns, black 3ft truncheons. They talk through black gas masks, which makes them incomprehensible. We turn left, not wanting confrontation, but are blocked again. At least 20 streets have been ringed. Seattle is under siege. On the other side of town another march is leaving the central community centre. Some 30,000 steelworkers and other trade unionists are due to leave later. The marches are meant to meet, but it never happens. By 9am every road block has at least 200 people in front of it.

The teargas starts at 9.15am. A few people occupying Union and Sixth streets are asked to move on. They don't. In seconds the police have come at them from two sides. The teargas goes up first, then the pepper spray. It mixes until your whole head hurts, but it clears the sinuses.

Then come the sting bullets. There are people lying on the side of the road, unsure if they have been wounded badly or not. Volunteer paramedics attend them.

City under siege as world looks on

John Vidal in Seattle

Seven in the morning. Dark, wet, cold. 1,500 people have gathered at Victor Steinbrueck park. It's innocent enough. Down with the WTO." "End Capitalism Now." "Free Tibet." "Fair Trade Not Free" read the banners.

We set off, led by steelworkers and loggers, shouting and singing and drumming. Anita Roddick is there. So, too, the Zapatistas, Tibetan monks, environmentalists, a few British veterans of the anti-GM and Newbury protest, and a rainbow collection of young America. A six-man Trojan cow. "Hey ho, hey ho, out with the WTO," shout the protesters.

Across Fifth Street is a line of 30 riot police, and behind them two more lines, horses, armoured cars and dogs. The protesters and police size each other up. The police look like something from Star Wars. Heavy black visors, black bandguns, black machine guns, black 3ft truncheons. They talk through black gas masks, which makes them incomprehensible. We turn left, not wanting confrontation, but are blocked by rows of police with armoured vehicles and horses.

der siege. On the other side of town another march is leaving the central community centre. Some 30,000 steelworkers and other trade unionists are due to leave later. The marches are meant to meet, but it never happens. By 9am every road block has at least 200 people in front of it.

The teargas starts at 9.15am A few people occupying Union and Sixth streets are asked to move on. They don't. In seconds the police have come at them from two sides. The teargas goes up first, then the pepper spray. It mixes until your whole head hurts, but it clears the sinuses.

Then come the stinging bullets. There are people lying on the side of the road, unsure if they have been wounded badly or not. Volunteer paramedics attend them. The police back off. The protesters form their own barricades and sit down. Both sides glare at each other.

Strains of Beethoven's fifth and Tina Turner drift in with the teargas as gangs of black-masked protesters overturn newspaper stands. They try to smash a Starbucks coffee house door, but go in quickly. A McDonald's window is broken, then one in Gap. They race through three streets followed by TV cameras.

The vast majority of protesters are peaceful, appalled at the hijacking of the demonstration. "The whole world is watching," they sing.

We reach the Sheraton hotel. Police try to barricade the doors and we're told half the delegates are inside. There are cheers. Inside the ring of force, the city centre is a ghost town, streets blocked by rows of

Only journalists, delegates, dogs and police are let in. "Just the scum left now," says one observer on the front line. The gas drifts through and we all choke.

The Paramount theatre is the calm eye of the storm, the venue for the opening ceremony. Outside, it swarms with security men. Protesters have clambered onto a barricade of buses.

John, from Washington, is not unfriendly. His earpiece crackles. On the other side of town, he says, protesters have been rolling barrels down a steep hill into a line of police. He expects trouble to spread across the city within the hour.

Delegates wander in, each with a tale. The Koreans have seen it all. "It's nothing. We shouldn't take it too seriously," says their chief negotiator. But two women from Venezuela are shocked. "We got to the barricades and [protesters] grabbed us. The police moved in and they tried to overturn a car. They led us through. I'm more worried about getting back," one says.

For the Chinese, here as observers, it's a lesson for the west. "If governments don't respond positively to something like this it will be trouble," said one of their team. "I cannot see how America will not be politically embarrassed. The world is watching. What do they see? A major city in disorder. It looks bad."

Inside the Paramount — due to show Miss Saigon, "the greatest love story of all time" — the US delegation of more than 900 is arriving. The US has 10 times as many seats as any other delegation.

As the delegates are sent home to their

'We've come thousands of miles for these talks. America is supposed to lead the world; what has happened?'

hotel, the opening ceremony postponed, there is deep embarrassment from the Americans and anger from the developing countries. "We have come thousands of miles for these talks," says a South American delegate. "America is supposed to lead the world — what has happened?"

Back outside, the teargas and pepper spray from 6th and Union streets is drifting east. It's impossible to see more than 80 yards as the white clouds settle over protesters and police alike. "Hell, man, this is America," shouts Chris, who has climbed a lamppost.

It's mostly calm. The crowd has sat down, created its own blockade in front of the police. They drum rather badly and try to sing through the smoke. Every few minutes a gang in black masks streams past, urging people to join them in looting or destroying property. "We've nothing to do with this. Go home," shout the peaceful protesters.

No one gives a damn.

> The police back off. The protesters form their own barricades and sit down. Both sides glare at each other.
>
> Strains of Beethoven's fifth and Tina Turner drift in with the teargas as gangs of black-masked protesters overturn newspaper stands. They try to smash a Starbucks coffee house door, but give up quickly. A McDonald's window is broken, then one in Gap. They race through three streets followed by TV cameras.
>
> The vast majority of protesters are peaceful, appalled at the hijacking of the demonstration. "The world is watching," they sing.

- *Par. 1*: Vidal is in a unique position: not only involved in the demo but also detached, observing. The narrative begins logically at the start; the time is given starkly. And then the factual details build up. The numbers present, the name of the meeting point; the banner slogans: all these are reported precisely. So none of the conventional five Ws here. Vidal is present at an exceptional event. His writing has to transcend the conventions of news reporting to capture the drama.
- *Par. 2*: again the build-up of observed details conveying clearly the fascinating breadth of support. Nowhere does the reporter say: 'I back this march' but his concern over the details conveys implicit support. Note the rhythm of the text: a short, 13-word sentence; then one with just 4 words; a 24-word sentence is next dense with details, another 4-word sentence (without a verb) seeming to frame that long sentence. And finally an 11-word sentence, the lilting rhythm of the slogan's jingle carrying extra interest. Roddick, the Zapatistas, the Newbury protest are not explained: Vidal presumes his readers need no explanation; he is partly flattering them with their knowledge – and in so doing, winning their support as he embarks on his dangerous trip.
- *Par. 3*: the details of the riot police, suddenly at the start of the new par., carry a shock effect. Perhaps as a way of coping with the reality of the threat posed by the police, he escapes into the fantasy world of films and compares them (in a rare literary flourish) to an imaginary 'thing' (probably Darth Vader) from *Star Wars*. The relentless build-up of closely observed details and the repetition of the word 'black' add to the sense of danger. Vidal is again with the marchers. 'We turn left, not wanting confrontation,' he says stressing their non-violent intent. Again, the use of a short sentence with its blunt message ('Seattle is under siege.') carries enormous impact. Next Vidal moves away from the 'eye-witness'/ subjective approach (reminding his readers he is present essentially as a reporter, not a participant) by carrying details about a march on the other side of town he clearly wasn't observing but which he had learned about through journalistic inquiry. The narrative, diary-like coverage (with the emphasis always on specific details) continues with the sentence: 'By 9am every road block has at least 200 people in front of it.'
- *Par. 4*: as in the previous par., this one opens with a significant, shocking shift in the drama. 'The teargas starts at 9.15am.' There is no over-indulgence in emotive language; the starkness of the prose conveys all the necessary horror. A small drama is enacted. People are asked to move on. They don't. And so the teargas goes up. And amidst all the panic Vidal can still see the funny side of things. The teargas makes his head hurt, but, he adds drolly, 'it clears the sinuses'.
- *Par. 5*: another significant, shocking shift in the narrative and another short, punchy sentence to begin the par.: 'Then come the sting bullets.' And people are hit. Four

short sentences convey a sense of drama and panic. The focus moves rapidly from side to side: first the police fire bullets; next the protesters are hit and aided by paramedics; then the police back off; next the protesters form barricades and sit down. At the end, the two sides are in a way drawn together: glaring at each other.

- *Par. 6*: Vidal describes not only what he sees and feels but also what he hears: the chants of the protesters and now the bizarre mix of Beethoven and Tina Turner. Again starting the par. this way helps convey the surprise element. Vidal no longer identifies with the 'black-masked protesters'. No longer 'we'; instead 'they try to smash a Starbucks coffee house'. The final sentence comes as a surprise too. We, the readers, expect the protesters to be chased by police. Instead, they are followed by TV cameras. It seems banal, almost. And yet in that concise way, Vidal reminds us that this is after all a media event.

- *Par. 7*: flows on from the previous par. After reporting on the violence, Vidal is concerned to stress the non-violent credentials of the 'vast majority of protesters'. They don't attack, they simply sing. And their song's lyric reflects an awareness of the importance of the media coverage to their protest. This par. stands out as the shortest so far. The importance of the point being made demands that kind of focus.

Consensual concerns: THE HUMAN INTEREST STORY

Human interest angles predominate in all sections of the press. Not in just the obvious areas: profiles, biographical extracts and reviews, showbiz features and throughout the popular press – but also in the heavies, local press and in all the specialist areas (Curran *et al.* 1980; Kennedy 1986; Sparks 1992). Politics coverage, just as much as sport and the arts, is dominated by the human interest focus. Many issues are represented as being duels between two people: Blair against Hague; Bruce Kent against Thatcher; Maxwell against Murdoch; Clinton against Saddam or Milosevic and so on.

This human interest consensus is rooted in the journalists' culture, which stresses the importance of human sources as opposed to abstract ideas. In stressing the human interest, newspapers are responding to a curiosity people have about others. Amidst all the complexities of modern living, the human interest bias serves to explain events in simply comprehensible terms. At the core of all human interest stories is the representation of basic emotions: love, lust, hatred, anger, tragedy, sadness, pity and joy. People can relate and identify with these emotions and the dramatic narrative structured around them.

Economic factors are fundamental. Since the emergence of the mass selling press in Britain around the beginning of the twentieth century, proprietors have been well aware that human interest stories sell. As competition has mounted so have the numbers of human interest stories. The human interest bias can often end up representing people's biographies as being untouched by the social, political, economic dynamics of history. Newspapers are said to provide the first draft of history. But it is often a distorted, elitist history. Exaggerating the power of a few individuals serves to eliminate so many other people and their struggles from the historical record.

Alongside this elitist dimension of the human interest story runs a significant 'democratic' element. The dramas, hopes, fears, tragedies or 'ordinary' people feature everyday in such stories – just as the press's tendency to seek to bring the powerful down to size (through scandals and revelations) promotes this 'democratic', 'subversive' dimension. The front page lead story (splash) of *Bury Free Press* (7 April 2000) is typical of the genre. Under the big headline 'Please end this misery' that carries an urgent, compassionate and campaigning tone, the report by Mark Baxter opens:

> A Bury St Edmunds man is desperately waiting for life-saving surgery after two operations were cancelled.
>
> Ray Orr, 58, has a brain aneurysm which could rupture at any time, killing or permanently disabling him.
>
> Addenbrooke's Hospital in Cambridge has cancelled the operation twice, and now Mr Orr is hoping he does not lose the chance of surgery on April 19.

A picture of a smiling Mr Orr being embraced by his loving wife provides extra impact to the story.

Analysis of 'Elton makes a wish come true':
Kent Messenger (30 December 1999)

Elton makes a wish come true

A DREAM CAME true for one of Elton John's youngest fans when he performed at Leeds Castle in September.

Minutes before the superstar stepped out on stage in front of 14,000, people he met seven-year-old Lorna Harvey and her family backstage.

Lorna, who went blind as a baby, was given the chance to meet Sir Elton when her parents, of Orchard Way, Horsmonden, contacted his management company to ask for tickets.

Her father, Paul Harvey, said: "It was a nice thing to achieve. It also restores your faith in the celebrity world to find that they do pay attention to other people's situation. It came from the heart, which was great."

It was the second time the family had trekked to Leeds Castle, after Sir Elton's earlier July dates had to be cancelled so that the singer could have a pacemaker fitted.

But Lorna didn't mind. She was thrilled to meet Sir Elton and take her presents of signed CDs, T-shirts and hats. Mr Harvey said: "He was a nice guy and very friendly although he was distracted by the fact that he was about to go on stage. He was very open. I asked him how he was and he said he was doing okay and was still playing tennis. I offered him a game but he didn't reply."

- This article is highlighted as particularly interesting in an end-of-year compilation. Indeed, it carries many the ingredients of a fine local story: a multimillionaire celebrity visits the area and meets a blind child. There is a touching story here and the chance for some colourful quotes. The media are increasingly fascinated by the world of celebrities; yet it is essentially unreal: their lifestyle, their wealth,

Man, 58, desperately waits for third chance of life-saving op

PLEASE END THIS MISERY

Ray Orr and his wife Margaret
0004-81/21A

by Mark Baxter

A BURY St Edmunds man is desperately waiting for life-saving surgery after two operations were cancelled.

Ray Orr, 58, has a brain aneurysm which could rupture at any time, killing or permanently disabling him.

Addenbrooke's Hospital in Cambridge has cancelled the operation twice, and now Mr Orr is hoping he does not lose the chance of surgery on April 19.

Mr Orr, of Sicklesmere Road, and his wife Margaret have complained to Addenbrooke's about the situation and the hospital's patient satisfaction department is investigating the complaint.

He lives with the constant risk of the cerebral artery aneurysm – a ballooning of the artery because of a weak wall – bursting.

"If it does burst there is a 50-50 chance of survival but you do not know what the quality of life will

be if you do live," he said. Mr Orr is also hoping the surgery will go ahead before his son Christopher's wedding in July.

Mrs Orr, a doctor's receptionist, said the first operation was cancelled two days before her husband was due to have surgery and the second date was scrapped on the morning of the operation.

She said: "Doctors say stress is one of the big killers in our society and yet they are giving Ray large amounts of it by cancelling his operation. He has to psych himself up to go into hospital."

Mrs Orr, 59, said that when she complained the third surgery date was not within the four weeks allowed under the Patients' Charter she was told the hospital regularly has to break the charter.

Clerical worker Mr Orr said: "The thing that put our back up was Myra Hindley getting treated so quickly for the same thing when I have had to wait months."

An Addenbrooke's spokeswoman said: "We very much regret Mr Orr's operation has been cancelled on a second occasion. Unfortunately it is inevitable that a unit which deals with emergency cases from the whole eastern region will cause routine operations to be cancelled."

their fame so removed from the daily lives of 'ordinary' folk. Hence our ambivalence towards it (so subtly exploited by the media) on the one hand we succumb to its seductive appeal; on the other hand we are offended by its superficiality and outrageous wealth in a world of mass poverty. Here Lorna has a 'dream come true' entering, however fleetingly, the dream world of super-celebrity.

- *Par. 1*: the 19-word opening par. stresses the local angle but delays mention of Lorna's name until par. 2 to help keep it concise. 'A dream came true' is a cliché, of course, but it works fine here.

- *Par. 2*: clever coverage. The par. flows logically on from the intro, embellishing it and adding necessary details and colour. 'Minutes before the superstar stepped out' carries narrative interest while the reference to the 14,000 spectators helps stress the uniqueness (and newsworthiness) of Sir Elton's attention to 7-year-old Lorna.

- *Par. 3*: background details and local angle stressed with home address.

- *Par. 4*: important direct quote from the father focusing on the drama of the meeting between the 'ordinary' family and the superstar. Significantly, the father expresses in one short sentence the archetypal ambivalence. His 'faith' in celebrity had foundered (perhaps as a result of so many tabloid sleaze exposés) but Sir Elton's charitable act had 'restored' it. The quote is snappy and supports the overall positive tone.

- *Par. 5*: more background, conveying determination of family as well of the suffering of the superstar (they are human after all). 'It was the second time' is a useful transitional phrase linking with the previous par.

- *Par. 6*: 'But Lorna didn't mind' is another excellent transitional, linking phrase bringing the focus back to Lorna. The father's final quote again captures the ambivalence. Sir Elton is a 'nice guy' but when Mr Harvey suggests they meet for a game of tennis, he doesn't reply. After all, the 'ordinary' and 'celebrity' worlds can meet for fleeting photo-opportunities such as this (which place the celebrity in the best possible light); but more than that is simply not possible. The two worlds are separated by an invisible wall.

Sexploitation of the human interest

Sex sells. At least that's what press proprietors believe. So day after day stories about sex fill pages of newspapers. Extra-marital affairs, prostitutes, sex-changes, bedroom secrets, ministerial and royal 'scandals', love-children of Catholic bishops, randy vicars, presidential passions, 'kinky' schoolgirls, full-frontal nudity on TV, Hollywood starlets who do or don't (strip for the cameras or in a West End show); how to do it; where to do – the list of subjects seems endless.

The sex lives of virtually everyone, from former FBI chiefs through media celebrities to truck drivers, seem fair game for the press. Nor is this sex obsession confined to the pops. The 'heavies' are equally interested though in more discreet ways, of course. Serialisation of biographies will usually focus on the bits about sex; photographs accompanying reviews of plays or operas in which nudity occurs will be far more explicit than anything in the pops. *Independent on Sunday* columnist and feminist Joan Smith comments:

The tabloids treat sex as something which has to be discussed in a kind of grown-up baby language – bonk, shag, boobs and so on while the broadsheets invented high-minded motives for what is essentially voyeurism. Both approaches are predicated on the unspoken assumption that sex is taboo, not to be spoken about. They leave us without a language to talk comfortably about desire.

On one level this sex obsession of the press is all escapist, titillatory trash. Significantly, when Rupert Murdoch bought the *News of the World* in 1969 and his mother expressed unease at his association with the scandal sheet, he explained that the poor Brits had to have such entertainment as their lives were so wretched (Shawcross 1992). But what distinguishes a lot of the sex coverage is its humorous tone. It is rather like grown-ups giggling with embarrassment over a taboo subject. John Fiske (1992) takes a different approach and argues that this witty approach carries a 'subversive' agenda critical of the elite and the hypocrisies of those who presume to be our moral guardians.

The pops are, indeed, virulent supporters of the status quo, usually rushing to support right-wing parties, whether Conservative or New Labour, by all means (fair or foul) at election times and other critical moments. At the same time they subtly tap some of the anti-establishment feelings held by many people. This tone of 'subversive laughter' is peculiar to many of the tabloids and accounts for much of their popularity. A lot of their contrived humour is built on down-right lies, sexism and racism. But in a complex way, people want to be lied to, to be seduced into a fantasy world while at the same time seeing through the lies. Ask someone why they read a paper like the *Sun* and they may well say: 'It is a laugh, isn't it?' That humour, that blend of fact and fiction leads to a curious, mass-selling product.

Analysis of 'Virginie's Secret':
Mirror (23 February 2000) Jenny Johnston

Chic Virginie Ledoyen strolls along the shore after turning her back on Hollywood's hottest heart-throb.

The French actress who filmed a passionate love scene with Leonardo DiCaprio in The Beach, has revealed that he left her cold.

While waves lapped at their sun-bronzed bodies and their lips met in a salty kiss, 23-year-old Virginie had only one man on her mind.

It definitely wasn't baby-faced Leo, 25. She could barely wait to rush home to her 40-year-old boyfriend, movie technician Louis Saint Calbre.

Louis, who shares a flat with her in Paris, is tall and dark with manly Latin looks. And he's the sort of partner Virginie prefers – mature.

She rolls her eyes in astonishment at the thought that she might have been sexually attracted by the pale young American.

"Leo and I got on very well as friends," she says. "He is very funny and very intelligent, but he did nothing to me on a romantic level. I suppose he is quite good-looking but Leonardo, is really not the kind of guy I go for.

"When we did our love scene, I got no physical pleasure from it.

"Sure I kissed Leonardo, but it did nothing for me. I was pretty unimpressed, if you must know.

"We had to repeat the scene a dozen times and it was hard work, but certainly not a turn-on.

"All I can remember is the taste of the salt because we were kissing in the sea and the water kept getting into our mouths."

Leonardo modestly agrees that he failed to make the ocean roar for his co-star as they filmed in Thailand.

"She simply wasn't interested in me," he confirms. "The fact that I was a Hollywood star meant nothing to her, and rightly so. She's a very sophisticated European lady."

Virginie has dated Louis for three years. She has also been closely linked to Paris lawyer Thierry Meunier, 40.

A friend said yesterday: "She ended her last affair with Meunier before she started the next one with Saint Calbre."

"The one thing both men have in common is that they are both much older than she is and both dote on her."

Virginie herself seems wise beyond her years. Indeed she is already a show-business veteran.

She appeared in a TV commercial at the age of three and made her first movie when she was nine.

At 16 she saved enough money to leave home and buy her own flat. Her beauty also won her a modelling contract with the cosmetics giant L'Oreal.

Featuring in 15 French films made her a big name in her own country. Now the phenomenal success of The Beach has opened the door to Hollywood's riches. Yet she is in no rush.

"It's true that since Leonardo, the film offers have been rolling in," she concedes.

"But I intend to choose my films carefully so I don't get typecast as just the pretty French girl in a short skirt. I am a tough person and want tough intelligent roles."

The Beach's British director Danny Boyle predicts a great future for Virginie, not least because of the way she coped with DiCaprio.

Danny recalls: "While other actresses might have been overwhelmed at sharing a lead role with the world's number one film star, she always remained cool and detached."

Since the emergence of the *Sun*'s topless 'pin-up' in the early 1980s, page three in the tabloids has always been associated with titillation. Here, the *Mirror* blindly follows that convention, presenting a picture of long-legged 'chic' Virginie Ledoyen striding down a beach – arms outstretched, tantalisingly, towards us, the readers. Her hair hangs wet and dishevelled; sand clings to her swimsuit and legs; she smiles warmly (though her eyes are merely dark splodges). This is an image of a beautiful, active, playful, assertive woman.

The story has all the typical tabloid ingredients: sex, film stars, gossip, secrets revealed, Hollywood hype. Yet at its core lies an archetypal non-event: a manufactured kiss between Ledoyen and Leonardo DiCaprio on the set of the latest Hollywood blockbuster *The Beach*. So often the media create heroes – and then soon afterwards mock and debunk them. Here, in that same style, DiCaprio, 'Hollywood's hottest heart throb', is 'revealed' as sexually cold. And beneath the appearance of sexual

Virginie's secret

EXCLUSIVE

By JENNY JOHNSTON

I PREFER MY MAN OF 40 TO DICAPRIO SAYS BEACH STAR

CHIC Virginie Ledoyen strolls along the shore after turning her back on Hollywood's hottest heart-throb.

The French actress, who filmed a passionate love scene with Leonardo DiCaprio in The Beach, has revealed that he left her cold.

While waves lapped at their sun bronzed bodies and their lips met in a salty kiss, 25-year-old Virginie had only one man on her mind.

It definitely wasn't baby-faced Leo, 25. She could barely wait to rush home to her 40-year-old boyfriend, movie technician Louis Saint Calbre.

Louis, who shares a flat with her in Paris, is tall and dark with manly Latin looks. And he's the sort of partner Virginie prefers – mature.

She rolls her eyes in astonishment at the thought that she might have been sexually attracted by the pale young American.

"Leo and I got on very well as friends," she says. "He is very funny and very intelligent, but he did nothing for me on a romantic level. I suppose he is quite good-looking, but Leonardo is really not the kind of guy I go for.

"When we did our love scene, I got no physical pleasure from it.

"Sure I kissed Leonardo, but it did nothing for me. I was pretty unimpressed, if you must know.

"We had to repeat the scene a dozen times and it was hard work, but certainly not a turn-on.

"All I can remember is the taste of salt because we were kissing in the sea and the water kept getting into our mouths."

Leonardo modestly agrees that he failed to make the ocean roar for his co-star as they filmed in Thailand.

"She simply wasn't interested in me," he confirms. "The fact that I was a Hollywood star meant nothing to her, and rightly so. She's a very sophisticated European lady."

Virginie has dated Louis for three years. She has also been closely linked to Paris lawyer Thierry Meunier, 40.

A friend said yesterday: "She ended her last affair with Meunier before she started the next one with Saint Calbre.

"The one thing both men have in common is they are both much older than she is and both dote on her."

Virginie herself seems wise beyond her years. Indeed she is already a show-business veteran.

She appeared in a TV commercial at the age of three and made her first movie when she was nine.

At 16 she had saved enough money to leave home and buy her own flat. Her beauty also won her a modelling contract with cosmetics giant L'Oreal.

Featuring in 15 French films made her a big name in her own country. Now the phenomenal success of The Beach has opened the door to Hollywood's riches. Yet she is in no rush.

"It's true that since Leonardo, the film offers have been rolling in," she concedes.

"But I intend to choose my films carefully so I don't get typecast as just the pretty French girl in a short skirt. I am a tough person and I want tough intelligent roles."

The Beach's British director Danny Boyle predicts a great future for Virginie, not least because of the way she coped with DiCaprio.

Danny recalls: "While other actresses might have been overwhelmed at sharing a lead role with the world's number one film star, she always remained cool and detached."

j.johnston@mirror.co.uk

TRUE LOVE: Virginie's heart is with 40-year-old Louis

FAKED LOVE: Her passionate scene with 25-year-old Leo

permissiveness, lies the assertion of a conventional moral code that prioritises commitment either in marriage, or here, in a long-standing relationship. In the end there emerges a fascinating tension – between the unreality of the central event (the film's 'passionate scene' which was not even passionate) and the conventions of journalism (the narrative structure, sourcing, 'balance') which are ultimately striving to represent a real world.

There are five thematic sections:

* *Section 1: pars 1–11*: 'mature' Virginie (her name tantalisingly close to 'virgin') finds DiCaprio cold in the sex scene on the set and is not turned on by him; she pines only for her current 'man' (intriguingly carrying the name 'Saint').
* *Section 2: pars 12–13*: Leonardo's views.
* *Section 3: pars 14–16*: Virginie and the men in her life.
* *Section 4: pars 17–22*: biographical background to Virginie, stressing her 'maturity'.
* *Section 5: pars 23–end*: comments of Danny Boyle on Virginie reinforcing theme of 'maturity'.

* *Par. 1*: just 15 words, the piece constantly plays on contrasts: here Virginie turns her back on Leonardo – but strides towards us. The alliteration in 'Hollywood's hottest heart-throb' adds extras emphasis at the end of the par.
* *Par. 2*: again just 22 words – the contrast between the 'passionate love scene' and Virginie being left 'cold'.
* *Par. 3*: here the central theme contrasting the 'maturity' of Virginie's 'man' (Louis Saint Calbre) and Virginie herself and their steady relationship with boy Leo (who symbolises illicit, immature sex) emerges. 'While waves lapped at their sun-bronzed bodies and their lips met in a salty kiss' has the feel of a Mills and Boon romance – but this romantic mood is quickly shattered.
* *Par. 4*: Leo's immaturity is confirmed by his looks: he's 'baby-faced' while, in contrast, Virginie's conventional credentials are confirmed: she can barely (a contrived pun) wait to rush home to her man. Similarly the two small inset pictures (to the left of Virginie) contrast Louis's 'true love' with the 'faked love' of DiCaprio.
* *Par. 5*: Louis's maturity is reaffirmed.
* *Par. 6*: DiCaprio well and truly debunked: he's described simply as a 'pale young American', not at all sexually attractive.
* *Pars 7–11*: the long direct quote seeks to add a note of authenticity to the story (for if she is being reported accurately, then the story must be real). First there is the contrast between friends and lovers (which they never became). The emphasis all the time is on the sex ('love scene', 'physical pleasure', 'kissed Leonardo', 'kissing in the sea') but the paradox is that none of it was a 'turn on'.
* *Pars 12–13*: Leonardo confirms the central line of the story (and so it must be true, real, it seems to be arguing again) and describes Virginie as 'a very sophisticated European lady'. The phrase 'failed to make the ocean roar' continues the 'sea' and 'beach' themes.

- *Pars 14–17*: Virginie has also been linked to a Paris lawyer. A 'friend' is needed to reaffirm her moral credentials.

- *Pars 18–22*: brief biography reaffirms her 'maturity': she is already a film 'veteran'. The direct quote adds a feeling of authenticity and immediacy.

- *Pars 23–24*: after the story has dwelt on the past Danny Boyle now predicts a 'great future' for Virginie. Above all he praises her for resisting the sexual allure of the heart-throb; amidst all the potential sexual heat of the beach she remained 'cool'.

8 More news assignments

Meetings, press conferences, reports, speeches and eye-witness reporting

Meeting the challenge: REPORTING MEETINGS AND CONFERENCES

Everyday there are thousands of meetings throughout Britain. Many are private, many are open to the public, but only a few are covered by the press. An underlying news value system operates to determine which meetings are covered, which are ignored. Some meetings, such as those of parliament, local councils and their various committees, occur on a regular basis and are covered routinely. Details are logged in news desk diaries and they are often covered by specialists. Many peace organisations (focusing on nuclear weapons, Iraq, Kosovo or East Timor) hold regular public meetings (and occasional conferences) throughout the UK but these are not usually covered on any routine basis, given their relatively low status in traditional news values.

In addition, there are meetings and conferences which are private but to which the press is invited. The CBI may hold a conference on building European exports, the Trades Union Congress (TUC) may call a meeting on developing European solidarity in the age of the internet. Unions, campaigning bodies, charities and professional associations may hold their annual conferences. All these events can provide a rich source of news to the press.

Be prepared: a useful journalist motto

The issues to be covered, the background of the speakers, the views of the organisers: these are some of the areas worth looking into before attendance. If the meeting is focusing on a running issue, the cuttings should be consulted. Because you are not faced with the demands of confronting a source face to face, as in an interview, there is a danger in thinking you can bluster through a meeting without any serious preparation. But just as with an interview, you could be confronted with some major issue you might be unprepared to tackle. Your note is untidy, you don't follow the subtleties of the debate, so a news angle goes missing or is carried inaccurately.

All that said, news-making is a hectic business and preparation is not always possible. General reporters can be assigned by their news desk to cover a meeting at short notice. They have a lot of rapid thinking to do. Practice certainly helps here.

So does constant immersion in the news. If the meeting or conference is considered of major importance, a backgrounder or advance story may be written highlighting the issues, personalities, any power struggles and possible decisions and outcomes.

Meeting stategies

Reporting strategies will depend on the length and news quality of the meeting. Covering all-day meetings and three-day conferences can be exhausting, given the degree of concentration required over such a period. Journalists may elect to cover all the contributions. Otherwise they may choose those they consider the most important and make inquiries about the others to make sure nothing was missed. If the meeting lasts more than three hours, a reporter on a daily will tend to leave it for certain periods while they alert the news desk over developments and send over copy for specific editions. An evening meeting lasting, say, two hours is generally covered from start to finish.

Never feel obliged to cover all the speakers in your copy. A small local paper, acting as the 'journal of record', might routinely cover all the speakers irrespective of news value. But then journalism is in danger of turning into a form of PR (for which, it might be argued, there is a place in small communities). Your news desk is likely to have briefed you over the kind of wordage required. If the story turns out to be worth far more or far less you should argue your case. If there is no hard news (mere platitudes, rhetoric or esoteric waffle) you should not feel obliged to provide any coverage.

Similarly, never feel obliged to cover the speakers chronologically. A report of a meeting by a non-journalist often begins with the first speaker and 'concludes' with the last. News values tends to subvert chronology. The most important point in your intro might emerge from the last words spoken. It might come from a brief aside. Never feel obliged to reproduce the priorities of the organisers or speakers. Some 95 per cent of a speech may be devoted to some un-newsworthy topic. You might consider just 1 per cent newsworthy. That 1 per cent may be the focus for your copy, the rest could be eliminated altogether.

The most newsworthy item may come from the floor rather than the platform or in response to a question from the floor. In this case, it is worth trying to contact that person to check the spelling of their names and their title. Sometimes it is difficult to hear a speaker from the floor, so go up to them afterwards to check any quote and maybe get more information and views from them. Some of the most difficult meetings to cover are those when the speeches are funny. You are tempted to sit back and enjoy it rather than engage in the mundane task of recording the joke. Your body tends to shake in laughter which adds to the note-taking problems. Incorporating the joke in a hard news story (which, by definition, is an 'unfunny' genre) is stylistically difficult too. One solution is to 'soften' the story carrying a witty, light tone throughout. Another is to carry the main report as straight hard news and contribute a second, wittier story to an existing diary column or a special one created for the event.

Responses from the audience are always worth noting. Including references such as 'was greeted with laughter/boos/jeers/applause/silence' adds a small but telling 'eye-witness' dimension to your copy. Even the dullest meeting or conference can be useful to the reporter. Contacts can be made, ideas for follow-up stories can emerge. National conferences can draw people from all over the UK. Someone from the other end of the country may talk to you and reveal a wonderful story you would otherwise have missed. Afterwards you will follow it up.

'Dullness', in any case, is a subjective notion. What is dull to you may be fascinating to someone else. One of the many challenges for a journalist is to report the 'dull' in an interesting way. Many public meetings contain informal discussion rather than set-piece speeches. Often a more 'feature-ish' approach is suited to this event where you may incorporate some comment and descriptive elements. While the meeting itself may not produce hard copy, a talk with one or more of the participants afterwards might.

After the meeting

Many meetings covered in the press are never attended by the reporter. The spread of 'phone journalism' (and increasingly email journalism) means they are often simply 'picked up'. A journalist will contact either one or more people present for their account of the decisions made and for their views on any possible consequences. They may follow-up a press release. Or a reporter may compile a retrospective, looking back at the meeting/conference or write an opinionated feature on the meeting and its implications.

Events or pseudo-events: COVERING PRESS CONFERENCES

Press conferences often provide important sources of news for journalists. They are useful for both the organisers and the journalist. For the organisation it marks an attempt to influence the news agenda. Journalists will be given a chance to look in depth at issues from the perspective of the organisation and to meet some of their important representatives. For the journalist, the event can provide the basis for a news report, for gathering background information, for developing contacts.

Organisations tend to send out press conference details three or four weeks in advance. If the news editor considers it possibly worth attending details will be noted in the diary for the day. Any accompanying literature, for instance, contact numbers and names will be filed. If there is likely to be a photo-opportunity ('pic op') linked to the event, the picture desk will be notified. Organisations often contact the newspaper again by telephone a few days before the event as a reminder. They can also send a press release (embargoed until after the likely end of the conference) giving an account of the event as if it had already occurred but not enough information to discourage journalists from attending.

When you arrive at the conference venue you are usually asked to add your name and that of your newspaper (or to indicate freelance) to a list. You may be given an agenda and a badge to identify yourself when meeting others afterwards. Transcripts of one or more of the speeches to be made and other background information on the organisation and relevant issues may be provided. It is important to compare the transcript with the actual speech. Occasionally small changes appear and there can be a story behind those alterations. For instance, there may have been a last-minute compromise to delete or amend some controversial statements or proposals. Equally, non-scripted asides can provide the most interesting quotes and angles.

It is important to establish, soon after arriving, the names, spellings and titles of the people on any panel. Contributions can often move rapidly among the speakers and without notes giving attributions to the various quotes clearly, writing a story afterwards can prove nightmarish. When a striking, intro-worthy quote or fact emerges, ring or star it to help identification later on. Conferences usually begin on time or just five minutes late so it is important to arrive on time. In any case, it reflects badly on your paper if you arrive late.

An organisation may spend most of the conference on an issue it considers important but which the journalist may regard as only marginally newsworthy. For instance, an organisation may use the press conference to spell out its '14-point charter for green consumerism'. A passing comment by a speaker may be more newsworthy. A prominent environmentalist may claim that a BBC documentary the previous night had 'seriously misrepresented the environmentalists' case' and that her organisation was planning to protest to the corporation. That angle may then dominate the intro with reference to the 14-point plan coming later or eliminated altogether.

Question of questions

It is often important to raise questions, particularly if you think later opportunities will be denied you. Perhaps an important source has indicated they will have to leave immediately after their contribution. Sometimes journalists, as a pack, co-ordinate on a series of questions to extract particularly complex and sensitive information. Sometimes they will swap around ideas for angles and quotes afterwards. When questions are asked out loud, it becomes difficult for the journalist to identify an 'exclusive' angle. Press conferences can promote a culture in which conformist, consensual news reporting is accepted too uncritically.

On many occasions, the most important part of the press conference for the reporter is during the informal questioning afterwards. This provides the chance for following up individual angles and delving into an issue more deeply. It provides the reporter with a chance to check details, quotes and spellings. Never feel embarrassed to ask for clarification of a complicated point. Better to get it right than botched up. Ideas for further follow-ups and contacts can emerge from these informal meetings. In addition to the speakers, other people from the organisation often attend who can provide useful sources of information.

Different circumstances will demand different strategies on handling the notebook or dictaphone during this informal period. Sometimes you will approach with your notebook and pen clearly visible. At other times it will be more appropriate to chat on in a relaxed way perhaps with a drink in one hand but aiming to remember everything said and only after a time bringing out your notebook or dictaphone (if at all).

Stage-management and manipulation

All press conferences should be treated carefully. Sociologists have called them the archetypal 'pseudo' news event (Boorstin 1962). It is not a 'real' event like a football match, a car accident or a court case. It is artificially contrived, aimed at gaining publicity. It has no status other than in relation to the media coverage it is seeking. An organisation calling one has a message to sell. It has gone to the trouble of sending out the details to the press, maybe booking a room, laying on drinks (and sometimes a meal) for journalists. It expects something in return. Namely publicity and preferably good publicity.

There is a danger that journalists will be used as glorified PR officers for the organisation. Press conferences are attempts to stage-manage the news. Since they are tightly managed affairs you should be thinking all the time: what are they trying to tell me and, more importantly, what are they trying to prevent me from knowing? The experience of the Australian war correspondent Wilfred Burchett is pertinent here (Kiernan 1986). At the end of the Second World War, following the bombing of Hiroshima and Nagasaki, 600 allied journalists covered the official Japanese surrender aboard the battleship *Missouri*. Only Burchett subverted the dominant news values and went, with great difficulty and courage, to Hiroshima. From there, he filed one of the most famous scoops of all times. His description of the devastation of the Japanese city after the nuclear bombing and the suffering and dying of people from radiation sickness was carried in the *Daily Express* of 5 September 1945 under the headline: 'The atomic plague: I write this as a warning to the world'. His reporting of radiation sickness was to be ferociously denied by the Allies for years afterwards. But he was right about radiation sickness – and right to report it (Burchett 1983).

Reporting reports

Reports constitute an important source for news stories and features. They can appear in book or leaflet form, as press releases, in specialist journal articles or in the agenda papers or minutes of meetings. Their value comes from the deep research which normally underpins them. Reports from such bodies as Shelter, the International Institute for Strategic Studies, Amnesty International, the Joseph Rowntree Foundation, Low Pay Unit, Child Poverty Action Group, Oxfam and other prominent charities provide a body of 'authoritative' details which journalists can use as the basis for their articles. Reports with a national focus will also provide opportunities for local follow-ups. They will usually argue a case or come to come conclusions which can lead to recommendations for action. These provide good copy. The reporter will aim to highlight the most important finding, conclusion or recommendation from the report in the intro and attribute it clearly to the source.

For instance, *The Times* (8 November 1999) introed: ·

> Smokers stand fewer chances of getting jobs because more employers discriminate against them, Forest, the smokers' rights group, claims.
>
> More than 300 companies advertising for staff in newspapers from January to August specified smoking as an issue. Some stated that only non-smokers should apply, says a report, *Smoking: The New Apartheid*, published by Forest today.

On the same day, the *Guardian* reported:

> An American study shatters the hopes of what feminism has sought to achieve and bleakly concludes that women are not yet free from oppression.
>
> The study, published by the American Psychological Association, pours cold water on the notion that girl power can put women in charge of their own destiny.

> It found that despite all the achievements of feminism over 30 years, women are still failing to control their lives.

Conventional reporting routines are followed. Both reports attribute clearly in the intro: in the first through the phrase 'Forest, the smokers' rights group, claims', in the second through the opening 'An American study shatters'. To avoid overloading the intro with details, the first story delays mention of the precise title until the second par.; the *Guardian* also delays naming the source, the American Psychological Association, until the second par. The first provides a straight, uncommenty intro; the second begins by making a general comment ('An American study shatters the hopes of what feminism sought to achieve') before settling on a general but striking conclusion drawn from the report ('women are not yet free from oppression'). Note that the most striking views from reports can be covered in direct speech; other important views and details can be summarised in reported speech.

Press conferences

Press conferences can accompany the publishing of reports. These provide journalists with the chance to 'humanise' their coverage, presenting views through the voices of spokespeople as well as the impersonal report. Background details can also be established. When press conferences are not held, reporters often ring up the writers for comments. In all cases they might contact others for follow-up responses. Publication details should always accompany reports, but normally they don't in the mainstream press (though websites may provide useful links to the publishers). In contrast, the monthly newsletter *Nonviolent Action* carries contact details at the foot of all articles, since it sees itself essentially as a political, campaigning, educational tool inspiring participation rather than just passive consumption of the news.

Reactions to reports

Reactions to reports are usually worth following up and can provide lively intro copy, as here in the *Daily Telegraph* (12 April 2000):

> Hairdressers reacted angrily yesterday to the Government's suggestion that girls should be discouraged, through assertiveness training at school, from turning to a career in the salon.
>
> Hundreds of them contacted their trade associations to complain about a Cabinet Office report on teenagers that expressed concern that young girls were being pressured to go into 'female' employment 'such as hairdressing, care work, health care' instead of engineering and other skilled careers.

Analysis of 'Jackpot winners are moaning lott':
Daily Star (15 November 1999)

Jackpot winners are moaning lott

By Thomas Harding

ONLY HALF those who win massive National Lottery prizes are happy, a survey revealed yesterday.

A study of millionaires found the win has made them fat slobs who quit work just to stay at home. Lottery operator Camelot released the findings as the game celebrates its fifth birthday this week with a £20 million superdraw on Saturday.

The findings show that 75 per cent of millionaire winners quit their jobs but very few take up new hobbies and can't be bothered to go to health clubs, despite having heaps of dough and spare time to spend it in.

A third of winners have piled on pounds of weight as well as in the bank and their lives are so dull that 91 per cent still play the weekly lottery. And only four out of ten stump up cash for charities.

The Mori survey of 249 players, which included 111 who scooped more than £1 million, also shows blokes give away more cash than women.

Just 55 per cent of winners were 'happy' since hitting the jackpot. Almost 10 per cent of marriages have broken down. Best friends still remain pals with winners, with men giving money, on average, £170,000 to three mates and women just giving to one pal, averaging £60,000.

Scots and Northerners were the most generous, followed by Midlanders and then Southerners who gave away a measly £17,000 to pals. But one unnamed winner has given away £3million. Half of £2 million winners remain in their original homes, but those who do move want to distance themselves from their former lives by buying country mansions.

Since its launch five years ago the lottery has created 866 millionaires and raised £7.5 billion for good causes.

One player scooped the £6,240,358 jackpot on Saturday with the numbers 7,10,21,28,29 and 39. The bonus ball was 2.

There is little punning in the copy, surprisingly so. The headline attempts a pun (though it is an exceptionally contrived one). The sentence lengths are typical of a red-top tabloid in being generally short: 15 words, 20, 22, 41, 31, 11, 23, 12, 9, 26, 21, 8, 26, 19, 18, 5. Very few sentences carry subordinate clauses.

The language is (typically for a red-top tabloid) often based on slang and vernacular: such as 'fat slobs', 'can't be bothered', 'heaps of dough', 'stump up cash', 'blokes', 'pal', 'mates', 'measly'. (Other tabloid variants are 'yobs'/'brutes'/'thugs' for 'soccer hooligans'; 'cops' for 'police officers'; 'boozing' for 'drinking beer'; 'aggro' for 'commotion'; 'boss' for 'manager'; 'blasted' for 'criticised'; 'mum' for 'mother'; 'cock-up' for 'mistake'; 'our boys' for 'British soldiers'.)

- *Par. 1*: a bit of journalistic licence here. Most of us, who have not won the lottery, secretly want to know that winning a million cannot automatically bring happiness (whatever that may be). We want to be reassured that our lifestyles are OK. Later in the copy, it is said that 55 per cent of winners feel 'happier'. In other words, more than half. But that is not what the reporter wants us to be told. And so he has averaged the figure down and begun with the qualifying word 'only'. Notice the clear attribution phrase 'a survey revealed yesterday' following news reporting conventions.

- *Par. 2*: focuses on the striking 'fat slobs' angle and then gives background on the survey (accompanying the fifth anniversary of the Lottery's launch).

- *Par. 3–4*: the 'fat slobs' angle is revealed as weak and unnecessarily contrived. Only a third 'have piled on weight' so it was wrong to exaggerate this statistic. Better to have cut the 'fat slobs' sentence and replaced it with par. 4 which provides the precise details. This par. also contains the text's only pun ('piled on pounds of weight as well as in the bank') though it is rather contrived.

- *Par. 5*: clear focus on precise details. Then shifts to the 'charity' angle, concentrating first on the gender distinctions. This is developed at the end of the next par. (with men giving on average £170,000 to three friends and women giving £60,000 to one). But ideally these details should have followed immediately after the reference to this in par. 5 and not been separated.

- *Par. 6*: the evidence to support the intro finally appears. 'Just' aims to deflate that figure as well as usefully drawing the number away from the start of the par.

- *Par. 7*: focus on regional differences in the charity stakes – particularly interesting for a newspaper with national circulation.

- *Par. 8*: background details. Unnecessary repetition of five years; we were told about the 'fifth birthday' in par. 2.

- *Par. 9*: wrap up providing Saturday's results.

Covering speeches

A speech constitutes a perfect event for news coverage: it has a tidy beginning, middle and end. A chosen speech will usually provide some copy so attendance makes economic sense. A complex and controversial issue may be usefully simplified through the voice of one person. The war in Kosovo in 1999 had its roots deep within the military and industrial complex of the US and UK and in the local animosities which followed the break-up of the former Yugoslav republic. A report of a speech on the conflict by a celebrity, peace campaigner or politician provided a focus for news coverage, reducing the complexities to a comprehensible event rooted in the 'now' of news.

Many covered speeches are not attended by the press. Publicity departments (of political parties, companies, campaigning organisations and the government, for example) distribute a regular supply of press releases (increasingly through email and over the internet) giving verbatim or edited accounts of speeches. A journalist attending a speech will often, then, attempt to incorporate some 'eye-witness' element to indicate their presence. They may report the responses of the audience or the mood of the speaker. They may place a dictaphone close to the speaker but this should never be entirely relied on. Problems can follow. Always back up with a written note, perhaps starring quotes which stand out as particularly newsy, interesting and maybe even worth following up.

A report will tend to combine reported speech with direct quotes, these being reserved for the most colourful expressions of opinion. As the story progresses extracts from the speech will decrease in news value; brief background details, comment, analysis and colour will be slotted in where relevant. Take these opening pars from the *Cambridge Evening News* (20 November 1999):

Graffiti heighten people's fears

VANDALISM AND GRAFFITI heighten people's fear of crime, Home Secretary Jack Straw was expected to say in his speech to a neighbourhood watch conference today.

Mr Straw was set to tell the annual National Neighbourhood Watch Association conference in London: "For some people anti-social behaviour, graffiti, vandalism and litter are an aggravating fact of urban living – a necessary evil to be reluctantly tolerated.

"But for many – particularly the elderly and vulnerable – it can heighten their fear of crime."

The newspaper has received an advance press release (clearly without an embargo) on the Home Secretary's speech and decided to run the account before the event. It comes from an elite source and focuses on an issue of major interest to the media: law and order. It was a Saturday, so a relatively quiet news day, and by the next publication day, Monday, the speech would have become 'old'. Coverage has, consequently, to be careful. The intro focuses concisely on the most newsworthy claim, attributes it clearly to Jack Straw and then follows with the 'where' (at a 'neighbourhood watch conference') and the 'when'. Only the 'was expected to say' appears somewhat convoluted. Notice the reporter writes 'was expected' and 'was set to tell' rather than 'is expected' and 'is set to tell'. Take this report from the *Newmarket Journal* (11 November 1999).

MP warns of alarming rise in drug abuse

By Ellee Seymour

DRUG ABUSE in Suffolk has risen dramatically, MP Richard Spring has claimed. He says the number of drug-users seeking care in the county rose by a staggering 35 per cent over the past year.

Mr Spring is patron of Adfam (Suffolk), which supports families of drug-users, and issued his warning at the group's annual meeting in Ipswich on Friday.

He said the figure continues to rise alarmingly, with a greater percentage moving towards harder and more dangerous drugs.

The number of 25-year-olds using heroin rose by 24 per cent over the past year, compared to the previous year.

"Two lethal drugs, heroin and cocaine, are growing in usage in Suffolk," warned the West Suffolk MP.

"Young Britons are more likely to use hallucinogens and amphetamines and be solvent abusers," he said. "Additionally, one third of British teenagers regularly smoke cannabis.

"This is no longer simply an urban problem. Substance misuse is growing everywhere. For families it can be extremely difficult."

Mr Spring, who founded the Newmarket Substance Misuse Group, said that the number of 15–16-year-old Britons experimenting with Ecstasy was three times higher than their French and German counterparts.

"We can only resolve this problem if everybody pulls together. That is what is happening with the countywide Drug Action team under Suffolk Health," he said.

"We have a national drugs strategy which can work. A similar strategy did succeed in reducing drugs misuse in the United States."

- *Par. 1*: all sentences and pars are kept concise. Clear opening focus on drug story, with local angle stressed and attribution to strong local source. Adverb 'dramatically' gives extra impact to intro. Note that 'said' not normally used to convey attribution in intros. It is too dull. Here 'claimed' is used. No specific 'when' or 'where' elements.

- *Par. 2*: following conventional routines, development of intro. Local angle reinforced with adjective 'staggering' carrying impact while 35 per cent is strong specific detail. Present tense ('he says') used to convey immediacy (though changing verb tenses from 'has claimed'; 'says' and 'said' in the story is best avoided).

- *Par. 3*: more background facts on the main source, with the 'where' and 'when' details delayed from the intro appearing now. (Mentioning 'Friday' in the intro would have dated the story and so reduced its impact.)

- *Par. 4*: the section 'He said the figure continues to rise dramatically' is a repetition of the intro (and following conventional reported speech rules it should be 'continued'). The reference to 'harder and more dangerous drugs' is strong.

- *Par. 5*: good details supporting the 'alarming increase' theme. Following reported speech rules should strictly be 'had risen'.

- *Par. 6*: three par. direct quote begins here (keeping to reported speech throughout would have been deadly dull) with clear spotlight on heroin and cocaine. Title of main source delayed until here (and avoids repeating 'Mr Spring' or 'he').

- *Par. 7*: strong, fact-based quote continues.

- *Par. 8*: quote continues with clear focus on 'non-urban' and 'families' angles.

- *Par. 9*: more relevant background details on main source while quote in reported speech adds interesting European angle.

- *Par. 10*: rousing call for 'everyone to pull together' with local angle stressed.

- *Par. 11*: ends on deliberate note of optimism.

Local newspapers sometimes follow up speeches made in private meetings. For instance, the *Newark Advertiser* (24 December 1999) led on a story about the Conservative prospective candidate, Patrick Merver, calling for a review of the medical benefits of cannabis. He had made the comments first during a debate at the Minster School, Southwell; reporter James Kelly later interviewed Mercer, giving him the space to expand on his argument.

All in the eye of the beholder:
EYE-WITNESS REPORTING

Journalists are the observers of history. When the Berlin Wall falls, they are there describing the tumultuous events. When the Americans invade Grenada (in 1983) and ban journalists from the island, the brave ones take to boats in an attempt to evade the censorship regime and see the attacks at first hand. More mundanely, a local journalist attends a football match and reports what he or she sees. The 'eye-witness' dimension (also known as 'direct observation') is one of the crucial distinguishing features of journalism. But it can become a cliché with the eye-witness journalist failing to explore the deeper underlying factors behind the events.

Reporters cannot possibly witness all the events they report. They have to rely on others for accounts. Editorial cutbacks of recent years have further reduced the eye-witness element in the news. Meetings, for instance, are often no longer attended but 'picked up' afterwards or handled on the basis of press releases. But when reporters are present at significant events, that witnessing can be used to dramatic effect, providing an immediacy, a 'human interest' and an appearance of authenticity to copy. Even a straight report of a meeting can be enlivened by the inclusion of an eye-witness element such as descriptions of participants' appearance, accounts of questions from the floor and responses from the audience. Take these opening pars by columnist Matthew Parris in *The Times*:

Analysis of 'Portillo hunting party targets early birds': *The Times* (24 November 1999)

HALF PAST SEVEN in the morning is no time to be out on the streets of Kensington and Chelsea. The first grey light was lifting over the smart rooftops, Entry-phone gates and magnolia trees as your shivering sketch-writer awaited the arrival of Michael Portillo's campaigning hit-squad for a dawn blitz on Holland Park Tube Station. Will these Portillo desperados stop at nothing?

By 7.45 – Outrage still abed – eager Tories were mustered, assembling piles of blue leaflets, bearing smiling snapshots of the great man and anchoring little flotillas of blue balloons to their sleeves. The youngest of these strange creatures sported only stubble on his head. "Shaved it for charity," he confessed. "Last week I was bald." The biggest Portillista wore a green waxed-cotton coat and curious felt hat. "Trilby or what?" I asked.

"I go shooting in it."

But his quarry today were unfeathered: the voters. And these birds were shy. Until El Numero Uno arrived, no commuter had been successfully apprehended.

"He's coming," hissed an excited Portillista. Down the pavement from Notting Hill steamed a lone Portillo, at a cracking pace. "Morning everyone," he growled sternly in his big Daddy Bear voice, readying himself to press the flesh by the station door. I slunk behind to overhear. Portillo has a massive neck. People kept slipping by, unapprehended.

Commuters were mostly a mixture of Filipino maidservants (baffled by Portillo's outstretched hand), hungover construction workers hiding beneath hard hats and the occasional expensive Suit, coat and scarf (who invariably turned out to be a Member of the Kensington and Chelsea Conservative Association already). "Where are you going," boomed the Candidate at a group of little boys in school uniforms. They gave him a withering glance.

- *Par. 1*: present tense used in first sentence to convey immediacy. But then the device is suddenly dropped ('was lifting') for no apparent reason. News is rooted in time and here Parris begins firmly by stating the precise time. Perhaps he betrays his privileged social position (and that of his readers whose sympathies he is trying to capture) by stressing immediately the 'ordeal' involved in getting up so early. For many (such as the 'construction workers' and 'Filipino maidservants' he notices later on) it is the normal time to be out in the streets. Then precise observations ('grey light . . . over the smart rooftops, Entry-phone gates and magnolia trees') set the scene. Again, Parris makes an appeal for his readers' sympathies addressing us intimately as 'your shivering sketchwriter'. And then comes the news angle: Michael Portillo, just elected as Tory candidate after a period in the political wilderness (and later to be William Hague's deputy) is due to join a group of Tory supporters campaigning outside a tube station. But Parris (somewhat unimaginatively) fixes on the biggest cliché of all (relating to war and violence) and describes the Tory group as a 'hit squad' preparing for a 'dawn blitz'.

There is an ironic, humorous tone here and throughout but at root, there is no biting political critique; it is all too friendly. Irony becomes a part of a strategy to help distance the writer from his sources. But it appears inauthentic and over-contrived. Parris (a former Tory MP) is like a court jester to Parliament and politicians: making fun of them, mocking them sometimes, but (with the mass media closely linked through economic ties to the dominant elite) always from a safe, insider position. Finally he calls the Tory faithful 'Portillo desperados'.

- *Par. 2*: there is almost a poetic feel to this text focusing on precise observations: 'abed', 'eager Tories', 'mustered', 'assembling', 'bearing smiling snapshots', 'anchoring little flotillas' is language untypical of traditional news coverage. Repetition of 'blue' stresses the Toryism of the event while 'great man' continues the ironic tone of the intro. His eye then focuses, in typical journalistic fashion, on the unusual: a man with just stubble on his head. 'Strange creatures' continues the leg-pulling tone, but how come he knew this chap to be the youngest? Did Parris ask him his age? If he did, why didn't he include it? Perhaps it was a piece of journalistic licence, aiming simply to brighten up still further the copy with a superlative. The short and snappy sentences in the dialogue add to its humour and impact. Then, striving hard for literary effect he invents the word 'Portillista' (to mean a female supporter of Portillo). Again, the dialogue helps convey the eccentricity of those present which the writer is at pains to stress.

- *Par. 3*: short, sharp quote varies the rhythm of the piece – and thus its overall interest. As his eye shifts, so does the rhythm of the text.

- *Par. 4*: to help the text flow, the copy builds on the shooting reference in the previous par. (with 'quarry', 'unfeathered', 'birds'). The cognoscenti will know that Portillo's father is Spanish – and the Spanish theme (begun with 'Portillista') continues with El Numero Uno, while 'apprehended' attempts ironically to compare the campaigning Tories to over-eager police officers. He mocks their lack of success.

- *Par. 5*: the over-contrived 'literary' feel to this text emerges with the use of 'hissed' here (and later on 'growled sternly'). A simple 'said' would have been inadequate: just as is later 'shaking hands'. It has to be 'press the flesh'. Similarly there is a deliberate emphasis on alliteration with 'Portillista', 'pavement', 'Portillo', 'pace'. And notice how most nouns have to be accompanied by adjectives. Portillo is transformed into 'Daddy Bear' (since bears growl) but that theme is neither anticipated – nor developed. Our intrepid reporter slinks (bear-fashion) behind the great man and notices the thickness of his neck. That's an unusual observation which works well here. The mocking of the Tories' canvassing failures continues.

- *Par. 6*: observations on the kinds of folk around early in the morning (even the Suits turn out to be Tory faithfuls). Again an over-contrived emphasis on alliteration with 'hungover construction workers hiding beneath hard hats'. 'Boomed' aims to mock the great man for his pretensions (as does the capitalising of Candidate). The contempt shown him by the 'little boys' mirrors the contempt felt by the writer. But how authentic is that contempt?

9 Powerful information

Reporting national and local government

John Turner

Politics is about power and information is power. Journalists are part of the information business and are crucial in a political process which involves the exercise of this potent force. People with power, whether they be Cabinet ministers, senior civil servants or chief executives of local councils, have a vested interest, not only in protecting their own power, buy also in obscuring the extent of their authority in the first place. The journalist occupies a pivotal position between those who make and implement important decisions and those who are often forced to comply with such decisions. Any democratic system depends on people being well informed and educated about politics by a media which give a full and accurate account of news, encompassing a wide and varied range of political opinions.

The media in general have a large and growing significance on politics. However, there is unclear evidence regarding the nature and extent of this influence. The political impact of the media, and the press in particular, is difficult to assess for various reasons:

- It is difficult to isolate the effect of the media from other influences like family, education, work and economic circumstances.
- There is a complex myriad of mutually influencing factors which complicate the relationship between newspaper and reader. The political impact of a paper will depend less on what is being read than on who is doing the reading and their level of knowledge and experience about politics in general.
- The media are fragmented, with television, radio and the national press having different effects compared with local coverage. A direct relationship between any media's influence on a political issue is therefore confused.
- Similar messages are received and interpreted in different ways by different people, hence a claim that the media are being used for propaganda purposes cannot be verified because one cannot be sure of the effect intended.

Before turning to aspects of local and national politics, it is important briefly to outline three ways in which the impact of the media has been assessed.

- *Agenda-setting and primary definers*: here the media are accused less of telling people what to believe, than in providing a more pervasive influence on what people think about and how they make judgements about different issues Agenda-setting involves a constant interaction between a newspaper and its readers. Newspapers also tend to take on board sources of information which control and establish initial definitions of particular issues. As such, a great deal of news coverage reflects the interpretations initially created by official sources.

- *Reinforcement and hegemony*: here the media are not so much creating attitudes but are involved in strengthening and reinforcing existing beliefs and prejudices. This can be linked to the notion of hegemony whereby consent is sought for those ways of making sense of the world which fit with the perspective of those in power

- *Independent effects*: there is a growing view that the media have a more direct and independent effect on beliefs and behaviour. Again evidence for such a view remains controversial. New media technologies have as much of an influence on attitudes and behaviour as the uses to which they are put.

Newton (1986) has pointed to a paradox in the media's impact on political awareness. Whereas political information is delivered faster to more people, nevertheless the mass tabloids contain only a little political content and what they report is personalised, trivialised, sensationalised and biased. Consequently, a large proportion of the public is provided with restricted news and knowledge of current affairs. This contradiction has been discussed by Seymour-Ure (1974) in his distinction of levels of readership between a mass public and informed political public. An information gap has been created with a small, well-educated public who use the media to become better informed and a mass public who mainly read gossip columns and sports pages and are therefore more readily influenced by biased news.

Local papers do not work in a vacuum. They are as much a part of the political system and process as anyone, and journalists working for them have assumptions about the way in which the political system operates. There is far less of a division between local and national politics today. Local government has increasingly become simply an arm of central administration and, as in the case of education policy, it is difficult to disentangle separate national and local agendas. Equally, there is nothing inherently local about local newspapers. Much of what is considered to be national news is local in nature and source. Indeed, Britain's tradition of a dominant national press has imposed a kind of artificial parochialism on the local press which has led to a number of criticisms about the rather narrow way in which local papers have covered local politics. The homogeneous and national nature of the British political system and political culture must not be underestimated in this respect. They have had an import tent effect on the way in which politics is reported by the local press.

The British political system

Previous studies of the British political system have pointed to its strong civic, culture, supported by a stable and cohesive system of politics (Almond and Verba 1963; Rose 1965). Power in Britain is centralised and, according to the traditional view, is concentrated in the Cabinet in Parliament and Whitehall, supported by political conventions, the cohesiveness of political parties, Treasury control, ministerial responsibility and the Crown prerogative. This strong and cohesive model of British government has been accentuated by a period of prime ministerial dominance, without the safeguards of accountability which might be imposed by a Bill of Rights or Freedom of Information Act. Before considering aspects of these institutions it is important to consider the underpinning nature of Britain's political culture.

The culture of deference

Deference and tradition

People in Britain have a remarkably deferential attitude towards the dominant political institutions (Kavanagh 1983). An appeal to tradition is used as a way of defending many of the institutions which have become a stable part of the political system. The monarchy, the House of Lords, the dominant role of the Prime Minister and pervasive secrecy are the ingredients of a political culture which has not been up-ended by revolution or war. Leigh (1980) has referred to the system as a huge mountain with abandoned monuments, with some still powerful and others forgotten. An example is the role of the royal prerogative. It is no longer abused by monarchical power but has been transferred to the hands of the Prime Minister and executive. Before MPs protested in 1993, the government considered denying Parliament the right to vote on the Maastricht Treaty. The Prime Minister's press office attempted to argue that under the Crown prerogative such treaties did not need the vote of Parliament, but could be ratified by the Prime Minister on behalf of the Crown.

Political participation

Such deference has made Britain a relatively law-abiding country. There is a general respect for authority and the law which complements a low level of political participation. Many social scientists were surprised that there were not greater social disturbances as a result of mass unemployment in the 1980s. Some 75 per cent vote in general elections, the figure falling to around 50 per cent for local elections. However, only about 5 per cent are members of a political party, with only about 2 per cent becoming party activists.

Centralisation and concentration of power

In Britain's unitary system of government decision-making power has been highly and centralised. Parliament, government, the administration, law courts, major companies and the BBC are all based in central London. Given the lack of a written constitution, save European law which Britain has had to sign up to as a member of the EU, Britain has failed to develop any notion of federal-style government. Therefore local government does not have the type of autonomy and independent powers which states have in the United States or Germany. Local government is controlled from the centre reinforced by party politics, which is similarly controlled from the centre. However, since 1997 we have seen the emergence of a Scottish Parliament, Welsh Assembly and a mayoral government in London. These innovations have increased, rather than assuaged, further demands for regional government in Britain.

Politics at the periphery

There has always been a tension between local government's administrative and political roles. Central government of whatever party has always safeguarded its powers to change politics at the periphery and determine the nature of service delivery. This has involved the abolition of significant parts of the local government system, like the Greater London Council (GLC) and metropolitan authorities; the reorganisation of the local taxation system, the reform of the management and operation of councils and the type of services which they can and cannot deliver. In 1986 the Widdicombe report warned of the increasing politicisation of local government which led to an unprecedented period of reorganisation. This process of permanent revolution has continued more recently under New Labour.

Supranational politics

The European Union now has a fundamental influence on the politics of Britain. Britain joined the then European Community in 1973 and in 1986 signed the Single European Act, which established an integrated single market 'without frontiers'. For federalists and those who wanted to see a political dimension to these economic reforms further political integration became an important part of the European agenda. In 1991 the Maastricht Treaty was signed establishing a three-pillar structure including first, the old European Community which would establish a single currency, second, a common foreign and security policy, and third, policing and immigration control. Britain initially obtained opt-outs from monetary union and the Social Chapter, although Tony Blair has now accepted the latter. Britain's entry to the single currency, the Euro (which was established in 1999) remains highly controversial, with all parties divided on the issue. Clearly the EU has moved towards greater interdependence and integration. Federalists especially want greater powers for the European Parliament and a more executive role for the Commission, alongside greater judicial authority for the European Court. Further EU enlargement and the development of the single currency will make Europe an ever-present part of British party politics (John Turner 2000).

Quango state

In recent years there has been a tendency to distance areas of administration from direct political control and public accountability. This quasi-government operates in a no man's land, occupying an increasingly crowded territory between central and local government. Quangos include public, private or voluntary organisations, or combinations of each. In Britain, examples include the Independent Television Commission set up as a statutory body by Parliament; the BBC established by Royal Charter; the Higher Education Funding Council, set up by the Treasury; and the National Consumers' Council, a non-profit-making company. A key issue for these bodies is the degree to which they are accountable to the public or to the political process of election. A further problem with the growth in quangos has been the process of patronage and the process of appointment to such bodies by ministers. Many posts involve some financial benefit and a large proportion of them have been filled by appointees supportive of the government The *Guardian* (11 April 1996) reported that the chairman of the London Ports Authority received a payment of

£4,000 a day for 12 days' work a year. In 1996 the Nolan Committee on Standards in Public Life recommended that there should be an end to payments for those sitting on public bodies (Nolan 1996).

Privatisation

The process of privatisation has seen public utilities which were formerly national-ized industries sold off to the private sector. These private companies, like British Telecom, British Gas and the electricity and water companies, are now huge monop-olies which have been able to make very large profits for their senior managers and shareholders. In a number of cases the problem of delivering public services in an efficient and cost-effective way has raised issues of accountability. The water com-panies, for example, have been criticised for failing to deliver services in Yorkshire and British Gas executives were criticised for paying themselves large increases in salary. In all these cases it has been difficult for politicians to regulate the activities of these bodies. Regulatory bodies like OFWAT and OFGAS have been powerless to interfere with their activities. New Labour has continued to extol the virtues of the private sector over the public sector, going ahead with the privatisation of air traffic control and rejecting completely any suggestion of the renationalisation of the railways following the October 1999 Ladbroke Grove train crash and the Hatfield train crash in October 2000.

Secrecy

Linked to this centralisation of power is the secrecy which pervades British politics and the patronising assumption that the government knows best. Britain's culture of secrecy is buttressed by harsh libel laws, weak rights of access to official informa-tion, the Official Secrets Act and the D-Notice system. Freedom of information legis-lation gives fewer rights to official information than those enjoyed by people in the USA, Australia, Canada, New Zealand or the Irish Republic. More rights were given under the last Conservative government's open government code. New clauses intro-duced by Jack Straw, the Home Secretary, explicitly ban the public from access to documents on policy-making. A 'catch-all' clause prevents disclosure on any matter which might reveal ministerial disagreements over policy. The clause applies to government, Parliament and all public bodies.

In addition further legislation will restrict freedom of information still further. For local government a new cabinet system has been proposed which will allow council-lors to take decisions about education, social services and planning in much greater secrecy. People will lose their right to know compared with the previous system which required councils to take decisions at open meetings of the full council or its com-mittees. The Terrorism Act goes one step further in putting journalists in danger of arrest, search and questioning if they cover the activities of campaigning groups like poll tax demonstrators, road protesters or environmentalist groups, Greenpeace, taking action such as against genetically modified (GM) crops. A further Act which will enhance secrecy is the Regulation of Investigatory Powers Act, which will threaten journalists' sources and confidential information. The state will be able to intercept email and telephone calls across private networks 'in the interests of the economic well-being of the United Kingdom'. This will be a powerful enhancement of what the Campaign for Freedom of Information has called 'the cover-up culture' of Britain.

Party politics

Since the 1880s Britain has been dominated by political parties and politics is still organised around a two-party system. In the 1980s some 80 per cent of people still identified with one of the two main parties and just over 50 per cent of the electorate voted for them in the 1997 general election. Parties control the political agenda through professional party machines and discipline, while party managers, through the Whips, dominate in Parliament.

The emphasis of *laissez-faire*

Britain has a strong state and free economy. There is active state intervention to ensure law and order and social control, but little to ensure full employment and increased social justice. In the past decade the trend since 1945 towards collectivism and corporatism has been halted and the Keynesian rationale for state intervention has been undermined by free-market philosophies

Language and symbols of politics

The use of particular forms of language defines political identities and reassures supporters. On the right terms are used like 'freedom of choice', 'patriotism', 'individuality', 'efficiency', the left is labelled 'extremist', 'communist', 'red' and 'unpatriotic'. For the left, terms like 'equality', 'socialism', 'class' and 'the state' are used, and the right is labelled as 'uncaring', 'capitalist', 'Fascist' and 'selfish'. Such terms have tended to highlight differences between the parties which have not in policy terms existed.

Consensus

Even despite the radical policy shifts of Margaret Thatcher there has been a high level of agreement on the main areas of policy in British politics. Over a range of policies, like foreign affairs (Iraq and Bosnia), Northern Ireland, race relations, there has been agreement between the parties, with governments being prepared to negotiate and compromise with pressure groups. Significantly, once elected in May 1997 Gordon Brown made an economic commitment to stay within the spending guidelines of the previous Conservative government.

Authoritarian populism

A more populist politics under Thatcher in the 1980s placed a new emphasis on self-reliance, individualism, market economics, curbing trade union immunities and encouraging private enterprise. There was also a more vigorous attack on many traditional institutions in the name of the market and efficiency. The civil service, health service and law profession were all targeted. Thatcher attacked important elements of the post-war consensus and was prepared to go beyond Parliament and the Cabinet by direct appeals to the electorate.

The shape of local government

Local government in Britain has two principal roles in the British political system. First, there is a political role as democratically elected bodies representing local people and giving legitimacy to local political demands and interests. Second, there is an administrative role in implementing policy, including the delivery of services, which have often already been determined by central government. There has always been a potential conflict between these roles and there were a number of reasons during the 1980s and 1990s why the political relationship between central and local government became more adversarial.

- *Partisanship*: local government has become increasingly politicised with parties in local government prepared to challenge the policies of central government and build up a power base in their own locality.

- *Polarisation*: there was increasing conflict between the right-wing policies of the Thatcher governments and many, especially urban, local authorities run by Labour groups who saw themselves as a last bastion of opposition during the eighteen years when the party nationally remained out of power.

- *Breaking the consensus*: the Thatcher governments in the 1980s proposed a radical shake-up in the ways that local government operated, generally attacking them as inefficient, over-staffed and undemocratic.

- *Economic cuts*: a major reason for these attacks on local authorities in the 1980s was because central government wanted to cut local government spending and their ability to raise taxes (the rates, poll tax, council tax). Local government spends over £75 billion a year, 80 per cent of which comes from the central Exchequer, and it employs over 2 million people.

Partly because of these factors local government underwent a constant process of change in the 1980s. There were important changes to structure, including in 1985 the abolition of the GLC and the six metropolitan authorities in Tyne and Wear, South Yorkshire, West Yorkshire, Merseyside, Greater Manchester and the West Midlands. These were seen as key Labour controlled authorities which had the ability to challenge the policies of central government at this time. Just before the 1997 general election there was yet another overhaul of the local government system in the non-metropolitan areas of England and throughout Scotland and Wales. In Scotland the old two-tier system of regions (or counties) and districts was replaced with a system of all-purpose unitary councils. In England reforms were more limited with the two-tier system being mainly retained in thirty-four of the thirty-nine existing counties. Avon, Cleveland, Humberside and Berkshire are now no longer part of the local government map and some thirty-five unitary authorities were established, like Milton Keynes, Nottingham, Southampton and Leicester, which now run all local services (see Figure 9.1).

During this period there were radical changes made to the system of local government finance, including cuts in block grant to authorities, the imposition of rate-capping and finally the introduction of a new local tax, the now infamous poll tax. This tax was seen as a major contributory factor leading to Thatcher's political demise; her successor John Major replaced it with a fairer council tax.

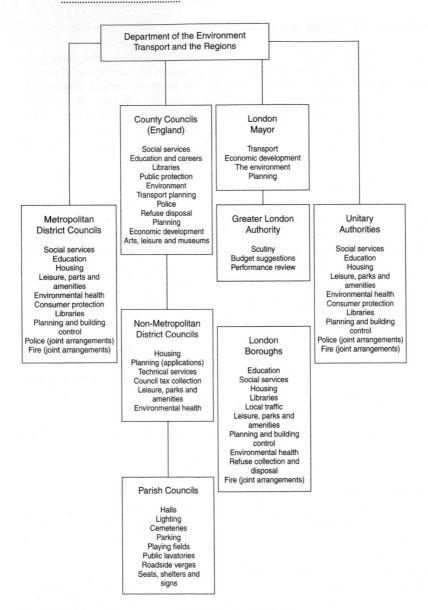

Figure 9.1 Local government in England and Wales

There were also important changes to the provision of services and organisation of councils. Councils were forced to move away from direct service provision, instead taking up what was termed an enabling role developing partnerships with voluntary, private sector companies and quangos. In 1980 the Conservatives introduced compulsory competitive tendering (CCT) which was designed to ensure that councils were forced to put out their services to tender. In many cases private sector companies took over the delivery of services like refuse collection, cleaning and school meals, usually with cuts in staff and wages. Many powers were also taken away from local government altogether, like housing provision to housing associations, local planning to urban development councils and education provision in relation to further education, technology colleges and the grant-maintained sector. In the 1980s governments claimed that it was also devolving powers away from councils and towards consumers, including the sale of council houses, parental preferences in schools and educational league tables.

In general powers have been moving away from local government and towards the centre or towards appointed quangos and to bodies such as school governors. Many of these changes were opposed by local government (of whatever party), but especially by Labour and the Liberal Democrats.

In May 1997 the Blair government came to power, with New Labour firmly in control of more local councils than any other party. Many of its new ministers and new MPs are former councillors with strong local government links. For example, David Blunkett, the Education Secretary, had been leader of Sheffield City Council. However, it is clear that much of the municipal terrain left by the Tories has been accepted by the new Labour government and it is important to concentrate on the continuities in general approach and policy towards local government. New Labour made a number of commitments in its 1997 manifesto which since then it has been in the process of carrying out. These have come under the control of the deputy prime minister, John Prescott, who is now head of a new Department of the Environment, Transport and the Regions (DETR). Following a number of consultation papers, a White Paper, *Modern Local Government: In Touch with the People* was published in July 1999 (DETR 1999). In many respects these proposals show a general continuation in policy direction as initiated by the Thatcher governments of the 1980s (Wilson and Game 1998). However, there have been important new initiatives, like devolution in Scotland and Wales and a new system of government for London, which have the potential to transform radically the political system in Britain as a whole.

Local government finance

The Blair government has accepted the council tax, although it remains a rather regressive tax, raising about £12.8 billion revenue (some 4 per cent of all central government receipts).

The government has ended 'crude and universal' rate capping with guidelines on how much local authorities should spend.

The government has also retained the national business rate, although it is limited by central government and there is a process of consultation on how such revenue should be used. It raises about £15.6 billion (some 5 per cent of central government income).

Enabling councils

The government has continued to expect councils to provide services in partnership with voluntary bodies, quangos and private firms. In the introduction to Labour's White Paper, *Modern Local Government*, John Prescott has argued that he wants 'councils to break free from old fashioned practices and attitudes ... There is no future in the old model of councils trying to plan and run most services. It does not provide the services most people want, and cannot do so in today's world' (DETR 1999).

Councils have been given a new statutory duty to promote economic, social and environmental well-being in their areas and councils have stronger powers to enter partnership arrangements (Lowndes 1999).

Powers removed from local government

The government has adopted a 'small carrot' and 'stick' policy threatening to take away services from councils that fall short of agreed standards. For example, in education it is envisaged that the private and voluntary sector will take over the running of 'failing' schools. So-called 'hit squads' have been sent into Hackney. The carrot is in the form of beacon councils, which are those that have been identified as centres of excellence. These councils will be given extra discretionary powers over capital investment and the way services are managed.

In the area of education Labour has gone much further than any reforms enacted by the Thatcher governments. In January 1999, David Blunkett announced a national advertising campaign inviting profit-making private companies to join a list of other voluntary organisations prepared to take over education services in failing local authority areas. In February 2000 a Labour think-tank, the Institute of Public Policy Research (IPPR), suggested the abolition of local education authorities (LEAs) and their replacement with new appointed quangos in the form of Local Learning and Skills Councils.

In April 1999 the government established eight regional development agencies (RDAs) which were given the responsibility of addressing the problems of Britain's poorest regions. Essentially the RDAs are business-led quangos, directly appointed by the Secretary of State, Prescott, with a budget of £1 billion. Some see these as a positive step towards full-blown English regional assemblies, addressing some concerns that Scottish and Welsh devolution will crowd out subsidies to poorer regions like the north-east.

'Best value' and the abolition of compulsory competitive tendering

New Labour's ambivalence towards local councils can be seen in its consumerist 'best value' regime designed to set performance indicators and improve the quality of services. Local authorities now face regular inspections from a unit of 400 staff based in the Audit Commission, created at a cost of £40 million. Councils will draw up local performance plans and central government has powers to intervene to remedy clear performance failure (Boyne 1999).

New ethical procedures

Labour announced a new 'ethical framework' for English councils in March 1999 in the wake of a much publicised fraud in Doncaster council where councillors had been imprisoned for expenses fraud and planning corruption, so highlighting the financial rewards allocated to committee chairpersons.

In response to the Nolan report on local government standards of conduct, a new independent standards board has been proposed to investigate all allegations that a council's code of conduct has been breached. Each council is required to keep a register of members' interests and a standards committee to oversee it. There will be regional standards boards and an appeals system to the national standards board.

Reinvigorating local democracy

In local elections in May 2000 turnout was around 30 per cent and only 33.6 per cent for the new form of London government (see p. 159). This followed the European parliamentary elections in June 1999 when only 23 per cent went to the polls. Indeed, the 1997 general election saw the lowest turnout since the war, with only 40 per cent of younger people bothering to vote. The government has been advised that turnout may fall below 70 per cent at the next general election (Page 1998).

To remedy such low public interest in elections, what some have called the rise of 'sod them politics', the Labour government wants to stimulate greater participation, more frequent elections to ensure accountability and innovations in electoral procedures. Gordon Brown, the Chancellor, has spoken of restoring 'civic patriotism'. It is intended to stimulate greater participation by giving local authorities a duty to consult with the public over local performance plans, including the public assessment of beacon councils and best value services. It is also envisaged that there will be a greater use of non-binding referendums by local councils on issues of local controversy like forms of council organisation and planning.

Labour has suggested that there should be more frequent local government elections – in two-tier structures half the county and half the district councillors being elected each year. In unitary councils a third of councillors should be elected each year.

The government also wants to encourage experiments in new forms of voting to increase turnout. This involves the introduction of electronic voting, including the use of the internet, mobile polling stations, entire elections by postal ballot and polling in supermarkets and shopping centres. The government is also looking at rolling registration to include people who have recently moved into a new local authority area. In the future the government wants to consider the introduction of proportional representation across all local elections. In the May 2000 elections there were experiments with new forms of voting. In Gateshead, for example, where overall turnout was 29.6 per cent, two wards chosen to test entirely postal elections (with freepost) saw the figure increase from 30 per cent to 62 per cent and from 19 per cent to 43 per cent. A tour of sheltered housing by a polling van achieved a 44 per cent poll of elderly residents. Also in Watford customers at Asda had a polling station open between Friday and Sunday to increase turnout.

New forms of political structure

Labour planned important legislation regarding the role of the committee system in local government. It sees the old system as failing to provide decisive leadership and accountability as well as being too time-consuming. Legislation was delayed in the House of Lords, where it was argued councils should have the discretion either to set up a new cabinet system or retain the old committee system (see Figure 9.2). Councils like Hammersmith and Fulham, Lewisham, Cardiff and Buckinghamshire were quick to move to a new system (Leach 1999).

Traditional committee system

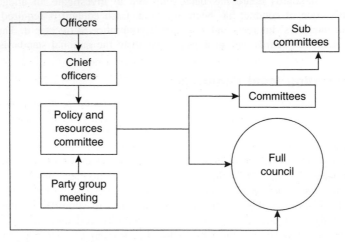

Proposed cabinet system

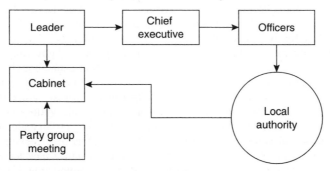

Figure 9.2 Old and new systems in the structure of local government

Blair has been greatly influenced by the US mayoral system and the government has proposed three models of reform:

- a directly elected mayor with a cabinet selected from among the councillors
- a cabinet with a leader
- a directly elected mayor with a council manager.

In each case it is proposed that a local referendum be held, especially if councils fail to propose any reforms.

There are, however, important criticisms of the new cabinet style of local government. First, where there is one strong party dominting this will affect the composition of the cabinet and relegate any opposition councillors to the role of backbenchers. Second, backbenchers will have limited powers to check the cabinet and gain access to key policy papers, especially where partisan politics dominates. Third, cabinets may lead to even greater secrecy and unaccountability. Cardiff's new civic cabinet arranged a £58,500 pay package for the lord mayor and council leader without wider council discussion and public accountability (Jones and Stewart 1998).

The first experiment in this new form of local government was the election of a London mayor and a Greater London Authority (GLA). This involved using a supplementary vote system (SV), with the GLA elected by an additional member system (AMS). Under these new systems councils are required to establish scrutiny committees of backbenchers to review and question the executive's decisions and performance. In general local councils have preferred the cabinet system to mayoral system, although the mayoral system is now being discussed in relation to other large cities like Liverpool, Manchester and Birmingham.

The powers of the new London mayor include responsibility for transport, economic development, the environment and planning, with a new Police Authority to

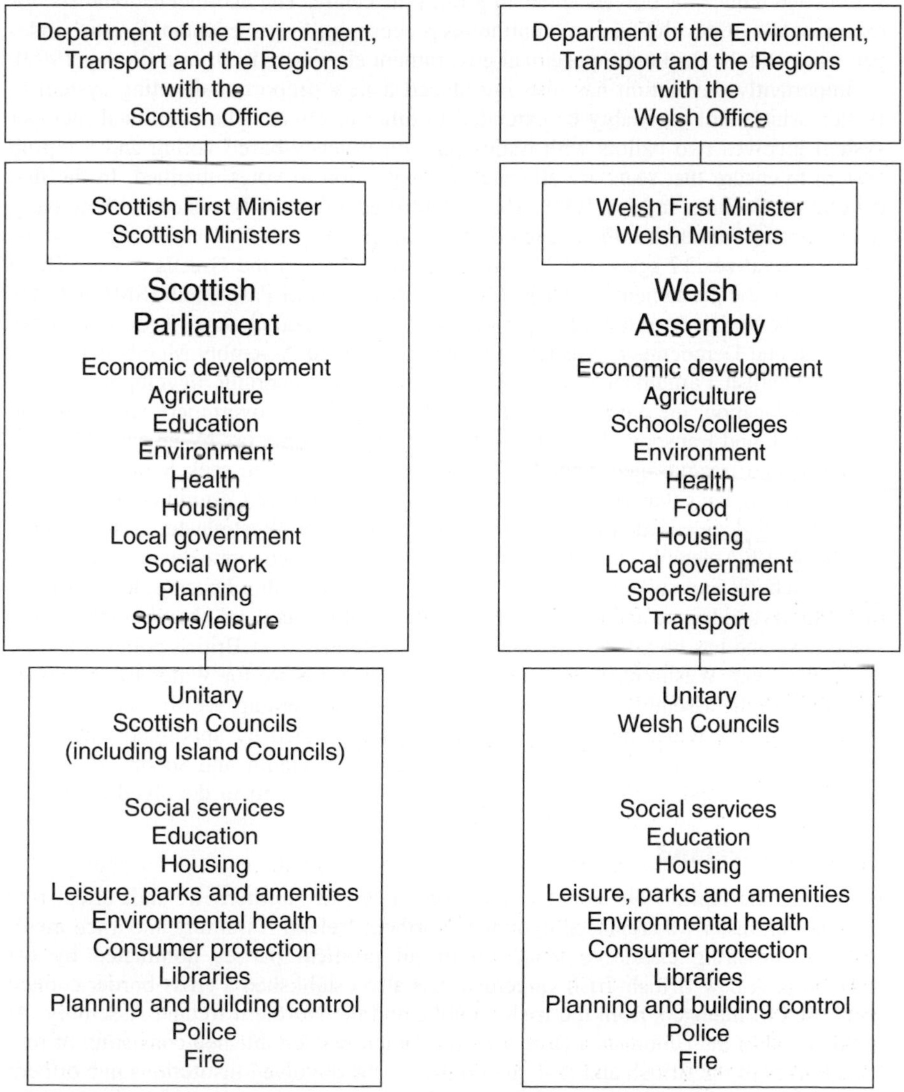

Department of the Environment, Transport and the Regions with the Scottish Office	Department of the Environment, Transport and the Regions with the Welsh Office
Scottish First Minister Scottish Ministers **Scottish Parliament** Economic development Agriculture Education Environment Health Housing Local government Social work Planning Sports/leisure	Welsh First Minister Welsh Ministers **Welsh Assembly** Economic development Agriculture Schools/colleges Environment Health Food Housing Local government Sports/leisure Transport
Unitary Scottish Councils (including Island Councils) Social services Education Housing Leisure, parks and amenities Environmental health Consumer protection Libraries Planning and building control Police Fire	Unitary Welsh Councils Social services Education Housing Leisure, parks and amenities Environmental health Consumer protection Libraries Planning and building control Police Fire

Figure 9.3 Scottish Parliament and Welsh Assembly structure

oversee the Metropolitan Police (DETR 1998). The mayor has a budget of about £3 billion. The mayor also has the right to choose a deputy mayor from the GLA, which has an advisory role. The new GLA has been given the tasks of suggesting changes to the mayor's budget, questioning policy and checking overall performance.

Devolution in Scotland and Wales

By far the most important and potentially most radical changes in sub-national government have been in the devolution of powers to a Scottish Parliament and a Welsh Assembly which now operate alongside a unitary structure of local authorities (see Figure 9.3). These have the potential to transform the character of the British political system and reduce the powers emanating from the centre. The Scottish nationalists, for example, talk of devolution as a 'continuous process' leading to eventual Scottish independence and the demand for regional government elsewhere in Britain (Stoker 1999).

Importantly devolution has also introduced a new proportional voting system to Britain which will inevitably be extended to other elections. The additional member system involves two ballots with traditional constituency-based voting and a top-up system to ensure that seats are allocated in proportion to votes obtained. In the first devolution elections in May 1999, AMS established a four-party system with no party in control. In Scotland, Labour gained 56 seats, the Scottish National Party 37 seats, the Conservatives 17 seats, the Liberal Democrats 17 and the Greens 1 seat. These members of the parliament are termed Scottish Members of Parliament (SMPs). In the vote for the Welsh Assembly, Labour gained 28 seats, Plaid Cymru 17, Conservatives 9 and Liberal Democrats 6. Elected members are termed Assembly Members (AMs).

The Scottish Parliament has devolved powers over economic development, agriculture, education, the environment, health, housing, local government and planning, social work and transport. It has the right to change income tax by up to 3 per cent. A convention is envisaged whereby Westminster will have to seek Scottish consent before making laws that affect devolved matters. The Judicial Committee of the Privy Council will decide which matters fall under Scottish or Westminster jurisdiction.

The Welsh Assembly can implement laws which affect economic development, agriculture, schools and colleges, the environment, food and health, housing, local government, sports and leisure and some transport policy. Unlike Scotland, the assembly cannot make laws and has no tax raising powers. Final authority over British policy affecting Wales lies with Westminster, although the Secretary of State for Wales has a duty to consult with the assembly and invite representations concerning Welsh matters.

Scotland and Wales now have first ministers supported by appointed executives (cabinets), including ministers of finance, agriculture, health and so on. These executives have responsibility for the day-to-day policy related to devolved matters.

Northern Ireland

Following the April 1998 Good Friday Agreement in Northern Ireland, direct rule from Westminster was replaced by a new Northern Ireland Assembly and a ten member power-sharing executive made up of all political parties nominated by the Assembly. A new British–Irish agreement has also established a cross-border council composed of ministers from the Irish republic and the Northern Ireland Assembly. At the demand of the Unionists a British-Irish Council was established consisting of representatives of the British and Irish governments, the devolved institutions in Northern Ireland, Scotland and Wales, and Jersey, Guernsey and the Isle of Man. Areas for co-operation include the environment, tourism, transport and organised crime.

Councillors

Bloch (1992) reported that about a third of councillors drop out of politics at each election. Most do so because of personal reasons related to family and work pressures. Unlike MPs, the 24,000 local councillors in the main local councils are neither full time nor paid for their services. Council work is often undertaken at the end of a councillor's normal day's work and, to be effective, they must master both policy detail and the work involved in looking after the interests of their constituents. A chair of a social services or education committee may be responsible for a budget of many millions of pounds. They are given limited expenses and allowances for loss of earnings and, unlike MPs, there are strict controls over gains. Councillors must declare an interest if any meeting deals with an issue which might lead to a personal gain. Smith *et al.* (1992: 31) have pointed out that 'one of the commonest of many misinformed criticisms of local government is that people only go into it for what they get out of it'.

A district, borough or city councillor represents a ward and a county councillor a county district. A ward may have more than one councillor. Most council matters need to be grounded in terms of a human interest. A local journalist will be able to obtain reaction to a school closure or a new day centre from a local councillor who represents people who are directly affected. The councillor will have knowledge of what is happening on the ground and may even have views conflicting with those of their local party. Elections take place every four years, although in some more urban county districts there are elections in three years out of four, when a third of councillors are elected each time.

Surveys show that councillors are mainly white, older, middle-class men, either retired or in professional jobs. In the big urban areas there has been an increase in councillors under the age of 45, and in the Liberal Democrat and Conservative parties there are slightly more women councillors. Labour has a larger representation of manual workers among its councillors, some 35 per cent.

The council system

Figure 9.2 showed the main parts of the traditional committee system of local government, contrasted to the new cabinet system which is proposed in current legislation.

Party group meeting

Most councillors are motivated by their support for a particular party and the Widdicombe (1986) report showed that the party group was the most dominant factor in local government. In Labour-controlled councils 99 per cent of groups voted together, and 92 per cent in Conservative councils; 87 per cent of councillors in Labour councils and 61 per cent in Conservative councils said their main task was to implement the party manifesto.

The party group meeting is outside the formal local government system but is the most important meeting. The ruling group is made up of members with the majority in the council and meets between the meetings of the full council and committees. The ruling group decides policy, elects the leader and deputy leader of the council and selects the committee chairman. The group develops a collective view and this line is then reinforced by the whips. These party managers, like those in Parliament, use the carrot (political preferment) and the stick (discipline and possible de-selection) to ensure party support for the leadership.

Group meetings are often held away from the town hall and other council buildings. Groups sometimes meet at the local party's headquarters. The local reporter should attempt to build up contacts with key members of the groups. Although held behind closed doors, journalists can obtain information about the meetings, often through leaks perhaps motivated by political infighting within the group. Political parties are coalitions of contending interests. Consequently, group meetings can be heated affairs, highlighting policy divisions which are hidden from the open council and committee meetings.

Full council meeting

This is often the least interesting meeting to attend as a journalist. The parties have already agreed their positions on policy and the meeting is devoted to ratifying decisions and reports made by the committees.

The full council is chaired by the (lord) mayor or chairperson (chair). They sit at the front of a semicircle of desks, with party leaders, deputy leaders and the committee chairs sitting in the front rows. The mayor is often joined by a chief officer while other officers usually sit in the back rows of the chamber. The council clerk is in administrative charge of procedure and an important person to cultivate if you are a reporter. Journalists may occupy a table outside this semicircle or be given a special place in the public gallery. Reporters should ensure they know the names of the principal speakers – the leaders, committee chairs and opposition speakers, though the clerk is normally available to help with names after the meeting.

Full council procedures

Councils have set procedures for dealing with points of order and votes. The council meeting will have an *agenda* which will outline matters to be discussed and indicate parts of the meeting open to the public and those parts when the public and press will be excluded. The full council meeting usually begins with the *approval of the minutes* of the last full council meeting. The mayor reports back on any matters arising and outlines any relevant correspondence, changes in the membership of the council or petitions from the public. Petitions from council-house residents or from parents of under-fives about the provision of services may be heard directly from the public in the council chamber itself.

The rest of the full council meeting is mainly taken up with the approval of committee minutes and reports arising from meetings which have been held since the last full council. Committee minutes are received, adopted and then approved by the full council. The committee chair may present the report and explain any details. There are four courses of action which the full meeting may decide:

- It may automatically accept items in the minutes which are *resolved* items. This is when the full council has already given delegated powers to the committee to decide on issues on its behalf.

- The meeting can *approve recommendations* made by the committee. The opposition may move that a recommendation should not be accepted and, in this case, there may be a debate and vote. Each recommendation is dealt with in turn, some meetings choosing to take them in blocks. It is important for the journalist to follow the proceedings carefully, making a note of the item number or the page reference given by the mayor.

- A *recommendation* may be amended, in which case there may be a vote.
- The meeting can ask the committee to look at the item again. In this case the matter is referred back to the committee.

Councillors do have the opportunity to ask the committee chair questions, and may give *written notice* where they require detail and further explanation.

The newsroom will be given three days' notice of the meeting and will be sent copies of the relevant minutes. Reporters need to read through these papers for items which may form the basis of a news story.

Committees

Most of the council's work is done in committees and subcommittees. Each is a microcosm of the full council, with the majority party taking most of the seats in the committee. Some councils have a tradition of allowing the opposition to chair some committees although, in the main, the dominant party takes all the chairs. Journalists are allowed to attend committee meetings, although their access to subcommittees may be restricted.

Committee work is detailed and greatly informed by officers. Heads of the council's departments, such as the director of social services or the education director, tend to ensure councillors do not go beyond their powers, *ultra vires*, and will often stop councillors from making decisions which break the law.

There are four main types of committees:

- *Standing committees*: an authority must have these if they run particular services. Hence a county must have an education and social services committee and a district must have a housing committee.
- *Ad hoc committees*: these are set up at the discretion of the council and cover areas which are seen as important but not statutorily required. For example, these may include a women's committee, an employment committee or a race relations committee.
- *Subcommittees*: these are smaller groupings of a committee handling specific issues or covering specific areas. The housing committee of Haringey Borough Council, for instance, has a subcommittee covering the Broadwater Farm housing estate.
- *Policy and resources committee (P and R)*: the most important committee, it is the cabinet of the council. Composed of the leader, deputy leader and committee chairs, it co-ordinates policy and allocates finance to other committees.

Procedures in committee

Each committee will start by approving the minutes of the previous meeting and go on to consider reports prepared by the council's departments. In a social services committee, the director of social services may present a paper on the implementation of the Children Act 1989. This may be about the issue of taking children into care when parental abuse is suspected. A recommendation may be passed which will he sent to the full council.

Journalists will be able to obtain such reports and may quote points made in the committee.

Officers

Officers are officially the servants of the council and try to resist attempts to politicise their role. However, as with civil servants in central government, politicians increasingly favour officers who are prepared to work with the policy of the ruling party group.

The work of officers is circumscribed by legal constraints and they are greatly influenced by their professional training. Many still think of themselves foremost as engineers, architects, planners, social administrators or accountants.

A journalist usually has to go through the public relations or press department of the council. They have their own agenda and the journalist must be careful to clarify the difference between publicity and news. Increasingly, press officers have found it difficult to be an intermediary between committed politicians and a more hostile national press and this has changed their role significantly. They are much more interested in negotiating a compromise between both sides.

The press office is likely to direct the reporter to the head of a department. The department will want to give a corporate view on an issue and will resent any attempt to contact and deal with a less senior officer who has only a partial view of the issue. Recent adverse reporting of issues related to social services and education have made officers much more sensitive as to what they say.

National politics

At the national level the main local contact is the constituency MP and there may be three or four in the local area. It is even better if a local MP is also a government minister or an outspoken critic on the backbenches. Speeches, general interviews, votes in the Commons, local party contacts and other public duties can provide material for stories. Background on an MP's personal and business life provides background for the local reporter.

A local paper will obtain a report of their local MP's speeches in the House from a stringer or news agency. Many regional and local papers have correspondents based at Westminster, some of whom are members of the lobby. The local newsroom will use Hansard Parliamentary Reports and local MPs will be more than forthcoming in sending journalists copies of speeches This may also include speeches at party conferences in October, when a local paper may wish to send a reporter or will again use a stringer.

Local political parties

The local party holds regular meetings, selects the prospective MP or de-selects the sitting MP, chooses candidates for the local elections and, with other constituencies, for the European Parliament (Ball 1981). Again, the journalist should build up a relationship with locals party activists because they can provide information about the content of local meetings.

Labour Party

The Labour Party has a federal structure controlled by a National Executive Committee (NEC): which is elected by the party conference. It meets at Millbank (on the Thames in London) which was opened in 1998 as a purpose-built political and media centre.

The NEC is made up of representatives from the trade unions, constituency parties, socialist groups, co-ops and a women's section. In recent years the NEC has strongly supported the process of reform in the party initiated by Neil Kinnock, and carried through by John Smith and Tony Blair. The leadership has moved power in the party away from the constituency parties and activists and has given ordinary members voting rights in the election of the party leader so replacing the old electoral college system which gave votes to the trade unions, MPs and constituency parties. The Blair leadership has also distanced the party from the trade unions, although most of its income still derives from the trade union political levy.

There are twelve regional councils with their own executive committees which coordinate activities in relation to local, national and European elections. At the local level the party is organised on a constituency basis, with an elected general management committee which has representatives from ward organisations. The ward may have twenty to thirty activists, whereas the constituency organisation may have a hundred representatives.

Blair has completed the process of policy reform, moving the party further to the right and away from policies which were associated with the left. This has involved, for example, a rewriting of the party's constitution, especially Clause 4, which advocated public ownership as an ultimate objective. After eighteen years in opposition New Labour won its largest majority in the 1997 general election.

Conservative Party

The Conservative Party has a more top-down structure with considerable power residing with the leadership. The party leader chooses the party chairman, who runs the party organisation at Smith Square, London. At the regional level there are the twice-a-year meetings of the Conservative Union, which has delegates from the constituency associations and which elects an executive committee. At the local level there are the associations made up of ward organisations and which appoint a committee.

The party conference is always a stage-managed affair. Speeches by the leadership tend to be orchestrated and representatives are mainly out to display their loyalty. It is not a policy-making body, although it is a good barometer of party feeling. The Conservative Party leader is elected by Conservative MPs, under an electoral system which requires a candidate to win 50 per cent of the vote plus a clear lead over other candidates of fifteen. In 1990 it was the failure to secure this threshold which led to Thatcher's resignation. After the election defeat in 1997 and Major's resignation as leader the party continues to use this election method, although most candidates have pledged themselves to widening the electoral process by involving constituency chairmen and possibly allowing one member one vote in future leadership elections.

Liberal Democrats

The Liberal Democrats also have a federal structure, with different organisations in England, Scotland and Wales. There are twelve regional parties who appoint representatives to the regional council. The conference is the most powerful body, electing a co-ordination committee to oversee the day-to-day running of the party. At the constituency level there is the local party. The party leader is elected by the party membership on the basis of one person one vote.

Scottish National Party (SNP)

The Scottish National Party was founded in the 1930s, although it began to make inroads into the British political system only with its victory at Hamilton in 1967. This gave the party a boost to membership and party organization across Scotland, although the party suffered a setback with the rejection of a Scottish Assembly in 1979. The SNP is the main rival of Labour in Scotland, especially with the general decline in Conservative support. The SNP campaign for Scottish independence has led them to take a more pro-European line, and Labour has had to toughen its arguments for a devolved Scottish Assembly to ward off further Nationalist inroads.

Welsh Nationalist Party (Plaid Cymru)

The Welsh Nationalist Party made a breakthrough at Carmarthen in 1966 and strongly contests seats against Labour in the valleys, West Rhondda and Caerphilly. Recently the party has moderated its illegal tactics, preferring constitutional means through self-government in the form of a Welsh senate. It has also dropped its linguistic nationalism, now accepting English as well as Welsh as national languages.

Ulster Unionist Party

The Ulster Unionist Party dominated Ulster politics from 1922 when Northern Ireland was established. However, unionism was fractured in the 1970s when direct rule was imposed from Westminster in the wake of increasing violence. Unionism is now divided between the more traditional Official Unionist Party (OUP) and the more hardline Democratic Unionist Party (DUP). Both have remained opposed to attempts to develop an Anglo-Irish agreement on the future of Ulster and argue for a return of self-government.

Social Democratic and Labour Party (SDLP)

The Social Democratic and Labour Party replaced the old Nationalist Party in 1971 and has been prepared to negotiate within the existing political framework despite its ultimate goal of a united Ireland.

Sinn Fein

Sinn Fein is often referred to as the political wing of the illegal Provisional Irish Republican Army (IRA) which has been engaged in an armed struggle against the British presence in Ireland since the 1960s. Sinn Fein received semi-illegal status when Thatcher imposed a ban on Sinn Fein politicians talking directly to radio and television. This ban was lifted when the Major government sought to involve Sinn Fein in all-party talks on the future of Northern Ireland.

Green Party

Founded in 1973, it was called the Ecology Party in 1975 and became the Green Party in 1985, emphasising its links with the more successful European green movement. The Greens had a partial breakthrough in 1989 when they took 15 per cent of the vote in European parliamentary elections, although their vote fell back to just 1 per cent in the following 1992 general election. Internally there has always been a basic division between those who want the Greens to be a conventional party and those who want to base the party's politics on alternative lifestyles. Recently Green representation has been improved by the use of the more proportional additional member system in elections. Greens now have three on the new Greater London Authority, one member of the Scottish Parliament, two members of the European Parliament (MEPs) and forty-three local councillors nationwide.

Elections

People are most aware of politics and political parties at election times and national elections especially provide journalists with a good source of stories. By-elections can be used as a barometer of government popularity and will always attract the leading MPs from all parties, including ministers and frontbench opposition speakers. The local agent for the candidates is the most important contact for the reporter, pointing them towards the appropriate meetings and photo opportunities. An agent may distribute a copy of a proposed speech in advance, highlighting the key passages which the party wants reported.

Otherwise most reports will be centred around candidates' comments on each other's parties' programmes and the personal stance taken by specific politicians. Journalists should be prepared to challenge candidates about issues and party commitments. Local issues are important and questions should be asked especially of candidates who have been brought in from outside the area by their respective parties.

Parliament

Houses of Commons

The House of Commons is the central focus for the reporting of national politics. Most political stories emanate from parliamentary reporting and many local papers have their parliamentary specialists, often located at Westminster. Otherwise, local papers will employ London-based stringers and the task of the local reporter will be to follow such stories up with a local angle and local interview.

Constitutionally, Parliament is the sovereign body having power to choose, maintain and reject governments. For the media in general the system of adversarial party politics provides a dominant agenda. This view overemphasises the role and powers of ordinary MPs.

The power of government and especially that of the Prime Minister has increased in recent years. The government controls the business and procedures of the Commons, the Leader of the House outlining the timetable of business after Prime Minister's questions. The guillotine and closure motions are increasingly used to push legislation through, curtailing debate by putting a time limit on the discussion of amendments to bills. The Commons acts with the permission of government, most of its time devoted to the passage of public (government) bills through Commons procedures with the government's control of its majority ensuring legislation is passed.

In three recent sessions of the committee stage of a bill, 906 out of 907 government amendments were accepted, whereas only 171 out of 3,510 backbench amendments were carried.

The work of government has grown in complexity. The state intervenes through economic and welfare politics and since 1945 this has led to a massive increase in public spending. Government requires more legislative time and the length of bills and Parliamentary sittings have grown in recent years. In one session there are about 150 government bills to be considered, most receiving the Royal Assent, and about 2,000 statutory orders and regulations. There were experiments with special standing committees to scrutinise policy during the passage of bills. Pressure groups were invited to play a part in the committee stage of the Education Act 1981 dealing with children with special educational needs. However, such experiments were quickly dropped (Norton 1991).

Backbenchers and the opposition parties can use the following limited devices for influencing government. Their interventions can provide copy for reporters:

- *Question time*: once a week for 30 minutes on Wednesday afternoons, Prime Minister's questions provide a set piece between government and opposition. There is little scrutiny here, with rhetoric crowding out information and the planted question from a government backbencher allowing the Prime Minister to attack the opposition.
- *Private Members' bills*: a good source of news. MPs ballot for the opportunity to introduce them and are then inundated with suggestions from pressure groups on suitable topics. There is very limited parliamentary time for such bills and few get through, the more controversial being usually talked out by the use of the filibuster.
- *Ten-Minute Rule bill, Adjournment debate and Early Day Motions*: ways for back benchers to draw public attention to specific issues.
- *Supply Days and Emergency debates*: used by the opposition parties to debate and vote on issues of importance. The government ensures it has a majority to ward off such attacks, the main intention of the opposition being to embarrass ministers and the government.

House of Lords

Since 1997 New Labour has been committed to the reform of the House of Lords, in 1999 doing away with all but 92 of the 650 hereditary peers and establishing a Royal Commission under the Conservative peer, Lord Wakeham. Essentially, there have been two options for reform, first, an upper chamber subservient to the government and so upholding executive power, and second, a second chamber like those in other western democracies which is directly elected and independent, designed to scrutinise the power of the government with no overlapping judicial or legislative functions. Critics have described Wakeham's report as an 'elaborate rabbit warren of systems and mechanisms' and as 'a fix from start to finish'. It wants a less partisan body, with part-time members, having a term of office for fifteen years. It suggests that a new appointed commission should be established for an eight-year term to select members, with a statutory minimum of 30 per cent women and representation for ethnic and religious minorities and the regions. Indications are that the Blair government has failed to think further than the abolition of most of the hereditary lords. Hugo Young has referred to the Labour government as 'agents of gesture, rather than reform'. Indeed, in a BBC2 documentary Lord Cranborne admitted to Michael Cockerell that 'Tony Blair wants a nominated house'. Hence, there has been much discussion of a half-reformed house of 'Tony's cronies'.

Select committees

In recent years the most notable attempt to increase the Commons' influence over government has been the introduction of new select committees. With the televising of Parliament these now have a much higher profile. They are made up of about twelve MPs and can call ministers, civil servants, union leaders and business chiefs to give evidence on particular topics. Since 1980 select committees oversee the work of the main government departments, including Agriculture, Defence, Education, Employment, Environment, Foreign Affairs, Home Affairs, Social Services, Trade and Industry, Transport, the Military and the Civil Service.

They produce reports, sometimes critical of government policy, but are weakened by the evasiveness of ministers and civil servants, hiding behind collective Cabinet responsibility. Select committees hold sessions which journalists can attend. Usually, officials and ministers are questioned by MPs about aspects of a contemporary issue. Sometimes discussions can be a little heated, and notes from the meeting can be used in conjunction with follow-up interviews with interested parties. Civil servants have a set of instructions, the Osmotherly Rules drawn up in 1977, which govern their evidence before select committees. They are instructed to be helpful, but guarded to ensure good government and national security. As a result many important issues relating to government are kept from select committees, including advice to ministers, how decisions are made in departments, the level of consultation, the work of Cabinet committees and how policy is reviewed.

The relative impotence of select committees was dramatically shown in the case of Clive Ponting, who leaked information to the Foreign Affairs Select Committee on the way Parliament had been deceived by the Ministry of Defence about the sinking of the *General Belgrano* during the Falklands War. The chairman of the committee, Sir Anthony Kershaw, instead of establishing an inquiry about government accountability, gave the documents to the Minister of Defence, who immediately set up a leak inquiry to punish the person who had provided the information. Other members of the select committee tamely acquiesced to their chairman's actions.

Standing committees

Standing committees of between twenty and fifty MPs are appointed to examine the details of bills as they progress through Parliament. The committee can be of the whole House, as with the Maastricht Bill or the Finance Bill, and amendments to a bill can be tabled.

A local MP may be on a standing committee or may have a particular interest in the legislation. There is a *First Reading*, when a bill is formally introduced without a vote; a *Second Reading*, when the general principles of the bill are discussed; a *Committee Stage*; a *Report Stage*, when committee amendments are considered by the House; and a *Third Reading*, when the bill is reviewed and further amendments added. The bill then goes to the *Lords*, the Committee Stage usually being of the whole House, and the bill returns to the Commons with *Lords' amendments* and these then need to be resolved before the bill receives the *Royal Assent* and becomes an *Act*.

Government and the civil service

The decline in the power of Parliament is matched by a growth in the power of the executive, and in particular the power of the Prime Minister's office. Much of this power emanates from party control and the growth of the Cabinet office since the First World War. The anonymity of civil service procedures reinforces this power at the centre (Ponting 1986). The Prime Minister appoints the government, dismisses ministers, chooses appropriate ministers for Cabinet committees, controls Cabinet agendas and chairs discussions with the Cabinet Secretary writing the minutes on behalf of the Prime Minister. The Prime Minister also controls the system of patronage, approving ministerial preferments to the chairmanship of quangos like the Independent Television Commission.

Cabinet government remains secretive and divisions between ministers are usually concealed by the notion of *collective Cabinet responsibility*. Under this convention decisions of the Cabinet are collective and ministers are not allowed to contest the view emanating from the Cabinet Office. This makes it difficult for journalists to record the true flavour of the political debates and discussions taking place at the heart of government. The work of the civil service is also kept secret by means of *ministerial responsibility*. This convention states that the buck stops with departmental ministers, ensuring that, when questioned in select committees, senior civil servants can dodge answering by referring to their minister.

Cabinet committees

The issues concerning the resignation of Nigel Lawson and Geoffrey Howe from Thatcher's government raised questions about the relevance of the notion of collective Cabinet government. In the 1980s the Cabinet met less often, some forty-five times a year compared with nearly a hundred times in every year since 1945, and the number of Cabinet committees and papers also fell (Hennessy 1986).

Under Thatcher a large proportion of Cabinet work was determined by Cabinet committees. Many major items of public policy were dealt with by committees including the abolition of the GLC and six metropolitan authorities, the introduction of the poll tax, the banning of trade unions at GCHQ, the privatisation of British Telecom and reforms of the NHS.

The three principal committees deal with economics, overseas and defence and home affairs. With more decisions made in committee, the whole Cabinet system has become fragmented with policy being decided by relatively isolated groups of ministers and civil servants.

Prime Minister's Office

Another recent trend has involved the bypassing of the Cabinet system altogether. Increasingly, policy has been determined by informal groupings centred around the Prime Minister. Government information flows as much through the Prime Minister's Office as it does through the Cabinet secretariat. As a consequence, policy reaches the Cabinet and departments in a fairly developed form, providing ministers with a *fait accompli* and little time to organise opposition to it. The Broadcasting White Paper of 1989 was developed in a series of breakfast meetings between Thatcher and like-minded newspaper editors.

Under New Labour there has been a burgeoning of political advisers and spin doctors. There has been a three-fold increase in advisers, some sixty-nine being taken on since 1997 with an increase in the salary bill from £1.9 million to £4 million a year. Lord Waldegrave, giving evidence to Lord Neill's public standards inquiry, pointed to a 'new political apparatchik system equivalent to an alternative civil service'. For example, Downing Street press secretary Alastair Campbell is both a civil servant on a public salary of £93,652 a year and a political appointee. The salaries of sixty-six of the sixty-nine political advisers paid by the taxpayer are kept secret by Number 10's Policy Unit. Attention has also been drawn to 'Tony's cronies' in the form of a New Labour establishment of supporting the great and the good elevated by appointments to peerages, taskforce jobs and quango posts. Tony Blair is becoming the most prolific creator of life peers ever, having appointed 176 since 1997 with over 50 currently in the pipeline.

Patronage still remains an insidious part of British government and culture, and with the wider culture of secrecy, places a question mark over democratic practice and accountability.

The lobby

The lobby is made up of some 200 journalists with privileged access to the corridors of power. Tunstall (1983: ch. 2) has outlined four types of access: off-the-record talks with MPs in the Commons' lobby; receiving embargoed copies of official documents; attending regular briefings by press staff; and having permanent offices at Westminster. The price that journalists pay is in their collusion with a system which reinforces the culture of confidentiality and deference. The lobby is particularly useful to government. For example, after the 1987 election Thatcher became displeased with one of her ministers, John Biffen. Through a press office briefing she let it be known that he had become 'a semi-detached politician'. He was then subsequently sacked.

Lobby journalists do not write reports about the proceedings in Parliament. Rather, they provide background on current political issues, culled from ministerial briefings and gossip from MPs and press officials. Journalists become insiders, keeping their sources anonymous. Public documents, like committee reports and White Papers are embargoed, with lobby journalists being given personal copies long before they are presented to Parliament.

A meeting of government information officers takes place every Thursday afternoon at the Cabinet Office, with the lead taken by the Prime Minister's chief press officer. Techniques involve ensuring that unwelcome news is managed in a way to reduce its damaging effect. No two ministers are allowed to announce unpopular measures on the same day, whereas bad news may be released on a strong news day when there are other important stories. Failing this, news can be released late on a Friday afternoon.

Under Thatcher, the press office became much more aggressive, mixing news management with public relations and advertising. Increasingly government has used lobby briefings to package policy and fly kites. For example, before the 1993 Budget, the Treasury let it be known that it was contemplating putting VAT on zero-rated goods, including food and books. This was then widely reported and there was much public concern. In the actual Budget no such measures were announced and the opposition were wrong footed, although the sting had been taken out of the issue. During the 1980s the government increasingly used advertising to sell policies. The budget for the sell-off of nationalised industries came at the same time as central government was restricting the right of local government to publicise its policies.

Every civil servant and journalist who has close links with Whitehall is subject to negative vetting. This involves an investigation by MI5 and Special Branch using the Criminal Record Computer of individuals' private lives, addresses, financial standing, politics and social views.

In March 2000 the prime minister's press secretary, Alastair Campbell, announced that he would drop his anonymity when quoted speaking on behalf of the prime minister. In future briefings would be on the record and journalists could quote the prime minister's official spokesman (PMOS). This followed criticisms from press, radio and TV reporters about Campbell's unilateral decision to give access to Michael Cockerell to film lobby briefings as part of a BBC documentary programme. In other EU countries government spokespersons are often seen on TV. Campbell also put summaries of his briefings on Number 10's new website, suggesting that the purity of the government's message will be less likely to be filtered into hostile coverage by what Blair has called a 'negative media culture'. Some journalists now argue that briefings should be broadcast on the internet and that TV cameras and microphones be allowed into briefings.

10 Law and disorders

Covering the courts

Henry Clother

Why court reporting?

The first time you are sent to court as a reporter can be daunting as well as exciting. Court buildings are like rabbit warrens and subject to security checks on entry. The police, lawyers and court officials are busy and speak in legal jargon. If you are lucky you may find an experienced court reporter to show you the ropes, introduce you to people and pass on tips. There is a lot to learn.

Court reporting is an important skill not only because the courts are a marvellous source of human interest and crime stories, but also because the law is the basis of a civilised society. The law should protect the weak and vulnerable and provide a check on naked power. Every citizen has a right to a fair trial, and the presumption of innocence – people are innocent until *proved* guilty – is a cornerstone of justice. The duty of a court reporter is to write nothing which could prejudice a fair trial. The strict rules of contempt of court, though irksome, are intended to protect this right. They should not hamper the journalist's duty to report the facts and issues accurately and fairly.

It is important to remember that in Britain reporters do not have any special status in the courts: their job is to be the eyes and ears of the public. Over the years special seats in press boxes have been allocated but journalists themselves have rejected special treatment in favour of independence. However, court reporters have one big advantage in law by what is called 'qualified privilege', effectively giving exemption from our swingeing libel laws for correct law reports. Privilege in this context does not refer to status, but means that journalists can report court proceedings without danger of libel. The 'qualification' is that court reports must be accurate, balanced and contemporaneous. Accuracy and balance are not always clear-cut, but getting facts right and giving both sides of the story are basic tenets of the reporter's craft. Contemporaneous means publication in the next edition, not usually a problem.

The reporter's job

It is sometimes argued that court reporting, following in the tradition of the stocks and public execution, is part of the judicial system. The reporter, by publicising a crime and its punishment, holds up the crime to public view, adding public shame to the punishment of the convicted. Reporters and editors are often approached by people found guilty asking them to 'keep it out of the paper', sometimes based on fears of suicide or harm to innocent parties. Such requests in practice should not be dealt with by the reporter but passed to the news editor or editor for decision based on the individual circumstances and the Code of Conduct.

The idea that the report is part of the punishment is wrong on two grounds. The first is that courts, like other public events, are not reported as fully or regularly as in the past. Newspapers do not have enough reporters to cover courts every day, even with the help of freelances. Good reporters use their sources and the telephone to keep track of interesting cases, but most cases cannot be covered today. Even large crown courts receive only the occasional influx of reporters for exceptional cases.

The second point is that reporters are not qualified to act as judges and juries: they do not have all the papers and facts available to the jury and, however experienced, they are fallible human beings. It is not the function of the press to add to the burdens of those who have suffered enough. There are few less edifying sights than the rat-pack of the popular press in hot pursuit of some poor man or woman who has drawn a few pounds of unjustified state benefit.

The lack of effective coverage means that not only criminal courts and coroners' courts have become less meticulous and even arbitrary in dealing with their case-load, to the detriment of ordinary people caught in the system. There are many complaints that the full facts of a crime, an industrial accident or miscarriages of justice, are covered up or suppressed. Witnesses may sometimes keep their oath to tell the truth and nothing but the truth, but the whole truth may be another matter.

How is court reporting different?

First of all, court reporting is not different: the basic rules of reporting apply, only more so. Accuracy is even more important because people's lives are being decided and your own professional reputation is on the line. A wrong name or address can cause serious harm for innocent people. A working knowledge of media law and the NUJ Code of Conduct is essential.

Remember the basics: a shorthand notebook with plenty of clean pages (tape recorders and cameras are not allowed in court) and two pens (always carry a spare) are tools of the trade. You will also need your trusty contacts book, with all those special numbers such as Amnesty International, Justice and Liberty, and a local street map for vital checking of addresses and place-names.

Dress should be appropriate to the job in hand. Neat and inconspicuous clothing is customary, generally a collar, tie and jacket for men and office wear for women. You will not be thrown out for wearing scruffy clothes, but you will get more help from officials if you are sensibly dressed.

Shorthand

Shorthand is especially useful in court reporting and is a skill required by the National Council for the Training of Journalists (NCTJ). However, it is possible to get by without it if you have a good ear and can subedit as you write, selecting the key facts and telling quotes. The approved shorthand systems such as Teeline, Pitmans and Gregg are better than speed writing. The NCTJ tests trainees at 100 words per minute, but in practice you need at least 120 wpm for a full note. One editor said: 'Shorthand should be a walking-stick, not a crutch.' Shorthand notes should be kept for six months in case of complaints. If there is a complaint, legal or Code of Conduct, a good shorthand note is a strong defence.

The most important piece of equipment is knowledge of, and respect for, the law. This chapter is intended to ease your way into court reporting, but to understand the law as it applies to journalists you need at least one reliable handbook: *McNae's Essential Law for Journalists* (Welsh and Greenwood 1999). It provides a clear and concise guide to journalism and the law. Other, more detailed books on media law can follow as your experience grows. Accounts of libel trials, from Oscar Wilde to Jeffrey Archer and Jonathan Aitken, are as readable as any thriller. To keep up with changes in the law and court practice, it helps to read the law sections and columns in the quality papers and listen to radio features such as the BBC's *Law in Action* and TV documentaries.

Order in court!

Now you are off to court, you need to know the cases being heard and planned starting times. The Home Office has recommended that lists be provided for the press and they are usually displayed on a noticeboard in the court lobby. Do not be surprised if cases are delayed because of legal argument, with press and jury excluded; courts can be switched at the last moment. The case list will give the name and age of the accused, with the charge and the Act and Section under which it falls. In some courts addresses are also given. In coroners' courts, lists of cases with name, age and address of the dead person can be collected from the coroners' offices; sometimes they are put on a side table.

Friends at court

Most journalists have little contact with magistrates or judges because of the need for judicial impartiality. The key contact in criminal courts is the clerk to the court, who unobtrusively but effectively controls its proceedings. In a small court with only one courtroom in operation, the clerk sits in front of the magistrates, keeping track of all the voluminous files and documents. In large courts, with multiple courtrooms, there is a clerk in every court, assisted by ushers. They are busy people but they have instructions to help the press and, approached with courtesy, they can be helpful. Barristers, for all their lofty manner and formal clothing, are perfectly aware of the value of publicity for their careers and are discreetly helpful.

The most important – and also difficult – area to cultivate contacts in and out of court is the police. Magistrates' courts used to be police courts, with police in charge and conducting proceedings, but now the Crown Prosecution Service is responsible for prosecutions while the police keep order in court. Journalists have developed a love–hate relationship with the police at all levels, and in local reporting they are a constant source of hard news. Just like every other source, they can let you down, and there is always the danger of becoming too close to your source and becoming dependent or alternatively alienating a vital informant. Journalists learn to live in this symbiotic relationship, gaining information without losing objectivity.

The police staffing courts or serving as coroners' officers are experienced and specially trained. It pays to cultivate both uniformed officers and CID (Criminal Investigation Department) detectives and to recognise their difficulties as well as their failings. However much you strengthen your police contacts, when a big story such as a murder breaks you will find that your best sources develop Trappist tendencies and the most stolid police constable guards the Incident Room (they are the hardest to talk your way around). This is where what Nicholas Tomalin called 'rat-like cunning' comes in. Detectives often talk in underworld slang, living in 'the manor', catching 'chummy' and 'doing a runner'. Another group who court reporters cannot avoid are the criminals, who are not always in the dock. They form a varied and colourful layer of society, but natural caution and careful checking are needed in dealing with them. There is no room for gullibility and every need for scepticism in reporting crime and punishment.

This dependence on contacts means that there is a big advantage for the regular court reporter who builds up experience and has the news sense to spot good stories. But any competent reporter who is sent out by the news desk to cover a part-heard case can turn in a usable report if he or she has sound training and common sense.

Court in action

The vital parts of a court case come at the beginning and at the end. The case opens with the plea (guilty or not guilty) and the case for the prosecution, set out by the Crown Prosecution Service, followed by the case for the defence. Counsel present their cases, with witnesses, statements and pieces of evidence for and against the accused. At the end the judge sums up the facts given and gives general guidance to the jury on the law. If the accused is found guilty, sentence is passed after any necessary social reports, with any comments the judge may make. However, a good story can appear at any time, sometimes during a plodding cross-examination when most of the press have slipped out for a cup of coffee. Old hands make sure that someone keeps an eye on things, just in case.

Keep as full a note as you can, as set out in the checklist below, with proper names clearly recorded. Watch out for significant detail. The prosecution says a man in a blue suit attacked a young woman, but there is clear evidence that the man in the dock was wearing a brown suit that day. Sometimes a young reporter can be so fascinated by a dramatic declaration or confrontation that they forget to take a note: this is when your pen should be flying across the page, passing it on to the reader.

Watch out for courtroom drama, with a witness breaking down or an outburst from the public gallery, which are all reportable.

Checklist

- Keep a full note, especially of the key facts, pleas, names, ages, addresses, dates, sentences and fines. The prosecution, defence and summing up.
- Note any possible direct quote. Quotes add life and credibility to any story.

- Check any facts of which you are not sure with the clerk of the court or other contact.

- Avoid jargon such as 'plaintiff' or 'defendant', which can puzzle the reader. And as for Latin – *sub judice* etc. – it is all Greek to the reader!

- Write your story as soon as possible, while it is fresh in the memory. Then put it on line as early copy for a good show in the paper.

- Read through your copy for literals and errors.

- Watch for the follow-up. Every story has a future as well as a past, and the story may well be there.

- Unfinished business. If the case is adjourned, give the date. If it is still going on, use 'The case continues'.

- Keep your balance. The law requires court reports to be balanced, but it does not specify whether that balance should be provided in each story or over the whole case. In practice it means giving equal prominence to both sides of the case.

Analysis of 'Nail bomber tried to start "a race war"': *Daily Telegraph* (6 June 2000)

This story, from the front page of the *Daily Telegraph*, has just about everything: mass murder, sex, race, violence – and an accused straight out of a horror story.

Nail bomber tried to start 'a race war'

By Sue Clough, Courts Correspondent

A NAZI SYMPATHISER killed three people after starting a campaign of nail bombings aimed at provoking a race war and venting his hatred of homosexuals, the Old Bailey was told yesterday. David Copeland, a loner who lived with his pet rat in a bedsit decorated with swastikas, planted two bombs in centres of London's black and Asian communities, said Nigel Sweeney, prosecuting. The third and most devastating explosion, in a West End pub frequented by homosexuals, killed three customers and injured 70 others.

Copeland, who appeared in court in an open neck blue shirt and dark trousers, learned to make the bombs via the internet.

He primed them with explosives from £1,500 worth of fireworks and packed each with up to 1,500 nails.

"These were plainly hate crimes, the motivation for the first two political and the last personal," Mr Sweeney told the jury.

Copeland, 24, an engineering worker from Cove, near Farnborough, Hants, denied murder.

He admitted manslaughter on the grounds of diminished responsibility, but the Crown refused to accept the plea, saying that what he did was "plainly murder".

For the first time, proceedings at an Old Bailey trial were transmitted outside the building. More than 100 relatives wanted to attend and only 40 could be accommodated in the courtroom.

Copeland told police that he wanted to cause "murder, mayhem, chaos, damage – to get on the news as the top story, really. The aim was to spread fear, resentment and hatred through this country."

Mr Sweeney said that he admitted planning to explode as many bombs as he could, "one per week".

Copeland told police: "I am a national socialist, or Nazi, whatever you want to call me. I believe in a ruling master race; I believe in race and country first, with the white race as the master race and Aryan domination of the world."

Mr Sweeney added: "He targeted gays because this was his personal reaction to his 'strange' parents who had put him through mental torture as a child – probably just stupidity on their part rather than malicious.

"Even as a racist, I would prefer the company of a black or Asian to a gay white man," he told police.

This was, of course, a major national story. The difficulty with stories like this is that there is so much detail and the news desk is barking 'let it run' and organising the story becomes a matter of priorities. This version is full of quotes and significant detail such as the pet rat in the intro.

The reporter demonstrates great professional skill in combining the political and racial themes with the facts of carnage in her tightly packed intro. She logically and carefully structured her piece to answer the questions in the reader's mind. Writing in short sentences and paragraphs, she includes plenty of precise detail and is meticulous in attribution of key facts and quotes, without losing the flow of copy. Her eye for detail comes out in her observation of precise colour: the accused 'appeared in court in a open neck blue shirt and dark trousers'. Quotes are carefully selected and melded with indirect speech and description. This reporter has not lost her news sense in the routine of court procedure: she spots that for the first time Old Bailey proceedings were broadcast outside the building. The precise way in which the charges and the nature of the defence on grounds of diminished responsibility are given show not only knowledge but also the ability to explain it simply. This work shows that court reporting can reach the highest standards.

Analysis of 'I want to get out of Town because of drugs – thief': *Chatham Standard* (6 June 2000)

This is a workaday story from a local weekly, the *Chatham Standard*. Distilling the news from stories like this calls for sound news sense and some ingenuity. I liked the clarity and element of background in it, although I invite you to spot the faults (see below).

The obvious summary intro for this story was that the thief's motive for stealing a video recorder was to finance his drug habit. The reporter decided to lead his story on the issue of a widespread drugs problem in the district. This adds a wider dimension to the piece and lifts it out of the ordinary. The writing is crisp and detailed, with prices given to the penny and the way the thief left the shop with a video recorder under his arm.

I WANT TO GET OUT OF TOWN BECAUSE OF DRUGS – THIEF

A MAN CONVICTED of theft wants to leave Medway for good because of its widespread drugs problem, a court heard.

Martin Cobley (31), of no fixed address, was jailed for six months by Medway magistrates on Thursday.

Kumud Singh, prosecuting, said that Cobley was at the Strood branch of Tesco on 8 January. Staff saw him pick up a video cassette recorder, worth £89.99, and left with it under his arm.

He claimed that he was going to show the video to his girlfriend before buying it.

On a second occasion, Cobley was caught on a closed-circuit television camera leaving Tesco's, in Gillingham, on 10 May with a compact disc system, valued at £49.99.

He admitted to police that he intended to steal the equipment to fund his £150-a-day heroin habit.

Cobley, who had been living rough, had several previous convictions, the court James heard.

James Burnham, defending, said: "His record does not make good reading and a lot is due to a drug habit. He is adamant that he is going to leave Medway and not come back. The drug scene in Medway is rife."

However, there is one glaring weakness which I hope attentive readers will have spotted. There is no direct quote to back up the man's declaration of intent to leave. A quote would have added colour and impact to a good story. I cannot believe that a subeditor would have cut it knowingly.

Even more important is the obvious signpost to a follow-up. This tale trumpets that the Medway area is a hotbed of drugs activity. It may or may not be true, but either way it is a heaven-sent subject for a feature or news feature. A quick memo to the features editor is in order, modestly offering your services, and you have notched up your first feature of the week.

After the case

Every story has a background against which it is set and consequences which follow from it, often giving it wider significance. Today's socially conscious journalists seek to provide this extra, more analytical dimension. The story may call out for an interview with a wrongly accused person who has been acquitted, or where a verdict is in doubt. There is nothing wrong with interviews after the case, although the rules of contempt apply throughout the hearing. Interviews with jury members about their deliberations are forbidden. When interviewing anyone else, it is a good idea to use the tea-room or a quiet corner.

In big cases there are often news features to be written giving the background – the extravagant lifestyle of the disgraced tycoon or the deprived childhood of the killer. Research for this cannot be left to the day of the verdict but must be done at intervals during the trial.

The court system

Journalists are not lawyers, but they are expected to have a working knowledge of the law as it affects their work. This means that while they are aware of the constraints of libel and contempt, but also how far they can go on reporting the facts within the law. The following is a brief guide to the court system.

There are two types of criminal courts: magistrates' and crown courts.

Magistrates' courts

Magistrates' courts are the courts of first recourse. All criminal cases start there, and most are heard and decided. They are presided over by at least two lay magistrates, non-salaried and briefly trained, or, in cities, by stipendiary magistrates, who are full-time professionals, sitting alone. These courts are heavily overloaded and only a small proportion of cases can be reported. This means that press attention has shifted to the first hearing of cases which are being transferred or 'committed' to the crown court for trial by jury. Only the bare essentials of the case can be given from the committal, including brief details of the accused, charges, name of counsel, bail arrangements and any lifting of reporting restrictions. However, if famous people are involved or the case has other news value, it is amazing what can be done with a very few facts, a photo and tabloid projection skills.

Crown courts

Crown courts are held in large towns and cities and sit with a judge and jury to try serious criminal cases. For 'either way' cases the accused person in the past was given a choice whether to be tried by the magistrates or to go to the crown court for trial by jury. This was changed by the Criminal Justice (Mode of Trial) Bill with effect from October 2000.

Always check the titles of judges in the crown court, who may be circuit judges, recorders or assistant recorders. Circuit judges are called Judge Joseph Oaks or Judge Joan Oaks, but never Judge Oaks. High Court judges are Mr (or Mrs) Justice Oaks.

Crown court juries of twelve are taken at random from the voters' list, minus peers, MPs, lawyers, felons and clergy, all barred for different reasons. Judges first ask juries to find a unanimous verdict, but if they cannot agree, a minority verdict of at least ten votes to two may be allowed.

Counsel for the prosecution and defence are normally barristers (trial lawyers) although solicitors have been granted right to be heard and the 1992 Law Commission recommended an end to the ridiculous class division between barristers and solicitors. The Old Bailey, as the Central Criminal Court is known, is essentially a crown court creaming off the more serious cases. A visit is usually worthwhile, if only for the barristers giving spirited imitations of John Mortimer's Rumpole of the Bailey.

Civil courts

Civil courts are concerned with disputes between individuals or groups seeking redress for claims and wrongs under civil law. A civil wrong which can be compensated by money is known in legal terms as a tort. There is a mass of civil law on breach of contract, negligence, libel and defamation, property, wills and family law. Given half a chance lawyers can argue these cases for months, and in the High Court in the Strand, they do.

County courts

County courts are cheap and cheerful courts to settle small claims. Some 290 county courts deal with every civil case except the complicated and expensive cases heard in the High Court. Presided over by circuit and district judges, they also act as arbitrators, encouraging neighbours and traders to negotiate out-of-court settlements whenever possible.

High Court

The High Court is to county courts what the Old Bailey is to magistrates' courts. It sits in a marble mausoleum just off the Aldwych in London and has its own press corps like the Bailey. Cases are heard by a High Court judge sitting alone, except for wrongful arrest, malicious prosecution, slander and libel, when a jury decides.

Court of Appeal

The Court of Appeal sits in the High Court and hears appeals, with three High Court judges sitting together. Appeals may be against the verdict, the sentence, or both. Each case is succinctly presented by counsel and after a brief recess the majority judgment is given by one of the judges, followed by any other comments or dissent from the minority judge. Since appeals need careful preparation, the success rate is high and frequently prisoners walk free from the court, their sentences quashed or reduced to 'time served'. There is a final court of appeal in the House of Lords – five law lords who decide the most difficult cases on a simple majority basis.

Coroners' courts

The coroner's job is to inquire into violent, unusual and sudden death. The key point about the coroner's court, often missed, is that it is inquisitorial, not accusatorial. This means that no one is on trial and the court is not allowed to attribute blame to any named person. Blame or guilt is a matter for criminal courts.

The purpose of the inquest is to find out three things: who was the dead person? How, when and where did the person die? What was the cause of death? There is normally no problem about the first two questions but the last is often difficult or impossible to answer, even aided by modern forensic medicine.

The court has a range of possible verdicts including natural causes, accidental death, misadventure, suicide, unlawful killing, lack of care and, if all else fails, an open verdict. Inquests must be held in the case of death on the roads, on the railway or in police or prison custody.

The coroner normally sits alone, but if there is any reason for public concern or doubt, he or she will sit with a jury of seven to eleven people chosen at random. Sitting alone, the coroner is said to record his or her verdict, while the jury by custom is reported to return its verdict. Coroners' courts are a rich source of stories, although they tend to have the same ending. Social ills, such as the plight of elderly people

d dying alone, depression, drunkenness and drug abuse, are described in all
nan poignancy, however sympathetic the coroner and his officers may be.
nes there may be four or five cases of old people who have died alone with
to know or care.

Times of change

In recent years, especially since the 1997 election, there have been major changes in
the legal system and, with rising public concern at crime rates, law and order has
become a prime political issue. One major change was the limitation on the right to
trial by jury in 'either way' cases under the Criminal Justice (Mode of Trial) Bill.
Serious cases such as murder, rape and robbery must be heard by a judge and jury
in a crown court, but in many less serious cases there has been a right for the accused
to choose (or 'elect' in the jargon) for trial in the crown court. The bill handed this
decision to the magistrates, although they must give their reasons and there is a right
of appeal. Home Secretary Jack Straw wrote in the *Guardian* that the goal of the
bill was 'a system that is fairer to victims of crime and to the community'. Another
change brought about in defiance of libertarian jurists was the removal of the absolute
right to silence, by which conclusions could not be drawn from the accused's refusal
to testify.

A sweeping ban on the identification of any young person under the age of 18
involved in adult court proceedings was enacted in the Youth Justice and Criminal
Evidence Act 1999, against protests from media organisations.

An extension of the law to ensure rights long accepted in other European countries is embodied in the Human Rights Act 1998. This brings UK law in conformity
with the European Convention on Human Rights. It has led to some useful checks
on British procedures, including the James Bulger case, when the European Court of
Human Rights found that both the trial of the two young killers and the mode
of sentencing were not fair. Other proposals for change, from weekend prisons
up to the abolition of magistrates' courts, have been mooted but need careful
consideration.

A reporter would have to be purblind or insensitive not to see that most of those
who end up in city courts are young, black, ill educated and unemployed. Their
crimes are motivated by ignorance and poverty. If they are criminals, they are not
very good at it, because they keep getting caught. If a middle-class youngster arrives
in court he or she is well dressed, with a good lawyer and respectable parents
promising it will never happen again. The child of the ghetto, inarticulate and alone,
expects nothing from the system and gets precious little. Courts cannot change society,
but they do provide factual evidence of what is wrong in our society.

There is more to court reporting than merely reporting the courts. The legal
reporters of the future will have to get out into the community and report the society
which so clearly shows its scars. What we need is less law and more social justice.

11 Investigative reporting

Why and how

David Northmore

Although the debate about journalistic standards in the UK continues to rage at the beginning of the twenty-first century, investigative journalism continues to gasp for breath. This form of inquiring journalism that challenges the activities of the dominant institutions in our society remains on death row.

In the 1980s and 1990s, the UK's political agenda was overshadowed by sleaze and disaster. The sleaze was epitomised by the 'cash for questions' scandal that dominated the political agenda in the dying days of the Conservative government of the early and mid-1990s. Such sleaze lead to political complicity that, in turn, allowed a catalogue of notorious business scandals to occur – Maxwell, BCCI, Matrix Churchill, pension funds and others spring readily to mind.

The disasters – such as those involving the sinking of the *Herald of Free Enterprise* passenger ferry, the *Marchioness* pleasure cruiser on the Thames, the Hillsborough football stadium disaster and numerous others in the late 1980s – continued with a series of fatal railway crashes to plague the privatised railway industry in the late 1990s. These included the Ladbroke Grove train crash just outside Paddington, a major central London terminus in October 1999, when two trains collided resulting in the loss of thirty-one lives, and the Hatfield train crash in October 2000, when four people died.

Spectacle

Yet throughout that tumultuous era, journalists working in the press and broadcast media invariably sat on the sidelines to simply watch the spectacle. There was little evidence that investigative journalists had taken a proactive role in exposing such activities and events – with the possible exception of the *Guardian*'s exposé of the misdemeanours of several prominent politicians before the 1997 general election.

In the American annual investigative tome, *Censored: The News that Didn't Make the News*, the American investigative reporter Danny Schechter observed such journalism in the following terms: 'Like blackbirds in flight, the sky darkens with packs of reporters moving in swarms, at the same speed and in predictable trajectory. When one lands, they all land. When one leaves, they all leave' (Project Censored 1998: 22). There is a growing mountain of evidence that prominent UK journalists see standards continuing to fall.

Writing in the tenth anniversary edition of the *British Journalism Review* (*BJR*) in the summer of 1999, editor Geoffrey Goodman observed:

Ten years on the *BJR* sees no reason at all to tone down its gunfire in pursuit of what we started for: to fight the battle for higher standards of journalism. No party political axes to grind; no vested interests to protect; no preconceived views except that good journalism is not an elitist concern of the 'chattering classes' but the absolute requirement of a healthy, thriving, fully-functioning democracy.

This was but one of many critiques of journalism standards to have been published at the time.

Also writing in early 1999, the former chairman of the Press Council – predecessor of the Press Complaints Commission – Sir Louis Blom-Cooper QC advocated the setting up of a Press Commission to monitor journalistic standards. He commented:

The dissemination of information is the one area of social life where the public is not constantly supplied with performance indicators. There is a standing Royal Commission for the Environment . . . a Food Safety Agency and there are methods of monitoring the Health Service. Why not the media?

[Sir Louis added:] It could, on its own initiative, carry out general investigations into media misinformation, misreporting and distortion of public events. A healthy press, infused with the ethos of freedom of information legislation, can behave responsibly if standards are set and complied with . . . Something much more is needed to instil an attitude of responsibility in newspaper owners, editors and journalists.

In late 1998 Granada Television was fined an astonishing £2 million for broadcasting a faked documentary on drug smuggling, *The Connection*. It was also fined £150,000 for a similarly faked documentary on Glaswegian rent boys, and subsequently faced another investigation over a disputed documentary production.

In March 1999 the Independent Television Commission warned ITV about the standards of its Channel 3 output following the demise of *News at Ten*. It called on programme commissioners to ensure that documentaries and current affairs programmes should not be sidelined by 'game shows and Hollywood films' between 9 p.m. and 11 p.m. By the middle of 2000 the ITC was threatening legal action to force the ITV network to reinstate its evening news bulletin to its 10 p.m. slot.

On the departure of *World in Action* at the end of 1999, the Independent MP for Tatton and former BBC foreign correspondent, Martin Bell, observed: 'It joins the galaxy of investigative programmes laid to rest . . . how much easier it is to run game shows and movies instead. They are simpler to make, cheaper to buy, make no waves; they are easy viewing, unchallenged and unchallenging; and they do not have politicians running for cover.'

Speaking at a Media and Public Confidence conference in February 1999, *Sunday Times* columnist Melanie Phillips (then with the *Observer*) commented:

Serious journalism has become boring. It has been reduced and relegated. Serious journalists feel as if they are standing on a small island whose sands are being eroded every week almost. A crucial part of the media's role is to expose wrong-doing, and one of my objections is that I think many journalists do not do that job properly but are content to be spoon-fed to far too great an extent.

Writing in the *Granta Book of Reportage*, former *Independent on Sunday* editor Ian Jack stated:

Newspapers and news organisations are now part of the 'media industry' and a subdivision of showbusiness. The old distinctions between the serious and the friv-olous – tabloid, middlemarket and broadsheet – have largely broken down. [He continued:] Stories are important because they sell newspapers; therefore they will be bought, stolen, distorted, spun, sentimentalised, over-dramatised and should all else fail – invented, to woo a public which has ten national dailies to choose from, and another nine on a Sunday.

Depressing

All very depressing. However, at about the same time these comments had surfaced, an attempt was made to halt the decline of journalistic standards in the UK and create a renaissance of investigative journalism. In April 1999 a dozen individuals working in journalism and television production met at the Great Northern Hotel, King's Cross, North London, to contemplate the future of investigative journalism.

The perception at the time was that the number of outlets for investigative journ-alism were rapidly shrinking. Journalists wanting to enter the profession – including a number of the first intake on the MA degree in investigative journalism at Nottingham Trent University – were finding it difficult, if not impossible, to obtain such work. Those old lags among them who had actually worked in this field were keen to see that decline halted, and the collective energy and enthusiasm channelled in a constructive way. So the Association of Investigative Journalists (AIJ) was born, and a small executive committee of half-a-dozen keen individuals was appointed to develop the organisation's plan of action. Part of the AIJ's remit was to highlight the demise of investigative journalism and proselytise the cause. Another part was the need actually to do investigative journalism – to write the articles and make the documentaries. The AIJ, therefore, was potentially both a campaigning pressure group and a news agency.

The early days were taken up with two key priorities: fund-raising and develop-ing the AIJ website – its main link to the group's members and to the rest of the outside world. The fundraising had an initial success. An application to the non-charitable Joseph Rowntree Reform Trust resulted in a small grant of £3,000. The http://www.aij-uk.com website, however, proved to be highly successful. Designed by a professional website journalist, its presence was certainly noticed. It attracted a total of some 20,000 hits from 7,000 visitors during its first year, largely due to the coverage it obtained in the *Guardian*, London *Evening Standard*, *Daily Mail*, *Press Gazette* and others from the production of a simple press release. And that attention resulted in the recruitment of several hundred AIJ members from around the globe.

Movement

One of the key functions of the website was to operate as a marketing device for journalism produced by AIJ members. For its launch the AIJ offered articles as diverse as MI5 records, fluoride, the UK heroin trade, Cypriot fascists, council fraud, a Colombian atrocity and many others. AIJ members were subsequently successful in placing a number of articles with one national broadsheet newspaper, the *Independent*, and one major news magazine, *Punch*. This then led to a trickle-down effect with other journalists and television producers taking an interest in the AIJ's work. And so a movement was born.

The AIJ executive committee then decided to launch an e-zine (a magazine on the internet) to enable investigative journalists to actually do investigative journalism. Thus the *Investigative Journalism Review* (to be found at http://www.ijreview.com) was launched in the summer of 2000. The strategy was for AIJ members to produce items of investigative journalism that would fit on the front page of any respectable quality newspaper. Produce investigative news items and features, the organisation's thinking went, and commissions will follow.

The AIJ had a few more successes. One priority was the promotion of education and training. After all, if journalists have no formal training in this area – and there is little such training in the UK – then it makes it even more difficult to practise the craft. The association took part in constructive meetings with senior officials of the National Union of Journalists and the Reuters Foundation. The plan was to produce one-day training courses for working journalists which could be conducted in the workplace. Working links were also developed with Sheffield University, Nottingham Trent University and London's City University. However, a long-term aim of the AIJ is to establish a formal link with one such centre to establish a Centre for Investigative Journalism and the pursuance of excellence in this field. Finally, one other major achievement for the AIJ is to have secured a book-publishing contract to produce a British equivalent of the highly acclaimed American investigative anthology, *Censored: The News that Didn't Make the News*. This annual tome is produced by Sanoma University's award-winning Project Censored and published by the New York-based Seven Stories Press. The UK version entitled *Censored: The News They Don't Want You to Read* was published in the autumn of 2000.

Exposés

The AIJ has been commissioned to produce another investigative title for Vision Paperbacks entitled *The Bitterest Pill: Lifting the Lid on the Global Pharmaceutical Industry*, which is due for publication in the early spring of 2001. This second title will be the first of a series of investigative exposés in the Vision list. But there was one low point to record. Back in the spring of 2000 AIJ member Julie-Ann Davies was arrested by members of the Scotland Yard Special Branch and detained for a number of hours under the Official Secrets Act while her home was searched and various personal possessions – including computer equipment – seized. To date neither Davies, her lawyer nor the association quite know why she was targeted. It is assumed that the operation was in response to a visit by Davies to Paris to interview reneg-ade ex-MI5 officer David Shayler. In fact, many journalists had travelled to Paris to interview Shayler, but only Davies had been targeted by the Special Branch.

Investigating into the Margaret Thatcher Archive Trust

Back to the practice of investigative journalism: here we look at one major scoop produced by an AIJ member and then posted on the website.

Thatcher archive probed by watchdog over secret charity scam

AN ARCHIVE HOLDING hundreds of thousands of personal papers belonging to former prime minister Margaret Thatcher is under investigation by the Charity Commission for refusing to allow public access to the files. The Margaret Thatcher Archive Trust, which is a registered charity based at Cambridge University, was established in April of 1997 to administer personal documents covering Lady Thatcher's entire life. Its trust deed claims the charity exists for "the advancement of the education of the public" and for "making it available to the public for the purpose of viewing".

But when a reporter from the *Investigative Journalism Review* applied to inspect the archive he was told that members of the public would not be granted access to the papers.

TAX BREAKS

Lawyers are now warning that the archive's trustees – which include Lady Thatcher, Lord Gowrie, Sir Charles Powell and three leading Cambridge University dons – could now be held personally liable to repay any tax breaks gained from the trust's charitable status. The Margaret Thatcher Archive Trust was set up two years ago with a donation of £100,000 from the Margaret Thatcher Charitable Trust – Lady Thatcher's personal charity which was founded in 1988. The archive trust's reported income to date totals £103,019 of which just over £23,000 has been spent.

The *Investigative Journalism Review* has learned that the archive spans Lady Thatcher's entire life, and currently occupies a 40-foot steel container at Churchill College, Cambridge.

CONTROVERSIAL

Of particular interest to researchers will be documents in the archive relating to Thatcher's 33-year period of office as MP for Finchley including her 11-year period as prime minister. They will include such controversial episodes as the campaign to secure her succession as leader of the Conservative Party in 1975, and the sinking of the Belgrano and the miners' strike in the early 1980s.

But the archivist responsible for the Margaret Thatcher Archive Trust, the eminent historian Dr Piers Brendon, has refused the *IJR* access to the papers. "The only items we have that are in the public domain are a very good collection of press cuttings and just odd bits and bobs," he said. "The papers virtually all come under the 30-year rule."

But the Public Record Office has denied that the Margaret Thatcher Archive will contain any official papers relating to her term as prime minister. It insists that the archive will only contain personal papers and therefore not come under the 30-year rule.

STRICT GUIDELINES

"There is no question of the prime minister's official papers being released to a private archive," said PRO spokesman

Nick Forbes. "There are strict guidelines on former office-holders keeping anything official," he added. "One or two former prime ministers have been granted access to documents to help prepare their memoirs, but they wouldn't be allowed to retain any documents."

The trustees' refusal to allow public access to the archive looked increasingly precarious when Dr Brendon confirmed that Lady Thatcher's official biographer, John Campbell, would shortly be granted access to the archive. This was confirmed by Julian Seymour, Lady Thatcher's chief of staff and fellow trustee of the Margaret Thatcher Archive Trust. He told us: "Part of the archive is now accessible to scholars. And the trustees have today granted a request for access to John Campbell, her biographer, to see the files. Otherwise it is a matter for the Cabinet Office."

'RIDICULOUS'
A leading expert in charity law, barrister Francesca Quint, believes the Margaret Thatcher Archive Trust could be acting illegally by refusing the public access to the files. "To claim that the public will be denied access to the Margaret Thatcher Archive is ridiculous given the terms of the trust's deed," she said. "Unless these materials are available to the public then they are fulfilling no charitable purpose at all. If they are just allowing her biographer access to these papers then it creates a very big question mark about whether they are acting in breach of trust."

Mrs Quint added: "Charitable status can be withdrawn if it can be shown that there never was any intention to allow the public access and it was all a sham. The appropriate official to investigate this matter is the Attorney-General, and the Inland Revenue may like to enquire to see if there is any irregularity from their point-of-view."

A spokeswoman for the Cabinet Office said the archive's secrecy was as a result of an informal agreement immediately prior to Thatcher's departure from Downing Street. "We are not fully aware of the agreement, but believe it was decided that the archive should not be open to the public without the agreement of Lady Thatcher and the Cabinet Secretary."

BEQUEATHED £2 MILLION
The archive was set up at Churchill College at a time when the Thatcher Foundation bequeathed £2 million to create the Margaret Thatcher Chair of Enterprise Studies at the university. In recent years Baroness Thatcher has undertaken a number of fund-raising lecture tours of the United States which have raised millions of pounds for Cambridge University. Last year she was invited to become a Companion of the Guild of Cambridge Benefactors in recognition of her work. This followed Oxford University's refusal to grant the former prime minister an honorary doctorate. Baroness Thatcher studied chemistry at Oxford's Somerville College in the 1940s.

Copyright © 2000 *Investigative Journalism Review*

Definition of 'investigative'

Before we look at how this piece of investigative journalism was undertaken, a quick reminder of what the 'investigative' in investigative journalism means. The most apt definition is offered by the Americans duo John Ullmann and Steve Honeyman in their book *The Reporter's Handbook*:

It is the reporting, through one's own work product and initiative, matters of importance which some persons or organisations wish to keep secret. The three

basic elements are that the investigation be the work of the reporter, not a report
of an investigation made by someone else; that the subject of the story involves
something of reasonable importance to the reader or viewer; and that others are
attempting to hide these matters from the public.

(Ullmann and Honeyman 1983: vii)

Despite that definition being published in the early 1980s, it has yet to be improved
upon and serves as a more than adequate guide for journalists conducting investigations anywhere. They then continue: 'Once defined, investigative reporting loses most
of its mystique. It is old-fashioned, hard-nosed reporting. What delineates it from
other forms of reporting is the nature of what is being reported and the amount of
original work involved.' Ullmann and Honeyman continue: 'A good reporter is
informed, perceptive, accurate, fair, careful, smart, and widely knowledgeable. He or
she is practised in the craft.' But, they warn, investigative journalism is no glamorous profession.

> On the average, it is nine-tenths drudgery, endless hours sifting through mostly
> meaningless documents, protracted negotiations with the defensive bureaucrats and
> lawyers, frequent meetings with dry sources and mentally disturbed crusaders,
> long nights, cold coffee, busted trails, bottomless pits and, occasionally, heady
> success.

You have been warned.

Background to the scoop

Back, though, to the exposé about the Margaret Thatcher Archive Trust. How did
the AIJ source this scoop? As we have previously noted, sleaze was a common factor
among Conservative politicians in the 1990s. All journalists must keep a sense of
political detachment at all times: grinding a party political axe would be highly
damaging to the work and reputation of any investigative journalist. Yet arrogance
was the hallmark of many Conservative politicians in the 1990s – the highly prominent cases of Neil Hamilton, Lord Archer and Jonathan Aitken proving that point.
But was there any unfinished business – from a journalistic point-of-view – concerning
the former Tory Prime Minister, Baroness Thatcher? This was a legitimate question
for an investigative journalist to ask. After all, any prime minister or former prime
minister is the legitimate target of the press. And so a journalist from the AIJ ran
the name Margaret Thatcher through a few routine public databases: the Companies
House index of company directors, the Data Protection Register, and the Charity
Commission database. All these searches could initially be carried out on the internet
at minimal cost. These were the findings:

* *Companies House*: a search of the Companies House database (http:
  //www.companies-house.gov.uk) revealed that 'The Lady Margaret Hilda Thatcher,
  OM FRS MP' [*sic*] of 73 Chester Square, London, SW1W 9DU, was a director
  of one registered company – The Margaret Thatcher Foundation. Much is known
  about the Margaret Thatcher Foundation as it was the major project that Lady
  Thatcher established following her departure from Downing Street. It hit the
  headlines when the Charity Commission refused to grant charitable status to the

foundation because of its overtly political agenda. So, little more to be discovered about the Right Honourable Lady from Companies House.

- *Data Protection Register*: the Data Protection Register (http: //www.dpr.gov.uk/ search.html) lists every individual and organisation registered to use a computer. Curiously, neither Baroness Thatcher nor the Thatcher Foundation are so registered, so clearly they stick to more traditional methods of communication. In the wider context bear in mind that the Data Protection Register can be a goldmine of information on the activities of a range of organisations – companies, local government, voluntary sector, academic, statutory agencies, government departments and the like.

- *Charity Commission database*: this, was the source of information that came up trumps. A search of the commission's internet site (http://www.charity-commission.gov.uk) showed that there were two charities registered with the 'Thatcher' name. The first was charity number 800225 – the Margaret Thatcher Charitable Trust set up by Margaret Thatcher in 1988, worth something in the region of £685,000 with an income of over £28,000 per year. This sum was donated by the trustees – Lady Thatcher and one Cynthia M. Crawford MBE – to a range of such worthy organisations as Buckingham University, Scope, Royal Artillery Museums, the Dementia Relief Trust, the Falklands Islands Memorial Chapel and others. One donation, for £100,000, was granted to the Margaret Thatcher Archive Trust.

The second charity registered under the Thatcher name was, indeed, the Margaret Thatcher Archive Trust – charity number 1061822, which was registered on 11 April 1997. According to the summary of the charity's objectives, which also appeared on the Charity Commission website, the Margaret Thatcher Archive Trust exists for the following purposes: 'The advancement of the education of the public in particular by acquiring, holding, restoring, cataloguing and maintaining the archive and by making it available to scholars for the purpose of research (and publication of the useful results of such research) and to the public for the purpose of viewing. General charitable purposes.'

Ambiguity

This was the key to the investigation – a charity that gives the public the legal right to gain access to Margaret Thatcher's massive personal archive. This is likely to include diaries, personal correspondence, files not deemed to be 'official' documents, and so on. The trust deed is clear about the purposes of the charity: 'the advancement of the education of the public' and 'making it available . . . to the public for the purpose of viewing' is sufficiently clear to prevent any ambiguity.

Because of the major implications of this investigation – either the journalist gains access to the archive or the trustees refuse such access – it is necessary to examine the complete trust deed. This can be done only in person at one of a handful of Charity Commission offices around the UK. In this case, it had to be done. A personal visit by the AIJ to the Charity Commission's London headquarters just off Fleet Street resulted in the files for both the Margaret Thatcher Charitable Trust and the Margaret Thatcher Archive Trust being ordered. There is no fee for this process.

A week later, the commission's office called the journalist to report that the files had surfaced from its archive. Note that such an investigation can result in some delays, so it might not produce overnight headlines. Still, it nevertheless makes a solid news item once completed. The file reveals an eleven-page trust document that provides detailed information about the running of the trust, but there appears to be nothing there that alters the key duties mentioned above. What it does do is reveal the identities of the trustees. In the document's own words, those trustees are:

> The Right Honourable Margaret Hilda Baroness Thatcher of Kesteven, LG OM PC FRS; the Right Honourable Alexander Patrick Greysteil Hope-Ruthven, the Earl of Gowrie PC; Sir Charles David Powell KCMG; Julian Roger Seymour; Professor Alec Nigel Broers PhD, ScD, FRS, FEng, FIEE, FInstP; Sir John Dixon Iklé Boyd, KCMG; and Michael John Allen.

The latter three figures, the trust document explains, are 'ex-officio trustees by virtue of their office: the Vice-Chancellor of the University of Cambridge; the Master of Churchill College, Cambridge; and the Bursar of Churchill College, Cambridge.' A quick reference to *Who's Who* reveals that Sir Charles Powell is a former key Downing Street aide to Lady Thatcher when she was Prime Minister and Julian Roger Seymour is chief-of-staff of her private office.

Respectable

All of which begs the question: are these very respectable academics going to allow a journalist access to the Margaret Thatcher archive? This question was answered simply by a telephone call to the keeper of the archive, who is duly recorded on the Charity Commission file as one Dr Piers Brendon – the highly respected historian.

The outcome is clear for all to see in the above piece. The responsibility of the journalist in this case is to establish that the two quoted representatives of the archive used in the piece are shown to be mistaken. This was done by simple press calls to the Public Record Office and to a barrister specialising in charity law. The Public Record Office has unrivalled expertise in the application of the Public Records Act 1958, which regulates the use of the thirty-year rule. If it says that the thirty-year rule would not apply in this case – given that all official documents relating to the ex-prime minister's term of office remained in the hands of the Cabinet Office – then that can be accepted as highly reliable advice.

Investigation

The entire proposition behind this piece was then run past a barrister specialising in charity law. Mrs Quint is the editor of the definitive law book on charity law and a senior officer in the Charity Law Association. The final call was to the Charity Commission to establish their position if they were informed that a registered charity had declined to comply with its stated objectives. They immediately launched an investigation.

An excellent piece of journalism – and not too demanding on resources. It takes a little time on the internet, a visit to a Charity Commission office and half-a-dozen telephone calls. The only additional point about the methodology in undertaking this piece of journalism was that the telephone conversations with the trustees and archivist were recorded on audio tape without their knowledge. This is permitted in such circumstances under the Press Complaints Commission's Code of Practice. If in doubt, check the code. This piece also demonstrates that a significant piece of investigative journalism can be conducted using fairly basic, public documents. Here are a few hints about undertaking such an investigation.

Launching an investigation

When launching an investigation, sketch out your rough plan of action. This can always be changed as the investigation progresses, but it is essential to have a plan setting out:

- what your starting point is
- where you see the investigation going
- a hit-list of sources to help you progress from one to the other.

Never overlook basic public sources of information such as *Who's Who* and Companies House records. And never underestimate the information available from a local main public reference library.

Always assume the information you are seeking has already been sourced by someone else at some time. The internet is ideal in making preliminary searches. Major search engines such as ixquick (found at http://www.ixquick.com) are ideal for such investigations. Whatever your chosen subject, it is likely that a pressure group or other specialist body, such as a trade association or official watchdog, has expertise in that area.

Keeping records

Always keep a record of your research. Every telephone call – both made and received – should be logged in a notebook or on a sheet of paper inside the file. This should contain the date and time of the call, the key issues discussed, any quotes to be used, other useful information provided, and the approximate duration of the call. This helps you enormously – not only to retain that information but also to challenge any denials or complaints at a later date. You will sound most authoritative if, months later, you can state the precise time and date a conversation took place and what precisely was said.

Keep all your papers relating to an investigation in either chronological or subject order in a ring-binder. These might include printouts of websites, photocopies, press cuttings and the like. This allows for easy accessing. Clearly label and store any audio tapes that might have been used to record telephone conversations.

Keep all your old notebooks used during your work as a reporter. It is good practice to write the date you started using that notebook in thick marker pen on the front cover, and number each one for easy access. Remember, to be a good journalist, you need to be a good administrator. The romantic notion of a busy journalist with a desk cluttered with endless yellowing press clippings and documents is something out of the movies. A successful journalist, like a successful lawyer, will be able to access any file or document in a matter of seconds.

Miscarriages of justice

Although the picture painted here about journalism standards and the future of investigative journalism might look bleak, an event occurred in recent years that gives one considerable hope in the journalism profession. A professor of journalism at the Northwest University of Chicago set his students a tough assignment. He suggested they use their journalistic skills to re-examine a number of cases when convicted prisoners had been given death sentences. The professor, David Protess, had a formidable track record of using his journalism skills as a campaigner and investigator to overturn miscarriages of justice.

His students devoted themselves full-time to investigating the case of one Anthony Porter who, in 1972, had been jailed for the murder of two teenagers. Porter had repeatedly protested his innocence, and he had been convicted on the evidence of only one eye-witness. His case had further been hampered when the public defender, given the task of presenting his defence in court, had fallen asleep during the trial on more than one occasion. The students even cancelled their holidays to investigate the case. They found that the sole witness for the prosecution had been 'threatened, harassed and intimidated' into identifying Porter as the culprit.

The students then investigated the background of the victims and found another suspect who had been in the vicinity at the time of the murder, who had known the teenagers and, crucially, had a motive for causing them harm. The students' investigation resulted in the murderer signing a confession and he was subsequently arrested. Porter was subsequently released from jail after sixteen years' imprisonment and given a grant of £3,000 to help rebuild his life.

A few years later, in the middle of 2000, Professor Protess and his students hit the headlines again – this time in the state of Texas. It was while the state governor and Republican presidential candidate George W. Bush was campaigning vigorously in favour of the death penalty. Governor Bush picked on the case of one Henry Watkins Skinner as a clear example of where the death penalty was justified. Skinner had been convicted of killing his girlfriend and her two mentally impaired children in 1993.

Professor Protess and his students embarked on a new investigation of the case to establish yet another miscarriage of justice. They claimed that Skinner was too drunk at the time of the incident to have committed the murders. They also claimed to have located an uncle who had previously raped Mr Skinner's girlfriend and who was seen stalking her just one hour before the murder. The investigation resulted in further demands for a moratorium of judicial executions across the United States. The Protess case proves that anyone with basic skills and resources can undertake investigative research. It is a credit to the journalism profession that these cases have been highlighted by student journalists. This, in turn, begs the questions: what were the professionals doing at the time? A question that every journalist – student or professional – should ponder during every working day of their lives.

12 Feature writing

Thinking visually, painting pictures with words

News features tend to contain more comment, analysis, colour, background and a greater diversity of sources than news stories and explore a larger number of issues at greater depth. It is the extra length that accounts for many of the distinguishing elements of features. In particular, their intro sections, where the overall tone of the piece is set, tend to be more colourful and varied in style than those of hard news. A news feature may argue a case; the personal views of the writer may be prominent. But the emphasis is still on the news.

The layout of a feature is often more colourful and imaginative than that of a news report. The headline, the standfirst (those few words that accompany most features summarising or teasingly hinting at its main point/s and carrying the byline), the intro, the picture captions, and sometimes the graphic's contents are worked on together by the subeditor to convey the overall message of the piece. It helps then if the reporter is able to think visually while composing the feature.

The intro

The news peg

Most news features do not start with the five Ws and the H of the traditional news opening section. The writing is more flexible – but the intro section still carries an urgency typical of straight news reporting. Occasionally a feature will begin in a news style but then break away to cover the issues in a distinctly 'un-newsy' way. For instance, the London *Evening Standard* (23 February 2000) began a feature on acquaintance rape with a straight news angle but moved on to carry the verbatim accounts of two women at length.

> Acquaintance rape is Britain's fastest growing crime, according to recent Home Office research. But the rising figures could well be the tip of an iceberg, women's groups believe, because many such attacks – where the woman knows, no matter how briefly, her attacker – go unreported.

The human interest focus

One of the most popular devices for helping the reader understand a complex event is to begin by focusing on the experiences or views of an individual. Thus in his *Mirror* report (11 April 2000) on the Ethiopian famine, Anton Antonowicz, alongside a large headline 'We said it must never happen again, yet the shadow of famine hangs over 8 million people . . . and the world has turned its back', began with this tragic observation:

A stick-thin woman stands with a bundle of rags in her arms. Sadly those rags are a funeral shroud covering the body of her two-year-old son.

For a week the child, Ramadan Safeh, had fought measles and human tragedy. He was already malnourished. He caught bronchial pneumonia. And he died two hours ago.

They had already started digging his grave here at the heart of the drought and famine which the United Nations has confirmed threatens up to 16 million people.

Similarly, in his report on the Russian–Chechen war, Ian Traynor in the *Guardian* (17 November 1999) began by focusing on the single woman's tragedy, following up with a striking direct quote from her:

Madina Khomzatova walked out of Chechnya and into Ingushetia yesterday clutching nothing but an embroidered purse containing six roubles (14p). It is six miles from her native village of Samashki to the border post. The trek took her six days.

"The Russians said on television they wouldn't bomb Samashki and that's when they started shelling," said the 42-year-old, who left her husband, son and brother at the Russian controlled checkpoint. She had already lost her livestock and tractor in the shelling.

Quote intro

Most news intros (as we have seen), do not start with a direct quote. In contrast, features can often begin with striking quotes: they set the scene and tone effectively and concisely as well as convey the human dimension. As here in *Socialist Worker* (12 November 1999) at the start of a news feature about 'flexploitation':

"We all sit in row after row. You have to log in and log out, even for your 15-minute coffee break. It's exactly like clocking in at a factory."

That's the reality of life on the white collar production line, according to a woman worker at Avis UK's call centre in Bracknell, Berkshire.

Eye-witness intro

Express reporter Esther Oxford (14 November 1999) visited a Liverpool school to discuss gender identities at the end of the millennium. Notice the rhythm of her writing, mixing short, striking sentences with longer ones built on a series of precise observations. She sets the scene with the narrative (the use of the present tense adding to the immediacy of the coverage) and then introduces herself as the 'I' of the journalist outsider, watching.

> The room is full of young women. There is an easy banter between them. Long legs cross, then unfold; manicured hands gesture, clasp, then flex with excitement. They are talking about their dreams, about jobs, men and prospects. They smile at each other and tease with up-front confidence.
>
> An hour later, five young men enter the room. They sit down, smirk with embarrassment, kick a leg, gaze out of the window, then catch each other's eyes. It is impossible to read their faces; their expressions switch quickly, before the coded language can be interpreted.
>
> I am at Calderstones in Liverpool, a popular school with 1,500 pupils and a sixth form to talk to the pupils about their ideas for the future.

Historical background

A focus on the past can often throw a particular light on the news of today. Thus a few opening pars focusing on historical background can be an effective way of leading into the main angle, as here in the *Sunday Mirror* (13 February 2000):

> For decades the world's tobacco industry has kept a tight lid on the list of deadly chemicals it uses to make cigarettes.
>
> And governments, whose coffers bulge with tobacco taxes, have conspired to keep secret the full horror contained in a single lungfull of cigarette smoke.
>
> Today, for the first time, the *Sunday Mirror* can reveal the deadly cocktail contained in cigarettes.

(The *Sunday Mirror*, incidentally, exaggerated when it claimed an exclusive for the story. Other newspapers carried details from the same health department report, due to be released later in the week.) Similarly, Matt Martel, in the *Guardian* (15 November 1999) began, using the historical background to highlight a striking contrast. Notice how the intro delicately avoids mentioning the precise details of Cagri's achievement, thus encouraging the reader to read on:

> Ten days ago, Mahir Cagri was an unknown journalist working in the Turkish city of Izmir. A man who apparently knew little of a world which cared less about him. Then, by virtue of a prank, a little sexual innuendo and the online community's sense of irony, he became the internet's answer to Forrest Gump.

Lucy Miles adopted a similar strategy in the *Sunday Mercury* (23 April 2000):

> Two years ago it seemed the death knell had sounded for Moreton Say Primary School.
>
> As with many other rural schools, falling pupil numbers were raising concern for its future.
>
> But now, for the first time in the Shropshire school's 129-year history, Moreton Say could be looking to expand to cope with increasing demand.

Striking contrasts

Highlighting striking contrasts in descriptive language can be an effective way to inject urgency and special interest in the intro section. Patrick Wintour and David Harrison reported in the *Observer* (25 January 1998):

> Near St Ippollitts village, the rolling fields and hills of Hertfordshire look green, calm, permanent. But this tranquil setting is the unlikely scene of a battle that pitches the Labour Party against itself. Labour versus Labour – a long and ignoble tradition in inner cities – has moved to the countryside.

The personalised intro

The 'I' of the reporter is only rarely prominent in news intros. But the tone of features can be far more personal, idiosyncratic, witty even. As David Newnham of the *Guardian* (21 November 1998) shows in his sparky, original, chatty style – combining slang, eye-witness colour and constant questioning.

> He's a dapper chappie my conductor – and a bit of a ladies' man, too. That pretty lady with the tenner, for example. She holds it up like a love letter and smiles a big red smile that matches the coachwork. Does he chuck her off into the rain? Does he lecture her on the need to proffer the exact fare? No chance. He sits down next to her – sits down, mark you, and counts out her change, nice as pie.
>
> Would I get the same care and consideration? I weigh the matter up and decide it's not impossible. For one thing, he's that type of conductor – a showman, a born party host. And for another thing, it's that type of bus.

Bury Free Press reporter Isabel Cockayne (7 April 2000) followed up news that a 'revolutionary' hair-cutting method had come to town by putting 'her head on the line to test the system':

> Split ends are probably the worst thing which can happen to my hair. It's thick, long and resilient as the inside of an oven but when I need a hair-cut, the ends start to feel like straw.
>
> So, when I heard that a new hair-cutting system had hit Bury St Edmund's, claiming to 'banish split ends', I jumped at the chance to try it out.

Questions

Questions rarely begin news reports. But in features they are OK. As for instance, in this report by Paul Wade in the *Sunday Express* (14 November 1999):

> Have you tried to get a ticket for your Christmas panto yet? You'd think that the box office at your local theatre was selling England/Scotland tickets not four together for Babes in the Wood, Aladdin or Dick Whittington.
>
> Pantomime is going through a resurgence, and it could all be down to TV.

The sex angle

Sex is the favourite focus of the red-top tabloids. But often a puritanical agenda underpins the coverage with the stress on sex outside marriage being dangerous and sinful or on 'kinky' sex being a threat to the stability of marriage. As here in the *News of the World* (9 January 2000):

> Clare Holtby slipped into sexy red knickers and stilettos and writhed seductively on the bed as her husband took photo after photo.
>
> The next night, she steamed up the camera lens again – only this time she was completely naked.
>
> It was all a bit of fun to spice up their sex life. But the sizzling snaps ended up plastered all over top-shelf mags – and the couple's "bit of fun" ended up leaving her feeling cheap and worthless and destroying their happy marriage.

The body of the text: THEMATIC STRUCTURE

While colour, description, opinion, analysis, narrative, quotes, dialogue and historical contextualising may be important in a news feature, they are all still built on the cement of factual detail and a sharp news sense. Just as in news stories the most important information comes first with the details declining in importance thereafter, so the same is true of news features.

At the same time, the writing style of features can be far more colourful and varied than that found in news stories. Emotional tones (angry, witty, ironic, condemnatory, adulatory) can vary along with the textual rhythms. Indeed, before launching into your writing, along with establishing the structure, it is crucial to identify the emotional core of your piece. Take these opening pars from a feature in the *Voice* (20 and 27 December 1999; see also pp. 200–1):

> # Youngsters flock to praise Christ
>
> **A Birmingham church is attracting large numbers from the city's youth.**
>
> **Kenneth Taylor finds out how**
>
> In his expensive Timberland sports jacket, designer jeans and trainers, Mark Tennant looks as though he is heading for the nearest street corner to hang out with his friends.
>
> The only indication that this trendy 22-year-old is actually making his way to Birmingham's Aston Christian Centre are a Bible in his left hand and the fact that it is 9.15am on Sunday.
>
> But Mark, who gave up hard drugs when he became addicted to the Lord, is not alone.
>
> He is part of a procession of streetwise youths, in cars and on foot, heading for the Thomas Street church to worship.
>
> The Pentecostal church, part of the Assemblies of God Churches of Great Britain and Ireland, is proving such a powerful magnet for young people that Pastor Calvin Young has to hold three services a day.

Souls

Recently an appeal was launched to raise £30,000 to buy a new building to house up to 1,000 people and leave enough space for various meeting rooms.

The church, on the embankment of the Aston Expressway and not far from the infamous Spaghetti Junction, is not much to look at from the outside, but inside is full of happy souls.

Pastor Calvin, in a maroon blazer, matching tie and slacks, looks more like a salesman than a minister.

Within minutes of the service getting under way, the congregation is whipped up into a spiritual frenzy.

Blessed

There is singing and clapping by the congregation while musicians are jamming away on keyboards, drums and guitars, accompanied by a trio of backing vocalists.

The Sunday I attended two people fainted when the 'Hallelujahs', 'Praise the Lords' and worshippers speaking in tongues reached fever pitch.

Pastor Calvin reckons about 80 per cent of the 250 people who regularly attend Sunday services are in their teens or early twenties.

He can't quite explain why his church – motto: 'A city church of many congregations, proclaiming God is love in the heart of the city' – is so blessed with youths at a time when others find it hard to attract them. But he feels the new millennium may play some role.

"If you look at human history, every 2,000 years something significant has taken place," he says. "I would not put a bet on it, but I believe this generation could be the one to witness the return of Christ."

The thematic structure is clear:

- *Section 1: pars 1–4*: focus on Mark Tennant
- *Section 2: pars 5–7*: focus on Pentecostal church
- *Section 3: pars 8–11*: inside the church
- *Section 4: pars 12–14*: Pastor Calvin.

This piece is particularly interesting for the way in which the flow between these thematic blocks is helped through the use of subtly deployed transitional phrases. The intro spotlights Mark and then the phrase 'But Mark . . . is not alone' leads effortlessly into the focus on the church and its popularity. The report first concentrates on the general facts about the church and then shifts its focus: 'but inside is full of happy souls'. That movement in the eye of the reporter (from outside to inside) helps provide an extra dynamic interest to the copy. It also provides the prompt for the new section of eye-witness description of people and events inside. Finally the focus falls on the Pastor. Factual details are combined with colourful description and striking quotes backing up the main theme of the piece. This is excellent writing. Moreover, the variety of genres displayed in these few pars (human interest intro, factual detail, eye-witness descriptions, shifting focus) adds to its overall vitality and interest.

6 VOICE DECEMBER 20 & 27 1999

Youngsters flock

A Birmingham church is attracting large numbers from the city's youth. Kenneth Taylor finds out how

WE ARE FAMILY: The Aston Christian Centre is pulling in ever greater numbers of young people.   Pic: Jason Tilley

IN HIS **expensive Timberland sports jacket, designer jeans and trainers, Mark Tennant looks as though he is heading for the nearest street corner to hang out with his friends.**

The only indications that this trendy 22-year-old is actually making his way to Birmingham's Aston Christian Centre are a Bible in his left hand and the fact it is 9.15am on Sunday.

But Mark, who gave up hard drugs when he became addicted to the Lord, is not alone.

He is part of a procession of streetwise youths, in cars and on foot, heading for the Thomas Street church to worship.

The Pentecostal church, part of the Assemblies of God Churches of Great Britain and Ireland, is proving such a powerful magnet for young people that Pastor Calvin Young has to hold three services a day.

Souls

Recently an appeal was launched to raise £300,000 to buy a new building to house up to 1,000 people and leave enough space for various meeting rooms.

The church, on the embankment of the Aston Expressway and not far from the infamous Spaghetti Junction, is not much to look at from the outside, but inside is full of happy souls.

Pastor Calvin, in a maroon blazer, matching tie and slacks, looks more like a salesman than a minister.

Within minutes of the service getting under way, the congregation is whipped up into a spiritual frenzy.

Blessed

There is singing and clapping by the congregation while musicians are jamming away on keyboards, drums and guitars, accompanied by a trio of backing vocalists.

The Sunday I attended two people fainted when the 'Hallelujahs', 'Praise the Lords'

and worshippers speaking in tongues reached fever pitch.

Pastor Calvin reckons about 80 per cent of the 250 people who regularly attend Sunday services are in their teens or early twenties.

He can't quite explain why his church – motto: 'A city church of many congregations, proclaiming God is love in the heart of the city' – is so blessed with youths at a time when others find it hard to attract them. But he feels the new millennium may play some role.

"If you look at human history, every 2,000 years something significant has taken place," he says. "I would not put a bet on it,

but I believe this generation could be the one to witness the return of Christ."

He also points to a range of activities from lone parents' groups and a Saturday school to a diabetic support group, pastoral clinics and drama classes.

He is also not afraid to use technology to spread the word.

"We try to communicate in a manner relevant to this present generation," he says.

Sexuality

"We try to address real issues. We address single people and their sexuality.

"A lot of young people have got problems but some churches don't address them."

Mark, who said he got his calling while watching the Vision Channel with a spliff in his hand, would certainly agree.

He readily admits to a past life of addiction to crack, marijuana, cocaine and lighter fluids, but within a few weeks of his calling he substituted them for the word of God.

"My mind was in a pretty bad way," he says. "My parents are Church of England but only in name.

"I had never been to church before I came here. It's like being in a family.

"This is the only church I've been to and it is the only one where I feel at home. It is God's will that no one should perish, but all

> **"Churches are changing and the face of Christianity is changing. It's not just about the way people dress and the fact that you don't have to wear a well-cut suit and matching handbag"**

DECEMBER 20 & 27 1999 VOICE 7

to praise Christ

should come to repentance."

Mark, who now works as a croupier on a ship – a colleague at a casino introduced him to the church – got baptised at the Aston Christian Centre just before last Christmas.

A'-level student Le Ancia Donaldson got baptised two years ago at 15.

Dancing

She started going to the Aston Christian Centre with her mum, Colleen, but insists she has not been influenced in any way to give her life to the Lord.

Le Ancia, 17, says: "I grew up in the church. I used to go to a Methodist church with my grandmother but there weren't so many young people there and it was very formal.

"Here it is lively, friendly and welcoming. We have lots of different ministries like dancing, drama, youth clubs and sports and the church supports them all.

"The atmosphere here is really good and I come here to get spiritually uplifted."

Estate surveyor Steve McDonald, 27, quit the New Testament Church of God three months ago to start worshipping at the Aston Christian Centre.

He said: "I needed something more from a church than just worshipping on Sundays. Here they have activities all week long.

"The New Testament Church had nothing to offer young people. There was not much encouragement. Rather than catering for young people, they catered for people who enjoyed the traditional type of service."

Alternative

Barrister Patricia Hawthorne said there were other inner-city churches in Birmingham, like Aston's King of Kings and the Ruach Inspirational Church of God in nearby Lozells, that also catered for young people.

Ms Hawthorne, 35, started worshipping at the Aston Christian Centre after becoming frustrated with the Baptist church where she was Christened.

"Churches are changing and the face of Christianity is changing," she said. "It is not just about the way people dress and the fact you don't have to wear a well-cut suit and matching handbag.

"It is the fact that people can go to church and be themselves and that the church also acknowledges that, as an individual, you have weaknesses.

"Here everyone seems to be genuinely worshipping the Lord and are not watching what each other are wearing. Also, young people can see the problems in the world for themselves and are searching for an alternative way ahead.

"At my old church, when I tackled [them] about changing direction, [I was told that] a lot of the congregation were middle class and had no great needs. Only when they were in a crisis did they turn to the church to seek God."

If the Aston Christian Centre is considered middle-of-the road, then the Ruach is much more radical.

Its praise and worship leader, Nikki Munroe, said the church often held services in places such as Balsall Heath, a known vice girls' haunt, and Constitution Hill in the city centre, a gay haunt.

She said only about five of its 195-strong congregation were older than 45.

"Ruach, which means breath of God in Greek, is very radical," said Nikki. "We go that extra mile. We like to meet people who don't always go to church. Those who want to hear the gospel, we go to them.

"We are very loud, very outrageous and music-oriented. We're following in the footsteps of Jesus, who often associated with the less desirables in society."

> ## "We are very loud, very outrageous and into music. We have this motto: 'Everybody is somebody' "

PASTOR CALVIN YOUNG: 'This could be the generation to witness Christ's return.'   Pic: Jason Tilley

Use of parentheses

Parentheses are rarely seen in news stories: they break the urgent flow of the copy. But given the more flexible rhythms of features they can work. For instance, Jonathan Glancey, in his *Guardian* report (10 January 2000) on the newly restored Pompidou Centre in Paris, wrote:

> Below shop and cafe are a children's rumpus room (the sort of mimsy you expect to find at Ikea) and a bookshop twice as big as before.
>   At the centre of this space is a stunted tree growing from a huge cube of earth rising from the basement (where four new performance and lecture spaces, including a second cinema, have been shaped) and a shoulder-shrugging information desk. (Don't try to speak a foreign language and, whatever you do, don't attempt your school French: this will only make matters all the more degrading for you.)

The final flourish

A hard news story carries information in order of news value. The last par. is the least important and is cuttable without destroying the overall impact. A news feature can be different (Hennessy 1993). News values still apply but the final section can often carry its own importance. A feature may explore a range of views on a subject and conclude by passing a comment on them; another may argue a case and come to a conclusion in the final section. A final par. may raise a pointed question; it may contain a striking direct quote or summarise an argument. Feature subs have to be particularly sensitive to this. Writers often include the words 'Must par.' in brackets before a final sentence to stress its importance to the sub (who will not feel obliged to follow the advice).

Negotiating the subjective: THE EYE-WITNESS SPORTING EVENT

Journalists often attend sporting events, not to record the happenings and results from a specialist perspective but to describe simply the experience of being there. As *Times* reporter Lynne Truss (1999: 127) comments: 'Uniquely in journalism, its appeal to the reader is entirely in the presentation of the simple fact: "I was there; I saw it with my own eyes; it happened once and it will never happen again".' The journalist becomes the outsider looking in. Such an assignment presents a varied challenge. You will need to extract a range of factual details relating to the event and highlight any news elements. It will provide you with opportunities for descriptive colour, eye-witness reporting, the development of sources and the use of quotes and for the exploration of you subjective response.

    The experience of attending an event as 'an ordinary member of the public' is very different from being a reporter there. As a journalist you are likely to have a notebook and tape recorder to record any interesting sights, interview and facts. You are on the look-out for the unusual, perhaps even the slightly bizarre, the newsworthy. You need to keep all your senses alive to collect a mass of details, quotes and impressions that will go towards the creation of your article. You are unlikely to provide a simple chronology of your experience: arrival, watching spectators, the highlights of the event, the results and departure. Instead, special journalistic values should come into play. You may want to intro on a lively quote or a striking incident which happens towards the end. It may be good to start with a colourful description of a participant and then pan out to take in the overall event.

Eye-witness writing is always overtly subjective. It should never be self-indulgent. If you are describing an underwater hockey match, the reader does not need to know at length your fears of underwater swimming originating in some early childhood trauma in Lake Ontario. This constraint does not apply to celebrity writers. Their own subjectivity is often, in journalistic terms, as interesting as the event they are describing and so their own self-indulgence is legitimate. But, in general, subjectivity works best when handled delicately. It is not easy striking the right balance between egotism and sensitive, effective 'subjectivity'.

Eye-witness features within this genre (and Lynne Truss's column in *The Times* is worth watching) are usually aimed at non-specialist readers. Thus, you may need to explain the rules of the game if it is an unusual one and the level of support in the UK. Evidence of class, race and gender bias run through whole segments of British life and is prominent in sporting activities. Certain sports are more distinctly working class (football, ten-pin bowling, rugby league, darts) than others (polo, hunting, grouse shooting). There may be opportunities in your feature to explore these aspects.

Unusual sports are played all over the UK: it is a challenge to search them out in your own area. Do not worry if you have never seen them played before. The newness of the experience will make it all the more intense for you. All the same it is advisable to prepare as far as possible before covering the event. Consult local libraries for contacts and information; ring the Sports Council or consult its website. Type your chosen sport into a web search engine and see what comes up. Ask friends and relations if they have any background information.

You may find the event boring and unintelligible. That merely poses you with the challenge of conveying that dullness in an interesting way. Always try to stay true to your feelings. Given the many pressures and constraints on journalists, that is not easily achieved. Try never to transform what you experience into a cliché you hope to be accepted to your news desk; try never to transform the 'dull' into something lively simply to 'beef-up' your copy. It will, inevitably, appear inauthentic. The tone will be an important ingredient of your piece. Humour, irony, wry self-criticism, mock chauvinism: any of these may be appropriate. But the tone has to emerge from your own experience. The eye-witness piece will work only if that tone is genuine. To explore the subjective element in eye-witness reporting, I shall examine critically a piece I wrote in 1977 while on the staff of the *Cambridge Evening News*.

Analysis of 'Bingo: Eyes down for that elusive jackpot': *Cambridge Evening News* (15 January 1977)

I am with more than 450 people packed in a hall in the centre of Cambridge. And I'm staring – in the silent thrall of my bingo fling – at a small piece of paper full of figures.

A man stands on a balcony and reads out nothing but numbers. He commands total attention as we sit poised with pens and pencils praying for the elusive jackpot.

"All the eights, 88," says the man on the balcony.

A cry of "Yes" is heard. A whistle is blown. Great chattering breaks out. A young man dashes (so quick it is as if his life depended on it) towards the crier, takes a card from him and reads out again nothing but numbers. The crier is £80 richer: another game is over, another drama has been enacted.

Indeed, it is the theatrical, almost surreal, aspects of the surroundings that I find so fascinating in the Central EMI Bingo and Social Club in Hobson Street.

This converted cinema could quite comfortably have found a place in the zaniest of science fiction movies – with its brash, psychedelic, mish-mash of colours (silver, yellow, red, green, rust, cream to name a few) and its huge, electrically operated board that rises high behind the caller, a confusing conglomeration of figures blazing out like the strange invention of a mad mathematician.

And then there's the peculiar bingo lingo – housey housey, full house, last'un, flyer, ling double, quickie – that flows so naturally off the lips of the cognoscenti.

Since the game first burst upon the British public 15 years ago the number of participants has been growing dramatically. It's an even bet that at some time or other you've had a bingo fling.

The four-year-old Cambridge Central club has 10,000 members. And Britain's big four bingo businesses – Mecca, Rank, EMI and Ladbrokes – have between them 422 clubs dotted about the country.

Britain is, in fact, going through a bingo boom. But bingo players remain the great unnameables. It's an almost dead cert that if you play bingo you don't want your neighbour to know it.

Last Saturday I could find no-one prepared to give me his or her name, so strong is the social stigma attached to the game.

EMI's Press officer, Mr Eric Sullings, blamed this on the "class consciousness of the town."

"If you go to Lancashire and Yorkshire, the real bingo playing country," he said, "people are happy to talk freely about playing bingo but the further south you go the more careful people become."

This wall of silence was not my only problem. Bingo, be warned, is almost submerged beneath rules and regulations.

Before you can play you have to be a member of the club. On my first approach to the Central I was membershipless and told I just could not play.

I had to sign like everyone else a free application card and wait a week for my membership. My second visit revealed still more hazards. I arrived at 8.15 p.m. expecting to launch into a game but was told it was impossible – no cards are sold after 7.45 and members are not allowed guests.

So last Saturday it was a case of third time lucky. Even then the manager Mr. John Jones, aged 41, first said I could not talk to any of the players or any of his staff. Then, after ringing his regional chief, he allowed me to talk to the players. His staff were to remain mute.

The bingo men are clearly still smarting from recent "bingomania revelations" in the national popular Press. Bashing bingo, they feel, has become a national newspaper sport and reports of women spending their rent money on the game have given it a bad image.

Certainly the Central is an addict's paradise – open every afternoon and evening except Sunday afternoon and with hundreds of pounds at stake at each session.

On Saturday the club linked up by phone to the EMI club in Oxford for a game which boasted a £400 jackpot.

Moreover the players I spoke to were quick to comment on the addictive aspects of the game: "That fruit machine is a disease," said one.

Indeed I looked on somewhat amazed at people dashing for the fruit machine (which spills out its £30 jackpot in 50p pieces) in the few seconds between games and then at the long queues forming in front of them during the interval.

But Mr. Jones was eager to stress the social aspects of the game. "We have people from all walks of life – police officers off duty, traffic wardens and doctors as well as housewives. It is a happy place. We get lots of pensioners in the afternoons who come for the warmth and companionship."

Clearly lots of people get lots of fun from bingo. I felt I had a good £1.80 worth playing in all the games – even though I did not come within a mile of winning any prize let alone the £400 jackpot.

But the final word goes to manager Mr. Jones: "I can't stand the game. It's too boring."

- *Par. 1*: the 'I' presence stated clearly at the start. Notice the use of the dramatic present tense. The tone is slightly ironic ('in the silent thrall of my bingo fling'), perhaps over-consciously literary with the use of alliteration 'full of figures'. And the local angle is stressed.
- *Par. 2*: more colour, eye-witness reporting and contrived alliteration.
- *Par. 3*: short direct quote to maintain the narrative flow.
- *Par. 4*: sense of drama is conveyed through contrasting sentence lengths: three short ones followed by a much longer one. Then comes a clear conclusion to the opening section's narrative 'another drama has been enacted'.
- *Par. 5*: a general comment about the subjective 'I' experience and the 'where' of the piece is detailed: the Central EMI Bingo and Social Club.
- *Par. 6*: an enormously long sentence whose home could only be a feature. There is an emphasis on the building up of descriptive details about what is seen. Again, the rather self-consciously literary and alliterative 'confusing conglomeration' and the simile 'like the strange invention of a mad mathematician'.
- *Par. 7*: an emphasis now on what is heard. And I am conveying some delight in the sounds of the unusual, jargon words.
- *Par. 8*: general British historical background details and I take up the gambling jargon with 'an even bet'.
- *Par. 9*: more background about bingo in Cambridge and in Britain generally.
- *Par. 10*: more general background with 'an almost dead cert' continuing the gambling theme. Social stigma theme emerges.
- *Par. 11*: social stigma theme developed and related to my own experience.
- *Pars 12–13*: strong quote to back up social stigma theme from good source.

Bingo: Eyes down for that elusive jackpot

I AM with more than 450 people packed in a hall in the centre of Cambridge. And I'm staring — in the silent thrall of my bingo fling — at a small piece of paper full of figures.

A man stands on a balcony and reads out nothing but numbers. He commands total attention as we sit poised with pens and pencils praying for the elusive jackpot.

"All the eights, 88," says the man on the balcony.

A cry of "Yes" is heard. A whistle is blown. Great chattering breaks out. A young man dashes (so quick it is as if his life depended on it) towards the crier, takes a card from him and reads out again nothing but numbers. The crier is £80 richer; another game is over, another drama has been enacted.

Indeed it is the theatrical, almost surreal, aspects of the surroundings that I find so fascinating in the Central

Membership card in hand, Richard Keeble enters the bingo hall.   827716

By Richard Keeble

EMI Bingo and Social Club in Hobson Street.

This converted cinema could quite comfortably have found a place in the zaniest of science fiction movies—with its brash, psychedelic mish-mash of colours (silver, yellow, red, green, rust, cream to name a few) and its huge, electrically operated board that rises high behind the caller, a confusing conglomeration of figures blazing out like the strange invention of a mad mathematician.

And then there's the peculiar bingo lingo—housey housey, full house, last'un, flyer, ling double, quickie—that flows so naturally off the lips of the cognoscenti.

Since the game first burst upon the British public 15 years ago the number of participants has been growing dramatically. It's an even bet that at some time or other you've had a bingo fling.

The four-year-old Cambridge Central club alone has 10,000 members. And Britain's big four bingo businesses—Mecca, Rank, EMI and Ladbrokes — have between them 422 clubs dotted about the country.

Britain is, in fact, going through a bingo boom. But bingo players remain the great unnameables. It's an almost dead cert that if you play bingo you don't want your neighbour to know it. Last Saturday I could find no-one prepared to give me his or her name, so strong is the social stigma attached to the game.

EMI's Press officer, Mr Eric Sullings, blamed this

on the "class consciousness of the town."

"If you go to Lancashire and Yorkshire, the real bingo playing country," he said, "people are happy to talk freely about playing bingo but the further south you go the more careful people become."

This wall of silence was not my only problem. Bingo, be warned, is almost submerged beneath rules and regulations.

Before you can play you have to be a member of a club. On my first approach to the Central I was membershipless and told I just could not play.

I had to sign like everyone else a free application card and wait a week for my membership. My second visit revealed still more hazards. I arrived at 8.15p.m. expecting to launch into a game but was told it was impossible—no cards are sold after 7.45 p.m. and members are not allowed guests.

So last Saturday it was a case of third time lucky. Even then the manager Mr. John Jones, aged 41, first said I could not talk to any of the players or any of his staff. Then, after ringing his regional chief, he allowed me to talk to the players. His staff were to remain mute.

The bingo men are clearly still smarting from recent "bingomania revelations" in the national popular Press. Bashing bingo, they feel, has become a national newspaper sport and reports of women spending their rent money on the game have given it a bad image.

Certainly the Central is an addict's paradise — open every afternoon and evening except Sunday afternoon and

with hundreds of pounds at stake at each session.

On Saturday the club linked up by phone to the EMI club in Oxford for a game which boasted a £400 jackpot.

Moreover the players I spoke to were quick to comment on the addictive aspects of the game. "That fruit machine is a disease," said one.

Indeed I looked on somewhat amazed at people dashing for the fruit machine (which spills out its £30 jackpot in 50p pieces) in the few seconds between games and then at the long queues forming in front of them during the interval.

But Mr Jones was eager

to stress the social aspects of the game. "We have people from all walks of life —police officers off duty, traffic wardens and doctors as well as housewives. It's a happy place. We get lots of pensioners in the afternoons who come for the warmth and companionship."

Clearly lots of people get lots of funs from bingo. I felt I had a good £1.80 worth playing in all the games — even though I did not come within a mile of winning any prize let alone the £400 jackpot.

But the final word goes to manager Mr. Jones: "I can't stand the game. It's too boring."

- *Pars 14–16*: details, rules and regulations of game drawn from my own experience.
- *Par. 17*: 'third time lucky' continues gambling theme as I continue narrative of my visits. Return to social stigma theme with indirect quote from manager.
- *Par. 18*: new 'bashing bingo/addiction' theme.
- *Pars 19–20*: extra detail about Cambridge club continuing addiction theme.
- *Par. 21*: short quote to support continuing addiction theme.
- *Par. 22*: eye-witness reporting supporting the addiction theme.
- *Par. 23*: quote to present positive view of the game in the interests of 'balance'.
- *Par. 24*: balancing comment from myself plus extra details about costs and prize money.
- *Par. 25*: short snappy concluding remark which is somewhat surprising: a 'sting in the tail' ending. In retrospect, I regret using this quote. Mr Jones did say it (a photographer was there to confirm after he protested) and it did provide me with a quirky finishing flourish. But it reflected badly on Mr Jones and caused him unnecessary problems. I should have exerted some self-censorship in that instance.

Looking back at the feature, written after I had been a journalist for around seven years, the detached, ironic tone is most striking. I think it probably emerged from my class orientation. Here I was, a middle-class man intruding into the world of the working class who felt themselves ostracised in academically dominated Cambridge. From this tension emerges the self-conscious, over-literary style of my writing. The tone of dry irony (common in the media), in fact, was my attempt to negotiate this feeling of being 'an outsider'.

Journalists' dilemmas

To what extent can and should journalists remain outsiders? How much do journalistic notions of neutrality, objectivity and balance conflict with inevitable feelings of sympathy, compassion, alienation, confusion and solidarity? George Orwell grappled with such dilemmas by going to live the experience he wanted to write about. He became a plongeur (a dish-washer in a hotel kitchen) and tramp before writing *Down and Out in Paris and London* (1933); he fought alongside the Republicans in the Spanish civil war and wrote of his experiences in *Homage to Catalonia* (1938). Later Orwell (often considered one of the twentieth century's greatest journalists) largely ignored the prestigious Fleet Street outlets for his journalism and concentrated his attentions on small circulation, left wing and literary publications. But even the 'Orwell solution' is not without its problems and paradoxes. The best the journalist can do is seek to understand their own histories; their own subjectivities as well as the broader political dynamics of their society. It is perhaps a tall order – but worth striving for.

Painting a picture in words: PROFILE WRITING

Open a newspaper and you are likely to find a profile somewhere. People, according to Harold Evans, former editor of *The Times* and *Sunday Times*, are news. The profile, the drawing of a portrait with words, is the archetypal manifestation of this 'people/human/interest bias' in the media. The portrait need not be only of a person: organisations, buildings, cemeteries, roads, parks, schools, Father Christmas, even weapons (rather obscenely) can be profiled. But people profiles are the most common. Profiles succeed in satisfying a wide range of interests:

- *Readers*: profiles are immensely popular. They feed people's curiosity about other people. What makes them tick, what hurdles have they overcome, what is the person really like behind the public face, what accounted for their downfall? This kind of questioning has great appeal. The tot (triumph over tragedy) story, in which people talk about their success against tremendous odds, is a particularly popular genre. We become voyeurs into private or professional lives.

- *Reporters*: writing profiles is fun, challenging and can often help a journalist to build up contact with a useful source. Reputations can be made on the strength of profile writing.

- *Editors*: profiles often appear in series which guarantee a certain space being filled each week. Readers like the series format also, perhaps because they provide a feeling of continuity, stability and order. They occupy the same spot at regular intervals and so simplify the reading process.

- *Proprietors*: there is an important commercial aspect to profiles. In terms of cost-effectiveness they are particularly attractive to newspaper proprietors. An interview with accompanying picture can easily provide half a page (broadsheet) or a page or more (tabloid or magazine). Compare this with the cost-effectiveness of investigative reporting. A journalist may spend hours, months even, investigating a story and get nowhere.

- *People*: being profiled can pander to their vanity. Profiles can help promote business. A writer, for instance, hopes the publicity will help sell more of their books. The PR industry is forever pressurising the press to profile their clients.

Types of people profiles

There are many kinds of profiles and no standard format. There are no profile rules. To highlight a few styles within the genre:

- A short profile may highlight some newsworthy feature of the subject. A variation on this theme are the tiny portraits of people drawn in diary or gossip columns.

- There is a profile focusing on the person's views about a contemporary issue or experience or highlighting a recent achievement or failure.

- A longer profile will aim to provide an overview of a life. The person will be chosen probably because of a newsworthy element (a new job, a new book/film/television series/political campaign or they are visiting the local region) which will be highlighted.

- A person may be profiled because of some unusual feature of their lives. They may have the largest collection of football or theatre programmes in the country or an unusual job such as travelling around advising gypsies on educational matters. The news element here is not significant.

- There is the 'authoritative' profile (such as in the *Sunday Times* and *Sunday Telegraph*) in which the newspaper tries to present its definitive view on the subject. These will tend to carry other people's views of the subject but will not carry any byline since it is the publication speaking.

- There is a whole range of 'special focus' profiles which build a picture of a person around a specific angle. The *Sunday Times* has its 'Life in the Day' series and 'Relative Values' in which two members of the same family give their impressions of growing up with the other person. (A similar feature in the *Independent* is called 'A Family Affair'.) *Night and Day*, the supplement of the *Mail on Sunday*, has a 'Lay in the life of' in which a celebrity talks about a memorable lovemaking session. The *Guardian* has a 'My Media' and a 'My Big Break' column.

- Becoming increasingly popular are question and answer profiles around various themes. *M* mag of the *Mirror*, for instance, has a 'Closet Confessions' column in which women talk about their clothes. Both the Birmingham-based *Sunday Mercury* and the *Daily Mail* have a 'Me and My Health' column while the *Express* has 'The Shape I'm In'. The *Guardian Weekend* supplement has its 'Questionnaire' in which celebrities answer a standard series of questions; the *Reality* supplement of the *Independent on Sunday* has a 'One minute in the mind of' feature while the *Newmarket Journal* has its 'My Way' column; the *Sunday Mercury* has a 'Facts of My Life' questionnaire and the London freebie, *Metro*, has 'The 60 second interview'. The *Independent* runs a regular questionnaire based on readers' submissions. Often these are commentaries rather than interview-based features. *The Times* has 'The Test' in which personalities are assessed in various categories. The *Guardian* has 'Pass Notes' in which the subjects are dissected through a jokey, conversational style of questioning.

- Occasionally a couple are profiled in the same article; they may be married, close friends, living together or in a business partnership. Some newspapers profile families.

Preparing the profile paint

Focus

The journalist has to be aware of the particular kind of profile sought by their publication. Is it to be an overview of the life or a focus on the latest achievements or affairs, or a 'life in the day' (very different from a 'day in the life')? In every case, the focus will influence the questioning. The journalist tends to identify to the subject during the initial contact the kind (and possible length) of profile envisaged.

Background research

Absolutely crucial. Quite simply the more knowledge of the subject and their special area you bring to the interview the more respect they will have for you and the more likely they are to 'open up'. Thus, if you are interviewing a writer/film director/television producer or sports personality/local council leader/political campaigner you should be aware of their previous achievements. People featured in *Who's Who* will not expect questions about fundamental details of their life. The challenge is very different when the subject is unknown. Then, the journalist needs to convey an interest in their subject and their specialist area.

Before (and if possible after) the interview, ask other people about your subject. You may want to include some of these views in your profile. Consult the cuttings; their website (official and unofficial, maybe); consult the online archive Northern Light (http://www.nlsearch.com) or, if appropriate, the celebrity site http://www.celebsites.com – but don't presume details are accurate without checking. Immerse yourself in your subject.

Place of interview/s

Most profiles are built on the basis of one-off interviews. Describing the time and place of the interview might provide colour to the piece. Good journalists use all their senses. Sometimes, the profile is the result of a series of interviews. On one occasion the subject may be relaxed, at another completely different. They may be extremely busy; describing snatches of conversation in various places can convey a sense of their hectic lifestyle. The journalist may meet the interviewee before the formal meeting by accident – and describe the experience in their copy. Occasionally a person is so famous they are extremely difficult to get hold of. Describing the hunt can provide colour to the profile. If the hunt ends in failure, the non-story can become the story. Again some people are very shy of interviews. When they finally agree, the 'rareness' is worth highlighting.

Sometimes personalities are unwilling to be interviewed. Profiles of them are still written, often containing comments about the person from other people. The person may have revealed something about themselves in a rare television interview and quotes and details from that may be used. Occasionally a profile might be built around a press conference but then the copy loses the feeling of intimacy that a face-to-face interview provides. Increasingly profiles are amounting to nothing more than rewrites of cuttings with some newsy element in the intro and concern is growing over the power of PR departments to shape celebrity profiles. According to Tad Friend (1998): 'Most profiles are almost scripted by the PR agency.'

Those important brush strokes: CONSTRUCTING THE PROFILE

The influence of the news

Profiles need not begin with the newsworthy aspect. They might seek to highlight a particularly significant or unusual event in the past. They might open with a particularly revealing quote. They might be descriptive, focusing on the appearance of the person or the environment in which the interview takes place. But many profiles are influenced by the news agenda and in these cases their news aspect will never be buried in copy. It will be near the start. Take for instance, this profile of artist John Hewitt by Mark Patterson in the Nottingham *Evening Post* (2 March 2000):

QUESTION: What is the connection between legendary KLF art terrorist Bill Drummond and Nottingham club The Bomb?

The answer is John Hewitt, the Nottingham artist who decorated the bus stops along the route of the city's No. 85 bus route in the name of the Now '98 festival two years ago.

That was then. These days, the 33-year-old is busy co-ordinating public art commissions along the new Sustrans bicycle path from Nottingham to Barnsley.

On March 19, he also begins a six day trek across 100km of the Sinai Desert.

And on Monday his fund-raising efforts will get a boost in a night of multi-media madness titled 2 × 8 at The Bomb.

The copy delays mentioning the main news angle until par. 5, slowly building up to that point. Other profiles, in contrast, are 'timeless' without a specific news angle. The person themselves may simply be newsworthy or there may be something particularly interesting about them.

The importance of quotations

Most profiles will carry the views of the person through the use of direct quotes. The importance of these to the profile cannot be overstated. Given that the profile is attempting to paint the most vivid portrait possible, the language of the interviewee is a vital ingredient of their personality. A profile in which all the views are in reported speech will be deadly dull.

Some profiles will carry snatches of conversation (sometimes remembered rather than noted) verbatim. It helps provide special insights into the subject as well as varying the rhythmic pulse and tone of the writing. As here from Joanna Coles's profile of the American novelist Joyce Carol Oates in *The Times* (7 April 2000): the novelist Edmund White, who has an office opposite at Princeton University, 'bursts in'.

"We're talking about the role of illusion," says Joyce by way of introduction.

"She's being very modest," I complain.

"Well she's great," says White.

"Oh isn't that sweet," Joyce giggles.

"Ever since I've been here, she's taken me under her wing and introduced me to everybody. She's incredibly sweet and has more energy than anyone I know," says White "And she's also incredibly smart."

"Oh my, *blush!*" cries Joyce.

"Very good, very good," beams White sweeping up his raincoat and bustling out. "See you later."

Hard news hardly ever begins with direct quotes but profiles quite often do. A striking phrase can encapsulate so much of the person's personality. As here, Nick Caistor begins his obituary of Jacobo Timerman in the *Guardian* (15 November 1999):

> "The cell is narrow. When I stand at its centre, facing the steel door, I can't extend my arms." With these words Jacobo Timerman, who has died in Buenos Aires of a heart attack aged 76, began what was for many the most important denunciation of the Argentinian military dictatorships of the 1970s, Prisoner Without a Name, Cell Without a Number.

Other profiles will merge quotes from a conversation into one long, direct quote such as the 'Life in the Day' feature in the *Sunday Times* colour supplement. The interviewee will often be consulted to see if they approve of the editing. Some profiles carry quotes from people about the interviewee, their personality and/or their work. This is particularly the case in 'authoritative' profiles which attempt to provide an overview of the person and their achievements.

Descriptive colour

Many profiles carry descriptions of the person, their appearance, their mannerisms perhaps, their asides, the environment where they live, work or are interviewed. All this adds colour and variety to the copy. Thus, to capture writer Norman Mailer's personality, award-winning interviewer Ginny Dougary described his home in detail (*The Times*, 2 June 2000):

> Inside you are blasted by the brightness of the light that fills the room, through a wall of glass, which leads on to a great deck, the size of a ballroom, and on to the blue dazzle of the sea beyond. There are several colourful paintings, a couple of them by local artists, an impression of cream and white furnishings, a table with biblical quantities of family photographs (Mailer has attended 27 graduation ceremonies) and an expensive looking chess set. It is not the kind of home, one feels, in which one would be encouraged to light up a cigarette, unexotic or otherwise, or, indeed, in which to become drunk and disorderly.

But do not be tempted to invent descriptive colour to brighten up a phone-based profile. In its 1992 report, the Press Complaints Commission criticised a reporter who said of the interviewee 'Watching her, sitting up in bed', though they had never seen her face-to-face.

Chronology

Only rarely do profiles begin at the beginning of a life and end with a focus on the present. That chronology will appear extremely dull since it reflects no concept of journalistic values. Instead, profiles can highlight a newsworthy/specially interesting aspect of the person and then, in the body of the article, take up the chronological theme, finally returning to the main theme. But be careful not to make confusing chronological jumps (first talking about 1975, then 1965, then 1999, then 1962).

Denis Staunton, in his *Observer* profile of Johanna Quandt and her family, owners of nearly half the shares in BMW (26 March 2000), begins by concentrating on the company's controversial plans, announced earlier that week, to sell off Rover. Then, in par. 9, he provides the historical background:

> The motor industry has certainly been good to the Quandts and the family's stake in BMW is now worth ten times what it was in 1982 when Johanna's husband, Herbert, died. Herbert was born in 1910 into a long-established industrial family and his father, Gunther, was one of Hitler's chief economic advisors. Gunther's second wife, Magda Friedlaender, later married Goebbels and the young Herbert spent part of his youth at the propaganda minister's home. By the time war broke out, however, Herbert was already an adult and was no longer in contact with Goebbels who poisoned himself, his wife and their six children in Hitler's bunker in 1945.
>
> Much of the Quandt family business was in ruins after the war and a great part of what survived had been commandeered by the invading Soviet forces. The task of rebuilding its fortunes fell mainly to Herbert, who proved to be a highly effective businessman, saving BMW from bankruptcy in 1959 by increasing his stake in the company and unflinchingly selling the family stake in Daimler-Benz when he judged the time to be right.

Newspapers often carry the biographical details briefly in a box accompanying the article leaving in the profile the space to concentrate on more up-to-date matters. Such 'fact boxes' are useful also for giving textual and visual variety to the page.

The presence of the reporter

In any representation of an individual there is bound to be a subjective element. Many profiles rely on an entertaining mix of quotes and background detail, the journalist subjectively selecting the material and remaining invisible in the copy. But some profiles exploit the journalist–interviewee relationship and make the journalist intentionally intrusive. Reporters may present their own views on the subject or on some of the issues raised in the interview. They may describe the dynamic in the relationship and how the interviewer responded to some of the questions (abruptly, hesitantly). This is how Anna Murphy, in the *Sunday Telegraph* (9 April 2000), described ballet dancer Sarah Wilder, creating interest by observing her subject outside the interview context:

> One minute she is sitting on the floor by the piano watching two other dancers – Jonathan Cope and Jaime Tapper, the second cast – rehearse the lead roles, the next springing up in the air as if she had jetpacks under those legwarmers to show how this particular jump should be just so. She sits back down, and then she is up again, spinning like a top, or twisting into an extravagant pose, still like a statue. Up, down. Up, down. I am exhausted just watching.
>
> Later in the canteen, I ask her about her latest role.

Top interviewer Lynn Barber, in the *Independent on Sunday* (30 January 2000), was not afraid to admit her insecurities to her readers when profiling Jimmy Savile. Notice how she makes no attempt to soften the impact of the question ('I hope you don't mind me asking, but'); she goes straight to the point:

> Still, I was nervous when I told him: "What people say is that you like little girls."
> He reacted with a flurry of funny-voice Jimmy Savile patter which he does when
> he's getting his bearings.

Notice here how Caroline Graham, in her profile of Vanessa Paradis (partner of
Hollywood actor Johnny Depp) in the *Mail on Sunday* magazine, *Night and Day* (19
March 2000), closely observes her subject's body language:

> My eye is suddenly drawn to a huge diamond ring on the third finger of Vanessa's
> left hand. Is it an engagement ring, I wonder?
> She blushes and looks down again, saying only, "it's a love ring."
> I ask if Depp gave it to her on a "special" occasion such as the birth of Lily-
> Rose. She twists the ring in her confusion, a rosy blush colouring her cheeks. "It
> didn't need a special occasion. It didn't require a date on a calendar. It's an antique
> ring, very old . . ."

The bias of the newspaper

When newspapers of the left carry profiles, they often promote strong political points,
rather than the subjective bias of the individual reporter. As here, *Socialist Worker*
(3 June 2000):

> Brian Souter, head of Stagecoach, has tried to pose as the voice of the people
> with his funding of the referendum over the anti-gay law, Section 28, in Scotland.
> Really, he is a shark who has spent the last 20 years building a multi-billion
> transport company by ruthlessly forcing other companies off the road.

The finishing touches

Profiles usually end on a significant note. Copy doesn't just die away, meaninglessly.
A common device is to end on a positive note, particularly if the subject has been
open in the interview about their difficult times. Thus a profile by Fiona James in
the *Sunday Mirror* (13 February 2000) of Ruth Harding, widow of the millionaire
football boss Matthew Harding, who discovered on his death he had two mistresses
– and a child by each – ends with this direct quote:

> Ruth is probably happier than she has ever been. She looks younger than she did
> when her husband died. She's a much trendier dresser under Richard's influence.
> "I've been very lucky," she says. "Anne Hoddle and Judith Mellor and I have
> all survived."

In Eileen Condon's profile of Mike Leigh, director of the film *Topsy-Turvy*, in the
Nottingham *Evening Post* (17 February 2000), a witticism and a sudden chuckle
provide a final lift to the copy:

And while Leigh is pleased with the accolades, he confesses his main aim with the film is to put Gilbert and Sullivan firmly back on the map.

"They've grown on me over the years but then so have a lot of things including grey hair," he says, his familiar hangdog expression brightening a little to allow a small chuckle.

The tone

This is the most vital ingredient of the piece. Is it to be an affectionate piece? Is it to be respectful, gently mocking, a damning exposé, intellectually discursive, witty, 'neutral' (hope you will never write a sycophantic one!)? In each of these the language used will be different. You may spend a couple of hours, even days, with your subject. They may offer you a meal. Some form of human contact is established. It is then very tricky to write a damning (though obviously non-libellous) profile of that person. Equally there is a danger of solving this dilemma by lavishing praise on your subject. There can be no standard response. At all times, passing judgement should always be handled delicately. A crook, a racist or a sexist needs to be exposed. But the interview is an extremely artificial environment and the impression that the subject provides should always be viewed as partial and superficial.

13 **Some specialist areas**

Personal columns, reviewing, freelancing

The 'I' witness: PERSONAL COLUMNS

All news emerges from a dialectical process in which the subjective confronts the objective. Its subjective element is particularly evident in the complex process of selection. Personal columns make this subjectivity overt. The 'I' speaks loud and clear. Personal columns 'work' when the voice speaks in particularly original tones. They may be witty, controversial, no-nonsense, hard-hitting, culturally eclectic, conversational, quirky, bitchy, whimsical, confessional, authoritative, subversive, irritating. At their worst they combine crude ranting with personal abuse. But the writer's personality should always shine through the copy.

The reader enters into a kind of relationship with the writer. Often accompanying the column is a head-and-shoulders picture or drawing of the writer to help 'personalise' this relationship further. Readers can come to love them – or hate them. The worst fate for a columnist is to be ignored. Yet, at the same time, as Christopher Silvester (1997) argues:

> a column appears in the same publication on a regular basis usually in the same position and with the same heading and by-line. The presence of the column is reassuring, therefore, not primarily because of what it has to say but because of its appearance in a particular spot, on a particular day or days and at an approximately predictable length.
>
> (Silvester 1997: xi)

Personal column styles, language and tones are also appropriate to their newspaper. They make up and are influenced by the overall 'personality' of the newspaper. Quotations from novels by contemporary East European novelists might appear in a column in the *Observer* but not in the *Star*. A slow moving narrative about a strange appointment at the hairdresser's may be appropriate for a local weekly but not for the *Guardian*.

The value of good columnists is acknowledged by all newspapers. *The Times* columnist Matthew Parris was rumoured to have turned down £300,000 a year to work for the *Independent*, while Suzanne Moore was reported to receive £140,000 a year for one column a week for the *Mail on Sunday*. Similarly local papers will use personal columns strategically. Rather than attempt to be journals of record like their daily rivals, a weekly may carry an opinionated column from either a staff journalist or reader. In this way, the paper is striving to make its mark on the local community, intervening with a column aimed at getting people talking and possibly provoking letters (either for or against).

There are many forms of personal columns. They might be straight opinion or involve a small amount of journalistic research. They might be a selection of short features or news stories reflecting the interests of the writer. Sketchwriters, such as Simon Hoggart, Matthew Parris and Frank Johnson, are associated particularly with light-hearted, eye-witness (and perhaps over-affectionate) pieces on Parliament. Most personal columns respond a little too slavishly to the dominant news agenda; too many journalists end up talking about other journalists, other media. Female confessional columnists, such as India Knight, Anna Blundy and Zoë Heller, became all the rage in the 1990s. Helen Fielding became the most famous exponent of the genre and her *Bridget Jones's Diary* went on to become a global best-seller. Kathryn Flett's outpourings in the *Observer* on her marriage breakdown drew an enormous response from readers. 'I wasn't resorting to journalistic tricks to fill the inches. There was no longer a place for endless puns, alliteration and smarty-pants irony; instead I was stuck with the truth,' she wrote (Flett 1997).

Also during the 1990s concern grew over the explosion of columns throughout the press. As Suzanne Moore commented:

As more and more people get their news from other forms of media, the role of newspaper journalism has become more interpretative and subjective. In these times of media saturation and its subsequent neurosis – information anxiety – columnists in their idiosyncratic ways wade through the mire of information about the world we live in.

(Moore 1996: x)

But, critics argued, instead of hard news and hard-hitting investigative pieces, frothy features full of the mindless musings of over-important, over-paid celebrity journalists were filling up the columns. According to Brian McNair (2000: 64): 'The rise of the political commentator is a direct consequence of the commodification of the public sphere which makes it necessary for news organisations to brand their output (give it exchange value in a market place containing many other superficially similar brands).'

Tips for budding columnists

Maintaining a constant stream of (ideally original) opinion is not easy. Indeed, according to Stephen Glover (1999: 290–1), the columnist's skill is 'in writing about matters of which one is ignorant'. Certainly, the columnist must be interested in, and reasonably informed about, a wide range of issues. Many journalists pick the brains of experts on their current subject – and then pass them on as if they were their own. The American columnist, Max Lerner, had this advice: 'I keep a notebook and a file into which I jot down ideas for columns as they occur to me. Before I write I look through the papers and often some headline event will converge with one of these ideas' (Silvester 1997: xxiii).

Keith Waterhouse (1995), the eminent Fleet Street columnist, has provided his own 25-step plan to writing the perfect column. It included:

*   Every columnist needs a good half-dozen hobby horses. But do not ride them to death.
*   On cuttings, he suggests: 'The more cuttings you accumulate, the more you will be tempted to offload them on to your readers. . . . Packing the column with other people's quotes is the columnar equivalent of watering the milk. Assimilate material and then discard it.'
*   Never try to fake it. 'Nothing is so transparent as insincerity – pile on the adjectives though you may, false indignation has the ring of a counterfeit coin.'
*   A column should not be used to pursue a personal grudge unless it is going to ring bells with most of your readers.
*   Allow your readers only a few restricted glimpses into your private life.
*   Columnar feuds are amusing to other columnists and may even yield them copy providing they don't mind living vicariously. The reader, or what Craig Brown describes as 'that diminishing minority of people who do not write newspaper columns', find them bemusing.

Analysis of Anne Robinson's column:
The Times (15 April 2000)

I can't quite work out why Kathleen Turner getting her kit off every night in *The Graduate* in the West End is causing such a stir. The first time around, when Dustin Hoffman starred in the film with Anne Bancroft, it was wonderfully radical for Mrs Robinson to shamelessly seduce her daughter's boyfriend. But now I am Mrs Robinson's age-plus, I think it would take no time at all to get Benjamin into the sack.

If only because these days Elaine, her daughter, would be a terrifyingly ambitious young woman with her sights set on merchant banking and million-dollar bonuses, doubtless scaring Benjamin witless with her power and desire for success. In contrast one can see the middle-aged Mrs Robinson as a very comforting alternative and needing to do little more than whistle to persuade an insecure lad to jump into bed alongside her.

● Madam Speaker has made it clear where she will and will not tolerate breast feeding in the House of Commons. Which surprised me because I thought we had sorted all that years ago when a young Labour MP called Helene Hayman fought to be allowed to bring her baby to Westminster.

By co-incidence the now Baroness Hayman, and an Agriculture Minister, was on *Watchdog* last week talking about Pet Passports.

After we came off air I raised the breast-feeding episode and she told me firmly that she held no particular brief for women wanting to feed in public. Her problem was a tiny ten-day-old baby, an even tinier Labour majority and an insistence by the whips that she be around to vote.

As she explained, her only hope of keeping baby and party happy was to fight to be allowed to nurse in between debates. Baby Ben, incidentally, is now 23.

Anne Robinson

'Now I am Mrs Robinson's age-plus, I think it would take no time to get Benjamin into the sack'

● I CAN'T quite work out why Kathleen Turner getting her kit off every night in *The Graduate* in the West End is causing such a stir. The first time around, when Dustin Hoffman starred in the film with Anne Bancroft, it was wonderfully radical for Mrs Robinson to shamelessly seduce her daughter's boyfriend. But now I am Mrs Robinson's age-plus, I think it would take no time at all to get Benjamin into the sack.

If only because these days Elaine, her daughter, would be a terrifyingly ambitious young woman with her sights set on merchant banking and million-dollar bonuses, doubtless scaring Benjamin witless with her power and desire for success. In contrast one can see the middle-aged Mrs Robinson as a very comforting alternative and needing to do little more than whistle to persuade an insecure lad to jump into bed alongside her.

● MADAM Speaker has made it clear where she will and will not tolerate breast feeding in the House of Commons. Which surprised me because I thought we had sorted all that years ago when a young Labour MP called Helene Hayman fought to be allowed to bring her baby to Westminster.

By co-incidence the now Baroness Hayman, and an Agriculture Minister, was on *Watchdog* last week talking about Pet Passports.

After we came off air I raised the breast-feeding episode and she told me firmly that she held no particular brief for women wanting to feed in public. Her problem was a tiny ten-day-old baby, an even tinier Labour majority and an insistence by the whips that she be around to vote.

As she explained, her only hope of keeping flabby and party happy was to fight to be allowed to nurse in between debates. Baby Ben, incidentally, is now 23.

● BACK to Covent Garden last week to see Sylvie Guillem in *Marguerite and Armand*.

It was sensational and, quite rightly, the audience howled its approval at the end.

My friend Sally, who was kind enough to get the tickets, was dreadfully disappointed with our view from Row D because the incline of the seats, intended to improve your view, is negligible so near the front and it was tricky seeing the footwork.

Then, at the interval, two women who turned out to be devoted fans of the Russian dancer Irek Mukhamedov, and had already seen him dance the role of Lescaut four times within a fortnight, came up to say hello. They looked pityingly at us when we told them where we were sitting.

"You have to go for Row A, or after Row H," said one of them shaking her head in disbelief that neither of us possessed such obvious House intelligence.

Why should we? When you book

no one offers you that sort of advice and it prompted me to step back into the auditorium early to ask one of the opera house staff where he would sit if he was paying.

"A22 upstairs," he said without hesitating, adding that when the Queen really wants to see the action she doesn't bother with the Royal Box. She and her party are there with the people in the front row of the circle.

● IT'S usually only Vivienne Westwood's most outrageous designs that are chosen by picture editors to feature in newspapers. A shame because it causes the public to view her, unfairly, as way out and silly.

A much better range of her work from the collection of Romilly McAlpine has gone on show at the Museum of London and is well worth a visit. Penrose absolutely fell in love with several of the numbers.

But then he loves women in men's clothes and would prefer me to dress the same as Katharine Hepburn in *On Golden Pond*. Even though I keep telling him that without the cheek bones, the hair and the slim hips, Katharine Hepburn would look like a bag lady.

● THE PARTY to launch the exhibition was swarming with glittery people. Nicky Haslam, the designer who looks about thirty instead of sixty and unlike Ms Westwood is still in his punk rock phase,

introduced me to Hilary Alexander, from *The Daily Telegraph*.

Ms Alexander does one of those daytime shows where housewives are taken out of their own clothes and put into daring new outfits. I often think half of them look better before-the hordes of makeover artists get to work. But the television team clearly believes it is taking part in important life-saving or at least face-saving surgery.

Dangerously so. Ten seconds after we were introduced, Ms Alexander started fiddling with my fringe and moving it around and telling me it was better "spread out". I was very tempted to give her a slap.

● THE DAUGHTER is due home from New York for Easter. I am taking time off to bake and to corset Kirsty Young, who knows a thing or two about television presenting but has yet to experience the joys of being a guilty working mother, will be delighting you for the next three weeks.

anne.robinson@the-times.co.uk

● Back to Covent Garden last week to see Sylvie Guillem in *Manon*.

It was sensational and, quite rightly, the audience howled its approval at the end.

My friend Sally, who was kind enough to get the tickets, was dreadfully disappointed with our view from Row D because the incline of the seats, intended to improve your view, is negligible so near the front and it was tricky seeing the footwork.

Then, at the interval, two women who turned out to be devoted fans of the Russian dancer Irek Mukhamedov, and had already seen him dance the role of Lescaut four times within a fortnight, came up to say hello. They looked pityingly at us when we told them where we were sitting.

"You have to go for Row A, or after Row H," said one of them shaking her head in disbelief that none of us possessed such obvious House intelligence.

Why should we? When you book no one offers you that sort of advice and it prompted me to step back into the auditorium early to ask one of the opera house staff where he would sit if he was paying.

"A22 upstairs," he said without hesitating, adding that when the Queen really wants to see the action she doesn't bother with the Royal Box. She and her party are there with the people in the front row of the circle.

● It's usually only Vivienne Westwood's most outrageous designs that are chosen by picture editors to feature in newspapers. A shame because it causes the public to view her, unfairly, as way out and silly.

A much better range of her work from the collection of Romilly McAlpine has gone on show at the Museum of London and is well worth a visit. Penrose absolutely fell in love with several of the numbers.

But then he loves women in men's clothes and would prefer me to dress the same as Katharine Hepburn in *On Golden Pond*. Even though I keep telling him that without the cheek bones, the hair and the slim hips, Katharine Hepburn would look like a bag lady.

The party to launch the exhibition was swarming with glittery people. Nicky Haslam, the designer who looks about thirty instead of sixty and unlike Ms Westwood is still in his punk rock phase, introduced me to Hilary Alexander, from *The Daily Telegraph*.

Ms Alexander does one of those daytime shows where housewives are taken out of their own clothes and put into daring new outfits. I often think half of them look better before the hordes of makeover artists get to work. But the television team clearly believes it is taking part in important life-saving or at least face-saving surgery.

Dangerously so. Ten seconds after we were introduced, Ms Alexander started fiddling with my fringe and moving it around and telling me it was better "spread out". I was very tempted to give her a slap.

Overview: critics might suggest this is a typical example of the 'dumbing down' of the broadsheet press: a TV celebrity penning a few gossipy thoughts based on her somewhat privileged lifestyle flitting from TV studio to Covent Garden and on to a glittery party. Until a decade ago this kind of column was reserved for the tabloid press (where Ms Robinson, in fact, developed her journalistic reputation). Others may argue it is all a necessary part of *The Times*'s moves to shake off its dull and sombre, pre-Murdoch past. Intriguingly Ms Robinson depicts a very feminine world: all her subjects are women, bar one.

Byline: The byline (in a large font) is accompanied by an unusual mug shot. Her expression is pleasantly cheeky-cum-whimsical. But most intriguing is the position of that right hand. It is held tightly around her front – as if protecting her from attack and that fist seems ready to punch anyone who dares intrude on her private territory. The few words drawn from the text (a 'pull quote' in a 'panel' in the jargon) accompanying the mug shot highlight significantly a passing remark that dwells on sex.

Gossip point one: 'I' is the first word setting the tone for the highly individualised copy. Significantly, to draw in her readers, she begins by focusing on a sexual theme. The largely male journalists of Fleet Street were, indeed, getting into something of a sweat over middle-aged Kathleen Turner, star of Hollywood (that ultimate dream machine), stripping on the West End stage. Acres of news, columnar and review copy (in both tabloids and broadsheets) were devoted to the event, even though it lasted for no more than a split second. (Similar hysteria later followed news that the former Mrs Mick Jagger, Jerry Hall, was to succeed Turner in the role.) Turner herself (and her publicists) fed the frenzy by turning up to a press conference draped in a towel.

There are many possible ways of explaining all this: a Freudian might focus on the failure of male journalists to outgrow their Oedipal adolescent fantasies about naked women – and particularly their mothers; a Marxist, for instance, might stress the commodification of women's bodies. Robinson avoids all these issues and moves on to a separate point: the supposed shock of seeing a middle-aged Mrs Robinson seduce the much younger Benjamin. It is intriguing to see how columnist Robinson sympathises and even identifies with Benjamin. Thus a determined careerist woman becomes, in her view, 'terrifying' – perhaps because she threatens men's traditional seats of power. Is there not a subtle anti-feminist agenda at work here?

Gossip point two: from sex we shift to the glittery world of TV celebrities and MPs. Betty Boothroyd, former Speaker of the House, had recently ruled against allowing MPs to breastfeed in the Commons chamber or committee rooms, though they were still permitted in their private rooms and in lavatories. Ms Robinson wants to convey this but her 'will and will not tolerate breast feeding' would be merely confusing to most of her readers. But she cleverly uses the column to give her readers a little insight into the goings on behind the camera, since what is unseen is far more interesting than the visible. It appears that her television guest Helene Hayman 'years ago' (a rather vague term) came to prominence over the Commons breastfeeding issue. But not through any sense of solidarity with her feminist sisters: she did it simply because of her concern to preserve the wafer-thin Labour majority. Robinson's failure to express any regret here is as significant as anything said.

Gossip point three: notice it's 'Back to Covent Garden' not ' To Covent Garden' Robinson is clearly part of that exclusive set who can afford regular visits. By reading her column we vicariously mingle. 'Dreadfully disappointed' uses alliteration to stress the point but it is not a phrase that would trip off the lips of the average man or woman on the Clapham Omnibus. An interesting narrative develops with a whiff of the investigative about it. She chats with two other Garden-goers about the best seats available. Dialogue helps vary the rhythm of the text. And it transpires that 'A22 upstairs' is the best. So you have been advised. But the most important fact is missing. Precisely how much is that seat? That kind of basic financial question is not raised in this dreamy, wealthy world by Robinson (who, a profile in the *Guardian* of 6 October 2000 revealed, had earned £2 million in 1999). Also, intriguingly, it appears that when the Queen mixes with 'the people' it is not out of any democratic instinct: she is simply aiming to get the best seat. Ms Robinson fails to draw out the irony here.

Gossip point four: and so to the launch of an exhibition of clothes by Vivienne Westwood. Tabloid values dominate this column – and yet here she takes a swipe at them for distorting the achievements of Vivienne Westwood. Then suddenly a 'Penrose' arrives on the scene with definite views about women's dress. Who is this person? Is it her lover, her husband, her butler? I think we should have been told. And why this reference to *On Golden Pond*? Katharine Hepburn was well known for wearing trousers but this preference has never been particularly associated in the public consciousness with this specific film.

Gossip point five: and so to her meeting another journalist at the exhibition launch party. Ms Robinson is critical of the kind of television programme her new acquaintance hosts, at the same time attempting to 'balance' her view. But in saying 'the television team clearly believes it is taking part in important life-saving or at least face-saving surgery' she exaggerates their case and thus subtly reinforces her own. Ms Alexander then attempts to invade Ms Robinson's personal space, fiddling with her fringe. From her mug shot we know how important that space is to Ms Robinson. It is no surprise, then, when she writes: 'I was very tempted to give her a slap.' Perhaps Ms Alexander should feel herself lucky not to have been punched in the face.

The art of reviewing

Reviews serve many functions. They provide basic information: for example, that a film has just been released and can be seen at the cinemas indicated. For people who intend to see, read or hear a work (or, in the case of broadcasting, have already seen or heard it) the review gives an opinion carrying some authority to compare with their own. Yet often the vast majority of readers will never experience directly the work under review. A concert may have been attended by no more than a few hundred people. The review must then exist as a piece of writing in its own right. It must entice in the reader through the quality and colour of its prose. It must entertain, though different newspapers have different conceptions of what entertainment means.

For the producers of the work the review (good, bad or indifferent) offers some vital publicity. Many journalists like reviewing. They often come from a humanities academic background where arts reviewing is common. Science is still on the margins of the journalists' culture. And for the newspaper, reviews can attract advertisers. A newspaper carrying substantial book reviews, for instance, is more likely to attract advertising from book publishers than one which largely ignores books.

On many local weeklies, the review might serve a different purpose. The newspaper is acting as a journal of record for the local community, carrying all the names of the performers, say, in a school play. Accompanied by a photograph of a scene, the report will serve as a souvenir for many. Just as in news, an overall consensus operates in the selection of works to review. For instance, in the area of films, the global economic power of Hollywood means that every week, its latest products receive automatic priority. In the area of books reviewing, a consensus means that out of the hundreds published every week just a few receive prominent attention throughout Fleet Street. At the heart of reviewing lie some basic journalistic challenges. A great writer does not necessarily make a great reviewer.

- Names of performers, producers, writers and of any fictional characters and places must be carried accurately. Where relevant their titles must be given.
- Direct quotes from the works, similarly, must be given correctly.
- Plots (or, say, the contents of an exhibition) should be summed up clearly and in accessible language.
- Any esoteric elements should be conveyed in a language likely to be understood by the majority of readers.
- In some cases, special sensitivity is required. A reporter, for instance, approaches a work by a group of committed amateurs or by children with different aesthetic standards from when reviewing a work by professionals. The reviewer may do the reader a service by not spoiling the suspense of a thriller; they may choose not to reveal a sudden twist in the plot at the end.
- In criticising the work, the journalist must not stray into libel by saying something that can damage a person's reputation.
- The journalist has to be true to their own experience and find the words to convey that accurately and concisely without falling into cliché.
- The reviewer must be able to write, handling variations of tone and sentence structure confidently in accordance with the overall style of the newspaper. The thematic structure (as in all features) must be clear and not contain any contradictions or repetitions.
- As in all journalistic writing, the intro section must carry sufficient weight to attract the reader. It might encapsulate the main theme of the piece, it may contain a striking quote or description, a joke or a narrative. If it is dull, pretentious, long-winded or off-target it has failed.
- Reviewers usually write to a specific length. As Irving Wardle, veteran theatre critic, commented: 'Reviewers soon learn to write to length knowing that if they overwrite it is their opinion that will be cut while all the plottery will be kept intact' (*Independent on Sunday*, 12 July 1992).
- The reviewer must be able to convey their enthusiasm for their specialist area. As critic Nigel Andrew comments: 'There is no such thing as an uninteresting film, wherever it came from, however much or little it cost and whatever it is trying to say' (*Press Gazette*, 15 January 1999).
- The style, length, content and tone of an arts review are influenced by many factors. Reviews in the popular press, often by celebrities, tend to be short, focusing on the entertainment level of the work. The language, as in the rest of the paper, is usually brisk and straight-to-the point. Any sexual, sensational, human interest elements are highlighted. The tone can be varied: mocking, ironic, damning, praising. But it is rarely analytical. In films and theatre/showbiz reviews, the focus is often on the performance of the leading 'star', particularly if they are British.

Many local papers tend to mix elements of the popular with those of the middle brow. The language and sentence length follow the style in the rest of the paper. But an extra overall length gives the chance for a more idiosyncratic approach. Plots can be explored in greater depth; themes can be explored further. Often in local and middle-brow papers, the emphasis tends to be more on the personalities involved. Heavies tend to put greater emphasis on reviewing, though there is a distinct London bias in their coverage. They draw important advertising from the arts and many of their readers, educated past the age of 18, have either an active or passive interest in 'culture'. Reviewers in the heavies aim to impress with the depth of their knowledge and appreciation. But as Edward Greenfield, for forty years *Guardian* music critic, commented (30 July 1993): 'My own belief is that the music critic must aim at appreciation above all, trying never to let the obvious need to analyse in nit-picking detail to get in the way of enjoyment.'

Analysis of a review of Simply the Quest:

News of the World (30 April 2000)

SIMPLY THE QUEST

TREK SYMBOL: Weaver

LET'S hope Star Trek fans have a sense of humour or the sci-fi spoof **Galaxy Quest (PG)** may have trouble taking off.

This 'comedy' relies on Trekkie jokes for laughs which, to be honest, are few and far between.

Sci-fi stalwart Sigourney Weaver plays Gwen DeMarco, the sex-bomb star of a TV series set on a spaceship.

As she and the crew, which includes Tim Allen as Commander Taggart, prepare for a Galaxy Quest convention they get a visit from aliens who believe the Galaxy crew are for real and the programmes historical documents.

The well-mannered Thermians from the faraway planet of Klatu Nebula are in dire straits and ask the Galaxy team to save them.

Can these stars of the small screen transform themselves into real-life superheroes before their friends are wiped out?

If you're a sci-fi fan, Galaxy Quest will probably have you falling off your seat with laughter. For the rest of the human race, I recommend the more Earthly goings-on in your local cinema.   ★★

This review appears at the bottom of the page: the caps headline, the pic of Weaver, ultimately the celebrity status of the reviewer, Mariella Frostrup, helping draw attention. The headline fits the space perfectly but the pun is inappropriate: Frostrup is critical of the film so an oblique reference to 'the best' through the pun hits the wrong note. There is another, better pun in the intro (the sci-fi spoof 'may have trouble taking off') and there is irony in the use of inverted commas around 'comedy' in par. 2. Otherwise, the writing is concise (sentence lengths being generally short: 22, 17, 18, 37, 22, 18, 17 and 17) and concentrates on telling the story simply. But Frostrup cleverly holds back from telling the whole plot, ending with a teaser in par. 6. There is no attempt at analysis. Cosmo Landesman, in the *Sunday Times* of the same day, placed the film critically within the context of previous Hollywood spoofs – such as *Blazing Saddles*, *Airplane!*, *The Naked Gun*, *Loaded Weapon*, *Fatal Instinct*. Frostrup has neither the inclination nor space to indulge in such musings.

Analysis of 'A Few Wisps of Smoke',
review of *Burning Issues*: Morning Star (4 May 2000)

[See p. 226] Compared to the Frostrup review, the sentence lengths here are much longer (25, 2, 44, 64, 44, 11, 38, 36, 61, 43, 35, 17, 16, 21, 22). In places they are too long. The piece is analytical and eclectic in its literary references. Larkin, Kafka, Proust, Powell, Rushdie, Orwell are all mentioned en passant without any explanations – the writer presuming a certain level of literary knowledge among his readers. There is a certain flattery involved which endears him to his readers. The text effectively mixes abstract musings (on say 'the nature of creativity', the 'credibility of biography', 'the source of great art') with slang and cliché ('the shit has really hit the fans', 'stabbing him in the back', 'whacky'). Though it appears in the newspaper which describes itself as 'the daily paper of the left', there is nothing particularly socialist or Marxist about the review. The London bias of the mainstream press is reflected here also in the *Star*'s choice of plays to review.

The review begins dramatically with a focus on Larkin. The piling on of the striking adjectives ('racist, misogynist, porn-loving and small-minded') effectively attracts attention. It is like the opening movement of a symphony which concludes with the staccato sentence 'It did'. But then the next pars ignore the Larkin theme and so the intro is left high and dry, bearing no apparent relation to the rest of the text. The intro implies that the play is primarily about Larkin. But it turns out it isn't; in par. 6 we learn it is only loosely based on Larkin as well as a number of other writers. Confusing. The reviewer also in many places appears to be attempting to cram in too many details. Sentences become overloaded with subordinate clauses and text in parentheses. Pars 2–4, in which Parker tells the story of the play, are particularly convoluted.

The structure is entirely clear. Par. 1: the Larkin allusion; pars 2–4: the plot; pars 5–9: analysis of main themes; par. 10: assessment of actors' performances; par. 11: conclusive remarks; final par.: booking details. Most of the analysis is constructed around contrasts (on the one hand this, on the other hand that) which becomes repetitive and clichéd. Thus, in par. 5, he writes: 'There are some incidental pleasure . . . But. . . .' In the next par. we hear about Mallowan. Par. 7 begins: 'But when we meet him'. Again the focus is on Hutchinson's argument. And the next par. begins: 'But with only hearsay to go on'. And so on. There is some imaginative writing based on acute observations, such as 'it is impossible to believe that this man, who keeps his custard creams in a lockable tin, could have written anything more profound than a complaint to the Gas Board [strikingly down-to-earth], let alone a 12-novel humanistic piece about art and morality'. And the short conclusive par. in which he playfully and almost poetically puns around the 'Burning Issues' theme works well (and provides the sub with a useful headline phrase).

Freelancing: A SURVIVAL GUIDE

Just as there are many kinds of staff reporters so there are many kinds of freelances. Some are the best paid and busiest writers. Many are finding life extremely difficult with widespread cuts in newspaper journalists' jobs intensifying competition among freelances. Such trends are not limited to the UK: an International Labour

A few wisps of smoke

BURNING ISSUES
Hampstead Theatre,
London NW3

WHEN poet Philip Larkin was revealed — after his death as racist, misogynist, porn-loving and small-minded, there was much debate about whether his reputation would survive. It did.

In Ron Hutchinson's new play, when a small publishing company newly acquired by a US conglomerate discovers that the diaries of its star author, Mallowan (Kenneth Colley) — a potential Nobel winner — contain little more than racist abuse, the shit has really hit the fans.

The publishers need the author's final instalment of his 12-volume novel; the contract to publish the journals is watertight; Mallowan's biographer, second-rate academic Watkins (William Chubb), failed to discover their existence; the US company's placeman, Richter (Rob Spendlove), sees a threat to profits; the editor who signed the contract fears for his Tuscan villa and his colleague is not-so-subtly stabbing him in the back.

When, in the space of a couple of hours, Mallowan is flattened by a gas boiler explosion and Watkins walks in front of a bus, the question becomes - by way of simplistic reference to Mein Kampf — whether the journals should go under the match.

There are some incidental pleasures, some funny lines and good performances. But for all Hutchinson's attempts to pose serious questions — about the nature of creativity, the credibility of biography, the morality of suppressing an author's beliefs to protect his literary reputation — his characters and situations are consistently unbelievable.

Mallowan, is constructed from bits of other writers — being a former insurance clerk (sort of Kafka), living "up north" in isolation except for his charlady (sort of Larkin), writing a novel sequence (sort of Proust/Powell).

But when we meet him, it is impossible to believe that this man, who keeps his custard creams in a lockable tin, could have written anything more profound than a complaint to the Gas Board, let alone a 12-novel humanistic piece about art and morality and the basic plot for The Satanic Verses, for which Rushdie has written to thank him.

Hutchinson is certainly arguing that the most banal life and personality can harbour the profound, a la Larkin, and - as one of the characters quotes from Orwell — that almost any world view, however whacky or extreme, can be a source of great art.

But with only hearsay to go on in respect of his literary talents, belief in Mallowan simply can't survive, particularly as his explanation for the disparity between his fiction and his journals is so unconvincing.

As the publishers, John Gordon-Sinclair and Andrew Woodall are entertainingly implausible but Miranda Pleasance's part is underwritten. As their accountant boss, Spendlove does well to make a last act double-U-turn only mildly preposterous. Chubb has the best turn as he discovers to his horror the extent to which his contemptuous subject has misled him.

But overall, Burning Issues is like the bonfire at its end, giving off little more than a few wisps of smoke.

Plays until June 3. Box office: 020 7722 9301.

MIKE PARKER

Organization world survey in 1999 on the economic and social status of freelances revealed a 'scandalous exploitation expanding rapidly over the globe'. All the same, if you are determined, organised, imaginative, talented and can cope with stress, opportunities are still available to break into the freelance world.

There are good and bad sides to the freelance life. To a certain extent freelances enjoy some 'freedoms' not permitted to staff writers. They can work from home, they are not forced to abide by a strict daily routine, they can avoid all the hassles of office politics. They may even be given the opportunity to pursue a specialism which no other journalistic route has allowed. They may be fascinated by food and wine. A full-time food specialist is a rare commodity on daily and weekly newspapers. Freelancing for a number of publications in this area is more of a possibility.

But freelances can rarely free themselves from the constraints of the market. You may be contemptuous of the capitalist rat-race of the newspaper world but freelancing hardly provides a refuge from this. Freelances have to go where the money is. George Orwell, for instance, committed himself to small-scale, left-wing, literary journals and largely ignored the seductive appeal of Fleet Street. But until his last two novels, *Animal Farm* and *Nineteen Eighty-Four* achieved global success, he lived in relative poverty. It was his ethical and political choice (Keeble 2000). If you are interested in progressive journalism then secure a steady job (with a charity, progressive think-tank or pressure group) and build up your freelance experience on that foundation.

A freelance's working day is in many respects more demanding and stressful than that of a staffer. Not only do they have the problems of finding work, promoting new ideas and meeting deadlines, but also they have a range of other issues to worry about. They have to sort out taxation problems. They may have to chase finance departments to pay up. They have to negotiate rates and make sure all their equipment is maintained properly. Without the regular inflow of money enjoyed by staff journalists, freelances have, in short, to be far more financially organised. On top of all this, the freelance has no job security. When jobs are on the line, they are invariably the first to suffer. Without the companionship that goes with a full-time job, the freelance's life can be lonely.

Starting up

Launching into a freelance career is not easy. Many freelances are former full-time staffers who have developed a specialism, sent out linage (freelance copy paid by the line) to nationals and then, through either choice or redundancy, taken the plunge and gone solo or started a small agency. Sometimes a non-journalist professional may build up contacts and a specialist knowledge. They may have enjoyed close links with the media and even contributed occasional articles to the press. On this basis they may decide to switch to journalism as a career. The feature linking all these examples is a specialism which can be exploited journalistically. Very few freelances are generalists.

As Stephen Wade comments:

The besetting sins of writing freelance are over-confidence and naivety. Never assume that editors are clamouring for your work. The competition is massive and there is a lot of talent around. Do not be naive enough to think that you can compete immediately with the full-time professionals. You have to put everything into your first article and submit to a realistic market, with a good covering letter. If you are sure of why you are writing, then these will all be more attainable.

(Wade 1997: 45)

Basic requirements

- A personal computer and printer: many freelances now have internet access and provide copy through email. A number of sites (such as http://www.smarterwork.com for writers seeking commissions, http://www.honk.co.uk/fleetstreet which covering a range of issues from job hunting to payments, and http://www.the-bullet.com offering a daily dose of media gossip) are specifically geared to the needs of freelances. Companies are increasingly supplying press releases through email.

- Telephone and answering machine; many freelances have mobile phones and pagers so they are contactable at any time. Some have a built-in facility for taping telephone conversations. For tax purposes it is necessary to keep separate records of business and personal calls.

- A fax machine: given the speed of newspaper operations, the normal mail is often too slow and many publications still like to see the original hard copy.

- A small tape recorder for interviews.

- A television: many freelances follow Ceefax and Oracle services to keep up with breaking news. And a radio.

- An accountant: to advise on tax and a pension plan. If you become particularly successful you will have to pay VAT. Most freelances keep in regular touch with their local tax inspector. Remember to log for tax purposes all relevant expenses such as stationery, office equipment, books and travel expenses.

- A solicitor: to help on copyright (see Howard 1994) and libel issues and looking into the small print of contracts.

- An office with a working desk: there are problems relating to capital gains tax if you sell your home and have used a room exclusively as an office. Consult your accountant on this. Your office will normally contain a library of reference books, dictionaries, collections of quotations, newspapers and magazines (often small circulation and specialist). In addition, the *Writer's Handbook* (Macmillan, annually) and *Writers' and Artists' Yearbook* (A & C Black, annually) are essential tools, providing tips, freelance rates and valuable lists of newspaper contacts. You may want on hand a collection of titles on freelancing such as Dobson (1992), Davis (1988), Dick (1998), Read (1992), Clayton (1994), Randall (2000) and (McKay 2000: 31–43). Access to public and specialist libraries is essential. Established freelances will also take the opportunity to use the library facilities at newspapers to which they file copy. You may choose to subscribe to the *Contributor's Bulletin*: Freelance Press Service, 5–9 Bexley Square, Salford, Manchester M3 6DB.

- A filing cabinet: this should be used to store cuttings, photocopies of crucial articles and chapters, notes from interviews and written sources, copies of correspondence and invoices. Organising a tidy filing system is a special art providing enormous rewards. So much time can be lost looking for information when the filing system is chaotic.

- Headed writing paper and business cards.

- Transport: most reporters drive (and set some of the costs against taxable income) but it is not essential. Some freelances rely on bikes, others on public transport.

- Membership of the freelance branch of the NUJ: the union, along with local education centres, runs courses for starting-up freelances which can help develop skills and confidence.

- Capital: Christopher Browne (1999: 17) suggests that beginning freelances should negotiate an overdraft facility of at least £3,000 to £4,000 with their bank manager after presenting them with a business plan drawn up by an accountant.

Finding an outlet

Get to know the market for your specialist area of interest. Study the different writing styles, the lengths of sentences and articles in the different publications. Try to establish by examining byline patterns the amount of freelance work accepted and in which specific areas: it may be in celebrity profiles, in authoritative, fact-based comment or in timeless features. Read carefully recent issues to make sure that you do not duplicate anything already done. It is not a good idea to ring a publication to gather this kind of information or even their general views about freelancing. You are expected to do all the basic groundwork and then approach the publication with a potential article.

With a hot news story you will obviously contact the paper by phone. But with other kinds of stories there are no rules. Some prefer contact by phone, others by letter or fax or email. Always direct your approach to the most appropriate person on the editorial staff. If you have a feature, ring the features editor (asking the switchboard operator their name before speaking). Expect to have to travel through a range of protective secretaries before speaking to them in person.

Explain the main point of your story and the likely length you envisage. In covering news, there is always a danger the paper will take down the details and then send out their staffer to handle it. Try to convey the story's importance and the fact that you have it ready to send over by phone, fax or email. Do not give too much away on the phone. Even if they use your call as a simple 'tip off' for a story they cover themselves, you are still owed a payment for that. If you are not known to the paper, they are unlikely to commit themselves to carrying a story on the basis of a rushed phone call. They are likely to say: 'That sounds interesting. Send in the copy but I can't promise anything.'

If you are submitting an idea for a timeless feature, explain your original angles, your main sources, the basic structure of the piece and wordage, why you are particularly suited to covering it and why you have chosen their particular publication. There are dangers here. The publication may steal your ideas and give them to someone else to follow up. And the freelance has absolutely no protection in law against this kind of theft. While written work can be copyrighted, ideas can occur to two people at the same time and can also be stolen. There is no easy solution to this problem. One approach is to provide only a bare minimum of background information before the idea is accepted. Personal contact with the commissioning editor also helps in creating mutual trust and confidence. The best solution is to prove your abilities to the newspaper in a series of stories sent on spec or to commission so they will be concerned not to lose your work to other competitors. It is also worth emphasising that you are the only person with the unique knowledge, contacts, idio-syncratic viewpoint or desire to complete the article. Clearly, freelances have to develop special negotiation skills.

Do not expect to have your hard copy returned. Even a stamped addressed envel-ope offers no guarantee. But always make sure you have a copy of all your submitted work. If it is rejected you may want to direct it to another newspaper or rearrange it with some new angles for a different outlet. Be persistent: remember *Gone with the Wind* was rejected 25 times before it was published and *Zen and the Art of Motorcycle Maintenance* 121 times. There may be queries over the story which can be cleared up only with reference to your original copy; you may need to protect yourself against libel where the paper has subbed in a comment or error.

Once the idea is accepted

If the commissioning editor has said: 'OK, I'll be pleased to look at your story but I can't promise we'll use it', they are free to reject your story without incurring any financial liability. But if they have commissioned your piece and then do not publish it, they should (though not all do) pay you a 'kill fee' comprising part or all of the original amount agreed.

How much should you expect to be paid for your hard work? Well, the NUJ draws up a list of minimum freelance rates which are regularly updated and which will give you some idea of what to expect. The union also at its 1986 annual confer-ence agreed a ten-point code on the use of freelance work. For example, Clause 1 stated 'Staff journalists hiring freelances have a duty to see that their freelances are treated reasonably'; Clause 2 ran: 'Conditions and rates of pay should be established clearly when the work is accepted or commissioned, preferably in writing'. According to Clause 3: 'Freelances should be paid in all cases for providing background infor-mation, tips, research materials, expertise etc.' Certainly make sure you also nego-tiate expenses when your piece is commissioned since without that agreement you may end up using the payment simply to fund your research. And send in an invoice soon after the appearance of your copy.

Remember that if you are a self-employed freelance you own the copyright in your work: it is your 'intellectual property' whether submitted on spec or commis-sioned. Thus you are strongly advised to hold on to your copyright. This does not mean refusing further use of the material; you can license it, giving permission for a specific use for an agreed fee. Freelances, however, have become increasingly concerned over newspapers' use of journalists' copy in a range of electronic outlets. In September 1999, a three-judge panel decided that the *New York Times*, Lexis-Nexis and other publishers could not re-sell freelance newspaper and magazine articles by means of electronic databases unless they had the author's express permission. And judges in Britain and Ireland were expected to follow the US lead.

14 New technology

How journalism can damage your health

Journalism can damage your health. Many in the industry find it extremely stressful. A survey of media workers by Anthony Delano and John Henningham (1995), found that 51 per cent considered that they experienced high levels of stress while 24 per cent felt that the levels were very high. Another survey, commissioned by Guardian Financial Services and published in July 1996, found that more than 75 per cent of media employees had seen stress play a significant part in causing physical ill-health. Migraines, headaches, ulcers, irritable bowel syndrome, digestive problems and heart disease were among the stress-related conditions suffered. Almost half of those surveyed felt their bosses were doing nothing to reduce stress levels.

Occupational psychologist Dr Stephen Williams (1996) has studied hundreds of workplaces but says journalism beats all for stress. According to government figures (published in 1996) journalists are out-performing other professions at booze and tobacco consumption, and dying young as a result. Deadlines can be short, competition can be fierce, criticisms from colleagues can be sharp. Get some information wrong and not only is your mistake very public but also a costly libel action may result. Pressures from all sides (news desk, editors, sources, advertisers, politicians, proprietors) are faced every day. As cutbacks in the industry deepen, job security dwindles and the pressures to conform and work harder to justify the job grow.

The introduction of new technology has, for many, brought new stresses. Over recent years the newspaper industry has gone through a revolution. In the late 1960s, photocomposition (by which page images were composed photographically) began to replace hot metal setting in the provincial press. The compositor would retype journalists' copy on a keyboard attached to a visual display unit (VDU). Text would be automatically hyphenated and justified while strips of bromide from the photosetter would be pasted down to form the page. But on Fleet Street, the introduction of photocomposition was delayed until the mid-1970s, the result of management incompetence and trade union conservatism. Even as late as 1985, three Fleet Street newspapers were hot-metal-set while five others used a mix of hot and cold systems. Then came Eddie Shah's launch of the new-tech, all colour *Today* on 4 March 1986 and the sudden shift of Rupert Murdoch's News International titles from Gray's Inn Road to Wapping. *Today* was launched with an editorial staff of just 130, less than a quarter of the staff levels then at the *Express* or *Mail*. So began a wave of editorial staff cuts throughout Fleet Street which are still continuing. One of the consequences of these jobs cuts is inevitably extra stresses for those remaining.

The silent sufferers

The journalist's VDU screen is an extremely flexible tool which has transformed the job. For instance, it can be split so that the reporter accesses on one side agency copy, the results of a database search or a previous edition story, while dealing with their own copy on the other side. Journalists have always suffered from writers' cramp (though this is little covered in the media). New technology has brought many new hazards. Indeed, research suggests that up to 25 per cent of the population as a whole suffers from techno-anxiety (Macleod 1999). Particularly notorious among journalists is repetitive strain injury. This swept the industry from the mid-1980s so that a decade later the NUJ was claiming that it knew of more than 1,000 sufferers. Nationally, with 7 million keyboard users, RSI became the biggest cause of time lost through illness in office work and in 1994 the TUC was claiming an 'epidemic' of RSI injuries, causing 200,000 people a year to take time off work. A 1997 survey at the giant IPC Magazines group in London found that one-third of journalists had some symptoms of RSI. Research by the GMB union in 2000 suggested that left-handers were particularly prone.

By the late 1990s most of the larger newspaper companies had come to terms with RSI and were dealing with affected journalists compassionately. At the *Guardian*, for instance, a technology committee was set up, combining management and the NUJ. The emphasis was on supporting people in continuing to work, not getting rid of them. As Tim Gopsill, NUJ health and safety officer, commented: 'The bigger the company the better. After all, they've got the money to spend. The *Financial Times*, for instance, has spent a fortune getting their newsroom up to acceptable ergonomic standards.' He said that apart from 'some judges and bent doctors', most people now acknowledge RSI as a serious injury. By mid-2000, the typical compensation payment ordered by the courts was between £2,000 and £7,000 for the pain and suffering caused. But in smaller newsrooms journalists could still be 'badly treated' and throughout the industry there remained many silent sufferers afraid that if they revealed their symptoms they could be unemployable or sacked.

What is RSI?

Research into RSI is already considerable but explaining its causes (why it strikes one person and not another) remains difficult. RSI and its associated symptoms have been around for more than 150 years. Piano players, factory workers, tennis players, farmers, anyone involved in repetitive activities with their limbs, are prone to suffer. But it is only recently, since journalists have been seriously affected, that concerns about it have been widely expressed in the media.

Symptoms can develop slowly over a period of time or appear suddenly as a devastating shock. One journalist recorded: 'I simply woke up one morning unable to move my neck or use my hands properly. I dropped newspapers, couldn't grasp a cup and, panic-stricken, didn't know what could be wrong.' While using a computer is often the main problem, first symptoms might appear while turning a screwdriver, mowing the lawn, writing, washing your hair, carrying shopping, turning taps, knitting or playing the piano.

How to avoid RSI

If you are a staffer, try to insist through your union that your employer follows the European Union regulations which came into force on 1 January 1993. These insist that chairs must have height-adjustable seats and backs that are height and tilt-adjustable. Employers are obliged to provide stands to raise screens and footrests when these are required.

Concentrate on getting your posture right at the keyboard. Your forearms should be parallel to the floor when you type and both feet should be firmly on the floor. If you have short legs, you may need a footstool, a specially adjustable chair or both. In front of the keyboard there should be sufficient space to place wrists during rest periods or while reading the screen. You should be able to sit straight, using the back-rest of the chair, with relaxed shoulders and chin up, looking down at the screen at an angle of 15 degrees. There should be no pressure on the thighs from the chair since this can limit circulation and put pressure on the sciatic nerve.

You need to take regular breaks from the screen. The NUJ recommends breaks of 15 minutes in every 75 minutes of continuous VDU work or formal breaks of 15 minutes after each hour. Lunches should be taken away from the desk. All the same, lunch-at-the-desk is an increasing trend among hard-pressed, under-staffed newsrooms across the UK and even in-built RSI warning sounds on computers are routinely ignored.

If symptoms emerge

If you suffer pain during or after working at the keyboard but not at other times when using your hands, take regular breaks, reduce your typing speed and adjust the height of your chair so that you can type more efficiently. And talk to your NUJ representative if there is one where you work. They should be able to advise on what to do.

If the pains persist during other uses of the hands, seek medical advice immediately: fear, anxiety and guilt do not help. Robert Jones, Emeritus Fellow at City University's journalism department, stresses the importance of being treated by an experienced doctor. He said: 'Physiotherapy can help but it can also make the condition worse unless there has been a diagnosis first and unless the physio is really experienced in dealing with RSI.' For some people RSI can have a devastating effect on their careers. The inflammation and pains remain and they have to quit regular employment. Subs are generally worse affected than reporters and where employers are sensitive, sufferers are moved to work in a reporter's post requiring much less screen work.

But not all RSI sufferers remain permanent sufferers. Some respond to treatment, others find a period of rest from the screen and careful attention to all possible precautions thereafter clears the pains. Often a change of job and a shift away from a stressful situation can remove the symptoms. Note there is an internet site for discussion on RSI. Subscribe, free, to Listserv@tictac.demon.co.uk. There is also a website at http://www.rsi-uk.org.uk

Other ailments

In addition to RSI, people have suffered eye complaints from sitting at VDU screens. headaches, blurred vision, fuzzy images, stress and irritability can result. The NUJ recommends that keyboard, desk, walls and other major surrounding areas should be non-reflective and avoid excessively bright or dark colour schemes. No VDU or operator should face a window.

Dust is attracted to a switched on screen and this, together with positive ions and static, can lead to blocked pores, dry eyes and irritated skin. Author Peggy Bentham (1991) suggests that every operator should have a dust cover to put over the screen when not in use, an antistatic floor mat and an antistatic desk mat. In addition, she advises people to wear natural fibres at the VDU to reduce static. Because of the radiation risks in sitting in front of VDUs, the NUJ recommends that pregnant women should have the right to switch to non-VDU work without loss of pay, status and career prospects.

Photocopiers and laser printers which produce ozone can pose health risks if they are poorly positioned or maintained or used for long runs. Areas in which they are sited should be well ventilated and no one should have to work within 3 metres of the machine. Health concerns have also been raised over the use of mobile phones. Research by US experts Dr Henry Lai and Dr Narenda Singh warns that exposure can damage the body's genetic building-block DNA, leading to Alzheimer's and cancer. A study by Polish scientists of soldiers (published in March 2000), found a direct link between mobile phone use and cancer. But a major report by twelve independent experts in Britain, in May 2000, concluded that mobile phones were not a proven health risk to users. All the same, if you have to use a mobile phone, keep calls short; if you have to make a lengthy call, then switch the phone from ear to ear.

15 On or off the job – or both?

....

Training and careers

The best way to learn about journalism is 'on the job'. You may have great ideas about the nature of reporting, you may know all about ideology and the history of the press in eighteenth-century England. But if you cannot bash out a quick story on a local murder you are useless. That was the dominant view in the industry at the beginning of the twentieth century. It remains largely the same at the start of the twenty-first. There have been slight changes. Training courses have developed with the support of newspaper managements and trade unions. They have even spread into the learned corridors of universities. But mutual suspicion persists between the press and academia.

On the one hand there is a prevalent belief that journalists are born, not made. You've either got the nose for news or, sadly, you haven't. As Sir David English, former editor of the *Daily Mail*, said: 'Journalism is a skill that can only be acquired on the job and at the end of the day it depends on whether someone has a burning individual talent.' On the other hand there is the belief that journalism is a profession with its own ethical and work-related standards which can be both taught and assessed. Thus, certain educational qualifications are laid down for entrants while the development of training courses becomes an essential part of the formation of the journalist's professional identity. Caught between these two views are students and trainers. A further twist emerges when attempts are made by trainers to promote reflective, critical approaches to dominant professional attitudes (as, for instance, reflected in this text). Scepticism about the value of theoretical studies for aspiring reporters remains widespread.

The contrasting US/UK traditions of training

The training of journalists in Britain is a relatively new phenomenon. In the United States, university training started at the beginning of the twentieth century with the first journalism school founded in 1908 at the University of Missouri. Ten years later there were 86 schools offering at least some journalism coursework while by 1940 this figure had jumped to 542. Currently about 400 colleges and universities offer programmes to around 100,000 students.

In Britain, in contrast, it was not until the mid-1960s that any major programme of journalism training was launched. A diploma course had run at King's College London between 1922 and 1939 but this was not restarted after the war. After the 1949 Royal Commission on the Press drew attention to the need for better training, the National Advisory Council for the Training and Education of Junior Journalists was set up in 1952 (Stephenson and Mory 1990). Three years later this body changed its title to the National Council for the Training of Journalists (NCTJ) and brought together representatives from the NUJ and the Institute of Journalists (the two trade unions), the Newspaper Society (owners of provincial newspapers in England and Wales and suburban London weeklies) and the Guild of British Newspaper Editors. Later they were joined by the Newspaper Publishers' Association (linking owners of national newspapers) and by the two bodies formed by the owners and managers of newspapers in Scotland.

Since the 1960s many colleges and universities have developed courses in journalism. Initially, the media were considered largely within their sociological or broader theoretical contexts in courses usually titled Mass Communications. But over recent decades the focus has shifted, largely in response to student demands, to the development of practical skills. Many mass communication courses have integrated a practical element while both postgraduate and (since the early 1990s) undergraduate journalism degrees have emerged. By 2000, there were more than 100 degree courses, with journalism being offered in one form or another by at least 32 universities and 16 higher education colleges (Hargreaves 2000). When media studies courses are added the number approached 1,500 catering for up to 35,000 students (Peak and Fisher 1999: 320). Yet despite all this, many newspaper journalists still learn the ropes on local papers.

Educational qualifications

In 1965 the trade unions and Newspaper Society agreed the minimum qualifications for entry to the profession was three GCEs, one being in English. Since 1970 the required minimum has been five passes at O level or GCSE at grades A, B or C with English language still being among them. Some other examinations have been approved by the NCTJ as being educationally equivalent and in exceptional cases (when the editor has their eye on an individual) the qualifications are waived. For those who seek to enter via a college course, the requirements are two A levels and two GSCEs including English at either level.

The trend over recent decades has been towards the formation of an increasingly graduate profession. In 1965 only 6 per cent entering local newspapers had a university degree while a further 33 per cent had one or more A levels. In 1990 53 per cent of entrants to provincial papers boasted degrees while most of the others had two or more A levels. By 2000, a survey of journalism intake by the University of Wales' journalism department found that 95 per cent of new recruits had degrees. Even so, academic qualifications in themselves have never been sufficient to guarantee a chance to become a trainee journalist. As Sarah Niblock (1996) comments: 'Some editors may feel journalists who are well read in media criticism may lead them to question editorial policy, so do not think having such a qualification will automatically give you a head start.' In addition to showing academic abilities, the successful applicant must be able to demonstrate a special commitment to working in the field. Many school pupils go to newspapers on work attachments, others manage to persuade editors to let them observe the newspaper operations during their holidays. Some students help with hospital radios; others send in letters and articles to their local newspapers. All this counts well for any applicant whether to a newspaper or college.

Pre-entry training: post A level

One year pre-entry courses are provided at centres dotted about the UK, such as at Brighton College of Technology; Clarendon City College, Nottingham; Crawley College; Darlington College; East Surrey College, Redhill; Gloucestershire College of Art and Technology; Harlow College; Lambeth College; Sutton Coldfield College; Warwickshire College. You may win sponsorship from a local paper or you may be able to secure a grant from your local authority to cover the fees and possibly living expenses. The grants are discretionary, dependent on the authority's willingness to support you.

Pre-entry training: the postgraduate diploma route

In 1970, the first university journalism course was launched at University College, Cardiff. Largely the inspiration of Tom Hopkinson, former editor of *Picture Post*, and modelled on a programme at Columbia University, New York, it initially attracted between fifteen and twenty postgraduate students. A similar one-year postgraduate diploma course was begun at City University, London, in 1976, initially with thirteen students. By the late 1980s postgraduate courses had grown in numbers enormously, spanning a wide range of diplomas and MAs: newspaper, periodical, broadcast, European (linking Cardiff and City with colleges in Utrecht, the Netherlands, and Aarhus, Denmark) and international. In the late 1990s, City University launched an electronic publishing MA.

Also during the 1990s, one-year postgraduate diplomas were started at centres such as City of Liverpool Community College; De Montfort University, Leicester; Strathclyde University; Trinity and All Saints College, Leeds, and the University of Central Lancashire, Preston. Trent University, Nottingham, launched a diploma in investigative journalism. Napier University, Edinburgh, launched an international journalism MA while in 2000 the University of Lincolnshire and Humberside began its Graduate Diploma in Print and On-Line Journalism. But suspicions of universities by the press persisted. As Professor Hugh Stephenson, of City University, commented: 'The academic community in this country has always been distrustful of courses in journalism and media employers have been distrustful of people with education.'

The degree route

In the early 1990s, for the first time the US-style undergraduate route to journalism emerged with the launch of degrees at five centres: Bournemouth University; University College, Cardiff; the University of Central Lancashire, Centre for Journalism; the London College of Printing, while City University offered a Journalism with a Social Science course (with an optional third year 'out' studying abroad or on work attachments). They were to be later joined by a host of others, including Teesside University, University of Sheffield, Staffordshire University, Wolverhampton

University, Liverpool John Moores University, Surrey Institute of Art and Design and Harlow College/Middlesex University. Some national and local newspapers offer awards (watch the publications themselves for details). For instance, the *Hull Daily Mail* and *Lincolnshire Echo* have linked up with the University of Lincolnshire and Humberside. There are also special awards for applicants from ethnic minorities.

On-the-job training

Roughly 40 per cent of entrants to newspaper journalism start by training on a local. Take a look at media directories (such as *Benn's* and *Willing's Press Guide*) which your local library should hold: these list all newspapers and periodicals in the UK. It is advisable before writing to ring any chosen newspaper just to make sure it is worth your while and to get the editor's name correct on the letter. Editors tend to come and go. Remember that trainees are appallingly paid, with some earning as little as £7,000.

Once accepted, a direct entrant for their first six months tends to take a course of home study in addition to receiving on-the-job training and experience. Most will then attend a twelve-week block release course (such as at Darlington College, Highbury College, Portsmouth or Sheffield College). Each trainee will have to pass seven qualifying examinations: newspaper journalism, handling handouts, law (two parts), local and central government (two parts) and shorthand to 100 words per minute. For direct entrants the qualifying period is two years, for pre-entry and post-graduate diploma students it is eighteen months. Once through all these hoops, the journalist can then take the NCTJ National Certificate Examination (NCE) to be fully qualified. A number of regional and national newspapers have set up their own training schemes including, Midland News Association, Trinity-Mirror, Eastern Counties Newspapers and Newsquest. Even the *Sun* joined forces with City University to launch a graduate training scheme.

National Vocational Qualifications

In the early 1990s, the National Vocational Qualifications (and Scottish Vocational Qualifications) in newspapers emerged. Organised by the Newspaper Society, the NVQs were almost entirely focused on work-based assessments. Following the setting up of the National Council for Vocational Qualifications in 1996, the Newspaper Society's steering group drew up a set of standards at Level 4 under three headings – writing, production journalism and press photography (a graphics journalism option at Level 3 followed). A reporter covering a diary event, for instance, is required to display accurate fact-gathering skills, an appreciation of any legal and ethical issues arising and the ability to file copy to a deadline. Students take from one to three years so candidates working part-time can complete the course.

In recent years, the NVQs (awarded by the RSA Examinations Board together with the Newspapers Qualifications Council) have come under severe criticism from the NCTJ, Society of Editors and the Periodicals Training Council. But some groups, such as Eastern Counties Newspapers, remained committed to them and by mid-2000 the number studying for NVQs was roughly equivalent to those studying for an NCE.

Other routes

In addition to these entry routes there are many others. For instance, there are two-year HNDs, BTECs and many evening class centres now run courses in freelancing, feature writing and press photography. There are privately run journalism training centres (most of them claiming extraordinary success for their graduates in gaining jobs in the industry) and you can even learn journalism via a correspondence course on the internet. The range of courses is, in fact, bewildering. Early in 2000, a National Training Organisation was set up by the leading bodies in the industry in an attempt to co-ordinate the training needs for newspaper and magazine journalists. It faced a daunting task.

Many universities provide media studies courses. In fact, during the 1990s media-related courses became the most fashionable to study and inevitably attracted the suspicions of Fleet Street once reserved for sociology and peace studies. Many editors argue that they require applicants with broad interests and knowledge rather than bookish experts in the narrow academic discipline of communications. Yet, increasingly, theoretical media courses are incorporating practical vocational elements. It is to be hoped that journalists' traditional reluctance to encourage the reflective, critical approach will dwindle as more media graduates enter the industry.

There are conflicting research findings over the job success rate of media graduates. But Angela Phillips and Ivor Gaber of Goldsmiths' College, London, conclude:

Despite myths to the contrary, employment prospects for graduates of communications and media degrees are good. The Standing Conference on Cultural, Communication and Media Studies, which brings together all relevant university departments, studied the destination of their graduates and found, gratifyingly, that the percentage of those in employment, six months after graduation, was slightly higher than the average for all graduates.

(Phillips and Gaber 1996: 63–4)

Further reading and contact addresses

Careers in Journalism: National Union of Journalists, Acorn House, 314–20 Gray's Inn Road, London WC1X 8DP. Tel: 020-7278 7916; fax: 020-7837 8143. (The NUJ also provides a list of useful books on journalism, drawn up by Humphrey Evans)

How to be a Journalist, Newspaper Society, 74–7 Great Russell Street, London WC1B 3DA. Tel: 020-7636 7014; fax: 020-7631 5119; email: ns@newspapersoc.org.uk; website: http://www.newspapersoc.org.uk

National Council for the Training of Journalists, Latton Bush Centre, Southern Way, Harlow, Essex CM18 7BL. Tel: 01279-430009; fax: 01279-438008; email: NCTJ@ techarlow.co.uk; website: http://www.nctj.com

Students' Guide to Entry to Media Studies: UCAS, Rose Hill, New Barn Lane, Cheltenham GL52 3LZ. Tel: 01242-222444; website: http://www.ucas.co.uk

The foot in the door: GETTING THE FIRST JOB

Journalism has always been a notoriously difficult world to enter. With staff cuts in virtually all newspapers since the late 1980s, the job hunt has become still more difficult. Admittedly, the internet is beginning to provide large numbers of new jobs for journalists, but not only are colleges producing more trained young aspirants but also the newspaper jobs market is becoming jammed full with experienced journalists made redundant and on the hunt for employment.

Contacts are crucial. Spend time while training concentrating on building up sources and links in the industry. Also try to get freelance work published. After completing work attachments on newspapers, get your supervisor to write you a reference. Compile an attractive portfolio of your cuttings and references and attach an up-to-date CV: that will provide an invaluable aid to you during job interviews. You may even want to post your CV on the internet, including links to other works you have completed. As Damian Barr (1999) advises: 'Provide the URL (the name of your website) in your prospective letter or email so that an employer can click to it easily without having to bother with attachments.'

The application

Because newspapers are inundated with job applications there is little need to advertise many of the jobs that fall vacant. But a number are still advertised in *Press Gazette* (published every Friday) and the *Guardian* Media section every Monday. Media jobs in general are advertised at the Media Centre (http://mediamasters. ndirect.co.uk/mediacentre/jobs.htm). Internet jobs are advertised at Recruitmedia (http://www.recruitmedia.co.uk) and local newspapers advertise on http://www.hold thefrontpage.co.uk (which also carries a section on journalism training). The letter of application should be brief and to the point. The accompanying CV should summarise your achievement to date. It should list your name, address, date of birth, education (school, college, university, evening classes etc.) with dates and qualifications (briefly), professional qualifications, work on student/university publications; any job/s you have held (perhaps on a local hospital radio), desktop publishing skills, publications, special interests, languages, references (with addresses and contact details) (see Corfield 1992). It is also advisable to have your CV printed out in an attractive font: it is an important document and you are more likely to impress if it looks good. (Websites advising on CVs include http://www.free-resume-tips.com; http://www. provenresumes.com; http://www.cvspecial.co.uk).

The interview

It is vital to prepare for any job or college interview. Find out about the paper, get some copies and look at them critically. The interviewer will also expect you to be able to speak confidently about the national media – both print and broadcast, and the internet. It also impresses if you can use some journalistic jargon. If words like 'follow-up', 'page lead', 'splash' and 'stringer' flow off your lips (at the appropriate moments, of course), this shows that your newspaper ambition is more than a Hollywood-induced fantasy. Dress tidily and be prepared to show off your portfolio. And always go prepared to ask questions. Good luck.

Glossary

....

ABC – Audit Bureau of Circulation: organisation providing official figures for newspaper *circulation*

access provider – a company that sells *internet* connections (also known as an internet access provider or *internet service provider*)

ad – abbreviation for advertisement

add – additional copy as when the Press Association (*PA*) follows lead of major story with new paragraphs

advance – statement/speech issued in advance to the media

advertorial – where distinction between editorial and advertising becomes blurred

agency – main news agencies are *PA*, Reuters, Agence France Presse, Itar-Tass, Associated Press. Also a large number of smaller agencies serving specialist and general fields. Copy known as wire copy. See also *snap*

agony aunt – women offering advice to people who write to newspapers with personal or emotional problems. Agony uncle is the male equivalent, but not many of these around

alignment – ranging of copy text (and headlines) over columns. Copy ranged/ aligned/set left begins on extreme left of column; all lines of copy ranged right are flush to the extreme right of the column and ragged on the left

alternative press – loose term incorporating wide variety of non-mainstream newspapers. Can include leftist, religious, municipal, trade union publications

ambush interview – when an interviewee is surprised by a suddenly different line of questioning or by a sudden appearance of a journalist (or group of journalists). Has dramatic flavour when done on television

angle – main point stressed in story usually in *intro*. Also known as hook. US: peg

AP – Associated Press news agency

apology – a newspaper may admit error and publish correction in apology. Complainant can still claim libel in court and publication of apology provides no defence for newspaper. But if newspaper loses case, fact that it took prompt and adequate steps to correct error and to express regret provides plea in mitigation of damages tending to reduce size of damages awarded

artwork – all illustrations, maps, charts or cartoons that accompany copy

asterisk – * occasionally used in text to link footnote or to indicate letters of words considered obscene

attachment or work experience – time spent by student journalists training (or occasionally just observing) at media organisation. US: internship

attribution – linking information or *quote* to original source

author's marks – changes made by author on *proof* of copy

backbench – group of top level journalists who meet to decide the overall shape and emphases in newspaper

background – section of news or *feature* story carrying information which serves to contextualise main elements. Also in computer jargon, indicates hyphenation and justification system is operating while copy is being input

backgrounder – *feature* exploring the background to main story in the news

back issue – previous issue of paper

back-up – fallback supply of equipment, data or copy

banner – front page headline extending across full page

baron – newspaper proprietor. Other words: mogul, magnate, boss

beat – when a story is gained before rival. US: refers to specialist area covered by reporter e.g. education, defence, health

bill or billboard – poster giving headline of main story of the day

black – in days of typewriters this was carbon, back-up copy of top, hard copy typed by reporter. Many contemporary computer systems still call copies of top story blax

blackout – organisation or government imposes ban on all news releases for specific period

blob par./s – follows small black marking (usually a square, outline of square, a circle or sometimes in tabloid a star) at start of paragraph. Bullet in computer jargon

body – copy following *intro*

boil down – shorten copy

bold face – heavy-face type (in contrast to lighter *roman* type of most stories' body text) used for emphasising in copy, headlines, subheadings; see also *italic*

box – copy with rules around all four sides; see also *fact file*

break – moment when news story emerges. But bad break refers to ugly looking hyphenation at end of line of text

breaker – any device (such as *crosshead* or *panel*) which breaks up text on page

brief – short item of news often of just one *par*. but occasionally with up to four or five pars. Other names: snip/nib/bright/filler; also short advice given to journalist before they cover a story

broadsheet – large-size newspaper such as *Daily Telegraph*, *The Times*, *Independent* as opposed to *tabloid*; also known as *heavies*

browser – software program for navigating the internet, in particular the World Wide Web

bureau – newspaper office in foreign country

bury – when important information or *quote* is carried within the body of text so its impact is lost

bust – when copy text or headlines run over allotted space

buy-up – see *chequebook journalism*

byline – gives name of journalist/s who have written article. Otherwise known as credit line. Subs sometimes call it blame line. When appears at end of story known as *sign-off*

calls (or **check calls**) – routine telephone calls (or sometimes face-to-face visits) by reporters to bodies such as police, ambulance, hospitals, fire brigade (usually supplying information on tapes) to check if any news is breaking

campaigning journalism – overtly partisan journalism promoting particular cause. US: advocacy journalism

caps – see *upper case*

caption – words accompanying any picture or *artwork*. A caption amounting to a small story is a caption story

casting off – estimating length of story

casual – journalist employed by newspaper on a temporary basis. Since it is cheaper for employers, numbers are growing

catchline – usually single word identifying story which is typed in right-hand corner of every page. Subeditor will tend to use this word to identify story on layout. US: slug

CD-ROM – abbreviation of compact disc-read-only memory. CD holding computer accessible data. For instance, dictionaries and back issues of newspapers are available in this form

centre spread – copy and pictures running over two pages in centre of newspaper

chapel – newspaper branch of National Union of Journalists. Chair, if male, is father of the chapel; if female, mother of the chapel

chequebook journalism – activity in which newspapers compete to purchase rights to buy up someone's story

circulation – total number of copies of each issue sold; see also *readership*

city desk – section of newspaper running financial pages

classified ads – small ads classified according to subject area and carrying no illustrations (cf. *display ads*)

clips or clippings – stories cut from newspapers and usually filed. Most newspapers have *cuttings* libraries to assist journalists' research. Individual journalists will have their own cuttings files. Increasingly computerised

colour – section of newspaper copy focusing on descriptions or impressions. Thus a colour *feature* is one which puts emphasis on description and the subjective response of the journalist though the news element may still be strong

column – vertical section of article appearing on page. Also known as leg

columnist – journalist who provides comment in regular series of articles

column rule – usually light line between columns of type

conference – meeting of editorial staff to discuss previous issue/s and plan future ones

contact – journalist's source

contacts book – pocket-sized booklet carried by reporter listing contact details of sources

copy – editorial material. Hard copy refers to editorial material typed on paper

copy approval – person allowed to see and approve copy before publication

copy tasting – see *taster*

correspondent – usually refers to journalist working in specialist area: defence, transport; or abroad e.g. Cairo correspondent

credit – byline of photographer or illustrator

crop – to cut a picture

crosshead – small heading usually of one or two words within body of text of larger type size than body text sometimes with *underline*. Used for design purposes to break up grey area of text. Word is usually drawn from text following but carries no great news value. Written by subeditor and not reporter

cross ref – abbreviation of cross reference: indicates story continues or begins on another page

cub reporter – trainee

cursor – usually dash or arrow on the computer screen indicating position of the next input

curtain raiser – story which provides background to forthcoming event. Otherwise known as scene setter

cut – remove copy from script, screen or page proof

cut-out – illustration with background cut, masked or painted out so that the image appears on the white of the page background

cuttings – stories cut from newspapers/magazines; cuttings job is an article based on cuttings; also known as *clips or clippings*

database – storage of electronically accessible data

dateline – place from which story was *filed* usually applied to stories from abroad

day in the life of profile – *feature* focusing on particular day of subject. Not to be confused with 'life in the day of' profile, which covers subject's life but in context of talking about currently typical day

deadline – time by which copy is expected to be submitted

death knock – when a journalist breaks news of a death to a member of the public

deck – unit of a headline

Deep Throat – secret *whistleblower* on major scandal. First given to secret source/s for Woodward and Bernstein in Watergate scandal. Derived from title of in/famous pornographic film starring Linda Lovelace

delete – to cut or remove

desks – departments of newspapers: thus news desk, features desk

diary column – gossip column; also a day-to-day personal account

diary piece – article derived from routine sources (press conferences, press releases, council meetings, parliament) listed in diary (originally in written form but increasingly on screens) which helps news desk organise news-gathering activities. Off-diary stories come from reporter's initiative and from non-routine sources

dig – to do deep research

direct entry – entry to journalism through publication which runs its own training programme

direct input – process by which text goes straight from editorial screen into computer for typesetting thus cutting out process in which printers typed out copy

discussion list – individuals communicating via email subscribe to the list and then receive all messages other subscribers send

disk – hard or floppy disk containing computer information (but note: compact disc)

display ads – large advertisements usually containing illustrations (cf. *classified ads*) and appearing on editorial pages. Advertising department will organise distribution of ads throughout the newspaper which is usually indicated on a *dummy* handed to subs before layout begins

district office – any office away from newspaper's main one

domain name – system of names to describe precise position of computer on the internet (e.g. city.ac.uk is the domain for City University, London)

doorstepping – journalists pursuing sources by standing outside their front doors. Now journalists often wait in cars

double column – text/headline/graphics over two columns. Double page spread is a feature occupying two facing pages

download – to transfer data from one computer to another

downpage – story appearing in bottom half of newspaper page

downtable – subs other than the chief and deputy chief subs (who often used to sit at the top table of the subs room)

drop cap – capital letter at start of *par.* occupying more than one line of text

dummy – small version of editorial pages used for planning overall contents and usually containing details of *display ads*

editor – person in overall charge of the editorial content of the newspaper

editorial – all non-advertising copy; also a column in which newspaper expresses its views on issues (sometimes known as leader)

email – electronic mail carried on the internet

embargo – time (often found on press release) before which information should not be published

exclusive – story supposedly unique carried by newspaper. System becomes devalued when attached to stories too frequently or when the same story is carried in other newspapers (as often happens)

eye-witness reporting – presence of reporter at news event can provide unique opportunities for descriptive writing

e-zine – electronic magazine

fact file – listing of facts (often *boxed*) relating to story. Useful way of creating visual and copy variety on page

feature – as distinct from news story, tends to be longer, carry more background information, *colour*, wider range of sources and journalist's opinion can be prominent

feedback – response from colleagues or public to journalist's copy

file – (verb) to send story from foreign country; (noun) anything stored on a computer such as a document, program or image

filler – short story, usually of one or two pars, filling in space when a longer story runs short (also known as brief)

fireman – person sent from newspaper's headquarters to cover major story (either at home or abroad). Notice gender bias in word

fit – when text, picture or headline does not overrun (bust) its allotted space

Fleet Street – though newspapers have dispersed from this street in East London (between the Strand and St Paul's Cathedral), national newspapers as a collective group are still known by this name. Often known as Street of Shame

floppy disk – flexible disk used for storage of information on computers

follow-up – when newspaper uses report in other media outlet as basis for its own news story

font – typeface of one particular size (incorrectly spelled as fount)

Fourth Estate – press supposedly occupying the position of fourth most powerful institution after Lords Spiritual, Lords Temporal and Commons (Lord Macaulay: 'The gallery in which reporters sit has become a fourth estate of the realm.')

free – free newspaper

freebie – range of services and entertainments (e.g. drinks, meals, trips abroad funded by organisations, concert tickets etc) provided free to journalists. Some journalists believe acceptance of freebies compromises 'objectivity' and refuse them

freelance – journalist contributing to several media outlets and not on permanent staff of any one organisation; see also *stringer*. US: freelancer

FTP – File Transfer Protocol, used to transfer files across the internet

galley proof – see *proof*

gopher – a menu system allowing you to navigate the internet, largely displaced by the World Wide Web

graphics – illustrations and drawings used in designing pages

gutter – space between pages in centre spread; also space between any two columns on computer screens

gutter press – sometimes applied to *tabloid* press

hack – insult word for journalists which journalists are happy to use to describe themselves

hamper – story displayed horizontally usually at the top of page

handouts – story sent to media outlets by press relations office of organisation or PR company

hard copy – copy typed on sheets of paper (usually A4 size). Each page is known as a folio

hard news – news focusing on who, what, where, when, why based on factual detail and quotes and containing little description, journalist comment or analysis; cf. *soft news*

heavies – *broadsheet* 'serious' papers such as *Guardian, The Times, Financial Times*

hold – instruction (usually known as set and hold) ensuring copy is prepared for publication but not printed, as for instance an *obituary* of some eminent person

home page – either the front page that is loaded at start-up by *web browser* or the main web document for a group, person or organisation

house – media organisation. Thus in-house (meaning within particular media organisation). House organ is company's own newspaper or magazine; see also *style*

HTML – hypertext mark-up language comprising the codes for writing web pages

human interest story – story focusing on success, failures, tragedies, emotional/ sexual histories of people, eliminating or marginalising more abstract and deeper cultural, economic, political, class-based factors

hypertext – divides a document into clickable links that connect web pages to each other

imprint – name and address of printer and publisher required by law on newspaper

indent – abbreviation for indentation providing white space at start or end of line

in-depth reporting – detailed coverage

index – front page (or sometimes elsewhere) listing of stories in rest of paper, to ease reading and 'sell'/'flag' the contents in prominent place

in-house – see *house*

input – to type copy into computer

insert – copy injected into story which is already written or set

inside story – reporter bases investigation on their experience and research within organisation/s at centre of controversy and/or quotes from insiders within organisation

internet – network of interconnecting computers communicating through the TCP/IP (Transmission Control Protocol/Internet Protocol)

internet service provider (ISP) – organisation providing access to the internet

intro – opening of news or feature story usually containing main *angle*. Not necessarily just single *par*. Also known as lead. US: nose

inverted pyramid – traditional representation of news stories (with main point at start and information declining in news value thereafter and ending with short background). Tends to oversimplify structure of news story. Better to imagine series of inverted pyramids within an overall large pyramid

investigative reporting – in one respect all journalism involves investigation. But investigative journalism tends to reveal something of social or political significance which someone powerful or famous wants hidden. US: muckraking

issue – all copies of the day's paper and its editions

italic – typeface sloping to the right *like this*; see also *bold* and *roman*

journalese – journalists' jargon

journo – jocular term for journalist

justify – line of text set to fit given measure

kill – to decide not to use (or drop) story or feature. Newspapers are supposed to pay 'kill fee' when they break an agreement to use freelance copy

knock down – to disprove story usually in rival newspaper

label – headline merely categorising the news e.g. ('Interview with PM')

layout – design of the page, originally by *subeditor* using pencil and sent to compositor for guidance but normally now done totally on screen

lead (pronounced led) – space between lines of type (derived from former 'hot metal' printing system when strips of metal, or leads, were used for this purpose). Leaded out copy has its lines spaced out to fit allotted space

lead (pronounced leed) – main story on page. On front page otherwise known as *splash*

leader – see *editorial*

legal (verb) – to send copy to lawyer to be checked for libel, contempt etc.

life in the day of – see *day in the life of*

lift – to use whole or section of story from one edition to the next; also to pinch story from other media outlet changing and adding only a little. When barest minimum is changed known as 'straight lift'

linage – payment to freelances based on number of lines of copy used

line drawing – drawing made up of black lines as in cartoon

listings – lists usually of entertainment events giving basic information: times, venue, phone numbers and so on

Listserv – software for organising an email discussion list

literal – typing error either misspelling or transliteration

lobby – specialist group of correspondents reporting House of Commons

lower case – small letters in *font* of type (as opposed to *upper case* or *capitals*)

masthead – newspaper's title on front page

middle-market – newspapers such as *Mail* and *Express* which lie (in overall style and appearance) between *heavies* and the *red-tops*

modem – telephone link-up for computers, most commonly used for sending email and accessing the internet

mole – a secret source for investigative journalist buried deep in the heart of organisation whose activities they are prepared to reveal

moonlighter – journalist who works during the evening for media organisation while holding another full-time job during day. Nice to be but it means moonlighter is depriving colleague of job

mug shot – photo showing just face (and sometimes shoulders), otherwise known as head and shoulders

must – editorial copy which must appear e.g. apology, correction

new journalism – literary form of reportage pioneered in US in 1960s and 1970s by Norman Mailer, Tom Wolfe, Joan Didion and Truman Capote

newsgroups – discussion groups on the internet

New World and Communication Order – a concept promoted by UNESCO in 1970s and 1980s to counter dominance of international news flows by five major news agencies. Western countries, particularly US and UK, saw it as 'threatening the flow of information'

obit –abbreviation of obituary, an account and appreciation of someone's life

off-beat – unusual story often with a humorous twist

offline – not connected to the internet

off the record – when statements are made not for publication but for background only. Information derived from comments should in no way be traceable back to source

online – connected to the internet

on spec – uncommissioned article submitted voluntarily to media

on the record – when there are no restrictions on reporting what is said

op ed – abbreviation of opposite editorial, being the page opposite one on which editorial/leader comment falls. Usually contains important features and commentary by prestigious columnists

opinion piece – article in which journalist expresses overt opinion

overline – see *strap or strapline*

PA – abbreviation for Press Association, an *agency* which supplies national news and features (as well as an international service from its link up with Reuters) to national and local papers. 'Page-ready' copy from PA is designed and can be slotted straight into newspaper

pack – collection of journalists (sometimes known as 'rat-pack') as in 'following the pack'

panel – text larger than body text with lines top and bottom. Serves to break up grey block of copy. Written by *subeditors*

paparazzi – horde of photographers

par. – abbreviation for paragraph. Also para

pay-off – last par. with twist or flourish

pic – abbreviation for picture meaning photograph; plural pix

pick-up – journalist attending function might pick up or take away a photograph supplied by the organisers, known as a pick-up job; also journalists following up an event after it has happened is 'picking up' news

picture-grabber – facility for taking pictures off television

podding – scheme originally promoted by Westminster Press in which multi-skilled subs, reporters and photographers worked in small teams

pool – privileged, small group of journalists with special access to event or source. Their reports and findings are distributed to those news organisations outside the pool

pops/populars – mass-selling national *tabloids*; now known as *red-tops* because their *mastheads* are in red

PR – abbreviation for public relations

press release – announcement made by organisation specially for use by media (not necessarily just press)

probe – investigation

profile – picture in words which usually focuses on an individual but organisation, cars, horses, a building, and so on can be profiled

proof – printout of part or whole page. This proof is read, corrected where necessary and the amended page (the revise) is then ready for final printing. Galley proof contains just columns of type

puff – story giving publicity

punchline – main point of story. Thus 'punchy' means story has a strong news *angle*

qualities – see *broadsheets*

quote – abbreviation for quotation; also when a reporter files copy over phone 'quote' then means first inverted commas. End quote marks are often known as 'unquote'

readership – number of people who read paper as opposed the number of copies sold

red-tops – tabloid newspapers such as the *Mirror*, *Sun* and *People*, so-called because their *mastheads* are red

re-jig/re-hash – rearrangement of copy provided by reporter usually by *subeditor* to produce a better structured piece

retrospective – *feature* looking back on event

re-vamp – change story or page in light of new material

revise – see *proof*

rewrite – to use information provided in story but compose it in completely new language. Known as rewrite job

ring-around – story based on series of telephone calls

roman – standard typeface (not *bold* or *italic*)

round-up – gathering together of various strands of story either under the same heading (otherwise known as umbrella story) or under variety of headings

roving reporter – reporter who travels around a lot

RSI – abbreviation for repetitive strain injury which journalists can suffer through their use of a keyboard and mouse

run – period of printing edition

running story – story which runs or develops over number of editions or days

run on – continue from one line, column or page to the next

scoop – exclusive

screamer – exclamation mark (usually in headline)

search engine – provides for subject searching on the internet through feeding terms on to a *database* and returning a list of 'hits' or correspondences

section – separately folded part of the paper

server – computer that makes services and data available on a network

set and hold – see *hold*

sexy story – story with popular appeal. But many 'sexy stories' give sex a bad name

sign-off – byline at foot of story

silly season – supposedly a time (usually in the summer holiday period) when little *hard* news is around and the press is reduced to covering trivia. For some newspapers silly season can last a long time. Wars and invasions often happen in silly seasons, too

sister paper – when company owns more than one paper each is described as sister. Thus *The Times* is the *Sun*'s sister since both are owned by Rupert Murdoch

sketch – light, often witty article describing event. Most commonly used with reference to reporting House of Commons

slip – special edition for particular area or event

snap – brief information given by news *agency* before main story is sent

snapper – photographer

soft news – light news story that can be more colourful, witty and commenty than *hard news*

soundbite – short, pithy quote used by journalists. First coined by US radio and television journalists in the late 1960s

spike – to reject copy or other information (e.g. *press release*). Derived from old metal spike which stood on wooden base on which subs would stick unwanted material. Had advantage over 'binning' since material was accessible so long as it remained on spike

spin doctors – people who attempt to influence news or political agenda (the 'spin' in the jargon) such as press officers, communications specialists and other propagandists

splash – lead news story on front page

standfirst – text intended to be read between headline and story which can elaborate on point made in headline, add new one or raise questions which will be answered in story (a teaser). Sometimes contains *byline*. Helps provide reader with a 'guiding hand' into reading large slice of copy – thus mainly used for features and occasionally long news stories. Also known as the 'sell'

stet – ignore deletion (Latin for 'let it stand')

stop press – column on back page of newspaper left blank and allowing for slotting in of breaking news just before publication

strap or strapline – headline in smaller type appearing over main deck. Otherwise known as overline

stringer – *freelance*, in provinces, in London or overseas, who has come to arrangement with news organisation to supply copy on agreed basis. Super-stringer will contract to devote most of working for one organisation but still be free to freelance for other media outlets for rest of time

style – special rules adopted by newspaper relating to spellings, punctuation and abbreviation. Often contained within style book though increasingly carried on screen. Many newspapers somehow survive without them

subeditor/sub – responsible for editing reporters' copy, writing headlines, captions, laying out pages etc. Stone sub makes final corrections and cuts on page proofs. US: copy editor

tabloid – newspaper whose pages are roughly half the size of *broadsheet*. All *pops* or popular papers are tabloids as are *sections* of some of the *heavies*. Serious tabloids exist on continent (*Le Monde* in France, for instance) and in US (*Los Angeles Times*)

tabloidese – shoddy, over-sensational, cliché-ridden copy most commonly associated with the *tabloids*

take – page or number of pages comprising a section of longer piece

taster – journalist who checks copy, selecting good and removing unwanted. Process known as copy tasting

think piece – analytical article

tip-off – information supplied to newspaper by member of the public

top – story at the top of a page

tots – abbreviation for 'triumph over tragedy story', particularly popular human interest genre

trim – cut a report

umbrella story – see *round-up*

underline – to carry a line or rule under headline or *crosshead*

upper case – capital letters when used alongside small (*lower case*) letters. When just capital letters are used (as in headlines) they are known as *caps*

URL – uniform resource location: a string of characters identifying internet resource and its location; the most common ones begin http://

vox pop – series of quotes on particular theme. From Latin *vox populi* ('voice of the people')

web – all websites on the *internet* linked to form a global 'web' (World Wide Web – www) of information

web browser – software for viewing websites, such as Internet Explorer and Netscape Navigator

whistleblower – person revealing newsworthy and previously secret information to media

widow – short line left at top of column

Bibliography

Aitchison, James (1988) *Writing for the Press*, London: Hutchinson.

Allan, Stuart (1999) *News Culture*, Buckingham: Open University Press.

Almond, Gabriel and Verba, Stanley (1963) *The Civic Culture*, Princeton, NJ: Princeton University Press.

Aubrey, Crispin (ed.) (1982) *Nukespeak: the Media and the Bomb*, London: Comedia.

Bagnall, Nicholas (1993) *Newspaper Language*, Oxford; Focal Press.

Ball, Alan R. (1981) *British Political Parties*, London: Macmillan.

Barber, Lynn (1991) *Mostly Men*, London: Viking.

—— (1999) 'The art of the interview', in Stephen Glover (ed.) *Secrets of the Press: Journalists on Journalism*, London: Allen Lane/Penguin Press: 196–205.

Barker, Dennis (1998) 'The question posers', *Press Gazette*, 11 September.

Barr, Damian (1999) 'Let them read all about you', *The Times*, 8 November.

Baston, Lewis (2000) *Sleaze: The State of Britain*, London: Channel 4 Books.

Beck, Sally (1999) 'Nice idea . . . but it's not really us', *Press Gazette*, 22 January.

Bentham, Peggy (1991) *VDU Terminal Sickness: Computer Health Risks and How to Protect Yourself*, London: Green Print.

Bird, S. Elizabeth and Dardenne, Robert W. (1988) 'Myth, chronicle and story', in James W. Carey (ed.) *Media, Myths and Narrative Television and the Press*, London: Sage.

Bloch, Alan (1992) 'Town Hall Turnover', *Municipal Review and AMA News*, 63(727): 40.

Bloch, Jonathan and Fitzgerald, Patrick (1983) *British Intelligence and Covert Action*, London: Junction.

Boorstin, Daniel (1962) *The Image: Or What Happened to the American Dream?*, New York: Harper and Row.

Bower, Tom (1988) *Maxwell: The Outsider*, London: Mandarin.

—— (1992) 'Maxwell: a very British experience', Sixth James Cameron Memorial Lecture, City University, London.

Boyne, Gerry A. (1999) 'Managing local services: from CCT to best value', *Local Government Studies*, special edition, summer.

Brown, Gerry (1995a) 'Fines are just fine by me', *Guardian*, 24 July.

—— (1995b) *Exposed! Sensational True Story of Fleet Street Reporter*, London: Viking.

Browne, Christopher (1996) *The Prying Game: The Sex, Sleaze and Scandals of Fleet Street and the Media Mafia*, London: Robson.

—— (1999) *The Journalist's Handbook*, London: A & C Black.

Burchett, Wilfred (1983) *Shadows of Hiroshima*, London: Verso.

Burgh, Hugo de (2000) *Investigative Journalism: Context and Practice*, London: Routledge.

Campbell, Duncan and Connor, Steve (1986) *On the Record: Surveillance, Computers and Privacy*, London: Michael Joseph.

Chalaby, Jean (1998) *The Invention of Journalism*, London: Macmillan.

Chilton, Paul (ed.) (1985) *Language and the Nuclear Arms Debate: Nukespeak Today*, London: Frances Pinter.

Chomsky, Noam (1999) *The New Military Humanism: Lessons from Kosovo*, London: Pluto.

Chomsky, Noam and Herman, Edward (1994) *Manufacturing Consent: The Political Economy of the Mass Media*, 4th edn, London: Vintage.

Chossudovsky, Michel (1998) *The Globalisation of Poverty: Impacts of IMF and World Bank Reforms*, London: Zed.

Christmas, Linda (2000) 'Road to enlightenment', *Press Gazette*, 10 March.

Clarkson, Wendsley (1990) *Confessions of a Tabloid Journalist*, London: Fourth Estate.

Clayton, Joan (1994) *Interviewing for Journalists: How to Research and Conduct Interviews You Can Sell*, London: Piatkus.

Cockerell, Michael, Hennessy, Peter and Walker, David (1984) *Sources Close to the Prime Minister: Inside the Hidden World of the News Manipulators*, London: Macmillan.

Cohen, Stanley (1980) *Folk Devils and Moral Panics*, London: Robertson.

Coleman, Terry (1993) 'Best chat lines of our time', *Guardian*, 6 November.

Corfield, Rebecca (1992) *Preparing Your Own CV*, London: Kogan Page.

Cramer, Chris (2000) 'I can still taste the cordite, 20 years later', *Independent*, 2 May.

Curran, James and Seaton, Jean (1994) *Power without Responsibility: The Press and Broadcasting in Britain*, 4th edn, London: Routledge.

Curran, James, Douglas, Angus and Whannel, Gary (1980) 'The political economy of the human interest story', in Anthony Smith (ed.) *Newspapers and Democracy: International Essays on a Changing Medium*, Cambridge, MA: MIT Press: 288–316.

Curtis, Liz (1984) *Ireland and the Propaganda War*, London: Pluto.

Davies, Nick (2000) 'Keeping a foot in the door', *Guardian*, 10 January.

Davis, Anthony (1988) *Magazine Journalism Today*, Oxford: Heinemann.

Delano, Anthony and Henningham, John (1995) *The News Breed: British Journalism in the 1990s*, London: London College of Printing.

Department of National Heritage (1995) *Privacy and Media Intrusion*, London: HMSO.

Department of the Environment, Transport and the Regions (DETR) (1998) *A Mayor and Assembly for London?* London: DETR.

Department of the Environment, Transport and the Regions (1999) *Modern Local Government. In Touch with the People*, White Paper Cm 4014, London: Stationary Office.

Dick, Jill (1998) *Freelance Writing for Newspapers*, 2nd edn, London: A & C Black.

Dijk, Teu van (1988) *News as Discourse*, Hillsdale, NJ: Lawrence Erlbaum.

—— (1991) *Racism and the Press*, London: Routledge.

Dobson, Christopher (1992) *The Freelance Journalist: How to Survive and Succeed*, Oxford: Butterworth-Heinemann.

Dorner, Jane (2000) *The Internet: A Writer's Guide*, London: A & C Black.

Dorril, Stephen and Ramsay, Robin (1991) *Smear*, London: Fourth Estate.

Dougary, Ginny (1994) *Executive Tarts and Other Myths*, London: Virago.

Ellwood, Wayne (1996) 'Seduced by technology', *New Internationalist*, December.

Fedler, Fred (1989) *Reporting for the Print Media*, 4th edn, San Diego, CA: Harcourt, Brace, Jovanovich.

Fiske, John (1989) *Understanding Popular Culture*, London: Unwin Hyman.

—— (1992) 'Popularity and the politics of information', in Peter Dahlgren and Colin Sparks (ed.) *Journalism and Popular Culture*, London: Sage: 45–63.

Flett, Kathryn (1997) 'When I bared all . . .', *Guardian*, 16 June.

Fowler, Roger (1991) *Language in the News: Discourse and Ideology in the Press*, London: Routledge.

Franklin, Bob (1994) *Packaging Politics: Political Communication in Britain's Media Democracy*, London: Edward Arnold.

—— (1997) *Newszack and News Media*, London: Edward Arnold.

Franklin, Bob and Murphy, David (1991) *What News?*, London: Routledge.

Friend, Tad (1998) 'Stars in their eyes', *Guardian*, 20 April.

Frost, Chris (2000) *Media Ethics and Self-Regulation*, London: Longman.

Gilster, Paul (1996) *Finding it on the Internet: The Internet Navigator's Guide to Search Tools and Techniques*, London: Wiley.

Glover, Stephen (1999) 'What columnists are good for', in Glover Stephen (ed.) *Secrets of the Press: Journalists on Journalism*, London: Allen Lane/Penguin Press: 289–98.

Goodwin, Eugene (1994) *Groping for Ethics*, Ames, Iowa: Iowa State University Press.

Gordon, Paul and Rosenberg, David (1989) *Daily Racism: The Press and Black People in Britain*, London: Runnymede Trust.

Greenslade, Roy (1992) *Maxwell's Fall*, London: Simon and Schuster.

—— (1995) 'Breaking the silence', *Guardian*, 6 February.

—— (2000) 'No more news of the screws', *Guardian*, 24 April.

Gripsrud, Jostein (1992) 'The aesthetics and politics of melodrama', in Peter Dahlgren and Colin Sparks, (eds) *Journalism and Popular Culture*, London: Sage: 84–95.

Halloran, James, Elliott, Phillip and Murdock, Graham (1970) *Demonstrations and Communications*, Harmondsworth: Penguin.

Hanlin, Bruce (1992) 'Owners, editors and journalists', in Andrew Belsey and Ruth Chadwick (eds) *Ethical Issues in Journalism and the Media*, London: Routledge: 33–48.

Hanstock, Terry (1999) 'The thirteenth pillar: the death of Di reconsidered', *Lobster* 38, 2–7.

Hargreaves, Ian (2000) 'In search of the elusive first rung', *Press Gazette* (journalism training special edition), 4 April.

Harman, Harriet (2000) 'A house of men', *Guardian*, 27 March.

Harris, Nigel (1992) 'Codes of conduct for journalists', in Andrew Belsey and Ruth Chadwick (eds) *Ethical Issues in Journalism and the Media*, London: Routledge: 62–76.

Harris, Robert (1990) *Good and Faithful Servant*, London: Faber & Faber.

Hay, Colin (1999) *The Political Economy of New Labour: Labouring under False Pretences?*, Manchester: Manchester University Press.

Hellinger, Daniel and Judd, Dennis R. (1991) *The Democratic Facade*, Belmont, CA: Wadsworth.

Hennessy, Brendan (1993) *Writing Feature Articles*, Oxford: Focal Press.

Hennessy, Peter (1986) *Cabinet*, Oxford: Blackwell.

Hicks, Wynford (1998) *English for Journalists*, 2nd edn, London: Routledge.

Hillyard, Paddy and Percy-Smith, Janie (1988) *The Coercive State: The Decline of Democracy in Britain*, London: Fontana.

Hogan, Daniel (1998) 'Sobriety in the last chance saloon', in *Self Regulation in the Media*, papers from the annual conference of the Association for Journalism Education, London.

Hollingsworth, Mark (1990) *The Press and Political Dissent*, London: Pluto.

—— (2000) 'Secrets, lies and David Shayler', *Guardian*, 17 March.

Hollingsworth, Mark and Fielding, Nick (1999) *Defending the Realm: M15 and the Shayler Affair*, London: André Deutsche.

Howard, Clive (1994) *Journalists and Copyright*, London: National Union of Journalists.

Howard, Philip (1984) *State of the Language*, London: Hamish Hamilton.

Hughes, Lotte and McCrum, Sarah (1998) *Interviewing Children*, London: Save the Children.

Johnson, Andrew (1996) 'The rising tide of shutdown culture', *Press Gazette*, 15 November.

Jones, George and Stewart, John (1998) 'Committees not all over yet', *Local Government Chronicle*, 6 November: 8.

Kavanagh, Dennis (1983) *Political Science and Political Behaviour*, London: Allen & Unwin.

Keeble, Richard (1998) 'The politics of sleaze reporting: a critical overview of the ethical debate in the British press of the 1990s', *Recherches en Communication*, Catholic University of Louvain, Belgium, 9: 71–81.

—— (1999) 'The three secret wars in the Balkans 1999', in Peter Goff (ed.) *The Kosovo News and Propaganda War*, Vienna: International Press Institute.

—— (2000) 'George Orwell – the journalist', *Press Gazette*, 21 January.

Kennedy, Paul (1986) 'A.J.P. Taylor and profound causes in history', in Chris Wrigley (ed.) *Warfare, Diplomacy and Politics*: *Essays in Honour of A.J.P.Taylor*, London: Hamish Hamilton.

Kiernan, Ben (ed.) (1986) *Burchett: Reporting on the Other Side of the World*, London: Quartet.

Kiley, Robert (1999) 'Easy as falling off a log', *Guardian*, 12 January.

Knightley, Phillip (1998) *A Hack's Progress*, London: Vintage.

Lashmar, Paul (2000) 'Is a good story worth a prison sentence?', *Independent*, 28 March.

Leach, Steve (1999) 'Introducing cabinets into British local government', *Parliamentary Affairs*, January: 77–93.

Leapman, Michael (1983) *Barefaced Cheek*, London: Hodder & Stoughton.

Leigh, David (1980) *The Frontiers of Secrecy: Closed Government in Britain*, London: Junction.

—— (1989) *The Wilson Plot*, 2nd edn, London: Heinemann.

Leigh, David and Vulliamy, Ed (1997) *Sleaze: The Corruption of Parliament*, London: Fourth Estate.

Leslie, Ann (1999) 'Female firemen', in Stephen Glover (ed.) *Secrets of the Press: Journalists on Journalism*, London: Allen Lane/Penguin Press.

Leyland, Adam (1998) 'The pen mightier than the sword but not the tape', *Press Gazette*, 17 July.

Lowndes, Vivien (1999) 'Rebuilding trust in central–local relations: policy or passion?', *Local Government Studies*, Winter: 116–36.

McCann, Paul (2000) 'Make way for TV briefings', *The Times*, 17 March.

McKay, Jenny (2000) *The Magazines Handbook*, London: Routledge.

Macleod, Louise (1999) 'Eek! It's a mouse', *Guardian*, 12 January.

McNair, Brian (1996) *News and Journalism in the UK*, 2nd edn, London: Routledge.

—— (2000) *Journalism and Democracy: An Evaluation of the Political Public Sphere*, London: Routledge.

McQuail, Denis (1992) *Media Performance: Mass Communication and the Public Interest*, London: Sage.

Mair, Peter (2000) 'Partyless democracy: solving the paradox of New Labour?', *New Left Review*, 2.2 (March/April): 28–35.

Mayes, Ian (1999) 'Disaster watch', *Guardian*, 16 October.

—— (2000) 'My word', *Guardian*, 1 July.

Melin-Higgins, Margareta (1997) 'The social construction of journalist ideals: gender in journalism education', paper presented at conference 'Journalists for a New Century', London College of Printing, 24 April.

Metzler, Ken (1997) *Creative Interviewing*, Boston:, MA: Allyn & Bacon.

Mills, Jane (1991) *Womanwords*, London: Virago.

Milne, Seamus (1995) *The Enemy Within: The Secret War against the Miners*, London: Pan.

Milner, Annalisa (2000) *Browsing the Web*, London: Dorling Kindersley.

Moore, Alison (1999) 'Articles of faith', *Press Gazette*, 2 February.

Moore, Suzanne (1996) *Head over Heels*, London: Viking.

Moore, Wendy (1999) 'Poverty still a killer', *Guardian*, 22 December.

Morgan, Jean (1998) 'Judge backs right of reporter and paper to protect source', *Press Gazette*, 3 April.

Morton, Andrew (1992) *Diana: Her True Story*, London: Michael O'Mara.

Naughton, John (1999) *A Brief History of the Future: The Origins of the Internet*, London: Weidenfeld & Nicolson.

Newton, Kenneth (1986) 'Mass media', in Henry Drucker (gen. ed,) *et al. Developments in British Politics*, London: Macmillan.

Niblock, Sarah (1996) *Inside Journalism*, London: Blueprint.

Nolan, Lord (1996) *Aspects of Conduct in Local Government in England, Scotland and Wales*, London: Committee on Standards in Public Life.

Norris, Bill (2000) 'Media ethics at the sharp end', in David Berry (ed.) *Ethics and Media Culture: Practices and Representations*, Oxford: Focal Press: 325–38.

Northmore, David (1990) *Freedom of Information Handbook*, London: Bloomsbury.

Norton, Phillip (1991) 'Committees in the House of Commons', *Politics Review*, 1(1).

Orwell, George (1984 [1957]) 'Politics and the English language', in *Inside the Whale and Other Essays*, Harmondsworth: Penguin: 143–57.

Oxford, Esther (1992) 'Pay your money and pick your man', *Independent*, 18 November.

Page, Ben (1998) 'Making Voting Attractive Again', *Local Government Chronicle*, 16 October: 16–17.

Paglia, Camille (1995) *Vamps and Tramps*, Harmondsworth: Penguin.

Peak, Steve and Fisher, Paul (1999) *The Media Guide 2000*, London: Fourth Estate.

Phillips, Angela and Gaber, Ivor (1996) 'The case for media degrees', *British Journalism Review*, 7(3): 62–5.

Pilger, John (1996) 'The hidden power of the media', *Socialist Review*, September.

—— (1998) *Hidden Agendas*, London: Vintage.

Platell, Amanda (1999) 'Institutionalised sexism', in Stephen Glover (ed.) *Secrets of the Press: Journalists on Journalism*, London: Allen Lane/Penguin Press: 140–7.

Ponting, Clive (1986) *Whitehall: Tragedy and Farce*, London: Sphere.

—— (1990) *Secrecy in Britain*, Oxford: Basil Blackwell.

Project Censored (1998) *Censored: The News that Didn't Make the News*, New York: Seven Stories Press.

Randall, David (2000) *The Universal Journalist*, 2nd edn, London: Pluto.

Read, Sue (1992) *The Complete Guide to Working from Home*, London: Headline.

Reddick, Randy and King, Elliot (1997) *The Online Journalist: Using the Internet and Other Electronic Resources*, 2nd edn, Fort Worth Harcourt Brace.

Reeves, Ian (1999) 'Reaping the whirlwind', *Press Gazette*, 18 May.

Robertson, Geoffrey (1983) *People Against the Press: An Enquiry into the Press Council*, London: Quartet.

Rock, P. (1988) 'News as eternal recurrence', in Stanley Cohen and Jock Young (eds) *The Manufacture of News: Social Problems, Deviance and the Mass Media*, London: Constable: 64–70.

Rose, Richard (1965) *Politics in England*, London: Faber & Faber.

Roszak, Theodore (1996) 'Dumbing us down', *New Internationalist*, December.

Rowlands, Barbara (1993) 'Don't call me, please, and I won't call you', *Independent*, 24 August.

Searle, Chris (1989) *Your Daily Dose of Racism*, London: Campaign for Press and Broadcasting Freedom.

Sereny, Gitta (1998) *Cries Unheard*, London: Macmillan.

Seymour-Ure, Colin (1974) *The Political Impact of the Mass Media*, London: Constable.

Shawcross, William (1992) *Murdoch*, London: Pan Books.

Silvester, Christopher (ed.) (1994) *Interviews: An Anthology from 1859 to the Present Day*, Harmondsworth: Penguin.

—— (1997) (ed.) *The Penguin Book of Columnists*, London: Viking.

Smith, Anthony (1978) *The Politics of Information*, London: Macmillan.

Smith, Geoffrey, Hemder, Derrick and Kett, David (1992) *Local Government for Journalists*, London: LGC Communications Information and Research.

Snoddy, Raymond (1993) *The Good, the Bad and the Unacceptable*, 2nd edn, London: Faber & Faber.

Spark, David (1999) *Investigative Reporting: A Study in Technique*, Oxford: Focal Press.

Sparks, Colin (1992) 'Popular journalism: Theories and Practice', in Peter Dahlgren and Colin Sparks (eds) *Journalism and Popular Culture*, London: Sage: 24–44.

—— (1999) 'The press', in Jane Stokes and Anna Reading (eds) *The Media in Britain: Current Debates and Developments*, London: Macmillan: 41–60.

Spender, Dale (1980) *Man Made Language*, London: Routledge & Kegan Paul.

—— (ed.) (1983) *Feminist Theories: Three Centuries of Women's Intellectual Traditions*, London: Women's Press.

Stephenson, Hugh and Mory, Pierre (1990) *Journalism Training in Europe*, Brussels: European Community.

Stoker, Gerry (1999) 'Slow road to regionalism', *Local Government Chronicle*, 22 January: 8.

Taylor, Norren (2000) 'The national ladies in waiting', *Press Gazette*, 7 July.

Tiffen, Rodney (1989) *News and Power*, London: Unwin Hyman.

Trelford, Donald (2000) 'The freedom to be irresponsible', *Press Gazette*, 24 March.

Truss, Lynne (1999) 'On the terraces', in Stephen Glover (ed.) *Secrets of the Press: Journalists on Journalism*, London: Allen Lane/Penguin Press: 125–32.

Tulloch, John (1998) 'Managing the press in a medium-sized European power', in Hugh Stephenson and Michael Bromley (eds) *Sex Lies and Democracy: The Press and the Public*, London: Longman: 63–83.

Tunstall, Jeremy (1983) *The Media in Britain*, London: Constable.

Turner, John (2000) *The Tories and Europe*, Manchester: Manchester University Press.

Ullmann, John and Honeyman, Steve (1983) *The Reporter's Handbook: An Investigator's Guide to Documents and Techniques*, New York: St Martin's Press.

Wade, Stephen (1997) *Freelance Writing*, London: Straightforward.

Wallace, Milverton (1996) 'Death of the deadline', *Press Gazette*, 12 April.

Wasley, Andrew (2000) 'Grief encounter', *Guardian*, 6 March.

Waterhouse, Keith (1981) *The Mirror's Way with Words*, London: Mirror Books.

—— (1991) *English our English (and How to Sing It)*, London: Viking.

—— (1995) 'Talking of which . . .', *Guardian*, 25 September.

Welsh, Tom and Greenwood, Walter (eds) (1999) *McNae's Essential Law for Journalists*, 5th edn, London: Butterworths.

Wheen, Francis (2000) 'The Sun's gypsy curse', *Guardian*, 22 March.

Widdicombe, D. (1986) *Report of the Committee of Inquiry into the Conduct of Local Authority Business*, London: HMSO.

Williams, Granville (1994) *Britain's Media: How They Are Related: Media Ownership and Democracy*, London: Campaign for Press and Broadcasting Freedom.

Williams, Kevin (1998) *Get Me a Murder a Day!*, London: Routledge.

Williams, Paul N. (1978) *Investigative Reporting and Editing*, Englewood Cliffs, NJ: Prentice Hall.

Williams, Stephen (1996) 'A job to die for?', *Journalist*, June–July.

Wilson, David and Game, Chris (1998) *Local Government in the United Kingdom*, London: Macmillan.

Wilson, John (1996) *Understanding Journalism: A Guide to the Issues*, London: Routledge.

Wingfield, John (1984) *Bugging: A Complete Survey of Electronic Surveillance Today*, London: Robert Hale.

Wintour, Charles (1990) *The Rise and Fall of Fleet Street*, London: Hutchinson.

Wright, Peter (with Greengrass, Paul) (1987) *Spycatcher*, Melbourne: Heinemann.

Zobel, Gibby (2000) 'Rights mess', *Guardian*, 3 May.

Index

accidents coverage 113–19
advertising 1, 35
Agence France Presse 18, 76
AgiliWriting 77
AIDS 34–5, 82, 92
Aitchison, James 42, 72
Aitken, Jonathan 26, 175, 189
Aitken, Victoria 27
Allan, Stuart 30, 33, 42, 95
Alliot, Mr Justice 54
Almond, Gabriel 148
AltaVista 57, 58
alternative media 1, 22, 23
Alternative Press Centre 56
ambush interview 63
Amnesty International 39, 43, 138, 174
Andrew, Nigel 223
Antonowicz, Anton 195
Article 19 39
arts reviewing *see* reviewing
Ashdown, Paddy 25
Asian Times 33, 45
Ask Jeeves 57
Associated Newspapers 2, 5; *see also*
    Daily Mail, *Mail on Sunday* and
    Evening Standard, London
Associated Press 18
Association of Chief Police Officers 114
Association of Investigative Journalists
    185–92
Astbury's shorthand system 77
Aubrey, Crispin 85
Automobile Association (AA) 118

Bagnall, Nicholas 83
Barker, Dennis 68

Baston, Lewis 28
BBC: 28, 36, 52, 59, 90, 121, 137, 149,
    169, 175, 184; World Service 13; *The
    World Tonight* 17; BBC Wales 39;
    BBC Online 16
Baig, Anila 32
Baird, Rachel 53
Ball, Alan **164**
Barber, Lynn 61, 65, 69, 70, 213
Barr, Damian 240
Baxter, Mark 126, 127
Beaverbrook, Lord 23, 26, 36
Beck, Sally 5
Beckett, T.R. 4
Bell, Martin 184
Bell, Mary 27
Bentham, Peggy 234
Bernstein, Carl 64
Bertrand, Claude-Jean 56
Bibby, Andrew 58
Bird, S. Elizabeth 113
Birmingham Evening Mail 15
Blair, Tony 9, 28, 42, 52, 85, 89–91,
    150, 155, **158**, **165**, **168–9**, **172**
Blake, George 38
Bloch, Alan **160**
Bloch, Jonathan 47
Blom-Cooper, Sir Louis 184
Blundy, Anna 217
Boorstin, Daniel 137
Bournemouth University 237
Bower, Michelle 30
Bower, Tom 36, 47
Box Productions 53
Boycott, Rosie 29
Boyne, Gerry A. 156

Brennan, Jim 56
Brendon, Dr Piers
Brett, Alastair 79
Brighton College of Technology 237
Bristol Evening News 54
British–Irish Council **160**
British Journalism Review 184
British Library 56
Broadcasting Standards Commission 56
Broadcasting White Paper 1989 **171**
Brockway, Fenner 61
Brown, Craig 218
Brown, Gerry 79
Browne, Christopher 26, 63, 229
BSkyB (British Sky Broadcasting) 3
Bulger, James 182
Burchett, Wilfred 138
Burton Trader 11
Burgh, Hugo de 64
Bury Free Press 126, 197
bugging 25, 79–80
Bush, President George 22

Cabinet Office 191
Caistor, Nick 211
Calcutt, David/Calcutt reports 24–5
Cambridge Evening News 8–10, 142,
    203–7
Camden Journal 15
Campaign for Freedom of Information 151
Campaign for Nuclear Disarmament
    (CND) 119, 120
Campaign for Press and Broadcasting
    Freedom 34
Campbell, Alastair 52, **171**, **172**
Campbell, Duncan 80
Caribbean Times 45
Carruthers, Oliver 18
catchline 93–4
Catholic Herald 45
censorship 35–9
Central Lancashire, University of 237
Chalaby, Jean K. 61
Charity Commission 189–91
Chatham Standard 178–9
Channel 4 53
Children Act 1989 **163**
Chilton, Paul 85
Chomsky, Noam 47, 91, 104
Chossudovsky, Michel 91
Church Times 45
Cincinnati Enquirer 50
City of Liverpool Community College
    237

City University, London, journalism
    department 13, 32, 55, 186, 237, 238
Clarendon College 237
Clarkson, Wendsley 75
Clayton, Joan 228
Clinton, President Bill 28, 76, 97, 125
clichés *see* language
Clother, Henry 173–82
Clough, Sue 177–8
CNN 121
Cockayne, Isabel 197
Cockerell, Michael 51, **169**, **172**
Cohen, Stanley 22
Coles, Joanna 211
columnists/column writing 12, 216–22
Coleman, Terry 67
Columbia University 237
Committee, The 53
Committee to Protect Journalists 56
Commons Privileges Committee 26
Companies House 189, 192
Condon, Eileen 214–5
Conservative Party 36, 37, 98, 119, 129,
    144–6, 152, 153, 154, **160**, **161**, **165**, 189
Confederation of British Industry 38, 42
confidentiality 52–3
conformism 1
Connery, Jason 79
Connor, Steve 80
Contempt of Court Act 1981 52, 53
Connection , The 184
Cook, Robin 27, 91
copy presentation 93–4
copyright 230
Corfield, Rebecca 240
Cornwell, Richard 115
Coronation Street 28
court reporting -173–82; magistrates'
    courts 175, 180; crown courts 180;
    civil courts 180–1; county courts 181;
    Court of Appeal 181; coroners' courts
    174, 181–2; *see also* High Court
Covert Action Quarterly 45
Cramer, Chris 121
Cranston, Nora 39
Crawley College 237
Criminal Justice Act 1994 122
Criminal Justice (Mode of Trial) Bill 182
Criminal Procedures and Investigations
    Act 1996 38
Crown Prosecution Service 175, 176
Curran, James 22, 36, 125
Curtis, Liz 97
CV 240

Dacre, Paul 5
Daily Express 23, 26, 27, 30, 100, 103, 105, 138, 195, 232
Daily Graphic 23
Daily Herald 36
Daily Mail 18, 23, 27, 52, 96, 185, 232, 235
Daily Sketch 23, 52
Daily Star 100, 106, 111, 140–1, 216
Daily Telegraph 27, 54, 96, 103, 139, 177–8
Dardenne, Robert W. 113
Darlington College 237, 238
Data Protection Act 114
Data Protection Register 189–90
Davies, Julie-Ann 186
Davies, Nick 6, 62, 66
Davis, Anthony 228
de-professionalisation 4
Deccan Herald 19
Delano, Anthony 32, 231
Demon Internet 59
demonstrations 54, 117, 119–25 *see also* risk assessment
De Montfort University 237
Derby Evening Telegraph 11
Derby Trader 10–11
Derby Herald and Post 11
Diana, Princess of Wales 25, 26, 40, 48
Dick, Jill 228
van Dijk, Teu 32, 81, 91
disability 33–4, 92
Diss Express 30
D-Notice 47, 151
Dobson, Christopher 228
doorstepping 63
Dorner, Jane 58
Dorril, Stephen 50
Dougary, Ginny 30, 65, 67, 212
drudgereport.com 56

Eapen, Matthew 27
East Anglian Daily Times 49, 115–16, 118
Eastern Daily Press 7, 53
EastEnders 24
Eastern Counties Newspapers 238
Eastern Eye 33, 45, 96, 111–12
East Surrey College 237
Economist 51
Education 17
Elliott, Chris 5
Ellwood, Wayne 55
email 10, 11, 51, 54–5, 57–8, 63, 136, 228, 229

Emap Regional Newspapers 2
Employment Rights Act 2000 4
Engineer 52
English, Sir David 235
English, Pat 30
Equal Opportunities Commission 31
euphemisms *see* language
European, the 11
European Commission on Human Rights 28, 53, 150
European Court on Human Rights 182
European Convention on Human Rights 28, 182
Evans, Harold 5, 208
Evening Standard, London 32, 76, 102–3, 185, 194
Excite 57
Express see Daily Express
eye-witness reporting 108, 120, 124–5, 135, 144–6, 195–6, 199; sporting event 202–7

fairness 22
Falk, Bernard 52
features 95–6, 194–215; the intro 194–8; structure of text 198–202; *see also* profiles
Fielding, Helen 217
Fielding, Nick 37
Financial Times 36, 97, 106, 121, 232
Fisher, Paul 1, 45, 236
Fiske, John 83, 129
Fitzgerald, Patrick 47
Franklin, Bob 27, 43, 44
Franzen, Peter 53
freelances/freelancing 1, 5, 45, 54, 94, 174, 225–30
freesheet 5, 35
Frostrup, Mariella 224
Fleet Street 2, 8, 13, 15, 30, 52, 61, 77, 93, 119, 218, 221, 223, 231, 232; consensus 42, 47, 90, 128
Flett, Kathryn 217
Flyn, Joe 50
Foot, Paul 14, 36, 62
Foster, Reginald 52
Fowler, Roger 81
Freedom of Information bill 39, 149
Free Pint 58
Friend, Tad 210
Frost, Chris 120

Gaber, Ivor 239
Gadafi, President Muammar 37, 93

Galvin, Adrian 53
Game, Chris 155
Gannett 2
Garavelli, Dani 53
Garner, Richard 14- 18, 92
Gay Times 45
Gemini News Service 18–20
General Council of the Press 24
Gilster, Paul *58*
Glancey, Jonathan 202
Glasgow Herald 45
Gloucestershire College of Art and
    Technology 237
Glover, Stephen 217
Godfrey, Lawrence 59
Goldsmiths' College 239
Goodman, Geoffrey 184
Goodwin, Eugene 40
Goodwin, William 52–3
Gopsill, Tim 232
Gordon, Paul 32
GQ 49
Graham, Caroline 214
Granada TV 184
Grant, Colin 8
Greeley, Horace 61
Greenfield, Edward 224
Greenham Common women 42
Green Party **160**, **166–7**
Greenslade, Roy 5, 28, 36, 47, 50
Greenwood, Walter 175
Gregg (shorthand system) 175
Gresham, Anne 77
Gripsrud, Jostein 22
Guardian, the 3, 5, 12, 13, 26, 28, 29,
    32, 37, 38, 51, 54, 57, 59, 68, 73, 84,
    92, 96, 99, 101, 102, 106, 107, 114,
    116, 117, 119, 120, 121, 122–5, 138,
    139, 150, 182, 183, 165, 195. 196,
    197, 202, 209, 211–12, 216, 221, 224,
    232
Guardian Financial Services 231
Guardian Group 18
Guild of Editors 38, 236
Gulf war 1991 47, 84, 85, 90

Hall, Phil 23
Halloran, James 120
Hamilton, Ben 53
Hansard Parliamentary Reports **164**
Hanstock, Terry 26
Harding, Thomas 140
Hardy, Rebecca 30
Hargreaves, Ian 236

Harlow College 237, 238
Harman, Harriet 30
Harris, Nigel 39
Harris, Robert 51
Harrison, David 197
Hastings, Max 32
Haverhill Echo 116
Hay, Colin 28
Hayman, Helene 221
Headway 119
Health and Safety Executive 118
Health Education Authority 34
Hearst, William Randolph 36
Heller, Zoë 217
Hellinger, Daniel 52
Hennessy, Brendon 202
Hennessy, Peter 51, **170**
Henningham, John 32, 231
Herman, Edward 47
Hicks, Wynford 72
Higgins, Stuart 51
Highbury and Islington Gazette 99, 109
Highbury College, Portsmouth 238
High Court 37–8, 39, 52, 53, 122, 181
Hillyard, Paddy 37, 122
hoaxes 51
Hogan, Daniel 28
Hoggart, Simon 217
Holderness, Mike 56
Hollingsworth, Mark 32, 37
Honeyman, Steve 188–9
Hopkinson, Tom 237
Hotbot 57
House of Lords **168–9**
Howard, Philip 85
Hughes, Lotte 70
Hull Daily Mail 238
Human Rights Act 182
Hurd, Douglas 38
Hussein, President Saddam 22, 44, 104,
    125
Hyman, Judge Michael 53

Ilkeston and Ripley Trader 11
Independent, the 37, 51, 52, 54, 93, 101,
    107, 108, 186, 209, 216
Independent on Sunday 27, 30. 50, 61,
    185, 209, 213–14, 223
Independent Television Commission 184
Index on Censorship 39
India Abroad News Service 18
India Express 18
India Today 18
infotainment 5

Ingham, Bernard 51
Ingram, Derek 18
Institute of Journalists 236
Institute of Public Policy Research 156
Intelligence Service Act 38
Interception of Communications Act 79
International Federation of Journalists
    54, 121
International Herald Tribune 45
internet 1, 11, 54–60, 92, 192; and
    copyright 58–9
InterPress Service 18
interviewing 57–8, 61–80, 210; *see also*
    ambush interview, doorstepping, vox
    pop
inverted pyramid concept 109–10
investigative journalism 5, 59, 78,
    183–93
Investigative Journalism Review
    186–92
IPC Magazines 232
IRA 38; Provisional 52, 98
Irish Independent 45
ITN 28, 121
ITV 184
ixquick 192

Jack, Ian 185
James, Fiona 214
jargon *see* language
Jempson, Mike 40
Jewish Chronicle/JC 33, 45
*Johannesburg Weekly Mail and
    Guardian* 12–14
Johnson, Andrew 38
Johnson, Angella 12–14
Johnston, Jenny 129–33
Johnston Press 2, 4
Jones, George **158**
Jones, Robert 233
Joseph Rowntree Reform Trust 185
Journal, Newcastle 53
Judd, Dennis R. 52
Julia Somerville Show 16
Justice 174

Kavanagh, Dennis 149
Keeble, Richard 28, 91, 203–7, 227
Kemsley, Lord 23
Kennedy, Paul 125
Kent Evening Post 15
Kent Messenger 126–8
Kenyan Standard 19
Kiernan, Ben 138

Kieran, Matthew 44
Kiley, Robert 59
Killen, Mary 96
King, Elliot 59
King's College, London 236
Knight, India 217
Knight, Sarah 10–11
Knightley, Phillip 71, 84
Kosovo war 1999 89–91, 141

Labour Party 26, 28, 36, 37, 43, 129,
    151, 156, 157, **164–5, 171**
Lai, Dr Henry 234
Lambeth College 237
Lampl, Peter 17
Landesman, Cosmo 224
language 81–94; acronyms 82, 85,
    clichés 84–5, 92–3, 103, 117, 225;
    euphemisms 85, 87; jargon 85–6, 87,
    177; meaningless modifiers 83;
    militarisation 84; neologisms 91–2;
    direct quotes 72, 74; reported speech
    72–6; simplification process 91; trade
    names 92; puns 83–4, 106;
    transitional phrases 199; *see also* style
Leach, Steve 157
Leapman, Michael 36
Leicester Mercury 32
Leigh, David 26, 50, 149
Lerner, Max 217
Leslie, Ann 31
Letts, Quentin 96
Lewinsky, Monica 28, 76
Lexis-Nexis 230
Leyland, Adam 79
Liberal Democrats 25, **160, 161, 165**
Libération 101–2
Liberty 174
Lincolnshire and Humberside, University
    of 237, 238
Lincolnshire Echo 238
Liverpool *Daily Post* 2, 100, 110–11
Liverpool John Moores University
    238
Liu, Betty 106
Llosa, Mario Vargas 19
lobby 51–2, **171–2**
Lobster 45
London College of Printing 32, 237
London Daily News 13
London School of Economics 25
Long Eaton Advertiser 11
Lunn, Marie 95
Lycos 57

McCann, Paul 52
McCrum. Sarah 70
McDonald, Trevor 18
McKay, Jenny 228
Mackay, Lord of Clashfern 27
McLaughlan, Lucille 27
Macleod, Louise 232
McNae's Essential Law for Journalists
    175
McNair, Brian 22, 46, 217
McQuail, Denis 42
Mayes, Ian 59, 119
Major, John 25, 27, **165**
Mail on Sunday, the 5, 37, 54, 209, 214,
    216
Mandela, Nelson 12, 74
Mandela, Winnie 12
Mandelson, Peter 27–8
Martel, Matt 196
Maxwell, Robert 11, 13, 36, 125, 183
Media Centre 240
meetings 134–6
Meikie, James 73
Meldrum, Andrew 106
Melin-Higgins, Margareta 30
Mellor, David 25
Mellor, Julie 31
Messenger Press and PR 10
Metacrawler 57
Metro (London freebie) 209
Metzler, Ken 58
Meyer, Christopher 51
MI5 37, 38, 39, 47, **172**, 186
MI6 37, 38, 39
Midland Independent Newspapers 10
Midland News Association 238
Miles, Lucy 196
Mills, Jane 31
Milne, Seamus 47
Milosevic, President Slobodan 22
Mirror, the 2, 5, 14–18, 25, 26, 27, 30,
    47, 92, 95, 101, 103, 106, 117,
    129–33, 195
Missouri, University of 235
Moloney, Ed 53
Mother Jones 45
Montgomery, Helen 6–10
Montreal Gazette 19
Moore, Alison 33
Moore, Pat 30
Moore, Suzanne 5, 216, 217
Moore, Wendy 116–17
Morgan, Piers 14, 16, 26, 30
Morning Star 45, 100, 225–6

Morton, Andrew 25
Mory, Pierre 236
Mossad 47
MSN Search 57
Mulholland, Brendon 52
Murdoch, Rupert 1, 2, 3, 16, 6, 26, 32,
    36, 54, 125, 129, 232
Murphy, Anna 213
Murphy, David 42
Muslim News 33

Napier University 237
National Advisory Council for the
    Training and Education of Junior
    Journalists 236
National Council for the Training of
    Journalists (NCTJ) 77, 174–5, 236,
    238, 239
National Training Organisation 239
Naughton, John 54, 59
Nekierk, Phillip Van 14
neutrality 22
neologisms *see* language
Newark Advertiser 144
New Internationalist 33
New Left Review 33
Newmarket Journal 102, 142–4, 209
New Nation 33, 45
Newnham, David 197
News Corporation 3; *see also* Murdoch,
    Rupert
News Line 45, 82
News of the World 2, 23, 26, 28, 29, 30,
    83, 84, 101, 129, 198, 224
News on Sunday 37
Newspaper Publishers' Association 236
news reporting 95–146, 202; intros
    97–106; structure of story 108–12; *see*
    soft news
Newspaper Society 2, 84, 236, 239
News, the, Portsmouth 5
New Straits Times 19
Newsquest 2, 238
Newton, Kenneth 148
New World Information and
    Communication Order 18
New York Times 37, 45, 230
New York Tribune 61
Niblock, Sarah 236
Night and Day 209, 214
Nolan, Lord 151
Nonviolent Action 139
Norris, Bill 39
Northcliffe, Lord 36

Northcliffe Newspapers- 2
Northern Ireland Assembly **160**
Northern Light 210
North London Press 15
Northmore, David 38; 183–93
Northwest University of Chicago 193
Norton, Phillip **168**
Norwich *Evening News* 61, 99
Nottingham and Long Eaton Topper 101
Nottingham Evening Post 32 , 74, 76,
    105, 210–11, 214–15
Nottingham Trent University MA in
    investigative journalism 185, 237
NUJ (National Union of Journalists) 4,
    24, 29, 31, 32, 35, 54, 186, 229, 230,
    232, 233, 234, 236, 239; Code of
    Conduct 39–40, 52, 174; code on
    freelance work 230; *Equality Style
    Guide* 31; ethics council 40; People
    First campaign 34
Nu News 11
NVQ (National Vocational
    Qualifications) 238

'objectivity' 22, 44, 45, 95, 109
Observer, the 35, 36, 37, 51, 54, 55, 59,
    106, 197, 212–13, 216
Official Secrets Acts 37, 51; OSA 1989
    38, 151, 186
Online Journalism Review 56
Organisation of American States 19
Orwell, George 81, 85, 207, 227
Osmotherly Rules **169**
Ottawa Citizen 19
Outcast 59
Oxford, Esther 49, 195–6

PA (Press Association) 6, 9, 10, 46, 56
Page, Ben 157
Paglia, Camille 31
Pall Mall Gazette 61
Panos 18, 19, 20
Parker, Mike 225–6
Parris, Matthew 84, 96, 144–6, 216
Parry, Deborah 27
Patterson, Mark 210
PCC (Press Complaints Commission)
    15, 25, 26, 27, 28, 32, 46, 76, 78,
    184, 212; Code of Practice 25, 26, 27,
    28, 40, 80, 191–2
Peace News 45
Peak, Steve 1, 45, 236
Penthouse 61
People's Daily 3

Percy-Smith, Janie 37, 122
Periodicals Training Council 238
Peterborough *Evening Telegraph* 102
Phillips, Angela 239
Phillips, Melanie 184–5
Picture Post 237
Pilger, John 47, 49, 55
Pinker, Professor Robert 25, 26
Pink Paper 45
Pirie, Jacqueline 28
Pitmans 175
Planet on Sunday 98
Platell, Amanda 30
Police and Criminal Evidence Act 54
Pollard, Eve 29
Ponting, Clive 38, **169, 170**
Porter, Anthony 193
Portsmouth and Sunderland Newspapers
    2
Powell, Sir Charles 191
Poynter Institute 56, 59
PR (press relations) 6, 64–5, 68, 135,
    164, 208, 210
'precision journalism' 59
Press Amalgamations Court 26
press conferences 136–8, 139
Press Council 26, 184
Press Gazette 25, 56, 185, 223, 240
PressWise Trust 40
Preston, Peter 26
Prevention of Terrorism Act 53
Privacy International 79
privacy: law 24; 25, 28, 29; invasions of
    25, 26
Private Eye 47
professionalisation 22, 45, 77
profiles 63, 68, 96, 208–15
Project Censored 183, 186
propaganda 22, 37, 47, 91
Protess, David 193
Public Order Act 122
Public Records Act 191
Public Record Office 191
Punch 38

Q News 33, 45

Race and Class 33
Race Relations Act 76
racism/anti-racism 32–3, 65
Ramsay, Robin 50
Randall, David 228
Reality 209
Reddick, Randy 56, 58, 59

red-top tabloids 3
Read, Sue 228
Recruitmedia 240
Reed, Rex 61
Reed Regional Newspapers 2
Regulation of Investigatory Powers Act
    60, 151
reported speech *see* language
Reporters Sans Frontières 121
Reuters 18, 34; Reuters Foundation 186
reviewing 222–5
risk assessment 121
right of reply 29
Robertson, Geoffrey 24
Robinson, Anne 218–22
Robinson, Geoffrey 28
Rock, P. 113
Rory Peck Trust 121
Rose, Richard 148
Rosenberg, David 32
Ross, Lillian 70
Roszak, Theodore 55
Rothermere, Lord 23, 36
Rowe, Bridget 30
Rowland, 'Tiny' 36
Rowlands, Barbara 64
Royal Commissions 23–4, 236
RSI (repetitive strain injury) 64, 232–4
Rusbridger, Alan 29
Ryan, Rocky 50

Saffron Walden Reporter 97
salaries (of journalists) 5
Sarkar, Dipankar De 18–20
Schechter, Danny 183
scanners 80
Scope 33
Scotsman, the 30, 45, 51
Scottish National Party **160**, **166**
Scottish Parliament 149, **159**, **160**
Scott, Selina 29
Searchlight 33
Searle, Chris 32
Seaton, Jean 22, 36
Sebba, Anne 95
Security Service Act 38
select committees **169**
Seneviratne, Gamini 18
Sereny, Gitta 27
sexism/anti-sexism 29–32
Seymour, Ellee 142
Seymour-Ure, Colin 148
Shah, Eddie 231
Shawcross, Lord 26

Shawcross, William 36, 129
Shayler, David 37, 38, 93–4, 186
Sheffield College 238
Sheffield University 237
shorthand 77, 174–5 *see also* Astbury's,
    Gregg, Teeline, Pitmans
Silvester, Christopher 61, 216, 217
Sinn Fein **166**
Sheffield University 186
Singh, Dr Narenda 234
Skinner, Henry Watkins 193
Sky Brazil 3
Sky Mexico 3
slang 140, 225
Slough Observer 13
Smith, Anthony 77
Smith, Joan 128–9
Snoddy, Raymond 21
Social Democratic and Labour Party **166**
Socialist Worker 33, 45, 107, 195, 214
Society of Editors 5, 238
soft news 101, 107–8
sources of information 41–60
Southnews 2
Spark, David 64
Sparks, Colin 1, 125
Special Branch **172**, 186
speeches 141–4
Sport First 1
Spencer, Earl 26, 28
Spender, Dale 31
Spycatcher 37
Staffordshire University 237
St Albans Herald 8
standing committees **169–70**
Star TV 3
Statewatch 39
Staunton, Denis 212–13
Stead, W.T. 61
Stephenson, Professor Hugh 236, 237
Stewart, John **158**
Stoker, Gerry **159**
Stream 3
stress 231–4
style 7, 20, 31, 34, 92–3, 118
subeditors 4, 6–7, 9, 20, 94
Sun, the 2, 32, 44, 51, 79, 130
Sunday Express 29, 49, 85, 99, 197
Sunday Mail 2
Sunday Mercury 85, 106, 196, 209
Sunday Mirror 2, 25, 30, 75, 106, 196,
    214
Sunday People 2
Sunday Record 2

Sunday Times 2, 5, 23, 25, 27, 37, 47, 51, 61, 79, 184, 208, 209, 211, 212, 224
Sunday Telegraph 209, 213
Sunday Tribune 53
Surrey Institute of Art and Design 238
Sutton Coldfield College 237

Tampere University 57
Taylor, Kenneth 198–201
Taylor, Norren 30
Teeline 175
Telecommunications Act 1984 59
Telegraph and Argus, Bradford 33, 84
Terrorism Act 151
Thames News 13
Thompson, Bill 57
Thomson Regional Newspapers 2, 10
Times Educational Supplement 16
Times, The 2, 5, 13, 27, 30, 36, 84, 86–91, 93, 96, 108, 138, 144–6, 202, 203, 208, 209, 211, 212, 216, 218–22
Thatcher, Margaret 24, 28, 51, 98, 125, 152, 153, **170, 171, 172,** 189, 190; Margaret Thatcher Archive Trust 187–92
Tiffen, Rodney 48, 49–50
Tisdall, Sarah 38, 52
Today 1, 231
Tomalin, Nicholas 3, 176
Tomlinson, Richard 38
Trade Union Reform and Employment Rights Act 1993 38
Trader Group 10
training for journalists 235–9
Traynor, Ian 195
Trelford, Donald 35
Trevor-Roper, Sir Hugh 51
Tribune 45, 99
Trinity and All Saints College, Leeds 237
Trinity International Holdings 2
Trinity-Mirror 2, 238
trivialisation 24
Truss, Lynne 202, 203
Tulloch, John 25
Tunstall, Jeremy **171**
Turnbull, Giles 57
Turner, John 147–72

UCAS 239
Ullmann, John 188–9
Ulster Unionist Party **166**

Unesco 18
United News of India 18
United Press International 18
University College, Cardiff 237
USA Today 2

Vanunu, Mordechai 47
Verba, Stanley 148
Vidal, 120, 122–5
Voice, the 33, 45, 198–201
Voisey, Karen 39
vox pop 62–3, 96
Vulliamy, Ed 26

Wade, Paul 197
Wade, Rebekah 30
Wade, Stephen 227–8
Wakeham, Lord 26, **168**
Wales, University of 236
Walker, David 51
Wallace, Milverton 55
Wardle, Irving -223
Warner, Jeremy 52
Warwickshire College 237
Washington Post 32, 45, 64
Wasley, Andrew 121
Watergate 64
Waterhouse, Keith 84, 93, 218
Waters, Pete
web *see* internet
Webcrawler 57
Welsh, Tom 175
Welsh Assembly 149, **159, 160**
Welsh National Party (Plaid Cymru) **160,** 166
Welwyn and Hatfield Times 8
Western Mail 30
Western Morning News 7
Westminster Press 2, 8
Wheen, Francis 32
White, Michael 96
Whiting, Alex 19, 20
Who's Who 210
Widdicombe, D. **161;** Widdicombe report 150
Williams, Granville 1
Williams, Kevin 2, 64
Williams, Dr Stephen 231
Willings Press Guide 57
Wilson, David 155
Wilson, Giles 59
Wilson, Harold 50
Wingfield, John 80
Wintour, Charles 36

Wintour, Patrick 197
Wireless Telegraphy Act 80
Woffindem, Bob 39
Wolverhampton University 237–8
Women in Journalism 30
Woodward, Bob 64
Woodward, Louise 27
word economy 82–3
Workers' Revolutionary Party 82
World in Action 184
Wright, Peter 37
www.bigfoot.com 57
www.celebsites.com 210

www.searchenginewatch.com
www.switchboard.com 57

Yahoo! 3, 55, 58
Yattendon group 9
Young, Brigham 61
Young, Hugo **169**
Younger Committee on Privacy 24
Young Person Act 1993 38
Youth Justice and Criminal Evidence
    Act 117

Zobel, Gibby 53